Chart Your Way to Profits

The Online Trader's Guide to Technical Analysis with ProphetCharts

Second Edition

TIM KNIGHT

WILEY

John Wiley & Sons, Inc.

To Alexander Dobrovolski, who made it all possible

For general information on our other products and services or for technical support, please
contact our Customer Care Department within the United States at (800) 762-2974, outside the
United States at (317) 572-3993 or fax (317) 572-4002.

Wiley also publishes its books in a variety of electronic formats. Some content that appears in
print may not be available in electronic books. For more information about Wiley products,
visit our web site at www.wiley.com.

Library of Congress Cataloging-in-Publication Data:

Knight, Tim, 1966–
  Chart your way to profits : the online trader's guide to technical analysis with
ProphetCharts / Tim Knight. – 2nd ed.
     p. cm. – (Wiley trading series)
  Includes bibliographical references and index.
  ISBN 978-0-470-62002-1 (cloth)
  1. Stocks–Charts, diagrams, etc.   2. Investment analysis.   3. Electronic trading
of securities.   I. Title.
  HG4638.K55 2010
  332.63′2042–dc22

                                                                    2010005946

Printed in the United States of America

10 9 8 7 6 5 4 3 2 1

Contents

Introduction

O ne of my favorite photographs was taken by my wife on our honeymoon. We were on the second leg of our trip, the first of which was in Dubrovnik, Croatia (part of the former Yugoslavia), and the second in central Italy. The photo shows me in bed, apparently asleep. The title of the book I am holding across my chest is clearly legible: *Technical Analysis of Stock Trends*, by Edwards and Magee.

Charting the financial markets has been my passion for over 20 years. The very first trade I ever placed in my life was on Black Monday, the crash of 1987—hardly a propitious start. But the markets and their vagaries have fascinated me ever since.

In 1992, I took my three main areas of interest—computers, trading, and business—and combined them to create Prophet Financial Systems. That was before the commercial Internet even existed (we used dial-up modems in those days for daily data updates). Over the years, we built a wide array of tools, all with the purpose of trying to help people make better trading decisions.

To be honest, I personally find books about technical analysis kind of boring. They are full of indicators, formulas, tables, and numbers. By and large, they put me to sleep (witness the honeymoon photo). I set out to make this book different. I wanted you to enjoy learning from this book, and I wanted to use as many real-life examples as possible. Hypothetical charts mean little, in my opinion. So you will find this book packed with hundreds of examples drawn from real trading in U.S. equity markets. This should give you a practical way to see how to apply the ideas presented in these pages.

SOME HISTORY

In 1998, we at Prophet took the first small steps toward creating a charting applet, which we called JavaCharts. My philosophy in product development has always been the same: have my engineers create a product that

I love to use. This had the happy side effect of attracting a lot of traders, because they liked what they saw, too.

JavaCharts became the foundation of the business in many ways. It was very popular on our own web site, Prophet.net, and we licensed it to a wide variety of brokerages and other businesses. The quality and reputation of the product was an important reason behind our securing the "Best of the Web" awards from both *Barron's* and *Forbes*, beginning in 1999 and continuing for years.

Over a nearly four-year period—from the beginning of 2003 to the end of 2006—we focused on our next generation of charting. Originally referring to this as simply JavaCharts 2, we later christened it ProphetCharts. Although this book will prove helpful to anyone interested in technical analysis, it will be especially instructive to ProphetCharts users.

HOW TO REACH ME

I would love to hear from you! I enjoy being in touch with other people interested in charting, so feel free to drop me a line with your questions and comments. My e-mail address is trader.tim.knight@gmail.com.

You also might enjoy my widely read blog, The Slope of Hope, which can be accessed via your browser at www.slopeofhope.com.

Whether you use any charting product, you should benefit from this book. I've tried to make it accessible, understandable, and practical for anyone interested in making better trading decisions. Let me know what you think, and good luck with your trading!

About the Author

T im Knight was the founder of Prophet Financial Systems, an online software company that was acquired by INVESTools in January 2005, which in turn was acquired by Ameritrade in the summer of 2009. He currently is an active trader and professional money manager.

Tim founded Prophet in 1992 to provide market data to self-directed investors using stand-alone technical analysis software. With the advent of the World Wide Web, he envisioned combining the power of these expensive software packages with browser-based convenience—enabling traders to focus on their analysis, instead of worrying about software upgrades and database issues. His online technical analysis suite at Prophet.Net delivered on this vision.

In his trading today, Tim relies on technical analysis as the primary basis for his investment decisions. He is the managing partner for the Tim Knight Organization, a money management firm, and writes the popular Slope of Hope blog.

Before starting Prophet, Tim was Vice President of Technology Products at Montgomery Securities in San Francisco, where he led the development of an institutional online-trading platform. Additionally, he held various positions in marketing management at Apple Computer and is the author of 20 computer books. Tim is a graduate of Santa Clara University's honors program and holds a bachelor's degree in business management.

He lives in Palo Alto, California, with his wife, children, dog, and three pampered chickens.

CHAPTER 1

Technical Analysis

What It Is and Why It Works

T echnical analysis is the study of past price movement for the purpose of predicting future price movement, which, if done correctly, can lead to substantial trading profits. The prices studied are typically those of financial instruments such as stocks, commodities, and foreign currencies. But no matter what market is being studied, the underlying principles are the same. Specifically:

- A price chart is the most perfect representation of the balance of buyers and sellers for any given entity.
- Prices tend to move in trends and patterns, which, based on historical analysis, can lead to statistically meaningful probabilities of future price movement.
- The close and skilled examination of a price chart can guide traders as to how long they should remain in a trade and when they should exit.

No matter what you trade, technical analysis can make you a better and more profitable trader. Price charts will consistently provide the most truthful picture that can be had of a tradable object, because everything that can be publicly known or speculated is already built into the graph. You will never get the same pure representation of a stock (or anything else) from a broker, a newsletter writer, or an analyst. A chart is as good as it gets.

THE BULLS VERSUS THE BEARS

Before we get into price charts—and there will be hundreds of them in this book—let's examine the basics about what forms a price chart in the first place: sellers (the supply) and buyers (the demand).

When buyers are more powerful than sellers, prices move up. When sellers are more powerful than buyers, prices move down. This tug-of-war, in these simple terms, is behind the trillions of dollars that get traded every week of the year.

What many people tend to forget is that every time a trade is placed, each side believes that they are right and the other side of the transaction is wrong. When person A buys stock from person B, person A believes the stock is going to go up in price (meaning B is selling too cheap), and person B believes he would rather have the cash than the stock (meaning A is buying an overvalued, or at least fully valued, stock).

As a group, the individuals who believe a given instrument is going to move higher in price are the bulls, whereas the opposing camp, believing prices for the same instrument will drop, are the bears. And the war between the bulls and the bears, fought over many thousands of different stocks, options, and commodities every day, is what creates price movement. Analyzing that movement well is what will give you a substantial edge in the markets you trade.

WHY IS A PREDICTION VALUABLE?

The astonishing thing about technical analysis is not only how far out its predictive power goes but also how, even with a future full of unknowns, it still seems able to see its way clear to make a meaningful prediction. A staggering number of great forces can wreak havoc with financial markets—scandals, war, governmental chaos, interest rates, terrorist attacks, earnings surprises, the social climate, and so forth. Through it all, the knowledgeable chartist can see what others cannot see and know what seems unknowable.

Let's take a real-life example with a very long time span: the Dow Jones Industrial Average over a period of more than 100 years. Figure 1.1 has two Fibonacci fans drawn on it. (Don't worry if you are not familiar with that term; it will be explained in Chapter 15.) These fans are drawn from an extreme low to an extreme high. The first is drawn from the low in 1903 (the "Rich Man's Panic," it was called) to the peak of the roaring twenties bull market in 1929. The second is drawn from the depths

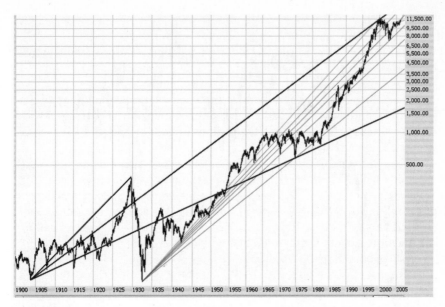

FIGURE 1.1 The Dow Jones Industrial Average from 1900 to 2005, enhanced with two Fibonacci fans.

of the depression in 1932 to the peak of the Internet bubble in January 2000.

There are a variety of astounding things to note in this chart:

- The point where the two major lines intersect in 1974 predicted the precise bottom of the massive 1973–1974 bear market.
- The steady climb from 1990 to 1995 was perfectly bounded by two of the fan lines.
- Most impressive of all, the ultimate market top in 2000 was established by the first fan (which, remember, began 97 years before).

Figure 1.2 is a close-up view of late 1999 and early 2000; as you can see, the almost century-old fan line creates impressive resistance to these prices moving higher on four different occasions. If we owned stocks at that time, this would be a vital warning signal that the top was established.

This is an extreme example, but the point is that being able to gain insight into the most likely future of a particular price is a vehicle for real trading profits. It is an edge that those not using charts will lack.

FIGURE 1.2   Highlighted here are four instances that the Dow bounced off the fan line established over a century earlier.

A WORD ON SHORTING

There will be many times in this book where we will refer to "shorting" a particular stock or "being short" a stock. It is valuable to understand this terminology, in case you do not already.

Most people participating in a market are "long" the market; that is, they own the security with the hope that the price will go up. So if a person owns 1,000 shares of Apple Computer (AAPL) which he bought at $50 per share, and later sells it for $90 per share, he has made $40,000 based on the long position ($40 per share gain times 1,000 shares).

A person who is short a security has done things backwards: he first sells a security he does not own for a certain price with the hope that the price will go down. The reason people are able to sell stock they do not own (essentially giving them a negative number of shares) is that their broker has so much of the stock already that it is available to sell with the promise that, at some point, it will be repurchased to replace the shares that were sold.

Taking the example of Apple again, an individual might sell short 1,000 shares of Apple at $90 per share. If the stock fell to $50 and the trader "covered" the position (that is, bought 1,000 shares of the stock, thus making the broker whole), he would have made $40,000 just as the other trader did, only he would have done it in the other direction.

The advantages and disadvantages of shorting markets will be discussed near the end of the book, but the principal benefit of shorting is that you can take advantage of a falling market as well as a rising one. If you are at the beginning of a bear market, and you can only buy stocks, it will be very difficult to make money. If you are able to short stocks at high prices and then buy them back later at low prices, you can make money in either an up or down market.

The key disadvantage to shorting stocks is that all the big money is made by going long. The most you can ever make with a short position is 100 percent (that is, if the stock goes to $0.00, which almost never happens), whereas the most you can make with a long position is unlimited. You can definitely make profits shorting markets, but unless you are a brilliant options trader, you will never get rich being a bear (that is, a person betting on a market going down).

SUPPORT AND RESISTANCE

The world of technical analysis can seem overwhelming to many. There are hundreds of complex mathematical indicators, studies, patterns, and rules. But there is absolutely no reason good charting has to be complicated. A trader can set aside all of the complexity and focus on some solid basics, starting with the ideas of support and resistance.

To illustrate this, think back to the children's game Red Rover. In case you don't remember it, kids split up into two groups, and each group forms a line by holding hands so that there are two parallel lines of kids standing across a field opposite one another. Then one team calls out, "Red Rover, Red Rover, send Ethan (or some other kid's name) right over!" and the named child rushes headlong into the other line, trying to break through. If he busts through the line, he gets to choose a person to join his team.

This image of "breaking through" is exactly what support and resistance are all about, because in the grown-up world of trading, buyers of securities tend to mass at certain price levels. And those owners will hold the line at those prices if the security tries to go above (in the case of resistance) or below (in the case of support).

Let's take a simple hypothetical example. Suppose a given stock traded at between $4.95 and $5.05 for many months. Day after day, week after week, it stayed in this range, accumulating owners of the stock at around the $5 level. Let's go on to assume the company has some good news, and the stock goes up to $6, but subsequent profit taking pushes the stock back down again.

Given this circumstance, you can rest assured that it's unlikely the stock is going to drop beneath about the $5 level. The reason is that there's a huge number of owners at that level, and they are simply not going to sell. Fear and greed are the primary drivers of the market, and in this case, greed is going to come first (meaning the owners are telling the market "I refuse to sell my stock at this price for a breakeven trade. I want a profit"). If something remarkable happens and it shoves the stock down to, say, $4.50, the fear starts to take hold ("I am worried my losses will get even worse, so I'm going to sell now while I still have the chance"), which means the selling will feed on itself.

Expressed in economic terms, the stock price found equilibrium at the $5 level, thus amassing a large number of owners. If the stock price challenges that level again, equilibrium will once more take hold, stabilizing the price. The people owning stock at this level constitute resistance—the "Red Rover" line will hold fast, unless a very powerful force punches through it.

Support, therefore, is a price level above which prices are prone to stay. Resistance is a price level below which prices are prone to stay. So these are reliable levels at which to count on a pause in price movement, unless the levels are violated, which is where the real action is.

WHAT HAPPENS WHEN PRICES PUNCH THROUGH?

One time when outsize profits can be made is when prices push through support or resistance and break out. The longer a price has been trying to push through a certain price level, the more forceful it will be if it finally does make it through. (Think back to our Red Rover game, and picture a particularly eager youngster who has tried 10 times to get through the line and is more determined than ever to do so.)

Figure 1.3 is an example of how potent this is. The first half of the stock chart for ALVR shows prices bouncing between about $2.00 and $2.50. For month after month, the stock was completely stagnant, and buyers were accumulating at these levels. There were several attempts to push through resistance (represented by the horizontal line), but they failed . . . until the midpoint of the graph, in April.

At that point, three important things happened: (1) buyers overcame sellers, pushing prices above resistance; (2) volume increased as excitement began to build around the stock; and (3) when some profit taking took place, prices eased back, *but they did not go beneath the former line of resistance.* From that point, the stock moved up about 500 percent in the course of a year.

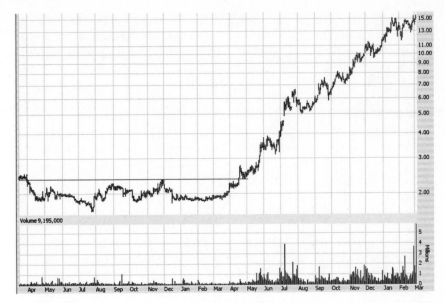

FIGURE 1.3 After breaking out of a saucer pattern, ALVR blasted ahead on much bigger volume to a 500 percent gain in about a year.

The concept of how resistance can change into support (and vice versa) is critical to your understanding of reading a chart. Any sort of line—be it a trend line, a channel, a horizontal line—has two faces to it: support and resistance. Once prices cross a line, the nature of that line changes. As you will learn later in this book, if a price crosses a line more than once, the line becomes meaningless and should probably be deleted.

Let's take another look at resistance to see how valuable it is to have an awareness of price behavior at certain levels. Figure 1.4 shows the chart for Chesapeake Energy (symbol CHK) over a period of about half a year. Early on, the price was blasting skyward to a new high, then it slumped down through August. It then regained its footing and mounted a new assault on higher prices, but it was repelled again at about the same level. A couple of months later, in November, a third attempt was made to push past the $34 barrier, but it failed a third time. You can imagine the frustration and exasperation of the owners of this stock as they kept seeing their stock getting shoved away from higher prices.

What the market was telling the owners of this stock was: "The price is probably not going to go any higher." The supply of stock (those selling it) represented what is known as overhead resistance. Perhaps some people who bought earlier at $34 promised themselves that the moment the stock recovered to a breakeven level, they would get out. Perhaps most people

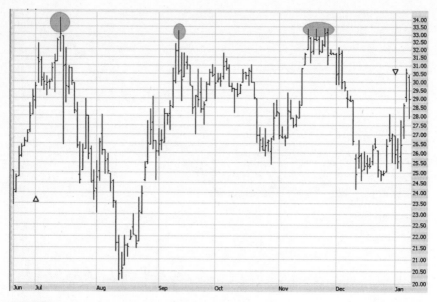

FIGURE 1.4 This is known as a triple top, where a new high happens three times, but the price can't get above it. Once the attempts at overcoming this resistance failed, the stock collapsed.

felt the stock was fully valued at $34. The reasons really don't matter; the fact is that over a six-month period, there was an invisible line drawn on the stock chart through which prices simply could not pass.

What happened afterwards is very interesting: far from pushing above the $34 price, the stock instead started collapsing. As Figure 1.5 shows, CHK withered away from $34 per share to about 50 cents, almost a 99 percent decline. Clearly the stock had worse problems than a triple top, but the important point here is that the market was *telling* the owners of the stock something, and the triple top was a warning that this was a stock to sell, not keep.

HISTORY REPEATS ITSELF

Another tenet of technical analysis is that human behavior doesn't change, and therefore price behavior doesn't change. If a certain pattern is predictable now, it will be just as predictable 10 years from now.

An excellent illustration of this on a single chart is Figure 1.6. The stock shown here is Red Hat (symbol RHAT) over a four-year period. For all of

FIGURE 1.5 After its triple top, CHK went on to a nearly 99 percent decline in price.

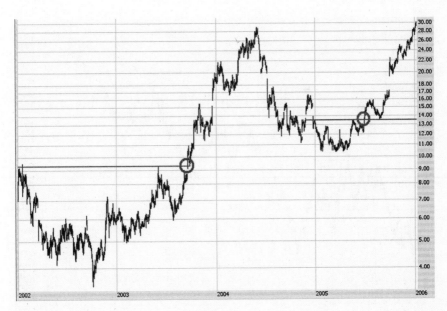

FIGURE 1.6 Patterns can—and often do—repeat themselves in the same chart.

2002 and most of 2003, RHAT was forming a rather large cup with handle pattern, indicated by the horizontal line. When it broke above this pattern, the stock just about tripled in price.

After it peaked, RHAT sank for about a year before establishing another pattern. This time, the pattern was quite similar, only smaller. And once again, after it broke above the pattern, the stock soared (this time *only* double its breakout price, which is typical of a smaller pattern).

As you can see, once you train your eyes to find patterns and understand what the important price points are, you can take advantage of what are relatively predictable price movements.

A variety of factors dictate the power of a breakout from a particular pattern. One is the pattern itself, because some patterns are simply more potent and reliable than others. Another is the volume accompanying the price movement; a stock moving higher on stronger and stronger volume is far more attractive than a stock moving the same direction on anemic volume. Another factor still is the length of the pattern. A breakout from a three-year-old saucer is going to have a lot more fireworks than a breakout from a tiny two-week saucer.

Figure 1.7 provides an illustration of both (a) repetition and (b) pattern size equaling potency. The chart is the Russell 2000. The symbol is $RUT. This chart is actually showing several patterns within a larger

FIGURE 1.7 An ascending wedge and, within that pattern, three nearly identical patterns indicated by the horizontal lines.

pattern. The broad pattern, shown by the two almost parallel lines, is an ascending wedge. This index is making a series of higher highs (bumping up against the upper line) and higher lows (bouncing off the lower line). So the index is in a general uptrend.

Within this pattern, though, are three smaller patterns, all of which are progressively smaller versions of the first. If you look at the shape of the prices beneath the horizontal line, you can see that this price movement is virtually identical in all three instances, although the second pattern is smaller that the first, and the third pattern is smaller still.

What's interesting, of course, is what happens after the prices break above each horizontal line—the stock moves higher. But not only can we see the stock moving higher, we can also observe that the amount it goes up is a little less each time. This is an example of how the oomph of the push upward is closely related to how sizable the pattern is in the first place.

HEAD AND SHOULDERS

Throughout this book, we'll be learning about a variety of patterns, a number of which are known as reversal patterns. They are called this because they forecast a reversal in price direction.

One of the most basic and powerful reversal patterns is called the head and shoulders. These formations are pretty easy to spot: on the left side is a hump in prices (gradually moving up and then moving down again to a certain supporting price). In the middle is a taller hump, again, slowly moving up and then down again to support; this is the head. Finally, there is another hump, the smallest of the three (ideally), which is the right shoulder.

The support line is what's key here. It even has a special name in the context of this pattern; instead of being called the support line, it's called the neckline. If prices break beneath the neckline, there are three general possibilities:

1. The prices will sink from there.
2. Prices will sink briefly, recover to touch the underside of what used to be support (now resistance), and then start to fall.
3. Prices will stabilize, push back toward the former support line, and then overcome it, thus negating the pattern.

The ideal circumstance is (2), since it allows a person to carefully enter the position at a very desirable price and set a stop just above the former support line. This is the ideal low risk–high reward scenario. Figure 1.8

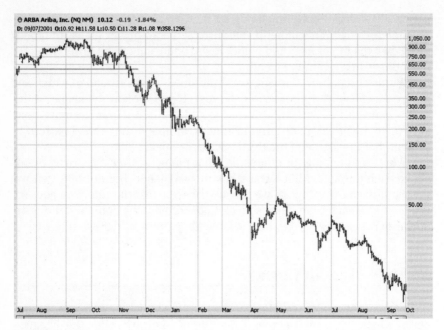

FIGURE 1.8 After a break beneath the neckline in November, Ariba lost virtually all of its value.

is an example of just this circumstance, with Ariba (symbol ARBA) forming a very nice head and shoulders pattern from July through November. Once prices broke beneath the neckline, the stock went from about $600 to $300. But for the first couple of weeks of December, buyers pushed the stock back to about $550, still below the neckline. (Note: these prices are adjusted for reverse stock splits.)

This is a test of the pattern. The pattern has already established itself, and the chart is bearish, but buyers are still trying to push the stock higher. You can almost picture the bulls and bears in a tug-of-war, with the neckline in the middle of the battle. In this case, shorting the stock at $550 would have been brilliant, because after testing the pattern, the price started to sink virtually without pause until almost all the equity was wiped out.

Take a look at Figure 1.9, which is a very similar chart. Broadcom (symbol BRCM) managed to survive the initial burst of the NASDAQ bubble in the first half of 2000. By October of that year, it broke beneath the neckline in a very well-formed head and shoulders pattern, and it didn't stop once to test that level again. The stock plummeted from $130 to under $10 per share in a couple of years.

⊖ BRCM Broadcom Corporation (NQ NM) 43.41 -0.03 -0.07%
D: 09/05/2002 O:10.131 H:10.296 L:9.9792 C:10.0386 R:0.3168 Y:34.4056

FIGURE 1.9 Broadcom, one of the hottest stocks of the Internet bubble, collapsed after a head and shoulders pattern in late 2000.

A BREAKOUT AND A FAILURE

Stock patterns are every bit as powerful on the upside as on the downside. When looking for bullish patterns, you need to be on the lookout for breaks above resistance, as opposed to breakdowns beneath support (as is the case with bearish patterns).

One such bullish breakout is shown in Figure 1.10, where a cup with handle pattern had been forming over the course of a year. At the mid-point of the chart, notice two important things happen simultaneously: (1) the price suddenly bursts well above the resistance line (drawn here for clarity), and (2) the volume in the stock increases substantially (as you can see from the volume graph located in the lower pane). Together, there is no more powerful positive statement about a stock's bullish direction, and this stock kept climbing by hundreds of percent afterward. As you will learn throughout this book, volume is almost as important as price movement, particularly with respect to bullish formations, which require a lot of volume to fuel the rise.

As you gain experience in recognizing chart patterns and anticipating the moves that stocks can make after a certain pattern is fulfilled, you may

FIGURE 1.10 A price breakout with accompanying high volume is an excellent predictor of future upward movement.

be tempted to mentally draw in a complete pattern where one hasn't fully formed yet. For example, if you see a shoulder, a head, and part of a shoulder, you might conclude that this is going to complete as a head and shoulders pattern, and you might as well get in now and enjoy the extra profits that exist between the current price and the neckline. Or you might see a saucer formation that is getting very close to breaking out, and you figure you might as well get a better price on the stock by not waiting for the breakout, since sometimes breakouts can rapidly push the stock up to much riskier levels.

It's important not to fall into this trap. Not all patterns that complete themselves perform as they are supposed to perform, and the chances for success are even lower if the pattern doesn't really finish forming. It's critically important that you wait for a pattern to complete instead of trading off emerging patterns.

A good example of this is shown in Figure 1.11. This stock was forming a very nice inverted head and shoulders pattern for nearly a year. The horizontal line indicates the neckline, which, had prices pushed above it, would have been an important measuring tool for the pattern.

However, about three-quarters of the way across the chart, you can see that the price stalled at about $25 and could not gather the energy to make a run for the neckline. Instead, the price started sinking, made a flimsy effort

FIGURE 1.11 Anticipating a breakout is almost always a mistake. The anticipated breakout, shown by the horizontal line, never happened, and afterwards the stock withered away.

to recover, and then started sinking hard. Had you bought at $25, contemplating a big breakout to much higher prices, you might have held on to the stock as it sank into the single digits. There are countless examples of this kind of event, and you must always remember to have the patience to wait for the pattern to complete.

A CHANGE IN DIRECTION

Most people have heard the maxim "The trend is your friend." One might supplement that by saying, "The trend is your friend, but every trend someday ends." Technical analysis is a means by which you can judge that trend change.

Many embellishments you can put on a chart, such as trend lines and channels, can be used to assess when an upward-moving stock is starting to head down, or vice versa. Look at Figure 1.12, for example, which is a 20-year-long chart of Harris Corporation. For well over a decade, the stock was trending down, making a series of lower highs and lower lows. You can see this downtrend more clearly because of the channel lines that have been drawn.

FIGURE 1.12 Breaking above the descending channel presaged a sea change in this stock's direction.

In late 1992, the stock price finally got the strength to push above this channel. It might have seemed risky to buy the stock at such a "high" price, but what the prices were indicating was that the downward channel was old news, and the stock had a new direction. Over the coming years, it went up many hundreds of percent in an uptrend that was just as well defined as its downtrend.

As with most technical studies, this cuts both ways—just as a downtrend can transform into an uptrend, an uptrend can be broken and change into a downtrend. Imagine driving down a straight highway, and all you are able to see is the median line in the road. As long as the median line is on the left side of the car, you know you're generally heading in the correct direction. But if that median line moves beneath the car and to your right, you know something has seriously changed!

In a similar fashion, look at Diebold's stock chart for the late 1970s and early 1980s in Figure 1.13. Year after year, the stock continued to climb, and it obeyed its ascending trend line, never letting the price go below it. That changed very early in 1984, when prices dipped under this very well-established trend line.

What's particularly fascinating is that this trend line switched coats, as trend lines often do when prices violate them, and changed from support to resistance. Diebold's price didn't fall far at all before it resumed moving

FIGURE 1.13 Here is one of countless examples of support changing into resistance, as the trend line did not permit the prices to go above it once it was violated.

upward. The average observer would breathe a sigh of relief that the stock was going up again. But the skilled chartist would know that the price was pushed up against resistance and, instead of being a solid stock to own, actually provided a fairly low-risk shorting opportunity. After nearly half a year of trying to poke through the trend line again, the price finally succumbed and lost nearly half its value.

Just because a channel or trend line is violated by price action doesn't guarantee that a trend change is in place, however. It simply suggests the possibility. Prices crossing a line almost certainly indicate the end of the prior trend or pattern. But what is beginning will take some time to know for sure.

As an illustration of this, examine the chart in Figure 1.14 of the large insurance carrier AIG. The stock was plainly in a downtrend from the end of 2000 to the end of 2003, as shown by the descending trend line. But at the very end of 2003, prices pushed through this line with force. This did not signal a new era of higher prices, however. The stock rallied, sank, rallied again, and sank again, and then rallied once more (in a series of lower highs and lower lows). Thus, instead of a new uptrend, the stock's downtrend was continuing at a much lower pace in the shape of an expanding wedge. Importantly, notice how the prices obey the support of the trend line, which had formerly represented resistance and now had changed coats into

FIGURE 1.14 The descending trend line here changed from resistance to support after prices pushed past it, and a new pattern—an expanding wedge—was formed.

support. Even though the line had been violated, it was useful in future years as a guideline for price behavior.

WHEN PATTERNS WORK TOGETHER

A pattern on its own can be a good indicator of future price direction, but two patterns working in concert, pointing to the same direction, can add even more credence to the prediction.

The patterns need not be similar, although they can be. For example, the right shoulder of a head and shoulders pattern might itself be a smaller head and shoulders pattern. Or you might find two bullish patterns (or bearish patterns) appearing on the same chart in approximately the same time frame.

Figure 1.15 is an example of this. The stock is the Utility HOLDRS Trust (symbol UTH). There are two bearish situations shown here: the first is that UTH broke beneath an extremely long ascending trend line, which indicates a possible change in direction from bullish to bearish. As the price meandered along during the last few months of 2005 and the first few months of 2006, it formed a very well-defined head and shoulders pattern whose neckline it pierced. Since these two patterns were both bearish and

FIGURE 1.15 This chart shows two patterns in action—an ascending trend line, which was violated, and a head and shoulders pattern.

happened roughly in the same period, it made a doubly bearish argument for UTH's direction.

MORE BREAKOUTS

Let us take some more time looking at examples of various breakouts to strengthen our understanding of what to look for and how potent these can be. Your "chart sense"—that is, your ability to recognize patterns in charts without their being pointed out to you—will mainly come from experience. The examples in this book are a first step toward that goal.

The first chart is for EMC Corporation (symbol EMC) from 1988 through 2000 (see Figure 1.16). For about four years, EMC formed a cup with handle pattern, whose resistance is illustrated by the horizontal line on the chart. There are a variety of things to notice about this chart:

- The volume was slowly picking up during the formation of the breakout pattern; it's always encouraging to see interest in a stock grow, even before the breakout.
- When the stock did break out (indicated by the circle), it paused for a little while, but it did not sink beneath the former resistance line; thus, the pattern was tested successfully.
- Subsequent to the breakout, volume increased steadily.

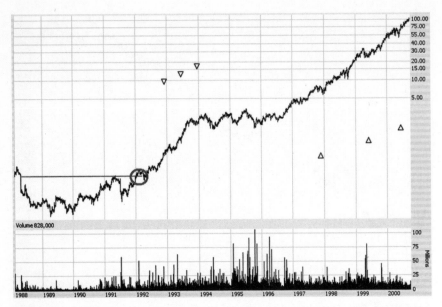

FIGURE 1.16 EMC's stock blasted thousands of percent higher after a breakout from a base. The volume picked up handsomely over the years.

From the point of the breakout, the stock went on to an almost unthinkable 40,000 percent gain. A mere $1,000 invested in this stock and sold at the top would have been worth $400,000.

The next breakout (Figure 1.17) illustrates how you never can tell when a boring stock is going to get exciting. The stock is Hansen Natural Corporation (symbol HANS), which, for a six-year period, must have been one of the most uninteresting stocks around. It bounced between a split-adjusted $1.50 and $2.50 month after month, year after year. And little wonder—this was a very small company selling fruit juice beverages in a world dominated by Coca-Cola and Pepsi.

That all changed in late 2003, about the time the company entered the market for energy drinks. It was clear that this was an important breakout point, because the basing pattern was so old and well-established. It should also be noted here that it's at times like these when a stock seems expensive. After all, think back to how the stock would have looked back then: it would be at an all-time high, and you would be paying more than anyone else had paid for more than six years. So you can imagine why people would be reluctant to pay $3.00 for a stock that so many others had bought for between $1.50 and $2.50. It would be tempting to wait for the price to ease back down again to the lower depths of its six-year-old range.

But this opportunity never came. The stock just started climbing, abandoning its old levels. Interestingly, volume continued to be thin, even while

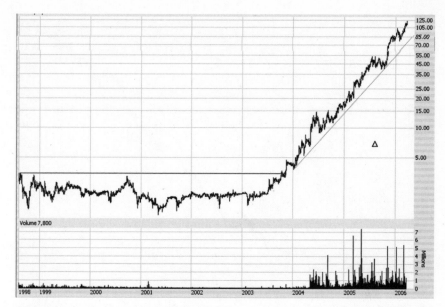

FIGURE 1.17 One of the hottest stocks of 2004 and 2005, Hansen Natural Corporation, made its move after breaking above a very well-formed saucer pattern in late 2003.

the stock doubled from $3.50 to $7.00 in the first few months of 2004. In May 2004, however, volume increased from 10 or 20 thousand shares a day to one or two *million* shares a day. You can see the tremendous increase in volume, which never abated. The stock stayed above its ascending trend line the entire time, increasing a handsome 4,100 percent from its breakout point as of the time of this writing.

It isn't just unknown little companies that can create amazing returns, however. Take a look at 3M Corporation, one of the solidest blue chip companies around, and certainly one that was widely known in the 1980s. Look at Figure 1.18 and see how the company's stock built an amazing cup with handle formation over more than a decade. From 1973 to 1986, the company's stock went essentially nowhere, but it was carving what turned out to be an incredibly potent base pattern.

In 1986 and 1987, the company's stock rose, but during the crash of October 1987, pretty much all the value that had been added to the stock was wiped out in a matter of a few days. What's especially interesting, though, is that 1987's crash is almost an inconsequential blip in the grand scheme of the chart, as 3M went on to an impressive 8,600 percent gain over the next 17 years. Once the basing and breakout were finished, the stock basically never went down and became one of the best-performing stocks of any kind, blue chip or otherwise.

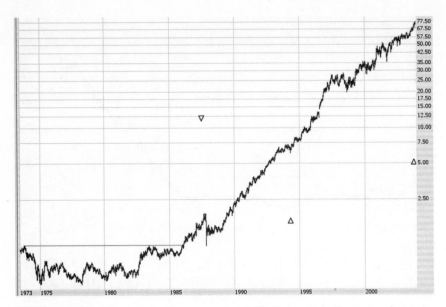

FIGURE 1.18 This very long-term graph of 3M Corporation illustrates that even over a long time period, technical analysis has tremendous weight. The breakout in the mid-1980s was the first step to a staggering rise in the value of 3M.

One last example of a breakout shows once again how vital volume is. A bullish move almost always requires volume to power it up, whereas a bearish pattern can make a stock collapse on its own weight. PetroChina (symbol PTR) had an explosion in volume perfectly correlated to its breakout from a cup with handle pattern in the spring of 2003. Notice the highlighted portion of the volume bars indicating this change in Figure 1.19. The volume is the gasoline that feeds the fire of higher stock prices. As buyers clamor to get into a stock, the excitement feeds off itself. It took a threefold rise in the stock's price before PTR paused at all and its prices eased for a while.

MORE BREAKDOWNS

The same principles that relate to ascending stock prices hold true for descending prices, except that volume isn't quite so important. But what you need to watch are the same simple guidelines of support, resistance, and pattern recognition.

CMS Energy (symbol CMS) is shown in Figure 1.20. The stock had been a top performer from 1985 through 1999, rising well over 10-fold. In 1998

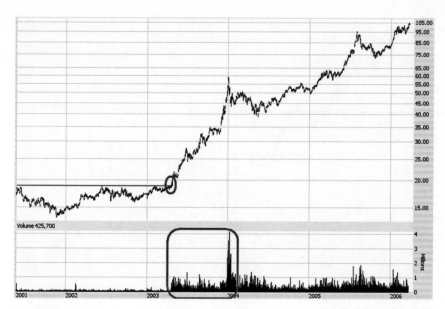

FIGURE 1.19 The gigantic rise in volume was an important factor in this stock's push higher.

FIGURE 1.20 Patterns can range in time from days to years—this head and shoulders pattern formed over a period of two years until it broke beneath its headline in the second half of 1999.

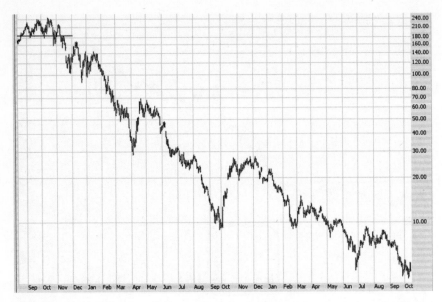

FIGURE 1.21 Juniper lost about 97 percent of its peak value once it broke beneath the neckline of its head and shoulders pattern.

and 1999, however, a head and shoulders pattern formed, and the price broke beneath the neckline. The price shored up and retested the neckline (which was the ideal time to short the stock, since the risk was the lowest) before beginning to fall in earnest. Notice that the fall took some time to fully unfold; the stock actually recovered most of its losses by the spring of 2001, only to begin its slide once more. By the time it was over, CMS had lost 90 percent of its value from its peak.

An even more amazing fall from grace is illustrated with Figure 1.21, which is Juniper Networks (symbol JNPR). This stock fell from $245 to $5 in just two years. A skilled technical analyst would have seen a bad fall coming based on the stock's behavior in 2000. Although the head and shoulders formation is somewhat more complex than normal, the neckline is well defined, and the prices did retest the neckline beautifully.

What made the fall of this stock so dramatic was its incredible rise beforehand. The stock had increased in value from about $18 in the spring of 1999 to $245 in the summer of 2000, so the ascent was very rapid. Because of this, there were very few areas of support on the way down when the stock started falling. Think back to the Red Rover game described earlier in this chapter; there simply weren't any lines of people chained together to slow the stock down. Once the price started falling, it rarely paused, until the buyers and sellers reached a state of equilibrium. But even by 2006,

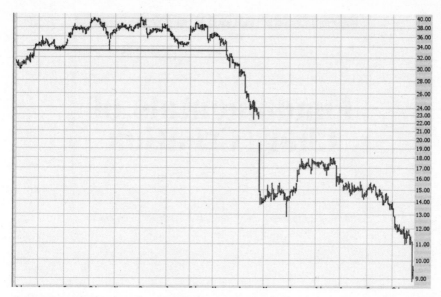

FIGURE 1.22 Not all price breakdowns include a pullback. For this chart, after the price broke, it didn't pause until it lost over half its value.

after the stock had recovered some, the stock price was basically the same as the initial public offering price from seven years earlier.

It has been mentioned a number of times that when a stock starts to fall, it may retrace some of the fall to test the pattern from which it had fallen. This isn't always the case, so you won't necessarily be able to get into a trade if you consistently wait for a better price. A final example of a stock's collapse, which illustrates this point, is Figure 1.22. Once the stock fell beneath its neckline at $33, it never looked back. The stock ultimately bottomed at $9, months later, but those who were waiting for the price to retest the neckline never would have had the opportunity to enter a position.

CHARTING FOR YOURSELF

In this chapter, we have focused on examples from the past. Now let's look to the future and learn how to make some graphs using ProphetCharts. Chapter 2 is going to introduce you to the program and its basic functions so you can start to build your own chart sense with your own computer and the stocks that interest you personally.

CHAPTER 2

Fundamentals of Chart Creation

I n this chapter, we get down to the business of actual charting. You are going to learn about different chart types, how to size and arrange charts, and the differences of charting different kinds of financial instruments, among many other topics.

The first task is to actually get to the charting system itself, which is ProphetCharts. To get to ProphetCharts, you'll need three things:

1. A computer with high-speed Internet access.
2. A browser equipped with Java (such as a recent version of Firefox, Chrome, Safari, or Internet Explorer).
3. Access to ProphetCharts via the Investools Investor Toolbox (www. investools.com) or the thinkorswim brokerage platform (www. thinkorswim.com).

For the purposes of this book, we assume that you are starting from scratch; that is, you have no saved chart styles, study sets, watch lists, or any other settings. There is no harm if you do have some settings already, but we approach this from the vantage point of having a clean slate.

ARITHMETIC VERSUS LOGARITHMIC

One of the most important properties of a chart is whether it is arithmetically scaled or logarithmically scaled. Now this may seem like a very

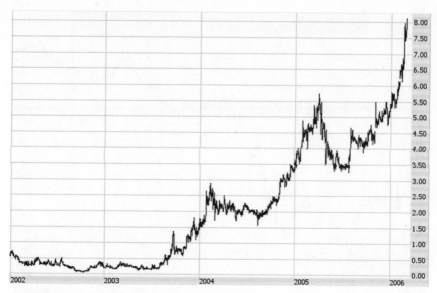

FIGURE 2.1 The arithmetic scale spaces all prices equally, which can create a distorted view for the technical analyst.

esoteric, arcane subject, but it's really quite important. Let's see what this is all about with an example.

First, Figure 2.1 shows an example of a stock that went from about six cents up to eight dollars, a huge 133-fold increase. Note that the chart is arithmetically scaled. Figure 2.2 shows the exact same stock in the same time period logarithmically (also called "log") scaled.

What are some of the differences you see? Generally speaking, the activity in 2002 and 2003 (when the stock was cheaper) is far more pronounced than in later years. On the arithmetic graph, 2002 and 2003 seem to be almost devoid of activity, whereas on the log graph, the stock is at its most dynamic.

The reason for this is simple—an arithmetic graph is constructed with the values of the y-axis (that is, the prices) equally spaced. The difference between 50 cents and $1.00 is the same as the difference between $10 and $10.50—or $100 and $100.50, for that matter. No matter what the price, the bars are scaled the same way.

A log graph, however, represents percentage changes correctly. So if you took a ruler and measured the distance from 50 cents to $1.00, it would be the same as the distance between $100 and $200, because they are both movements of 100 percent.

To be more direct about it, there is no reason you ever need to use an arithmetic graph when looking at a stock chart. It can badly misrepresent

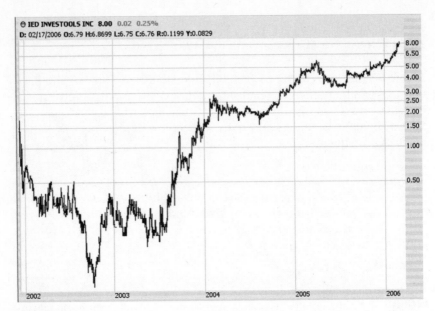

FIGURE 2.2 The log scale represents price movement in terms of percentage change, which is far more appropriate for analysis.

the movement of a financial instrument (be it a stock, a future, or a mutual fund), because it treats all price movements as identical, even if they are not.

If you were given the opportunity to own $10,000 worth of stock that moved from 50 cents to $1.00 and an alternative opportunity to own $10,000 worth of stock that moved from $100 to $100.50, which would you rather have? If you are economically rational, you would take the first choice because you'll make $10,000 in profit, whereas in the second instance you'll make a $50 profit. But an arithmetic graph would represent these price movements as identical, which clearly they are not.

So check the "Log" checkbox in the upper-right corner of ProphetCharts as shown in Figure 2.3; you'll never have to touch it again. (Actually, the default is Log. You have to make an effort to get out of this mode of charting!)

FIGURE 2.3 Check the log checkbox so that all your charts will use log scaling instead of arithmetic scaling.

DIFFERENT INSTRUMENTS, DIFFERENT CHARTS

Before delving into charts, you should understand some subtle differences that exist among different financial instruments that can be charted. Although the vast majority of the readers of this book will be charting stocks, take a moment to understand these differences about charting various kinds of investments:

Stocks—Data will include the open, high, low, and close of a stock for each given day (or whatever time period is chosen)m as well as the volume for that same time period. It is also important to note that stocks are adjusted for splits and dividends, which means that values for some stocks will change over time to take these events into account. So if a given stock was $50 on a certain day, and later that stock has a 2-for-1 split, then the price will be adjusted to $25.

Indices—The data may be identical to stocks (open, high, low, close, volume), but some indices do not have all of this information. Most typically, index data will not have accompanying volume data. In some cases, only the closing price will be available.

Mutual Funds—Only the closing price will be available, which in the world of mutual funds is known as the Net Asset Value (NAV). There is no volume for mutual funds. Mutual fund distributions are taken into account, so that fund prices are adjusted for these distributions in a similar manner as stocks that are adjusted for splits.

Futures/Commodities—These markets contain the same price data (open, high, low, and close) and volume data as stocks. They also have one extra field, known as open interest, which is displayed in the volume portion of the chart. Open interest represents the number of open contracts on a particular market and is shown as a line in Figure 2.4.

Options—The data fields for these charts are identical to futures; you should note, however, that both options and futures tend to have fairly short life spans (usually just a couple of months), so the graphs tend to look quite different from those for stocks, which can span decades.

Forex—Here the information is only one data point per time interval, and unlike any of the other instruments, it defines a relationship of one thing to another. For example, the popular EUR/USD currency pair defines the ratio of the euro to the U.S. dollar.

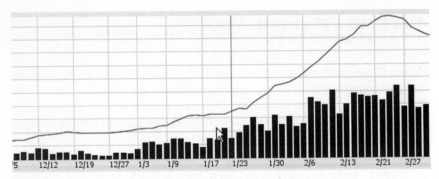

FIGURE 2.4 The black line illustrates the open interest for the commodity being charted. It appears in the same pane as the volume bars.

Regardless of what you are charting, one other fact to understand is that each bar (or point) represents a specific segment in time. That segment could be as little as a single minute or as great as a year. We will go into much more detail about these instrument types in Chapter 5.

LET'S START CHARTING

Once you are on the ProphetCharts page, go ahead and type in a symbol (such as QQQQ) and press Enter. In a moment, the data should load, and the chart should be displayed on your screen.

It's valuable to understand that the data need only load once for a given symbol. Once you have a chart on your screen, any modifications you make to that chart—such as applying studies, putting drawn objects on it, zooming in to it, or rearranging the elements of the chart screen—do not require another download of the data. The only time ProphetCharts has to fetch data again is if you want to load in a new symbol or if you load in a different amount of data for the same symbol (for instance, if you load two years of data when before you had just one).

In the lower-left corner of ProphetCharts is a button labeled Detach. Clicking this button detaches the applet (which is a term we will consider synonymous with ProphetCharts) from its place on the browser window and allows you to resize it any way you like. Double-clicking the title bar of the applet will maximize it, causing it to fill the entire screen. Because screen real estate is helpful when charting, you may find it useful to detach the applet any time you use ProphetCharts in order to give it the maximum available workspace.

ZOOMING FOR A BETTER VIEW

Once you have a chart on the screen, you can zoom in to look at it in more detail. There are a couple of different ways to do this: the zoom tool and the cursor selection.

The zoom tool is located in the lower-right corner of the screen; there are actually two icons related to zooming (Figure 2.5), both of which look like magnifying glasses. The one with a plus sign (+) zooms in to the chart, whereas the one with the minus sign (–) zooms out.

Clicking on the zoom-in tool will show you the rightmost half of the chart each time you click it. So, for example, if you are looking at two years of daily data, clicking zoom-in once will change the chart to just one year of data, and clicking it again will yield six months, three months, and so on. Conversely, clicking on the zoom-out tool will produce the opposite result (three months, six months, and so forth) until the entirety of the chart data you originally selected is displayed.

The other method of zooming is more flexible, since it allows you to home in on any visible part of the chart. This swipe method is simple:

1. Point to the portion of the chart where you want to begin zooming, then click the mouse button.
2. While holding down your mouse button, drag the mouse to the point where you want the zooming to stop (it doesn't matter if you swipe to the left or the right, although usually it's more intuitive for people to go from left to right, since that is how time progresses on the chart).
3. Release the mouse button, and the highlighted area of the chart will instantly be displayed.

During the zooming-in process (Figure 2.6), you will see the portion you are swiping highlighted. You can drag the mouse left or right until you are satisfied with your selection, at which time you can release the mouse.

To revert to the original, complete chart, double-click the mouse anywhere in the chart area.

FIGURE 2.5 The zoom-in and zoom-out icons are in the lower-right corner of ProphetCharts.

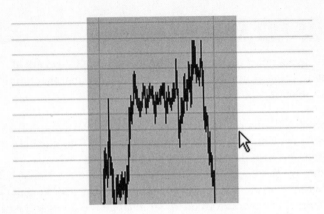

FIGURE 2.6 Dragging the mouse over a portion of the chart will zoom in to that part of the graph.

DATA DETAILS

One of the most basic but useful features of ProphetCharts is the ability to see precise information for any single point on a graph. This information is displayed on the data line (Figure 2.7) just above the graph.

The information in the data line corresponds to wherever the cursor is pointing on the chart (or, if the cursor is not inside the chart, it displays the information for where the cursor was most recently in the chart). There are one-character labels preceding each element of the data line, and here is what they mean:

D: The date (in the example shown, November 4, 2002). If you are look-ing at an intraday graph, this data point includes both the date and the time.
O: Opening price for that price bar.
H: High price for that price bar.
L: Low price for that price bar.
C: Closing (or last) price for that price bar.

⊜ **QQQQ Nasdaq −100 Trust Ser 1 (NQ NM) 41.37 0.00 0.00%**
D: 11/04/2002 **O:**26.05 **H:**26.82 **L:**25.80 **C:**25.90 **R:**1.02 **Y:**40.9408

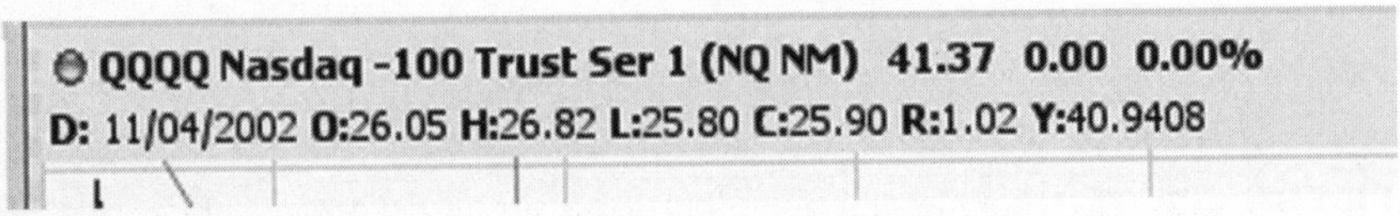

FIGURE 2.7 The data line shows the price data for the one price bar where the cursor is pointed.

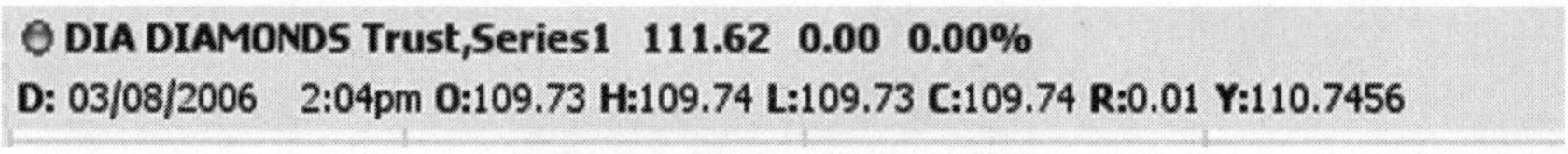

DIA DIAMONDS Trust,Series1 111.62 0.00 0.00%
D: 03/08/2006 2:04pm O:109.73 H:109.74 L:109.73 C:109.74 R:0.01 Y:110.7456

FIGURE 2.8 The data line for intraday graphs also shows the time of the bar whose prices are displayed.

R: Range, which is the difference in price between the high and the low. This can be useful information if you are seeking securities with a large amount of volatility. The larger the R value, the more price volatility took place during that time period.

Y: Y-value of wherever you are pointing. In other words, this reflects the price value at the place where you are pointing. So if you are looking at a chart and point at a part of the chart where you think the price will fall or rise, the Y figure tells you the price at which you are pointing.

In Figure 2.8, for example, is a data line from an intraday chart. Notice how the time has also been added to the data. The time will represent the starting point of the intraday bar. For example, if a particular price bar represents the activity from 11:15 until 11:30 (a 15-minute bar), the time on the data line would say 11:15. The data line in Figure 2.8 is from a minute graph, so it shows that one particular minute: 2:04 P.M.

The data line isn't shown just for price data, however. Technical studies, both overlaid (that is, appearing in the same area as the price data) and those in separate panes have their relevant data displayed as well (Figure 2.9). What is shown will depend on the indicator, but the concept is

MACD3(12,26,9)—MACD 0.0150832 signal 0.0126976 delta 0.0150832 last=-0.0142816;-0.0171122;-0.
Wed
Thu
Fri
Mon
Tue

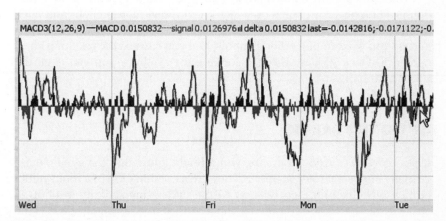

FIGURE 2.9 When technical studies are displayed, the information for the segment of time where the cursor is pointed is displayed in the data line.

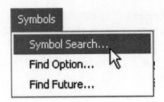

FIGURE 2.10 The Symbols menu lets you find any stock, option, or futures symbol.

the same: the relevant information for that study will appear for whatever day of data to which your cursor is pointed.

SEARCHING FOR SYMBOLS

ProphetCharts provides many different kinds of financial instruments, but you may not always remember the symbol associated with what you want to chart. There are three helpful symbol search tools built into the program. To get to any of these, click on the Symbols menu (Figure 2.10) at the top of the applet.

The first selection, Symbol Search, lets you search for any equity symbol (which includes mutual funds) based on its name. You don't have to know the entire name of the company—just a portion is all you need to enter. Type in as much of the name as you like, and either press Enter or click Search. The results are shown in Figure 2.11.

Once you find the name (and symbol) you want to chart, you can either double-click on your choice or select it (with one mouse click) and click on the Get Chart button. The Symbol Search dialog box will remain open in case you want to find other symbols, and you can see the resulting chart behind it. Once you are through looking for symbols, you can click the Close button.

OPTIONS SEARCH

If you have ever traded options, you already know that the symbols are virtually impossible to remember. They are a combination of a root symbol (which often has little correlation to the underlying security symbol), a strike symbol, and an expiration symbol. Added to this complication is the fact that it's difficult to know what strikes and months are available for any given stock or index.

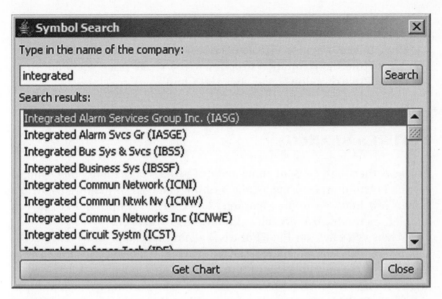

FIGURE 2.11 Entering a portion of a company's name will yield all the company names that have that as part of their name.

The Options Search wizard in ProphetCharts eliminates this problem. Choose "Find Option . . ." from the Symbols menu, and the Options Wizard appears.

The only information you need to provide is the stock symbol whose option you want to find. Enter the symbol in the Symbol box and click the Set button (Figure 2.12). This will cause the Options Wizard to query the

FIGURE 2.12 The Options Wizard makes it easy to locate an arcane options symbol based on a small amount of information.

database for all expiration months and strike prices available for a particular stock.

Once this information is loaded, choose the expiration month and year
you want from the Expiration dropdown, the strike price you want from
the Strike Price dropdown, and click Get Chart.

FUTURES SEARCH

Because there are tens of thousands of stocks and funds, the Symbol
Search is based on entering as much of the name as you know. There are
only a few hundred futures markets, however, so it's possible to take a
simpler, hierarchical approach to finding what you need.

When you click on Find Future, a dialog box appears (Figure 2.13)
that is mostly blank, except for a dropdown menu labeled "Groups." These
groups are general categories of futures (such as "Grains" or "Currencies")
from which you can choose.

Click on the Groups dropdown and select the group of interest to you.
Once you do, the dropdown beneath Groups is filled with the individual
markets that comprise that group. For example, if you choose Grains, markets such as Corn, Soybeans, and Wheat will appear for your selection. You
should therefore choose which market in particular is of interest to you.

When you do this, the Futures Wizard does something very helpful: it
ascertains for that market what years and months are available from the

FIGURE 2.13 The Futures Wizard guides you through the process of finding the
futures contract you want to view.

FIGURE 2.14 As you select different choices from the dropdown menus in the Futures Wizard, the available contracts for that market will be presented to you for selection.

database. This can be a real time-saver, since the months and years for different markets vary widely. In Figure 2.14, for instance, Wheat has been chosen, so all of the possible years (from 1959 forward) and months for Wheat are loaded into the Year and Month dropdown menus, with the front month automatically selected as a suggestion for what you might want.

At this point, you can click on Get Chart to see that particular month. So in this example, the March 2006 Wheat contract will be displayed if you click Get Chart. There are several other choices available to you, however:

> *Continuous.* Futures contracts expire, and the amount of time any given futures contract is active is typically quite short—usually just a couple of months. So, unlike stocks, which can span decades, most futures contracts don't have much data and therefore aren't very helpful in determining broad trends. A continuous contract, however, chains together individual contracts to create a synthetic, never-ending contract. So a continuous contract of the S&P 500 would chain together March 1987, June 1987, September 1987, December 1987, March 1988, and so on. This gives you the opportunity to view decades of markets such as wheat, gold, and Treasury bonds.
>
> A nonadjusted continuous contract is one in which all the regular contracts are simply chained together without any alternation in price. However, some markets have fairly large gaps between contracts. This is often the result of a market being seasonal

(in other words, markets that are crops, not financial commodities). You can distinguish which kind of continuous contract you want—adjusted or nonadjusted—by selecting your choice from the dropdown menu next to the Continuous radio button.

Cash Only. Some of the futures markets have corresponding cash markets available in ProphetCharts. If you want to see the cash market (also known as the spot market), click the Cash Only radio button. There is no guarantee that the cash data are available, however. But a proper symbol for it will be constructed.

Cash Overlay. Instead of seeing just the cash market, you can overlay a futures market with its cash market in the same graph. Click the Cash Overlay radio button to do this so you can see, for example, how the S&P futures contract correlates to the underlying S&P 500 cash index.

STREAMING CHARTS

One of ProphetChart's most useful features is the ability to stream data. In other words, you can make the chart come alive with real-time quotes that also display the chart in motion during the trading day.

To change a static chart to a streaming chart, click the Stream checkbox (as shown in Figure 2.15). When you click Stream, two things happen. First, the chart comes to life with a dynamic price bar on the rightmost part of the chart. So as quotes come in, the bar will grow and change to reflect the open, high, low, and last price data for that particular bar. Once that time period has passed, the bar becomes part of the historical chart and a new bar begins.

The length of time represented depends on the kind of chart you are using. If you are looking at a minute bar chart, the streaming bar will represent anywhere from one second of information (when it first begins) to one minute of information (when it is complete). And all the bars to its left will also represent one minute of time. So the graph will grow during the course of the day, as the stock you are watching bobs up and down with price activity.

FIGURE 2.15 Clicking the checkbox next to Stream will change the graph into a streaming chart.

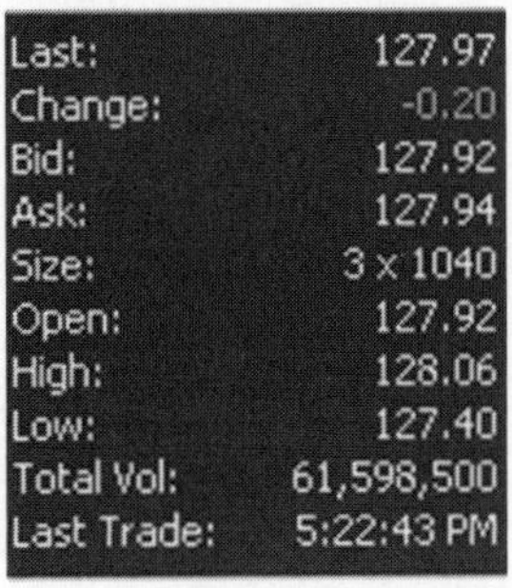

Last:	127.97
Change:	-0.20
Bid:	127.92
Ask:	127.94
Size:	3 x 1040
Open:	127.92
High:	128.06
Low:	127.40
Total Vol:	61,598,500
Last Trade:	5:22:43 PM

FIGURE 2.16 The upper-left portion of ProphetCharts becomes a streaming quote panel when the Stream box is checked.

The other thing that happens (shown in Figure 2.16) when you click Stream is that the upper-left corner of ProphetCharts changes into a streaming quote panel.

This panel shows you the most recent information for the security you are charting. Each data point is clearly labeled, and the Last Trade line shows you the time stamp for the quote being shown, which will tell you how recent the quote is.

CHARTING DIFFERENT TIME PERIODS

ProphetCharts has access to two broadly different kinds of data: intraday data, which can be in segments as short as one minute each, and daily data, which is typically presented as daily bars but can also be shown in cruder granularity (such as weekly or monthly).

When you select how much time you want to see in a chart, you have two choices to make: the duration of the chart and the frequency. The duration (Figure 2.17) is simply how far back in time the data go. The dropdown menu to the right of the symbol entry shows you the available durations. For intraday, the range is from 1 day to 60 days, and for daily, the duration can be anywhere from 1 month to all (which, although ambiguous, will fetch all the data available in the system for that symbol).

The bottom choice on the Duration dropdown is called Custom. This lets you select a specific date range, which doesn't necessarily have to end at the present. For instance, perhaps you want to chart the stock market crash of 1987 and nothing more.

When you select Custom, a dialog box appears with two calendars displayed. The calendar on the left is for you to choose the start date, and the calendar on the right is for the end date. For clarity, any days that are a

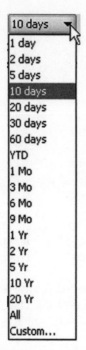

FIGURE 2.17 Choose the duration from the dropdown menu to indicate how much time you want to see in the graph.

FIGURE 2.18 The frequency menu controls how much time is represented in each price bar of the graph.

weekend day or a holiday are displayed in red instead of black. To chart a customized date range, simply select a start date and an end date; then click Get Chart.

Once you choose a duration, ProphetCharts automatically loads that amount of data using the frequency it considers appropriate. So choosing "1 day" will automatically select a frequency of "1m" (that is, one-minute bars); choosing "5 days" will select "5m" (five-minute bars); choosing "1 Yr" will choose "D" (Daily) bars, and so on.

You can choose a different frequency, however. Perhaps you want to see more detail on the chart. For example, if you choose All, the frequency will automatically be set to M (for Monthly data). Perhaps you want to see every day instead. You could therefore choose D from the frequency menu to get more fine-grained information. Or if you chose a 60-day graph, it would automatically provide the prices in hourly bars, but perhaps you want 10-minute bars instead—so you would make this selection from the frequency dropdown, as shown in Figure 2.18.

You may find that the frequency you want isn't displayed on the drop-down. For instance, you might want to look at a 3-minute bar or a 17-minute bar. For intraday charts, you can double-click at the top of the frequency dropdown and manually enter any whole integer you want. This lets you enter any customized frequency you want for an intraday chart.

As you create charts with different combinations of duration and frequency, you will determine there are certain kinds of charts that work well for you. Instead of having to make these choices every time you want to see a certain kind of chart (such as a 5-year-daily chart, a 30-day-minute chart, and so on), you can create what is known as a chart style to automatically conjure up a preselected duration, frequency, and other properties (such as whether the chart streams, whether the volume is shown, and what kind of graph style it is).

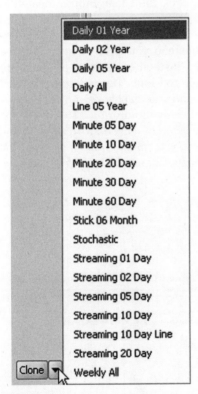

FIGURE 2.19 Chart styles give you one-click access to a wide variety of settings you establish in advance to control the appearance of the chart that works best for you.

FIGURE 2.20 The Clone button, located in the lower-left of the applet, makes another instance of ProphetCharts where you can create different charts.

We will explore how to create and save styles in Chapter 4, but it is valuable to know that this feature is available. As you create different styles (Figure 2.19), you should give them meaningful names that suggest what the styles will invoke.

CLONING CHARTS

When you are using ProphetCharts, you are not limited to just one chart window. You can create multiple windows, and these windows do not have to correspond to one another in any way. Each can have whatever symbol, style, study set, or other properties you choose.

Clicking on Clone (Figure 2.20) will create another instance of ProphetCharts. To create extra charts, click the Clone button located in the lower-left corner of the applet for each new instance.

The chart created will indeed be a clone of the original chart. Perhaps you don't want it to be identical, but instead you want to see the same symbol with a different style. If you do, instead of clicking on the word Clone, click the down-pointing arrow next to Clone. This will bring up a list of all the chart styles you have created, and you can choose any of them.

This can be quite handy if you are closely monitoring a stock. For example, if you are looking at the past five years of daily data on a stock, and you want to see live market activity on it, you might create a clone of the past two days on a minute-by-minute basis (Figure 2.21). If you had such

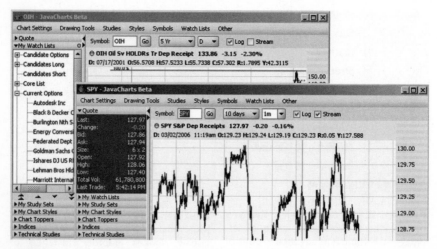

FIGURE 2.21 Multiple charts give you a more complete view of the market's activity.

a chart style available, clicking that style name would create a new chart with that style.

NEXT UP

We have covered a lot of ground in this chapter, including basic chart properties, different kinds of financial instruments, viewing detailed data on a chart, searching for symbols, streaming, and cloning. In the next chapter, we will dig deeper into what else can contribute to a chart style and how we can save and manage these styles for easier, more productive technical analysis.

CHAPTER 3

Modules and Preferences

P rophetCharts has four areas that offer control: general settings, modules, menus, and the tool bar. The second of these, modules, will be covered with this chapter.

The module list is located on the left side of the ProphetCharts applet, and although it has a variety of functions, the principle is similar for each of them. That is, each module provides a list of choices, and each module can be either expanded or collapsed, depending on whether you are interested in it. You therefore can avoid cluttering your screen with items not currently of interest.

Figure 3.1 shows what the module list looks like when all of the modules are collapsed. The arrows on the extreme left can be clicked to expand a list (if it is collapsed) or collapse a list (if it is expanded). Clicking anywhere on the module title will perform this action.

Notice the pair of arrows in the upper-right corner of the module list. This indicates that the entire list of modules can be collapsed in case you do not want access to any of the modules for the time being. This also points out the dividing line where you can make the module list wider or narrower by dragging it.

Figure 3.2 gives an example of resizing. When you point your mouse to the vertical area to the right of the module list, the cursor becomes a two-headed arrow. Once it does, you can hold down the mouse button and drag to the right (for a wider module list) or the left (for a narrower list). Doing this is a trade-off between giving the modules plenty of space (so there is more room for names of technical studies, stock names, and so on) and reducing your chart space. This figure shows

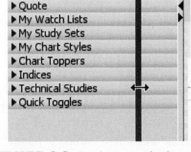

FIGURE 3.1 All the module titles are shown with no content beneath them when all the modules are collapsed.

FIGURE 3.2 By dragging the bar on the right side of the module pane, you can resize it to your liking.

a user reducing the size of the modules so that the chart area has more room.

As mentioned previously, there is a one-click method of instantly changing the module size: clicking either the left-pointing ("collapse") or right-pointing ("revert") arrows in the division bar. If you click the collapse arrow, the module will instantly shrink to nothing, maximizing the space you have for charting. If you click the revert arrow, it will return to whatever size it was before you collapsed it. Figure 3.3 shows what happens when collapse is clicked: there is no module at all on the left, and only the arrows within the dividing line remain.

BASIC MODULE BEHAVIOR

As you know already, clicking the title bar of a module will make the module expand (if collapsed) and collapse (if expanded). Typically, only one

FIGURE 3.3 If the left-pointing arrow on the module area is clicked, the entire module pane collapses, giving you more room for your chart.

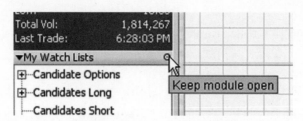

FIGURE 3.4 Holding the mouse pointer over the module's pin causes a tool tip to appear. Clicking this pin toggles between forcing the module open or permitting it to be closed.

module will be open at a time. For instance, if My Watch Lists is open and you click the Chart Toppers, then My Watch Lists will collapse and Chart Toppers will expand. This is ProphetCharts' way of giving you as much information in the module as possible, since it assumes whatever you most recently clicked is what interests you.

However, you might want more than one module open at the same time. To do this, you can pin any module you want to remain open, even if others are opened. You can pin as many modules as you want, up to the extreme of having every single module open simultaneously.

As shown in Figure 3.4, the pin button is a small circle on the right side of the module's title bar. When you put your mouse cursor on top of it, a tool tip will appear, reminding you that clicking this will keep the module open. If you click it, it will turn black (and the module will be pinned). Clicking it again turns it back to an empty circle (and the module will no longer be pinned open).

In Figure 3.5, you can see four modules open at the same time: Quote, My Study Sets, Indices, and Quick Toggles. Notice that the pinned-open modules have the solid black circle on the right part of their title bar. Also note that the Quote module doesn't have such a circle. The reason is that Quote has the special behavior of remaining open even when other modules are open because it's very common to want to see the quote data, even if you are looking at other modules.

THE DETAILS OF EACH MODULE

Let's take a look at each of the modules in detail. Although they have a number of features in common (collapse/expand, ability to pin), each of them is unique in both function and features.

FIGURE 3.5 By clicking several pins in the module pane, you can keep several of the modules open at once.

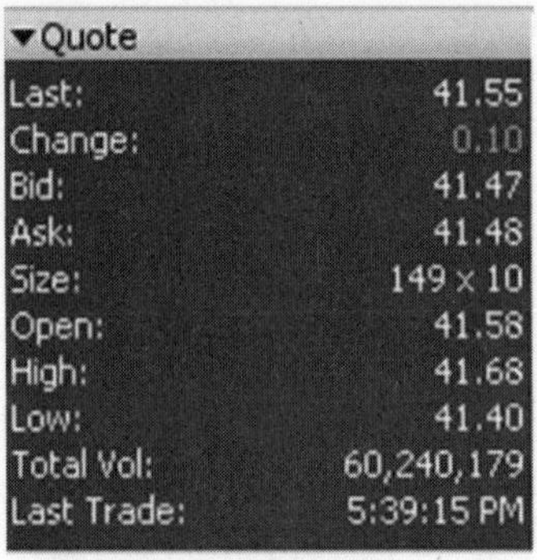

FIGURE 3.6 The Quote panel shows all the most recent price information, including the time stamp of the last trade.

Quote

The Quote module provides you with streaming price information on the security you have charted. Whether the quote is real-time or delayed depends on whether you are entitled to receive real-time data. When the Quote module is on, it will provide you the most recent price information to which you are entitled.

The information provided in the Quote panel (Figure 3.6) includes:

Last: the most recent quote available to you.
Change: the change in price compared with the prior day's close.
Bid: the highest price someone is offering for this security.
Ask: the lowest price at which someone is selling this security.
Size: the quantity of shares offered (in 100s) being bought (first) and sold (second).
Open: the first price of the day for this security.
High: the high price of the day so far.
Low: the low price of the day so far.
Total Vol: the total quantity of shares (or contracts) traded so far today.
Last Trade: the time stamp of the most recent trade; this is most typically in whatever time zone the exchange is located (which, for stocks, would be EST), but this time stamp will display in your own time zone if you have set that in preferences (which will be addressed later in this chapter).

Patterns: Symbols

In Chapter 14, you will learn about the pattern recognition tools that are built into ProphetCharts. This module is where the symbols resulting from a pattern search are housed. Unless you perform a pattern search, this module will be devoid of content.

Candle Patterns: Symbols

Similarly, this module is specifically used to house the results of a pattern search—specifically, a candlestick pattern search. You will learn how to execute this kind of search in Chapter 14 also.

Phase 1 and 2 Scores

Used mainly by fundamental analysts who have been trained with Investools education, the phase 1 and 2 scores represent in a very shorthand way the fundamental strength or weakness of a particular stock symbol. You can learn more about this data at www.investools.com.

Currency Pairs

Foreign exchange trading is based on currency pairs, such as the euro versus the U.S. dollar or the Japanese yen versus the Canadian dollar. All of these figures are ratios of one currency to another, and you can get instant access to any of the available pairs with the currency pairs module.

The module is simply a list of dozens upon dozens of different currency pairs. The main benefit to this module is that you need not remember the arcane symbols that accompany FOREX markets.

Ratio Charts

Ratio charts are covered in Chapter 16. In this module, you can store custom symbols you create with the ratio charts function. This module will be blank at first, but as you create customized symbols, it is much less time-consuming to preserve those symbols in this module than to enter them by hand every time you want to see your chart.

My Watch Lists

Of all the modules, My Watch Lists is probably the most important and the most frequently used. This is where you can view, modify, and use the contents of your watch lists in ProphetCharts. (The subject of watch lists is covered in Chapter 4.)

The content of this module is easy to understand and use. Each watch list you have created is displayed, and if there are any securities inside the

FIGURE 3.7 If a plus sign appears next to a watch list name, it has content. Otherwise, it is an empty list.

watch list, the name of the list will have a plus sign (+) to its left, indicating the list can be expanded to reveal its contents.

For example, in Figure 3.7 there are a variety of watch lists (Candidate Options, Candidates Long, and so on). Four of these have a plus next to them, meaning that any of these four can have their plus sign clicked, which would reveal the securities contained in each of those lists. Those without a plus sign are empty watch lists.

Unlike the modules panel, watch lists are not shown one at a time. When you open a watch list, it will remain open, even if you open others. You can see the contents of all of your watch lists by clicking each of the plus signs. You also have a choice whether you want to see the securities shown by their full name (such as the company's name, in the case of stocks) or only as symbols. This is controlled by the Watch Lists menu, where you can choose either View By Symbol or View By Company Name. By default, View By Company Name is chosen (and therefore a check mark is next to it).

One very useful feature in My Watch Lists is the ability to drag-and-drop items between lists. This lets you control the content of the lists so that your trading world can stay organized.

For example, assume you had three watch lists set up. One was named Candidates Long (which had stocks you were seriously considering buying), another was named Current Long Positions (which had the stocks you actually owned), and another was named Stocks I Follow (which was everything else, neither owned nor being considered for purchase).

Being able to drag-and-drop between these lists is clearly valuable, since what belongs in these lists changes over time. If Apple Computer (symbol AAPL) was in your Stocks I Follow list, and you were seriously considering buying it, you would drag it to the Candidates Long list. Later,

FIGURE 3.8 The four different kinds of arrows at the bottom of a module let you easily move the contents of a list up and down within that module.

if and when you actually bought some of this stock, you would drag it to the Current Long Positions list.

The mechanics of dragging and dropping will be addressed in this chapter, since it applies to other modules as well. Another helpful feature in My Watch Lists, as well as in most other modules, is the arrows that appear at the bottom of the module. There is a pair of up-arrows and a pair of down-arrows on the left and right, and a single up-arrow and down-arrow in the middle, as shown in Figure 3.8.

Clicking these arrows while in a module will do the following:

- *Double-Up Arrow* (keyboard equivalent: Ctrl-Up Arrow): Will either go to the previous tagged item in the current list or to the top of the list if no item is tagged. A tagged item is one that shows up in boldface, and items are tagged by choosing "Tag" when right-clicking a symbol. If you are at the top of a list, clicking the double-up arrow will go to the last item in the previous list, if there is one.
- *Up Arrow* (keyboard equivalent: Up Arrow): Will go to the previous item in the current list. If you are at the top of a list already, it will go to the last item in the previous list. For instance, if you have two watch lists, "list one" and "list two," and the current selection is the first item in list two, then clicking the up arrow would select the last item in list one, since that is the next item "above" your current location.
- *Down Arrow* (keyboard equivalent: Down Arrow): Moves down to the next item in the current list. If you are at the bottom of a list, and another list follows, it will open up the next list and choose the first item on that list.
- *Double-Down Arrow* (keyboard equivalent: Ctrl-Down Arrow): Moves down to the next tagged item on the current list or, if there is none, moves to the bottom of the current list. If you are at the bottom of a list and another list follows, it will go to the first item in the subsequent list.

The arrow sets provide a quick and easy way of navigating within lists, particularly long ones. These arrows are especially useful if you make use of tagging symbols. For instance, you may have a list of 200 stocks you follow, but only 20 of them are of great interest and are therefore tagged. Being able to click through this list-within-a-list is a great time-saver.

My Portfolios

If you manage your portfolios on Investor Toolbox or Prophet.net, the information you enter is automatically available in ProphetCharts via the My Portfolios module. Within this module will be displayed the names of all the portfolios you have created, as well as their contents.

By opening any single portfolio, you can see the symbol, quantity, and entry price of each item within that portfolio. For instance, if you bought 700 shares of Apple Computer at a price of $72.63, there would be a line item reading "AAPL 700 @ $72.63" underneath the name of the portfolio containing that entry.

Deeper information, such as profits and losses and net changes, is not displayed here, since that information is more appropriate to the Market-Matrix or Portfolio pages. This module provides you a view into your holdings with a single glance, which saves you the trouble of having to refer to a different page.

My Study Sets

A study set is a collection of one or more technical studies that work together. For instance, you might have put together a series of three different moving averages (15-day, 50-day, and 100-day) plus a MACD study and called this the "Bullish Breakout" study set. This name would appear in the list of your study sets for easy access. Creating and naming study sets will be addressed in Chapter 7.

The module named My Study Sets is simply that—a list of your study sets that you can double-click to apply to the current chart (and any subsequent symbols you may enter). You can also right-click on any particular study set name to choose "Use this Study Set" (which is the same as double-clicking) or "Delete this Study Set." Figure 3.9 shows an example of

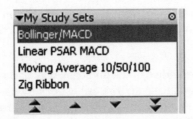

FIGURE 3.9 My Study Sets shows the names of the technical study sets you have created. When you first start using ProphetCharts, this will be an empty module.

the expanded module showing four study sets. When you first start using ProphetCharts, this module will have nothing in it.

My Chart Styles

This module is as easy to understand as My Study Sets, because it is a simple list of customized objects you have created and can access with a double-click of the mouse. In this module are your chart styles. (The subject of creating chart styles will be covered in Chapter 4.)

A chart style is a collection of properties that define the appearance and settings of a chart. For example, suppose you created a chart that had a duration of 10 days, a frequency of 1 minute, had no volume displayed, had streaming data, and used the candlestick style of graph. It would take you time to get this style of chart again later unless you preserved all of these settings into a chart style. You could save all of these properties (and there could be many more, for this is just an easy example) and name them as a chart style.

My Chart Styles displays, in alphabetical order, all of the chart styles you have created. As with the study sets, when you first start using ProphetCharts, this module will be empty. But, as in Figure 3.10, you can create as many useful styles as you like.

This also helps illustrate why it's important to give meaningful names to each style and to name them in such a way that they are well ordered. If some of the names in the figure were "Ten-Year Daily" and "5-Year Daily" and "10-Minute Graph" and "Single Day Streaming," the list would be more jumbled, and it would be harder to locate the style you really wanted.

Chart Toppers

The one module with constantly changing lists throughout any trading day is Chart Toppers. This is not a list that you construct. Instead, it is a live, up-to-date report of the securities that are trading and are doing extraordinary things; each list contains 10 stocks. This chart module provides live scan results on:

- *Percent Gainers*: stocks priced higher than $1 that are up the most for the present day (or, if you are looking at the chart module on a weekend or holiday, the most recent trading day) on a percentage basis.
- *Dollar Gainers*: stocks priced at higher than $1 that are up the most in absolute dollar terms for the present day.
- *New 52-Week Highs*: stocks that during the present day reached a price higher than any previous closing price for the past year.

FIGURE 3.10 The Chart Styles module gives you quick access to all the customized collections of parameters that control the appearance of a chart.

- *New 52-Week Lows*: stocks that during the present day reached a price lower than any previous closing price for the past year.
- *Dollar Losers*: stocks priced at higher than $1 that are down the most in absolute dollar terms for the present day.
- *Percent Losers*: stocks priced at higher than $1 that are down the most for the present day on a percentage basis.
- *Most Active*: the most actively traded stocks, measured by share volume.

As you can see in Figure 3.11, the Chart Toppers module covers the three U.S. stock exchanges: NYSE (New York Stock Exchange), NASDAQ, and AMEX (American Stock Exchange). Each of these has its own set of seven live-scan results.

When you open the Chart Toppers module for the very first time, only the exchange abbreviations will appear. Clicking the plus sign (+) will

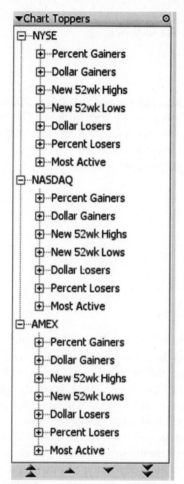

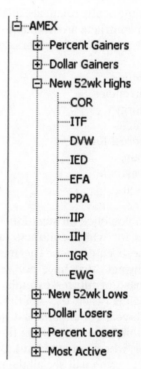

FIGURE 3.11 All three major U.S. exchanges are represented in the Chart Toppers module.

FIGURE 3.12 You can click on any plus sign to see the detailed results of the scan for that particular exchange.

reveal the seven scan lists beneath that exchange. You can then click the plus sign for any particular list to see the individual stock components. In Figure 3.12, the 10 symbols that are making new yearly highs on the American Stock Exchange are shown.

You can right-click on any stock symbol to add it to a watch list. Because the markets move through the day, these lists in turn change throughout the day. Looking at the Chart Toppers module is not only a way to discover where the action is but is also a great way of uncovering highly dynamic stocks that you might not yet be following.

Futures

There are hundreds of futures contracts available at any one time, and remembering the complex symbols behind them can be very difficult. The futures module neatly organizes all the futures markets, as well as the months for which contracts are available, into a three-tier hierarchy.

The first tier are the general kinds of futures, which are:

+ E-Minis
+ Currencies
+ Energy
+ Indices
+ Interest Rates
+ Grains
+ Livestock
+ Metals

When you click on any of these categories, you will see all the months and years for which contracts are available for the markets that reside within these categories. The month-year combinations will be only for those contracts that have not yet expired. In other words, even though the database of futures extends back to the 1950s, you will only see, in chronological order, the months and years that have not gone by yet. So the month-year combinations displayed are the second tier of this module.

The third and final tier is the markets themselves (such as pork bellies, silver, wheat, and the like). By clicking on a particular month (such as March 2011), you will see all the markets for which contracts are available on that given month. Double-clicking on one of these contracts will fetch the data for that chart.

Indices

Having an understanding of where the broad market is, and where you think it might be going, is vital to good investing. There are many hundreds of different indices and indicators available, but only a relatively small number are widely followed.

Many of these are household names (such as the Dow Jones Industrial Average), but the symbols that represent some of them are not easy to remember (such as $XMI, $COMPQ, and $NDX). ProphetCharts provides a quick way to access any of the most popular with the Indices module

FIGURE 3.13 You can have easy access to the chart of any major U.S. index with the Indices module.

(see Figure 3.13). You can double-click on any of the items in the list (or drag-and-drop the item from the list into the chart area) to get access to that index.

Technical Studies

ProphetCharts has almost 200 different technical studies you can apply to price data. These studies are covered later in the book, but for now all you need to know is that you can access any of them from the Technical Studies module.

When you expand this module, all of the studies are displayed in alphabetical order, as shown in Figure 3.14. You can double-click on any study to apply it to the price chart (or drag-and-drop it onto the chart). Once a study is applied to a chart, any other symbols you enter will have the same study. If you double-click another study, it will replace the study currently being used. (You will learn how to apply multiple studies in Chapter 7.)

Breakout Studies

This module contains seven predefined study sets. They are called breakout studies because the arrows indicating when a study has broken above or below a signal area are present (green up-arrow for upward breakout; red down-arrow for downward breakout). As with Technical Studies, any of the following seven studies can be applied by double-clicking the name

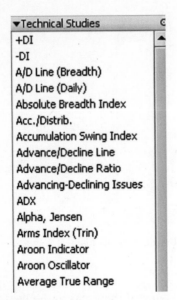

FIGURE 3.14 There are nearly 200 different technical studies available in ProphetCharts, any one of which is available in the Technical Studies module.

FIGURE 3.15 The Quick Toggles module gives you one-click access to turn settings on or off.

or by dragging and dropping it into the price chart.

1. CCI with Breakout Signals.
2. EMA with Breakout Signals.
3. MA with Breakout Signals.
4. MACD Hist. with Breakout Signals.
5. Momentum with Breakout Signals.
6. RSI, Wilder with Breakout Signals.
7. Stochastics with Breakout Signals.

Quick Toggles

The next module on the list is Quick Toggles. A toggle is sort of like an on-off switch. In this case, there are five different items that can be toggled on or off by checking a box (Figure 3.15). These five items are:

1. *Color Bars:* When checked, this makes all of the price bars representing downward movement in price turn red, as well as the corresponding volume bars.

2. *Hide Expansion:* In Chapter 9, you will learn about expanding the white space in a chart in order to give you more room on the time axis (to the right of the chart) and the price axis (above and below the chart). When this item is checked, any expansion you have done with the expansion tool is suppressed, thus yielding a normal chart without any extra white space. Unchecking the box puts the chart back into expanded mode. Ctrl-F yields the same result.

3. *Hide Drawn Items:* When checked, this will hide all of the trend lines, Fibonacci studies, highlights, and other items drawn with the tool bar. This item is similar to Hide Studies in the sense that you can temporarily clean up a chart of embellishments and just look at the prices. You can use Ctrl-D for the same results.

4. *Hide Events:* When checked, this will hide any corporate events, such as stock splits, dividends, conference calls, and earnings announcements. You can use Ctrl-E for the same result.

5. *Hide Grid Lines:* Normally, ProphetCharts displays the familiar Cartesian coordinate grid of horizontal lines and vertical lines that are on most charting programs. You may want to eliminate these lines for a cleaner, simpler chart, which you can do with this checkbox or the keyboard equivalent, Ctrl-G.

6. *Hide Studies:* When checked, any of the technical studies being displayed will disappear. Checking this on and off is a quick way of seeing the pure price chart temporarily if you are using technical studies. You can use Ctrl-S for the same effect.

7. *Hide Volume:* When checked, this toggle will eliminate the volume graph. This frees up more room for the price chart, and if you're looking at a chart that doesn't have volume data (or you simply aren't interested in examining the volume at that time), you should check this box. You can use Ctrl-Space for the same effect.

Option Controls

If you trade options, you will probably find this module extremely helpful. In it are four checkboxes that offer options charting features that are difficult or impossible to find anywhere else. The four checkboxes and their functions are:

1. *Avg. Imp. Volatility:* Clicking this on will plot on a new graph pane (beneath the price pane) the average implied volatility for a stock graph. This data begins February 2005 and works only with stock charts.

2. *Bid-Ask Overlay:* Most options are extremely thinly traded. This means that 99.9 percent of options charts are virtually unreadable, since they typically consist of just a few lines here and there. However, the bid price and ask price within these options markets do change, even if there is no trading, and the ProphetCharts servers store the bid and ask information at the close of every day for every option. This means that a meaningful graph, showing the true market motion of an option irrespective of its popularity, is possible. Checking the Bid-Ask Overlay box will leave the price data on the chart, but it will also overlay two line graphs (the upper one being ask, the lower one being bid) so you can see what the market was actually doing during this time span. This feature works only when you are viewing an option chart.

3. *Compare with Stock:* Checking this (when viewing an option graph) will automatically load the underlying stock corresponding to this option and plot it on its own distinct axis. The stock axis will be on the left side of the screen (to indicate price), and the option price axis will be on the right side. This is an outstanding way of viewing how a stock's price movement affects an option, since the widely disparate prices of these two instruments are reconciled by providing an independent price axis for each.

4. *Implied Volatility:* This checkbox will work only for an option graph. Turning this checkbox on will plot an implied volatility for an option in a separate pane.

PREFERENCES IN PROPHETCHARTS

The last item in the Chart Settings menu in ProphetCharts is called Preferences. This is probably not something you will access very often, but it has some important features that you may find helpful, some of which are directly related to modules. Figure 3.16 shows the dialog box that appears when you choose this item, and the following sections describe each part of the preferences.

Appearance

This portion of Preferences controls four different elements. Let's take a close look at this section to understand each one. See Figure 3.17.

The Font Size dropdown menu lets you choose between Small, Medium, and Large Fonts. The default is Small Fonts, but you may find it difficult to read the characters on the chart, such as the data line, the

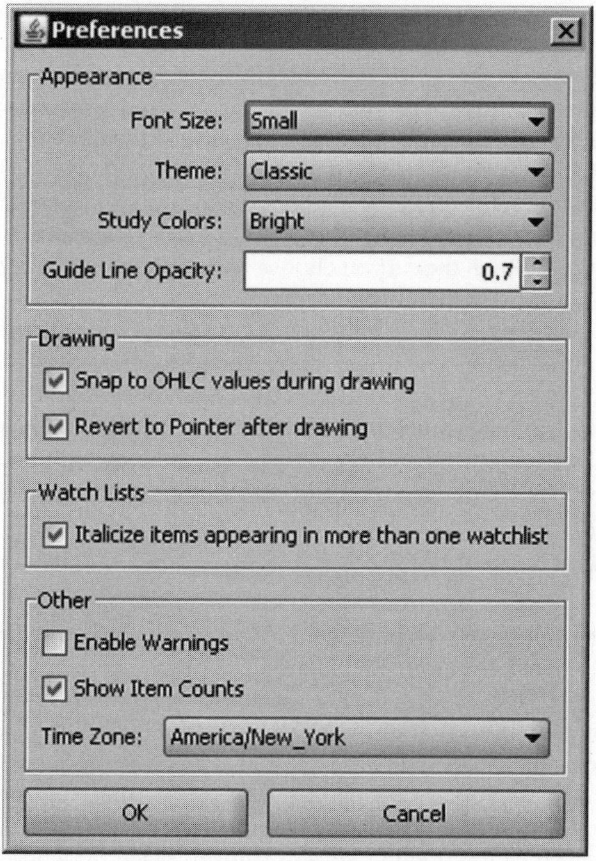

FIGURE 3.16 There are many different preferences you can set in ProphetCharts. These will be retained in your account so you don't have to set them each time you use the program.

FIGURE 3.17 You can control the general appearance of ProphetCharts with the appearance portion of the Preferences section.

quote panel, and the contents of the other modules. You can make all of this easier to read with a larger font setting.

The Theme is the color scheme used by ProphetCharts. You can choose a different theme to change the colors used within the program. You should try each of the themes so you can select whatever is easiest for you to read and most pleasing to the eye.

Study Colors lets you apply a color scheme only to the technical studies (if any) present on a chart. The choices as of this writing are Bright, Earth, and Soft. Which theme you choose is strictly an aesthetic preference and will not otherwise affect the chart.

Guide Line Opacity controls how heavy the guide lines (that is, the vertical and horizontal lines that follow the cursor around) are. You can click the up and down arrows to move this figure anywhere from as low as 0.1 (the lines will be virtually invisible) to 1.0 (the lines will be solid). Here you can balance the trade-off between plainly visible guidelines against the visual noise they create for you while examining a chart.

Drawing

There are two checkboxes here, each of which is extremely important to the behavior of the program. See Figure 3.18.

"Snap to OHLC values during drawing" will, when checked, make drawn objects snap so that drawing accurate objects is much easier. Each price bar on a chart has an open, high, low, and close price (OHLC). If this is not checked, as you are trying to put a drawn object on the chart, the program will let you freely pick any pixel on the screen.

However, it's most likely that you want to place the end point of the drawn object on a specific part of the price bar (most typically the high or low price). Checking this feature frees you from needing surgeon's hands to accurately place a drawn object on the price bars. It is usually a wise idea to have this item checked, particularly if you do a lot of drawing.

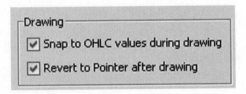

FIGURE 3.18 You will probably want to have both of these boxes checked, since they make using drawn objects much easier in the program.

"Revert to Pointer after drawing" controls the behavior of the tool bar. If this is not checked, the tool bar will be in what is known as a persistent mode. In this mode, once you have selected an object, that object will remain selected until you choose another one.

In persistent mode, if you select the Trend Line tool, that tool will remain selected until you choose something else. So every time you go to the chart and click the mouse, a new trend line will be created. If you intend to draw a lot of trend lines (or any other particular object), this persistent mode is handy.

Typically, since you'll want to revert to the pointer mode after you have drawn an object, you'll want this checkbox checked. Most of the time you will want to draw a single item (such as a trend line) and then be in a position to zoom in or perform some other cursor-related function, as opposed to drawing a succession of new objects.

Italicize Items Appearing in More Than One Watch List

Depending on how you organize your watch lists, you might want to know if there are any duplicates among the contents of your lists. For example, suppose you had one very large list called Core List, another called Short Positions, and another called Long Positions. Further suppose you only wanted a symbol to be in any one of these three lists at any given time.

If the lists are large, it is difficult to keep track, but if you mark the checkbox to Italicize Items Appearing in More Than One Watch list, ProphetCharts will do just that—put any symbols that are not unique to a Watch list in italics. This will help you spot symbols appearing in multiple places.

Enable Warnings

If checked, this will instruct ProphetCharts to provide warnings about certain functions in the program, such as the deletion of an item from a watch list. Warnings are helpful when you are first starting to use the program so that you have a chance to think about what you are going to do before committing to it. As you gain expertise in the program, however, you may not want to waste time reading these warnings, and checking this box will suppress them altogether.

Show Item Counts

If you mark this checkbox, a sum total of the symbols in each Watch list will appear next to the name of each Watch list. So if you have 157 symbols in the Watch list called Focus, then the list name will appear as Focus (157) in the Watch Lists module. Keeping a count is handy for many reasons; for instance, if you wanted to track all the components of the S&P 100, it is helpful to have a checksum next to the watch list you create so that you know there are indeed 100 symbols housed in that list and that you haven't missed any when entering them.

Time Zone

Time is displayed in two different places on a chart—one is in the Quote module, and another is on the x-axis of the chart when intraday data are being displayed (and, in turn, on the data line as you move the cursor left and right). Normally, the time used in these places is based on the local time of the exchange where the security is traded. If you are looking at a chart of IBM, which trades on the New York Stock Exchange, the times shown will be in Eastern (meaning the market opens at 9:30 A.M. and closes at 4:00 P.M.).

Perhaps you live in San Francisco. From your point of view, the market opens at 6:30 A.M. and closes at 1:00 P.M. You can choose your time zone in Preferences so that you don't have to do a mental conversion of the time when you look at it. Just choose an appropriate time zone from the list provided.

As you can see in Figure 3.19, there are a lot of time zone options in Preferences. Once you are satisfied with your choices, click the OK button to apply your changes (or Cancel if you want them all ignored).

One final point is that you can also use the Other menu in ProphetCharts as a shortcut to changing the font size, color theme, or line color setting, as shown in Figure 3.20.

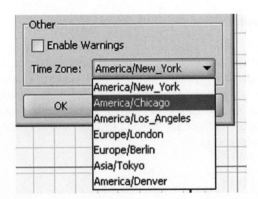

FIGURE 3.19 If you want to set the time shown for trading events to be the same as your local time, you can do so here.

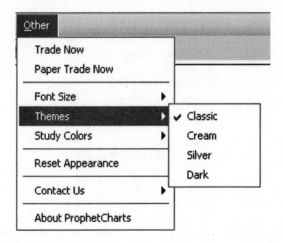

FIGURE 3.20 A shortcut to some of the appearance controls in ProphetCharts is available from the Other menu at the top of the program's screen.

DRAGGING AND DROPPING

Because ProphetCharts uses the latest Java technology, it has access to the most sophisticated user interface features. One of these is the ability to drag-and-drop items from place to place.

As an illustration of what a time-saver this is, you could compare the method of moving a stock from one watch list to another in JavaCharts (which was ProphetCharts' predecessor) to the current product. In JavaCharts, you would need to:

1. Right-click on the symbol you want to move.
2. Choose the menu item "Move to Watch List."
3. A dialog box of available watch lists will appear.
4. You choose a watch list from the dropdown and click OK.

With drag-and-drop, you simply click on the symbol you want to move and drag it to its destination. As you do this, a faint ghost of what you are dragging appears so you can easily tell what you are doing. In this example (Figure 3.21), the stock Affiliated Managers Grp is being dragged from the Current Options watch list up to the Candidate Options list.

You can also drag any security from any module (not just watch lists) onto the chart area to automatically load that symbol. This is often easier than manually typing in the stock symbol (which you might not even

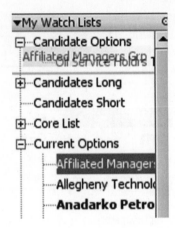

FIGURE 3.21   Moving an item from one watch list to another is simply a matter of dragging it from place to place.

know). Again, a ghost image shows in the price chart area until you release the mouse button, causing the new chart to load. See Figure 3.22.

RIGHT-CLICKING FOR MORE ACTIONS

One last aspect of the modules section is that you can access other functions by right-clicking on the item inside most of the module lists. These functions vary by module, so here is a snapshot of some of them.

If you store study sets, the names of those sets are in the My Study Sets module (see Figure 3.23). Right-clicking on any of these names gives you three choices: (1) Use This Study Set, which will apply that set to the current chart; (2) Delete This Study Set, which, after confirmation, will remove it from your settings; and (3) Rename This Study Set, which will present a dialog box in which you can rename any of the study sets as you wish.

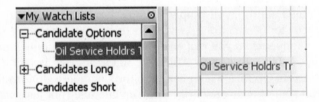

FIGURE 3.22   When you drag an item from a watch list into the chart area, it will automatically chart that item for you once you release the mouse button.

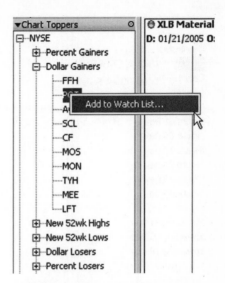

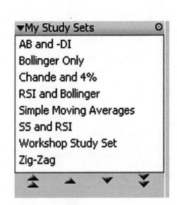

FIGURE 3.23 Right-click on any study set to apply, delete, or rename it.

FIGURE 3.24 Right-clicking on a symbol from Chart Toppers lets you add it to any of your watch lists.

Chart toppers gives you access to all the unusual trading activity on the various exchanges, such as new highs and lows, biggest dollar gainers and losers, most active securities, and so forth, all partitioned by exchange. Going through the lists in this module, especially on days when the market is making a major move, will usually yield at least a few interesting symbols you would like to add to a watch list. A quick way to do this is to right-click on the symbol, such as in Figure 3.24, and choose Add to Watch List, which will provide you a list of your lists so you may click the appropriate recipient.

My Chart Styles, shown in Figure 3.25, has offerings similar to My Study Sets when you right-click on its content. That is, you can Use, Delete, or Rename whatever chart style on which you right-click. If you have warning messages activated, ProphetCharts will confirm whether you're sure about deleting anything.

The longest right-click list is within My Watch Lists (Figure 3.26). The choices given are:

- *Copy to List:* Lets you take a stock and copy it to another list while at the same time leaving it in its current list. When you select this, a dialog box of available watch lists appears. You can choose the destination for the selected symbol from this list.

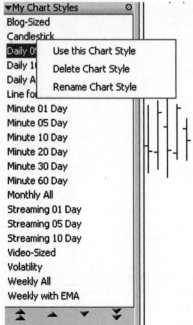

FIGURE 3.25 The chart styles module gives you a quick way to apply or delete a chart style if you right-click on any existing style.

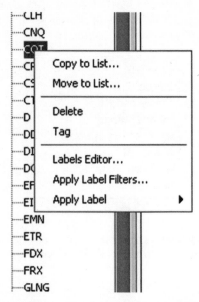

FIGURE 3.26 Right-clicking an item in a watch list provides a variety of functions, including the ability to copy, move, delete, or tag the item.

- *Move to List:* This is like Copy to List, except that the stock is removed from its current list. This is identical in outcome to dragging and dropping.
- *Delete:* Removes the symbol from the list.
- *Tag:* Makes the symbol (or company name) boldface so that it stands out from the others. This can be a very useful feature if applied properly. Tagging is a way of calling out certain stocks within a list. If you want to pay special attention to certain securities, you can tag them, which not only makes them easier to discern because they are bold but also makes navigating the watch list with the arrows more powerful since you can leap directly from tagged symbol to tagged symbol. If the symbol you are right-clicking is already tagged, this menu item is Remove Tag.
- *Labels Editor:* You will learn about labels in detail in Chapter 16. This item invokes the dialog box that lets you edit, add, and delete labels for symbols.

- *Appy Label Filters*: Brings up the dialog box that lets you restrict the contents of watch lists based on the labels of the items within each one.
- *Apply Label*: Lets you choose which, if any, of the available labels you would like to apply to the selected symbol. Labels that are selected will have a check mark next to them.

You have learned a great deal about modules and preferences in this chapter. You have learned how to exercise control over many aspects of the chart's appearance and how to use some of ProphetCharts features to make applying these controls quick and easy. In the next chapter, we will explore watch lists and chart styles to make using ProphetCharts more efficient.

CHAPTER 4

Watch Lists and Chart Styles

Watch lists are a way of keeping your trading world organized. As you become a more experienced trader, you will have a variety of ideas about what to trade. Sometimes you will come across a stock you are thinking about buying. Other times you will see stocks you might want to short. Or you might want to start a list of companies whose products you like, and another list of companies whose stock you already own.

No matter how you want to organize your trading ideas, the effective use of watch lists is the best way to handle the goal in ProphetCharts. And this certainly doesn't mean putting all the stocks into a single group called "My Watch List." This chapter will show you the mechanics of managing watch lists (as well as chart styles) and how to use them effectively.

WATCH LIST BASICS

At the top of ProphetCharts are the various menus, one of which is named Watch Lists. Within it are all the controls you need to manage your watch lists. A watch list is a compilation of financial instruments that you collectively name and manage. You control what is inside the list, and you can move things to and from various lists to keep them well organized.

You might not necessarily *own* the stocks in your watch lists. Some watch lists you create might be along the following lines:

Candidates Long—Stocks you are considering buying.
Candidates Short—Stocks you are considering selling short.

FIGURE 4.1 The Watch Lists menu provides all the basic controls needed for Watch List management and viewing.

Current Long—Stocks you currently own.
Current Short—Stocks you currently are short.
Core List—The main list of stocks you track regularly.
High Fliers—Volatile stocks.
Steady Performers—Stable, steadily rising stocks.

The lists and their contents are really up to you. But the watch lists should be given names that suggest their content, and they should be unique enough to be useful.

The Watch Lists menu (Figure 4.1) includes six choices:

1. *Add to Watch List:* Add the stock displayed in the chart to a watch list of your choice.
2. *Create New Watch List:* Create and name a new watch list.
3. *Delete Watch List:* Delete the watch list of your choice and its contents.
4. *Apply Label Filters:* This topic will be covered thoroughly in Chapter 16, but this function bases the contents of the watch lists on the filters you apply.
5. *Delete Label:* This topic also will be covered in Chapter 16, but this function lets you delete a label you previously defined.
6. *View by Symbol:* View all of the securities in the watch lists by their ticker symbol.

FIGURE 4.2 When adding a symbol to a watch list, you can choose from any of the watch lists in the dropdown menu.

7. *View by Company Name:* View all of the securities in the watch lists by their company name (this is the default choice).

8. *Import:* You can import a text file of symbols into a watch list with this function, which can be a big time-saver. For instance, let's say you find a list of all the symbols in the S&P 100 on the Internet. You could save that list of symbols to your hard drive and then import that text file via ProphetCharts' import command, saving you the time and trouble of entering all those symbols individually.

When you choose Add to Watch List, ProphetCharts will take whatever symbol is displayed currently and add it to whatever watch list you select. Figure 4.2 shows the Add Favorite dialog box, which contains a dropdown menu of all your watch lists, sorted alphabetically. Choose the list to which you want the symbol added and click OK to finish the task.

To create a new watch list, choose Create New Watch List, and enter the name you would like it to have (Figure 4.3). Remember to give it a name that helps identify its contents, because once you have a large collection of these lists, you will want them to be easy to organize. Also keep in mind that your new watch list will be empty at first.

FIGURE 4.3 Type in whatever name you would like to give the watch list, but try to make it something that describes the contents you intend for that list.

FIGURE 4.4 Deleting a watch list permanently removes all the symbols and the watch list name. ProphetCharts will confirm you want to delete a list before actually doing so.

If you decide to completely eliminate a watch list from your account, choose Delete Watch List from the menu. A dropdown menu of all the watch lists available (Figure 4.4) will be shown. Choose the one you want to delete and click OK. Because the deletion is permanent, ProphetCharts will double-check with you to make sure you want to go ahead with the deletion. If you confirm it, the watch list will be gone.

MY WATCH LISTS

Although the Watch Lists menu is useful, you will probably find that the My Watch Lists module is a more efficient place to manage your lists. From the module you can move items from one list to another, perform drag-and-drop operations, copy items from place to place, rename lists, and perform many other functions.

When you expand My Watch Lists, all of your watch lists will be shown in the state you last left them. The lists are shown in alphabetical order, and you can either expand them (which means the contents are shown, and there will be a minus sign next to the list name) or collapse them (meaning only the list name will be shown, and a plus sign will be next to it).

Figure 4.5 shows a portion of a hypothetical My Watch Lists. The list called Candidates Long is expanded, and some of the company names in that list are boldfaced, meaning they have been tagged. The list above it (Candidate Options) is empty, so there is no plus or minus next to the list name. The list beneath it (Candidates Short) is collapsed, so there is a plus sign next to it.

If you were to choose View by Symbol from the Watch Lists menu, the same list would resemble Figure 4.6. Note that although symbols are shown instead of company names, tagged items still appear in boldface. Note also that alphabetically sorted symbols may not necessarily appear in the same

FIGURE 4.5 This expanded watch list shows the stocks expressed as their company name. Some of the securities have been tagged, and they are displayed in boldface.

FIGURE 4.6 This is the same list of securities shown in Figure 4.5, except they are displayed by symbol instead of name.

order as alphabetically sorted names, since company names and symbols do not always correspond (an example being symbol T, which corresponds to the company name AT&T).

DRAGGING-AND-DROPPING

One of the most useful features in ProphetCharts is the ability to drag an item from one watch list to another. This makes it quick, easy, and convenient to keep your watch lists organized as you move things from place to place.

For instance, assume you had five watch lists—Candidates Long, Candidates Short, Current Long, Current Short, and Favorite Stocks. Further assume you were an active trader and were often examining stocks and

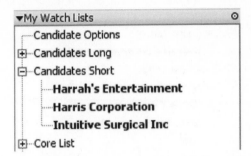

FIGURE 4.7 This shows three tagged symbols in the Candidates Short module.

opening and closing positions. You can imagine how dynamic these lists would become. By being able to drag symbols from one list to another as their status changes, you would be able to keep your trading world organized. So a stock you regularly follow (in the Favorite Stocks list) might be moved to the Candidates Short list if you were considering selling it short. And when you actually sold the stock short, you would move it to Current Short. Finally, when you covered the short (hopefully at a lower price) you would return it to its regular home, Favorite Stocks.

Dragging and dropping is as easy and direct as it sounds. Figure 4.7 shows a list of three tagged stocks in Candidates Short. Assume you wanted to drag Harrah's Entertainment to the Candidate Options list.

All you need do is point to Harrah's Entertainment, hold down the mouse button, and drag it to the Candidate Options list, as shown in Figure 4.8. ProphetCharts shows a light ghost of the company name as you are dragging it so it's easy to aim at your target (that is, the name of the watch list to which you want to drag the symbol).

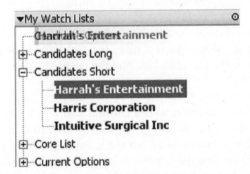

FIGURE 4.8 In this case, the stock Harrah's Entertainment is being dragged from the Candidates Short watch list to the Candidate Options watch list. A light ghost image can be seen during the drag-and-drop operation.

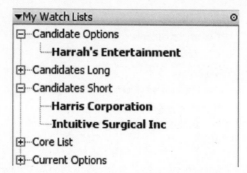

FIGURE 4.9   Once the drag-and-drop is complete, the stock has been moved from Candidates Short to Candidate Options. The quantity of stocks is still the same, but their arrangement is different.

After you release the mouse button, the symbol has been moved from one place to another, as shown in Figure 4.9. You can also drag-and-drop into the chart area if you want to simply chart a symbol. It's accomplished in exactly the same way: just click on the symbol you want to chart and drag it into the chart area. Unlike moving a symbol from one list to another, dragging-and-dropping for charting will not remove the symbol from its list.

RIGHT-CLICKING ON SYMBOLS

Besides the menu and the module, there is a third way of modifying watch lists: right-clicking on a symbol within a list. If you do so, a variety of actions for that symbol will appear (Figure 4.10):

Copy to List—Lets you choose another watch list to which you would like to copy this symbol. Unlike drag-and-drop, the symbol will remain in both the original list and the destination list once the action is complete.

Move to List—Similar to the drag-and-drop operation, this lets you choose a destination watch list and will remove the symbol from the original list and insert it into the destination list.

Delete—Deletes the symbol from the watch list.

Tag—Makes the symbol appear in bold so that you can highlight it as a symbol to which you want to pay special attention.

Labels Editor: The three labels-oriented items on this menu will be discussed in Chapter 16; choosing this item brings up the labels editor dialog box.

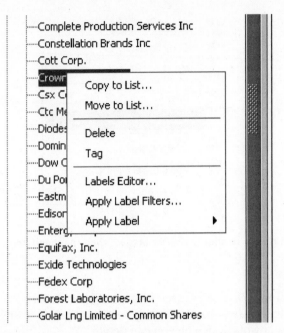

FIGURE 4.10 Right-clicking a stock name in a watch list brings up a menu with a variety of possible actions.

Apply Label Filters: Modifies which items in the watch lists are displayed by applying the label filters you choose.

Apply Label: Lets you apply a specific label to the symbol being right-clicked.

The Tag menu item is unique since it renames itself if the symbol is already tagged (Figure 4.11). In this case, the menu item is Remove Tag, and clicking it will make the boldfaced stock change back to its normal plain appearance.

The right-click menu is most convenient for deleting and tagging symbols. Unless you want to make copies of symbols from one list to another, using drag-and-drop between lists is much faster and more efficient.

Besides right-clicking on an individual symbol, you can also right-click on a watch list and take any of the following actions, based on the menu that pops up:

Rename Watch List—Lets you type in a new name for the selected list. You can also double-click the list name and make the change directly, without the menu's help.

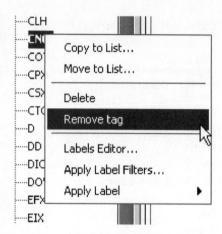

FIGURE 4.11 If a symbol is already tagged, then the menu item Tag is instead called Remove Tag.

Create Watch List—Creates a new, empty watch list.

Delete Watch List—Yields a dialog box showing you the existing watch lists, any one of which you can delete.

Export Watch List—Lets you take the contents of the selected list and save it into a text file on your hard drive.

Add Current Symbol to Watch List—Adds the charted symbol into the selected list.

View in Grid—Grid charts are covered later in the book; this displays the first four charts in the list in a two-by-two grid format.

Tag All—Tags all the symbols in the list.

Untag All—Untags all the symbols in the list.

Copy All—Lets you copy all of the symbols in the list to another list.

Move All—Lets you move all the symbols from the current list to another list, leaving the original list empty.

Labels Editor—Again, labels functions will be covered in Chapter 16; this brings up the labels editor.

Apply Label Filters—Lets you apply the label filters to all the lists.

Apply Label—Lets you apply a label to every symbol in the selected list.

CHART STYLES

Chapter 2 explained the basics of chart creation. There are a great many ways in ProphetCharts to adjust a chart's appearance to your liking. Over time, you will probably find certain kinds of charts that work well for you. You might like a six-month daily candlestick chart, a 10-day minute-by-minute streaming chart, or a 10-year weekly chart.

Changing the parameters that control a chart to get a different view of a security is tedious and time-consuming. That's why ProphetCharts allows you to preserve a wide variety of settings into a chart style. When you create a style, you give yourself instant access to whatever properties a given chart has, without having to spend time adjusting menus, checkboxes, and other settings.

A chart style will preserve just about every aspect of a chart. Some of the key parameters that make up a chart style are:

Graph Type—There are seven different kinds of graphs: OHLC, HLC, HL, Candle, Line, Area, and Percent. Your chart style will remember which of these you selected.

Quick Toggles—Are color bars in the chart? Is volume displayed? Are drawn items shown? Are studies shown?

Streaming—Is the chart streaming?

Log—Is the scale type logarithmic or arithmetic?

Duration—What is the duration of the chart?

Frequency—What is the frequency of the chart?

Technical Studies—What technical studies, if any, are used?

You don't have to do anything special to create a chart style except create the chart you want and then save it as a style. The Styles menu (Figure 4.12) is where this happens; the top two choices let you save a style or delete a style, and beneath that are all the styles you have created (if any).

Besides the Styles menu, the chart styles you've made are also listed in the My Chart Styles module (Figure 4.13). You can apply a style from the menu by selecting it, and you can apply a style from the module by either double-clicking it or dragging and dropping it into the chart area.

CREATING AND SAVING A STYLE

Once you create a chart whose properties you want to preserve, choose Save Settings as a Chart Style from the Styles menu. A dialog box (Figure 4.14) will appear, asking you what name to give the style.

You can either type in a name and click OK, or if you want to replace an existing style with the present one, you can click the Update an existing Chart Style radio button and choose the style you want to replace from the dropdown menu (Figure 4.15).

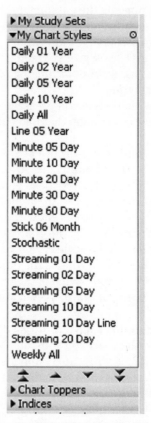

FIGURE 4.12 All of the styles you have created are in the Styles menu, along with the ability to save or delete a style.

FIGURE 4.13 The chart styles are also listed in the My Chart Styles module, and any one style can be invoked with a double-click or a drag-and-drop into the chart area.

It's important to remember to give your style a meaningful name. Don't use names like Style 1, Style 2, My Style, Stock Chart, and other meaningless terms. Instead, use descriptive language such as Candlestick 6-Month, Streaming 10-Day, or Daily 5-Year.

Another suggestion: because the style names appear in alphabetical order, you should use consistent names to group similar styles. For instance, if you have a few minute graphs (that is, intraday graphs), a few daily graphs (longer term), and a few streaming graphs, you might choose

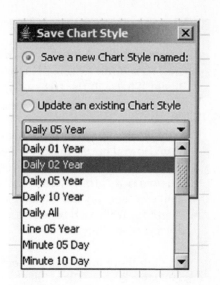

FIGURE 4.14 The Save Chart Style dialog box lets you save a new style or replace an existing style.

FIGURE 4.15 To replace a chart style, choose the style from the drop-down menu.

style names such as Minute 5-Day, Minute 10-Day, Daily 2-Year, Daily 5-Year, Daily 10-Year, Streaming 2-Day, Streaming 5-Day, and Streaming 20-Day. That way, when the style names are shown in alphabetical order, it will be easier to find the style you want.

TRADING STYLE

A different kind of style has nothing to do with a software feature, but instead this style is about developing yourself as a trader. My belief is that learning how to trade is one of the richest processes of self-discovery a person can undertake, provided that person is highly dedicated to learning the art of trading and has enough introspection and flexibility to learn and grow. For myself, the process has been long—measured in decades—and difficult, but I can say with confidence that I am a little bit better at what I do with each passing year.

But in the course of trying to learn to be a good trader, you are going to need to adopt your own personal style. By style, I don't mean a bromide like "a trader who makes a lot of money" or, less glibly, "one who trades what he sees." I think those are empty characterizations, no better than saying your philosophy of life is to try to be a good person and do the right thing.

My point of view is that trading style encompasses several areas:

- **Quantity:** How many markets and/or positions do you plan to trade? One? A handful? Dozens? Hundreds?
- **Basis:** What will the basis of your decision be with respect to what positions you will undertake?
- **Frequency:** How often do you plan to enter and exit positions? In other words, are you a day trader, a swing trader, or an investor?
- **Bias:** Do you have a bullish or bearish bias? I believe the vast majority of people have a bullish bias, in spite of their declarations of neutrality. (The old saw "I trade what I see" is the safe route, similar to a political stance of "socially liberal and fiscally conservative"—meaningless.)
- **Security:** What kind of securities do you like to trade? E-minis? Penny stocks? Blue chips?

I'm sure there are other elements, but that's not a bad start. My own personal style is along these lines:

- **Quantity:** I like a lot of small positions in order to spread my risk. There are times when I have a couple of hundred positions.
- **Basis:** I'm a chartist, pure and simple. I use my experience of having viewed hundreds of thousands of charts as the rationale for my decision making.
- **Frequency:** My preference is holding periods measured in weeks or months, although volatile markets can make that unrealistic.
- **Bias:** I tend to be somewhat bearishly biased, although I am always striving to be as balanced and open-minded about charts as possible.
- **Security:** I gravitate toward stocks that trade at least half a million shares a day—hopefully much more—and are typically priced between $20 and $90.

You may not have adopted a style of your own yet, but these parameters are worthy of some thought. As you trade in the coming months and years, return to this topic, since learning to be a successful trader requires being in a constant state of self-evaluation and, hopefully, improvement.

ON TO TECHNICAL STUDIES

You have learned about two vital features of ProphetCharts: the management of watch lists and the creation of chart styles. Now it's time to begin exploring the powerful library of technical studies at your disposal.

CHAPTER 5

Market and Data Types

There are tens of thousands of financial instruments that ProphetCharts can display, and it will help you as a trader to understand what these instruments are and how they differ in a chart. Although just about any kind of time series data can be charted, there are some subtle but important differences between these data types that we discuss in this chapter.

INDEXES

An index is typically an amalgamation of various instruments that are subject to some kind of mathematical process to yield a meaningful number (typically in the form of an average). Well-known examples include the Dow Jones Industrial Average (also known as the Dow 30), the Standard & Poor's 500 (also known as the S&P 500 or simply the SPX), and the Gold and Silver Index.

Another similar chartable item is an indicator, which—instead of being computed using individual instruments—is more typically an independent summary of a fact, such as the number of stocks on an exchange that rose on a particular day or the total number of shares that traded on a particular exchange. For simplicity's sake, we will refer to both indexes and indicators as "indexes" since they are treated the same way in ProphetCharts.

In ProphetCharts, index symbols are preceded by the dollar sign: $INDU represents the Dow 30, $UTIL represents the Dow 15 Utility Index,

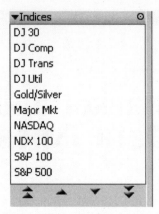

FIGURE 5.1 The index module provides easy access to popular index data.

$NDX represents the NASDAQ 100 Index, $HUI is the Gold Bugs Index, and so forth.

There is an Index module built into ProphetCharts to make the task of accessing indexes simpler than memorizing a bunch of arcane symbols. If you choose to display the Index module, you will see the list shown in Figure 5.1. Double-clicking any of these items will make that index appear, using the time duration and frequency you have selected. Some indexes go back for a long time; the Dow Jones Industrial Index goes back the farthest, with data back to the beginning of 1900. (As an aside, we actually had data from the nineteenth century, but Java cannot comprehend time prior to 1900, so we had to forgo using it).

As of this writing, the vast majority of indexes in ProphetCharts lack volume data. There are a handful of exceptions, but on the whole, the volume pane will be blank for any indexes (and all indicators). There are some instances where ProphetCharts has volume data, but they begin only later in the time series. Figure 5.2, for instance, shows the Dow Utility Index with volume data commencing early in 2007. Before that, the volume is all zeros.

Looking at indexes in ProphetCharts should probably be a daily routine for active traders, since the movement of major indexes is a major influence on the direction of individual equities. You will probably want to create a watch list to store the indexes you most frequently examine.

EQUITIES

Equities are most typically shares of common stock in public companies, although for the purposes of our discussion, they include any instrument

FIGURE 5.2 Most of the index data in ProphetCharts have no volume data or only partial data.

that is traded on a stock exchange (including, for instance, Exchange-Traded Funds, commonly known as ETFs).

When people speak of equities, they are usually talking about stocks such as Google (GOOG), Apple Inc (AAPL), Kelloggs (K), and Johnson & Johnson (JNJ). They are also talking about funds such as the NASDAQ 100 ETF (QQQQ), the gold trust (GLD), the silver trust (SLV), the S&P 500 "spyders" (SPY), and other popular trading vehicles.

Symbols for equities range in length from one alphabetic character (such as C, which stands for CitiCorp) to five characters. They typically only have alphabetic characters (examples: HD, IBM, F, SHLD), although for preferred stocks and other special issues, there may be other symbols (for instance, BRK.A for Warren Buffett's Berkshire Hathaway). You can use the search item in the symbols menu to find the symbol of any security.

The data fields for equities are:

Open—The opening price (that is, the first traded price) for the given time period (usually one day, but in the case of intraday graphs or other frequencies, it will be longer or shorter)

High—The highest price for that time period

Low—The lowest price for that time period

Close—The last price for that time period

Volume—The total number of shares traded during that time period

Something unique to equity symbols in ProphetCharts are event icons, which are automatically displayed on the price chart. Figure 5.3 shows an example of a stock with many event icons. Mousing over any of these will provide more information about the meaning of the event for that stock.

Because active ProphetCharts users tend to be technical traders, the event icons aren't something that you will probably be using a lot. By pressing Ctrl-E, you can toggle between showing and hiding the event icons. However, there are times when it is helpful to have an awareness of events—particularly market-moving events such as earnings announcements. The four different kinds of event icons displayed are:

Dividends—This looks like an up-arrow and denotes when a dividend is paid and its value.

Stock Splits—This looks like two overlapping squares and indicates when a stock has split and by what amount.

Conference Calls—This looks like a telephone and indicates a conference call between a company's management and stock analysts.

Earnings Announcement—This looks like a dollar sign and shows when a company's quarterly earnings were (or will be) announced.

An example of a dividend event is shown in Figure 5.4. Mousing over this arrow icon shows that a 22-cent dividend was paid on September 22, 2005. As you can see, there are five dividend icons in this particular example, so the span of time displayed is about five quarters (since dividends are usually paid on a quarterly basis).

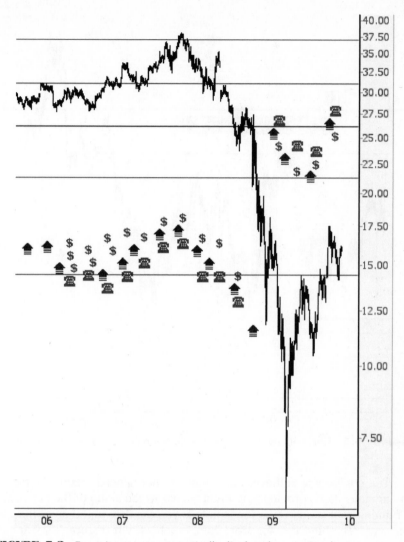

FIGURE 5.3 Event icons are automatically displayed on equity charts.

The stock split icon, shown in Figure 5.5, is placed on the date when a stock split took place. This includes historical splits as well as forthcoming, announced splits. Mousing over this icon shows the split amount and date. A 2-for-1 split, for example, means that shareholders prior to that date would, after that date, be holding twice as many shares as before (which are probably each worth about half what they were before, exogenous events notwithstanding).

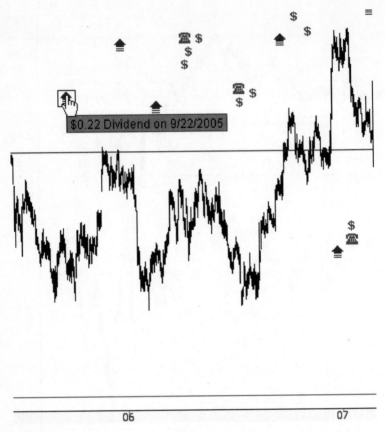

FIGURE 5.4   The dividend icon shows the date and amount of each dividend.

The conference call event icon has a rather special feature, in that it can in many cases provide you direct access to the audio of the call itself. If running your mouse over the icon tells you the date and time of the call *and* says "Double-Click for More Info," such as with Figure 5.6, you can double-click the icon to activate an audio playback of the conference call itself.

Finally, the earnings report icon, shown with a dollar sign, indicates the dates of prior and forthcoming earnings announcements. Understandably, these event icons often correlate with major price moves, particularly with highly volatile growth stocks. A positive surprise (or negative disappointment) during an earnings report can create large gaps in a stock's price movement. Figure 5.7 shows a stock with a large number of earnings icons (spaced a quarter apart), any of which yields the date of the earnings release.

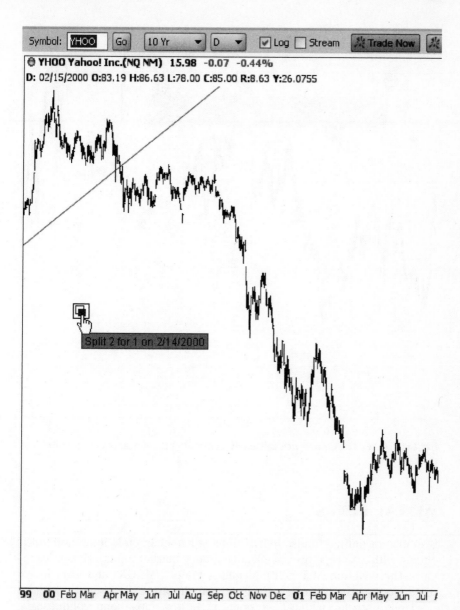

FIGURE 5.5 Here we see a 2-for-1 stock split for Yahoo! issued at the end of the Internet bubble. Yahoo! has, understandably, not had any stock splits since that time.

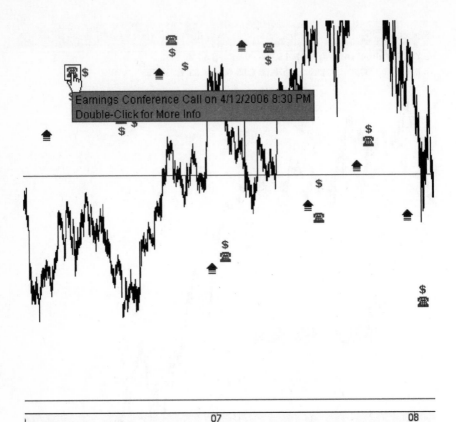

FIGURE 5.6 The conference call event icon often provides access to the audio of the call.

MUTUAL FUNDS

Symbols for mutual funds are five alphabetical characters long (and those ending with XX are, more specifically, money market funds). Examples include the well-known Fidelity Magellan Fund (FMAGX) and ultra index funds, such as the Ultra-Bear ProFunds Small-Cap (UCPIX).

Unlike stocks, which have open, high, low, close, and volume data points, mutual funds have only one data point per day, the Net Asset Value (NAV). Because of this, when you chart a mutual fund, you will see a graph with only one small dash per day, such as Figure 5.8, which can be difficult to read.

Because of this, we advise using a line graph instead. Just go to the Chart Settings menu, choose Graph Type, and then choose the line type

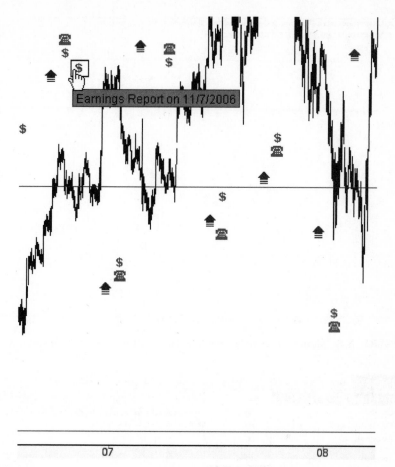

FIGURE 5.7 Earnings announcements can often be accompanied by large price moves.

of graph. This setting makes any mutual fund graph much easier to interpret, as illustrated in Figure 5.9. You should also note that fund NAVs typically are not available until two hours after the regular close of the stock market.

Another aspect of mutual funds is that they often experience distributions, which are cash payments to participants in the fund. The data platform supporting ProphetCharts is rather special in that it adjusts for these dividends. Most charting platforms show a large gap in instances of distributions, which renders the chart much less useful. Failing to adjust for a distribution is just as bad as failing to adjust for a stock split. ProphetCharts applies a coefficient to all data preceding a distribution so that the chart is

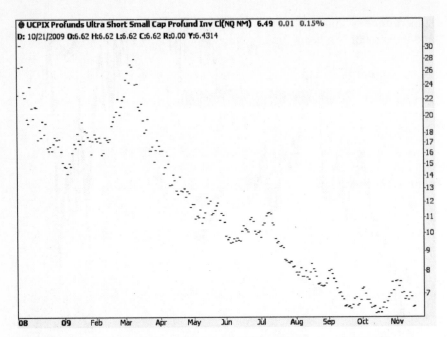

FIGURE 5.8 Mutual funds only have one data point per day, and no volume.

FIGURE 5.9 A line graph is the best choice for charting mutual funds.

smoothed and adjusted, more accurately reflecting the true performance and movement of a given fund.

FOREX

The foreign exchange (FOREX) market, as is mentioned in probably every advertisement that's ever appeared for the industry, is the largest dollar-volume market on the planet. Trillions of dollars of currencies are traded worldwide every day.

Even if you never intend to trade in the FOREX markets, you will find that a basic understanding of these markets will be helpful in your trading in other realms. Intermarket analysis has value, and having an awareness of what the euro–U.S. dollar ratio is doing is important in the world of modern trading.

A huge number of currency pairs are available in ProphetCharts, and all of them are listed in the Currency Pairs module, shown in Figure 5.10. As with all the other modules, you can activate this module by going to the Chart Settings menu and choosing it from the list of modules shown.

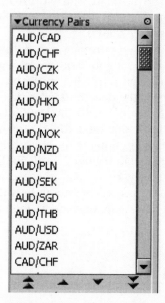

FIGURE 5.10 The Currency Pairs module provides easy access to dozens of FOREX ratios.

FIGURE 5.11   The EUR-USD is the most widely watched FOREX market.

You can either double-click, drag-and-drop, or manually type in any of these currency pairs to see the chart. The data are available on both a daily and an intraday basis, and unlike equity markets, FOREX trades virtually around the clock (except weekends).

The most widely followed currency pair is the EUR-USD, shown in Figure 5.11. The EUR-USD is a good way to get a glimpse of the relative strength of the dollar to the euro (the higher the price, the weaker the dollar is, because the dollar is the denominator in this instance). Other good pairs to follow include NZD-USD, USD-CAD, and EUR-JPY.

As with e-mini futures, our next topic, streaming intraday FOREX data give you a good sense in nonmarket hours what the next day might hold. Events that take place after hours, particularly important economic reports, have immediate reverberations in these markets, and you can get an accurate and timely assessment about how the equity markets will probably react to such news announcements long before regular trading commences.

E-MINI FUTURES

One of the most successful products—perhaps the most successful—ever introduced by the Chicago Mercantile Exchange is the e-mini future. These are electronically traded almost around the clock, and they cover all kinds of different markets, but far and away the most popular of these is the S&P 500 e-mini, colloquially referred to as the ES.

There are a number of advantages to this instrument. As stated, it is electronic, and it trades almost 24 hours a day. It is a highly leveraged product, so profit potential (and loss potential!) is substantial. It provides an excellent way for those proficient at anticipating index moves to make money doing so.

The Futures module houses both the regular futures data and the e-mini data. You do not need to have this module open to access the charts, but it makes it easier to see which contracts are available and to double-click on the item of interest instead of having to enter an arcane symbol such as @ESZ9. Figure 5.12 shows an example of an e-mini contract that has been chosen from the module and whose chart is being shown in the price pane.

Looking closely at the various e-mini instruments available in the Futures module (Figure 5.13), you can see that it covers the gamut from Asian indexes to sector indexes to currency futures.

In addition to the standard price data (open, high, low, close, and volume), e-mini futures also contain open interest, plotted as a red line graph on top of the volume histogram. As with most futures, these markets are extremely thinly traded until they become the so-called front month, as shown in Figure 5.14. The S&P e-mini, for instance, has expiration months of March, June, September, and December. So the September contract for

FIGURE 5.12 The e-mini futures symbols are housed in the Futures module.

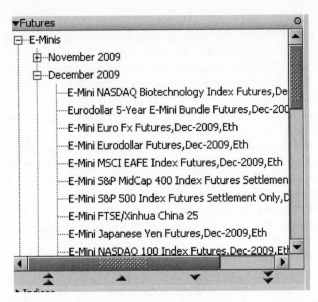

FIGURE 5.13 To chart a particular e-mini, choose the month and then the market within that month from the dropdown menu.

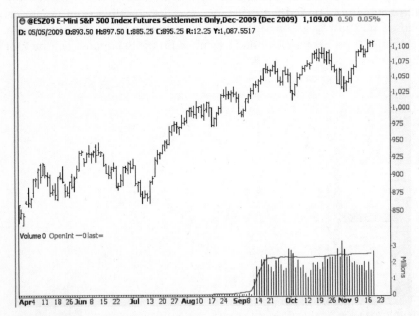

FIGURE 5.14 As shown in the volume pane, there is very little trading in a futures contract until it becomes the front month, at which time volume and open interest both surge.

FIGURE 5.15 E-mini futures trade around the clock, although most of the volume is during regular market hours.

a given year would tend to be active from about the second week of June until the first week of September, a three-month span.

As mentioned earlier, the e-mini markets trade extended hours. In the case of the ES (and the important but not as popular NASDAQ equivalent, the NQ), the trading is virtually constant, except for weekends. As you can see in Figure 5.15, the volume during the evening and nighttime is extremely thin, but it nonetheless provides valuable insights and indications as to what the next trading day will be like.

FUTURES AND COMMODITIES

Almost all ProphetCharts have access to the basic financial instruments, such as U.S. stocks and indexes, mutual funds, and e-mini futures. Some classes of data are available only to those who have signed up for certain exchange agreements. Your entitlements (based on the platform on which you are using ProphetCharts) dictate whether the data you see is delayed or real-time, or whether you can see a particular class of data at all.

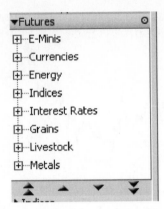

FIGURE 5.16   The Futures module organizes hundreds of markets into industry-oriented categories.

Therefore, do not be concerned or confused if, by chance, you are not able to view futures or options data. It may simply be that your particular platform doesn't permit you to see it. For the sake of completeness, we will briefly discuss these data types as well.

Futures and commodities data (which will be referred to simply as "futures" here) cover markets from around the world in hundreds of different forms. Everything, from pork bellies to orange juice to crude oil, is traded on futures markets, and although there are many more stock traders than futures traders, the opportunities for profit from the highly leveraged world of futures have captured the imagination of many traders.

The futures module, shown in Figure 5.16, puts the hundreds of different individual markets into a sector-based hierarchy. If you wanted to see what wheat contracts were available, for instance, you could click on the plus sign next to the word *Grains*. Crude oil, on the other hand, would be under *Energy*, while Silver would be under *Metals*.

The construction of a futures symbol tends to be in the format <root><year><month>. For example, the June 2010 S&P 500 contract would be represented as SP1006, since SP is the root symbol, 10 is the relevant portion of the year 2010, and 06 is the numeric representation of the month June.

Futures contracts are ephemeral creatures, however. Most of them last just two or three months. Therefore, ProphetCharts provides access to synthetic futures contracts as well, more popularly known as continuous contracts. These are individual futures contracts that are chained together so that you can get a longer-term view of a market's direction. If you were interested, for example, in the wheat market, and you looked at

FIGURE 5.17 The unadjusted contract shows many years of data chained together.

only one specific contract, your understanding of wheat would be extraordinarily limited. Looking at the continuous contract, however, you could see wheat's price action over a period of half a century.

There are a couple of styles of continuous contract: unadjusted and adjusted. The unadjusted contract, as the name implies, chains the raw contracts together. So if there were four contracts per year for a particular market, then March would connect to June would connect to September would connect to December, and so forth. The period of time in which each of these was the front month would also be the portion of time when the price data for that market would be presented in the continuous contract.

Figure 5.17, for instance, shows the continuous unadjusted contract for crude oil. The symbol for such a contract is the root symbol followed by the number 1600. Therefore, CL1600 is the continuous unadjusted contract for crude, W1600 is for wheat, NG1600 is for natural gas, and so forth.

There are some markets, however, in which the price difference from one contract to the next might be substantial. Some agricultural markets in particular might have months that represent different crops whose prices

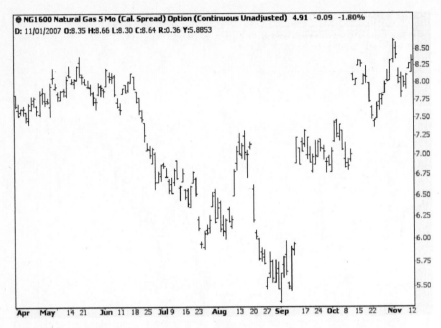

FIGURE 5.18   Unadjusted continuous contracts can have large price gaps.

are far apart, and chaining these contracts together would create many misleading price gaps in the graph. Therefore, ProphetCharts provides for adjusted contracts, which do a better job of merging such disparate data together into a more useful graph.

Take natural gas, for example, shown in Figure 5.18. As you can see, there are some very big price gaps, which usually come about when another month takes over as the front month.

The same market adjusted for these irregularities, shown in Figure 5.19, is much smoother. Adjusted graphs are far more useful when combined with standard technical studies and drawn objects because they provide a more realistic representation as to what the market is really doing. The symbol for these is slightly different: 1700 instead of 1600 (examples: JO1700, HU1700, PB1700).

OPTIONS

Stock and index options have some very unusual symbology, but luckily ProphetCharts has a helpful Wizard feature to make charting options a snap.

FIGURE 5.19 In some markets, the adjusted version of the contract provides a cleaner and more useful representation of the price action.

The first thing you need to do is choose the Find Option item from the Symbols menu, which will reveal the Options Wizard dialog box, like the one in Figure 5.20. The way to use this Wizard is:

1. Enter the underlying symbol. In the example shown here, the symbol being used is IWM, which is the exchange-traded fund for the Russell 2000 index.

FIGURE 5.20 The Options Wizard greatly simplifies the task of finding an option chart.

2. Click the Set button. After you do, ProphetCharts will take a few moments to query the price database and determine all the available expirations and strike prices. You will see these dropdown menus become available once the query is completed.

3. Next, choose what kind of option interests you—a Put (which is the right to *sell* a given security at a given price) or a Call (which is the right to *buy* a given security at a given price).

4. Then choose the month and year expiration from the Expiration dropdown menu, as well as the strike price from the Strike Price dropdown menu. You will often find a large number of strike prices available.

5. Finally, click on the Get Chart button, which will show you the daily or intraday price chart (depending on what you've selected in the Frequency and Duration dropdowns).

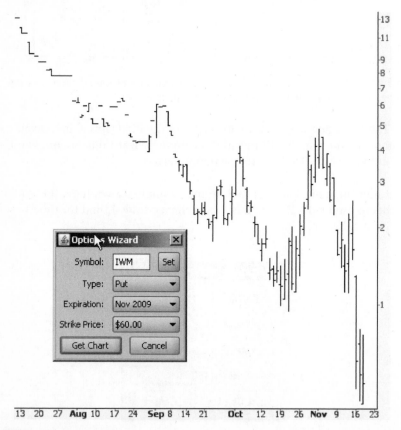

FIGURE 5.21 Options tend to be thinly traded except for the last couple of months prior to their expiration.

After you have clicked Get Chart, you can use the Wizard to find other options, or you can click Cancel to close the Wizard. An example options chart, the IWM $60 put for November 2009, is shown in Figure 5.21. As is so often the case with options, trading is very light and spotty early in the history of the contract, but as the expiration date nears, the price bars become more regular and easier to read.

As with futures contracts, options have open interest, which is plotted in the volume pane. You can press Ctrl-Spacebar to toggle volume and open interest on and off, as illustrated in Figure 5.22.

For the purpose of trading, an options chart isn't particularly useful. Not only is its history quite short but also only the final couple of months

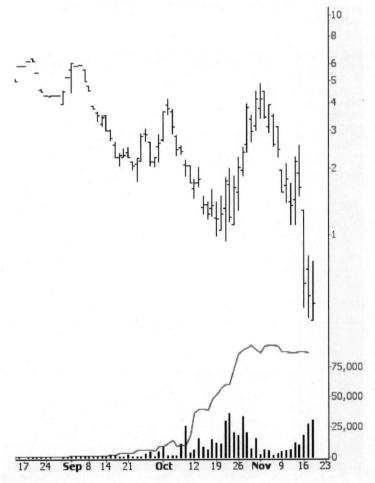

FIGURE 5.22 Open interest is plotted for options, as well as volume data.

of an option have enough trading activity to create a decent graph. It is almost always more valuable to examine the underlying security (that is, the principal instrument on which the option is based) to make an assessment as to the probable future direction of a security.

OPTION CONTROLS

There is another module you can access—Option Controls—that gives you one-click access to four useful tools when looking at options charts. These four checkboxes, shown in Figure 5.23, are:

- Avg. Imp. Volatility (that is, averaged implied volatility).
- Bid-Ask Overlay.

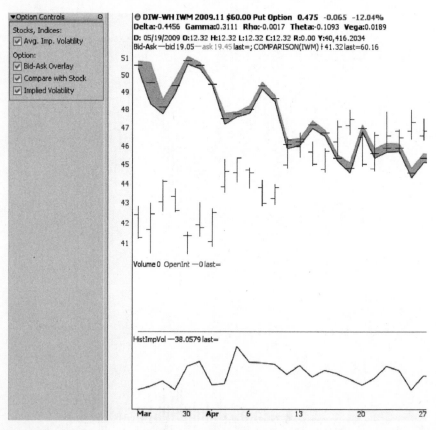

FIGURE 5.23 Use the Option Controls module for one-click access to more options-oriented functions.

- Compare with Stock.
- Implied Volatility.

An unusual and interesting feature is the Bid-Ask Overlay. In the world of options trading, a huge majority of the tens of thousands of options on the market don't trade every day. Those that do trade might trade just a few contracts.

Because of this, most options have little or no trading data. In a given week, maybe only one trade will take place. So the other four days of that week have no data at all. ProphetCharts has a novel solution to this problem. In the price data, the bid price and ask price are retained for every single day and every single option. That way, you can get a good sense as to the market for an option, irrespective of its activity.

Look at Figure 5.24, for instance. This is an option with very little activity, which is why the price chart has just a series of little tick bars and flat lines. Once the Bid-Ask Overlay checkbox is on, however, the price chart is much more meaningful, because a green line chart (representing the ask) and a blue line chart (representing the bid) are plotted, as illustrated in Figure 5.25.

Of course, options are based on something else, since they are derivative instruments. You can make use of the Left Axis function automatically with Option Controls, combining a given option with its underlying

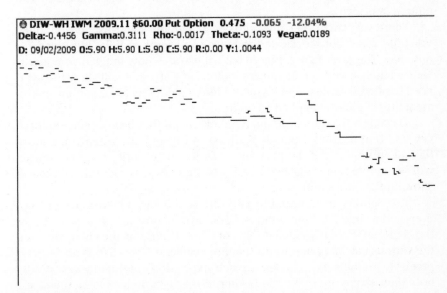

FIGURE 5.24 Most options charts look a lot like this—very little data, and very hard to interpret.

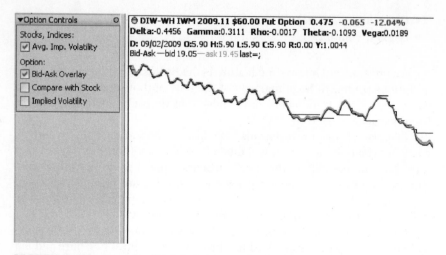

FIGURE 5.25 Once the Bid-Ask Overlay is checked, the graph is much easier to read.

instrument, which ProphetCharts will deduce for you. Look at Figure 5.26, for instance. The option (plotted in black) is a put on IWM. By checking Compare with Stock, you can cause ProphetCharts to plot in the same graph the security on which the option is based (in this instance, IWM, plotted in brown).

There are two other checkboxes in Option Controls: Avg. Implied Volatility (used for stocks and indexes) and Implied Volatility (used for options). The prior figure, Figure 5.23, illustrates how implied volatility is charted in its own pane. If you are looking at a stock, it will show the averaged implied volatility, and if you are looking directly at an options instrument, it will plot the implied volatility.

There is a third item on the Symbols menu that hasn't been explored yet, and that is Show Options, featured in Figure 5.27. When you choose this menu item, all of the puts and calls for the security you are viewing will be denoted on the chart. It will not show expired options, but it will show all the future options.

The options are denoted by two different icons: a large C for call options and a large P for put options. Looking at Figure 5.28, you can see that the chart of IWM has yielded dozens of C and P icons on the chart, showing the various call and put options that are available. These icons are located precisely on the x-axis (to denote their expiration time) and y-axis (to denote their strike price). So the farther to the right an icon is on the chart, the farther out in time it expires, and the higher the icon is on the graph, the higher its strike price.

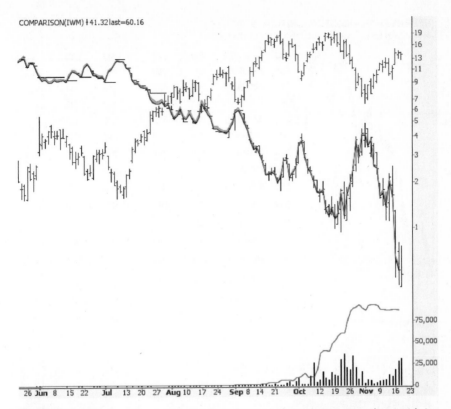

FIGURE 5.26 Overlay with Stock plots the underlying instrument along with its option.

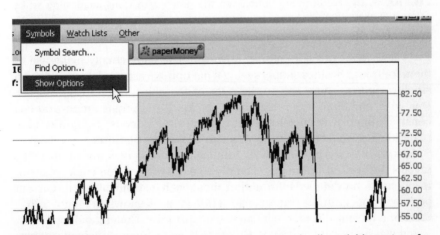

FIGURE 5.27 Choosing the Show Options item reveals all available options for the security shown.

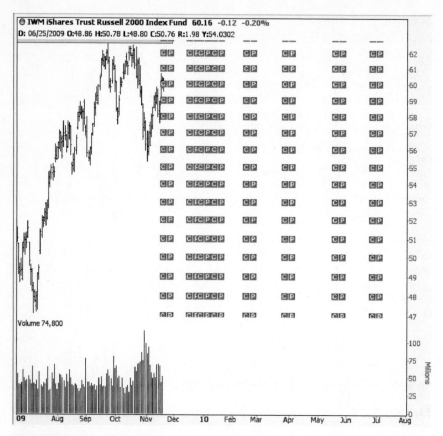

FIGURE 5.28 Forthcoming options on the graph with icons suggesting strike prices and expiration dates.

These icons are not passive, however. You can actually make use of them for things besides simply seeing what options are available for a given stock or index. There are, to the right of the chart, three tabs—Singles, Dual-legs, and Multi-legs—suggesting the kinds of options orders you can construct simply by clicking on any of the C or P icons. This order construction is specific to the think or swim brokerage platform.

As you can see in Figure 5.29, running the mouse over any of the icons reveals the symbol, strike price, type, and expiration. If you click on any of the icons, richly detailed information about each instrument and its current price will appear in the order construction area, as shown in Figure 5.30.

For a technical trader, data means opportunity. Understanding the different classes of data in ProphetCharts will, at a minimum, help you appreciate intermarket relationships regardless of what you trade, and it might

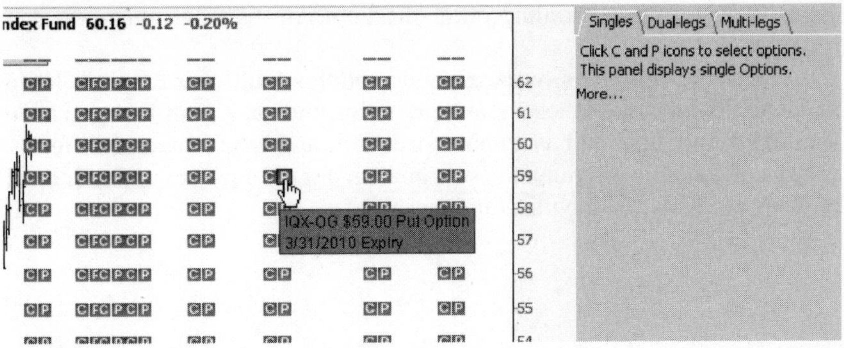

FIGURE 5.29 Running the mouse over any of the options icons will yield basic information about them.

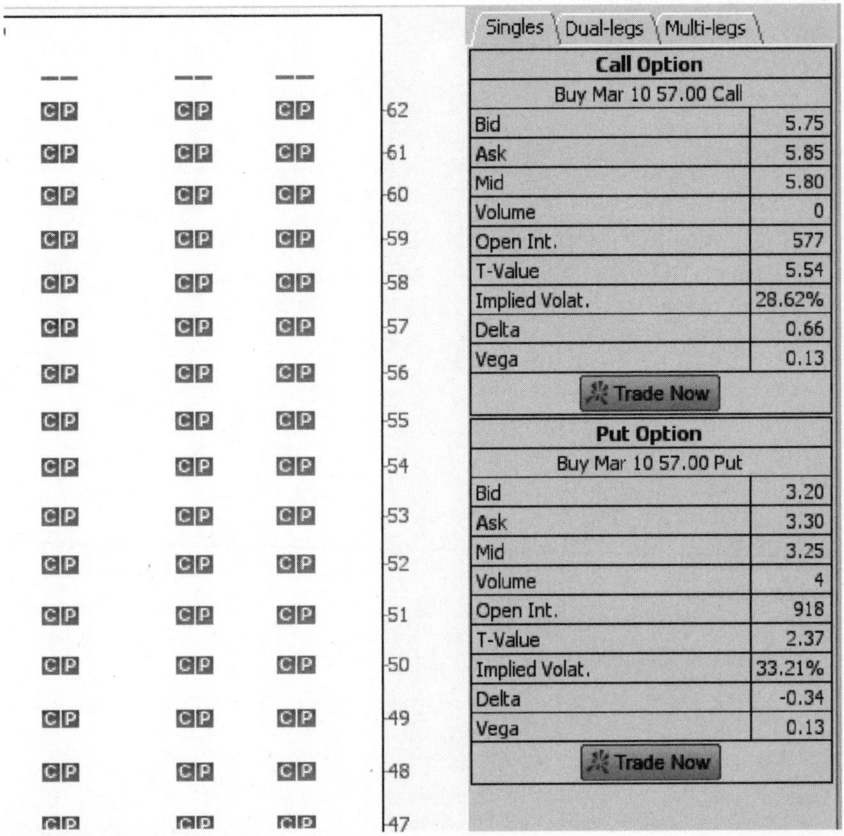

FIGURE 5.30 Clicking on any of the icons will make deeper data appear in the option order construction pane.

even open you up to trading other markets you had not considered in the past.

The menu functions, wizards, and modules built into ProphetCharts make accessing any of these data types quick and easy. Now that you have a solid grounding as to basic chart formation and how to access different classes of tradable instruments, we can turn our attention to a deeper level of chart analysis, the technical indicators.

CHAPTER 6

Indicators in Action

I n the world of charting, the most basic way to look at a stock (or any other financial entity) is with the price data. The prices make up the trends and patterns of value as it moves through time, and there is a great deal that can be learned and predicted based on price movement.

However, there is another deeper way to look at this price movement, and that is with the use of technical indicators. An indicator is essentially an embellishment on the graph derived from price and/or volume data. This embellishment might take the form of up-arrows, down-arrows, a line graph overlaid on top of a price graph, a histogram, or any of many other forms.

There are literally hundreds of indicators that have been created. ProphetCharts provides access to nearly 200 of these. And many of these indicators can themselves provide different parameters and tweaks to their settings. So the number of possible indicators at your disposal theoretically is in the hundreds of thousands.

The purpose of this chapter is not to delve into each and every possible indicator. There are far too many, and there are many excellent books already written about the specifics of these indicators. Instead, this chapter provides you a basis for understanding the philosophy behind indicators, highlighting a small sample to help you understand the reasoning. It also has the purpose of showing you how, within ProphetCharts, to access these indicators.

SINGLE VERSUS MULTIPLE INDICATORS

Indicators can be used one at a time or in combination. To better understand this, it is important to know that indicators come in two very different types: overlaid and independent.

An overlaid indicator is one that is put in the same space as the price chart itself. A good example is the moving average indicator. This line is plotted directly on top of the price chart and is thus laid over the original chart. An independent indicator, on the other hand, appears in its own separate window. This window can appear above or below the price window so that the time series lines up, but it is not within the price chart itself.

If you choose to use more than one indicator, those that you choose can be any combination of overlaid or independent indicators. For example, you might choose to put (1) a 20-day moving average, (2) a 50-day moving average, (3) a 200-day moving average, (4) a MACD histogram, and (5) an RSI study on a chart. Of these five indicators, the first three are overlaid, and the last two are independent. (Thus, you would wind up with three stacked chart panes: one with the price chart and the other two with the MACD and the RSI.)

This chapter focuses on using just one indicator at a time. In Chapter 7, you will learn how to edit the parameters of individual indicators as well as how to combine indicators into Study Sets.

MOVING AVERAGES

One of the most popular and simple indicators is the moving average. There are a number of kinds of moving averages (simple, exponential, displaced, bands, and so on), but as was mentioned earlier, the purpose of this chapter isn't to address every possible permutation of every indicator; instead, its purpose is to understand the basics so that you can apply that knowledge to any of the hundreds of indicators available.

The purpose of a moving average is to smooth the price data in such a way as to filter out the noise—the daily up-and-down price movements. The computation of a simple moving average is the sum of "n" number of prices (typically, the closing price) divided by "n." For instance, suppose that over a five-day period, the following closing prices existed for a given stock:

Day 1: $12.50
Day 2: $13.75

Day 3: $13.27
Day 4: $14.23
Day 5: $14.05

The five-day moving average, as computed for Day 5, would be the sum of the prior five days ($67.80) divided by 5, which equals 13.56. By computing this value on a continuous basis, and plotting the line graph of the moving average, ProphetCharts is able to display a smoothed representation of price action.

Look at the chart in Figure 6.1, which is a price chart of Nucor Corporation (symbol NUE) with a plot of its 20-day simple moving average (which is the smooth line). Creating this study is simply a matter of (1) opening the Technical Studies module and (2) double-clicking on the study desired, which, in this case, is Simple Moving Average.

There are a number of things to notice about this chart:

- In the upper-left corner of ProphetCharts is the notation MA(20) last=110.4075. This is a shorthand way of ProphetCharts indicating that the smooth line is a 20-day moving average whose last value is $110.4075. If you are using multiple studies, a legend will appear with an abbreviation for each study used and a colored line to indicate which color corresponds with what study.

FIGURE 6.1 The price of Nucor, which has stayed above the 20-day moving average for many months, crosses beneath it, indicating a sell signal.

- The moving average is represented as a smooth line graph, as opposed to the open, high, low, and close bars of the price chart. By its very nature, this line is a lagging indicator; in other words, it is based on old data (in this instance, the past 20 days) and is therefore behind the price trend. But that is the value of this indicator: because it lags the prices, it provides a slower-moving representation of the general price action and can suggest important directional change when the price crosses above or below it.
- Once the price pushed above the moving average in January, it stayed above that level until late April, denoted with a large arrow in this graph. This is known as a crossover, and in this instance, the price crossing below the moving average would be interpreted as a sell signal. So if you were long this stock at about $70, when the price moved clearly above the indicator, you would have held it until about $110, when the price finally dipped below the moving average.

The basic principle at work here—and you will see this many times with technical indicators—is that positive crossovers generate bullish signals and negative crossovers generate bearish signals. The more sensitive an indicator, the more volatile it is, which means that whipsaws are a common and dangerous phenomenon. A whipsaw takes place when signals are so common that you would, in theory, be jumping in and out of a stock far too frequently, and with poor results. The chart in Figure 6.1 illustrates a smooth and useful indicator, because the price was plainly above the moving average until a very clear signal was generated. If the price had crossed under and over the indicator 10 times during the course of the chart, it would obviously be much less useful.

Moving averages can be set to virtually any length of time. To take an extreme example, a one-day moving average would match the closing price exactly (and would therefore simply be a line graph of the price chart). The shortest time span typically seen with moving averages is 10 days, and other common lengths include 30-, 50-, 100-, and 200-day moving averages.

The longer the period, the slower (and smoother) the moving average is. A 200-day moving average is going to lag the price far more than, for instance, a 30-day moving average. Generally speaking, the longer the time period you use, the less frequent the signals will be. If you are a relatively conservative trader, a 200-day moving average will be far better suited to you than a shorter time horizon.

Figure 6.2 provides a good example of this. The security OIH made a broad upward movement, nearly doubling in price during the time frame shown. A buy signal, highlighted with the arrow, took place early in December when the price moved above the 200-day moving average. Even though it dipped close to this moving average a couple of times, it stayed

OIH Oil Sv Holdrs Tr Dep Receipt 157.54 2.54 1.64%
D: 12/06/2004 O:82.1626 H:82.4411 L:80.6705 C:81.4365 R:1.7706 Y:54.752
DMA(200,-14) — last=131.11832

FIGURE 6.2 The buy signal is generated here when the price of OIH crosses above its 200-day moving average.

above it, which means you would have stayed in the position if you were using this indicator as the basis of your trade. A shorter moving average would have generated sell signals much earlier.

Zooming in much closer on the same graph (Figure 6.3), it is much easier to see exactly when the crossover took place. In this instance, the price got very close to the moving average, touching it exactly on the day before the crossover. But until the price truly crosses over, there is no signal. On December 5, the price pushed over the 200-day moving average, and the stock ultimately tripled in price after the crossover (only the first portion of the move is shown in these graphs).

The simple moving average is the easiest to calculate and understand. However, it treats all price data equally; in other words, with a 20-day moving average, the price 20 days ago is just as important as the current day. If you would prefer to give a greater weighting to more recent data and a lesser weighting to older data, use an exponential moving average (EMA). The mathematics need not be understood here—the computer does all that work—but the concept is that the indicator does not lag as severely since recent price data have a heavier weighting.

FIGURE 6.3 A close-up of the OIH graph, highlighting the point where the price crossed above the 200-day moving average.

There is even a kind of moving average that can be shifted forward or backward in time to compensate for the lag in the indicator. It is called the displaced moving average (DMA). No matter which moving average is used, the basic principles are the same in how to apply it to trading.

Figure 6.4 provides an example of the DMA in action. This graph is a somewhat more realistic example than the earlier moving average graphs, because prices do not always behave perfectly with respect to indicators. In other words, whipsaws are very common, and some amount of discretion is needed to ascertain when a crossover has taken place and whether a crossover in the opposite direction negates the earlier signal or is simply noise.

In this case, symbol ESRX crossed beneath the 100-day DMA. This signaled the end of a rather long uptrend in the stock and could have been interpreted as a sell signal. The price moved above the DMA, then below, then above, then below again before staying clearly beneath the indicator and falling in earnest. In this example, interpreting the violation of the DMA as a change in trend was the right move, since ultimately the stock fell hard, even though it took a few weeks to truly do so.

To understand the premise behind crossovers, remember that there are three basic directions that a stock (or any financial instrument) can be heading: up, down, or sideways. A market moving up makes a series of higher lows and higher highs, creating stairsteps that generally push prices higher. A market moving down makes a series of lower lows and lower highs, also creating stairsteps, but moving lower. A market that fits neither of these trend definitions is going sideways.

FIGURE 6.4 Symbol ESRX crossed beneath the moving average early in March and started falling in earnest by late April.

Indicators such as moving averages are useful during trending markets, be they up or down. If used in a sideways market, a lagging indicator will create little more than false signals, frustration, and capital losses.

Until now, the examples shown have been for bullish moves. Figure 6.5 illustrates the DMA as a bearish signal, which would be useful to either (1) close a long position or (2) sell the stock short, aiming to buy it back later at a lower price. At a minimum, such a signal would at least let you know not to be long the stock in the first place.

For this stock, Home Depot (symbol HD), the price briefly dipped below its 200-day DMA early in May, popped back above the DMA for a few trading sessions, and then once again fell below the DMA, staying beneath the indicator for many months to come. This signal preceded a nearly 60 percent fall in the price of the security.

About 11 months later, the stock had formed a fairly decent base in the low 20s, picked up steam, and crossed back above the DMA. As before, the price initially crossed the indicator, fell to the other side for a few sessions, and then very clearly crossed to the other side. This kind of noise is very common, and it is up to your judgment and discretion whether to make

HD Home Depot Inc 39.93 -0.29 -0.72%
D: 08/04/2003 O:30.1937 H:30.5172 L:29.5075 C:30.3407 R:1.0097 Y:24.4129
DMA(200,-14) — last=40.72966

FIGURE 6.5 How crossovers work in both directions. After Home Depot crossed beneath its moving average, it fell for many months afterward. The price firmed up and crossed above the moving average again, preceding a handsome move higher.

a trade at the first sign of a crossover or whether to wait for a very plain confirmation that the price is well away from the indicator and is not likely to be crossing it again.

Because lagging indicators by definition will trail the price movement of a security, you will not get in or out of a position at the optimum time. That is the price you pay for catching broad trends. It is virtually impossible to pinpoint the precise top or bottom of any market. But if you are able to capture 80 percent of the movement from one extreme to another, you will do very well as a trader.

Figure 6.6 shows a good example of this with the stock Yahoo! (YHOO). The indicator used is a slow-moving 200-day DMA. The price of this stock bottomed at about $4.50 (which, as with all the examples in this book, is a split-adjusted price) and crossed above its DMA at about $7.50. So the price of the stock had moved up handsomely before a buy signal was generated. The stock got as high at $40 and then started softening up, and eventually the price crossed beneath the DMA at about $34.

The move from $4.50 to $40 was about a ninefold move in the stock, whereas the move from $7.50 (the entry point, based on the DMA) to $34

YHOO Yahoo! Inc. (NQ NM) 32.78 -0.42 -1.27%
D: 03/08/2005 O:33.55 H:33.73 L:33.14 C:33.16 R:0.59 Y:34.8773
DMA(200,-14) — last=35.16183

FIGURE 6.6 An owner of Yahoo! might have held on to YHOO from $7 to $34 using just a moving average, since the stock stayed clearly above it during most of this graph prior to the crossunder.

(the exit point, based on the DMA) was only about a fivefold move. But the fact is that only in hindsight could one pinpoint these precise low and high values, and with a relatively conservative approach, the majority of the upward movement was still captured.

BOLLINGER BANDS

Bollinger Bands is a widely used indicator, which, like moving averages, is an overlaid indicator. As the name implies, Bollinger Bands are made up of more than one part—there is an upper band (which is two standard deviations above the simple moving average) and a lower band (which is two standard deviations below the simple moving average).

Figure 6.7 illustrates what Bollinger Bands look like in ProphetCharts. As with any other indicator, applying these bands is simply a matter of double-clicking the study from the Technical Studies module. ProphetCharts makes it easy to see where the price is relative to the

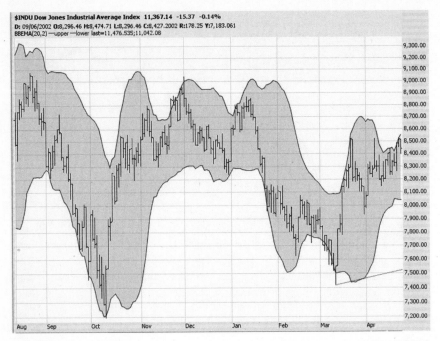

FIGURE 6.7 The Bollinger Bands are shaded to make the price's relative position easy to see.

boundaries created by the Bollinger Bands since it shades in the area contained by the bands. These bands make it easy to view both volatility and price levels (relative to past history) over any period of time.

Bollinger Bands aren't particularly useful for ascertaining future price movements. Instead, they provide insight as to where a price is relative to its past action. If prices are mashed up against the upper band quite tightly, it indicates that the price is relatively high. If prices are pushed down hard against the lower band, it indicates that prices are relatively low. Just because prices are at the upper band doesn't mean they will soon be going down, nor does it mean prices will go up if prices are at the lower band. But you can at least understand which direction is more likely based on the prices' relative position to the shaded portion of the banded area, as shown in Figure 6.8.

Bank of America's stock (symbol BAC) moved outside the Bollinger Bands in Figure 6.9. It is possible, although not very common, for a price to do this when it is making an extremely fast move either up or down. A price can sometimes stretch and even break its bands in this manner, but eventually, the price will return to the range-bound domain.

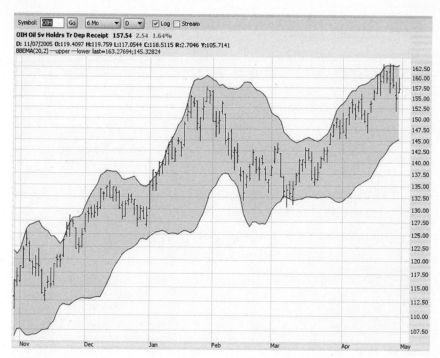

Symbol: OIH [Go] 6 Mo ▼ D ▼ ☑ Log ☐ Stream
OIH Oil Sv Holdrs Tr Dep Receipt **157.54** 2.54 1.64%
D: 11/07/2005 O:119.4097 H:119.759 L:117.0544 C:118.5115 R:2.7046 Y:105.7141
BBEMA(20,2) —upper —lower last=163.27694;145.32824

FIGURE 6.8 A price can cling to an extreme for many trading days.

THE RIBBON STUDY

One of the most interesting—some might even say beautiful—studies available in ProphetCharts is known as the Ribbon Study. This study is comprised of any number of moving averages of various periods. In Figure 6.10, a Ribbon Study made up of 16 different moving averages is shown, each of which has a different time period (10-day, 20-day, 30-day, and so on).

The Ribbon Study is unusual in that it creates somewhat of a three-dimensional representation of price movement (Figure 6.11). When a price is moving generally higher or lower, the moving averages eventually all move in the same direction and get evenly wide from one another. When a price begins to move sideways (or change direction altogether), the moving averages get tighter and coil up into a band, almost as if the threads of the study are forming a rope. During direction shifts of a security's price, you can actually see the band turn as it twists from one direction to another. This coiling and turning is helpful in knowing when prices are consolidating and, ultimately, changing direction.

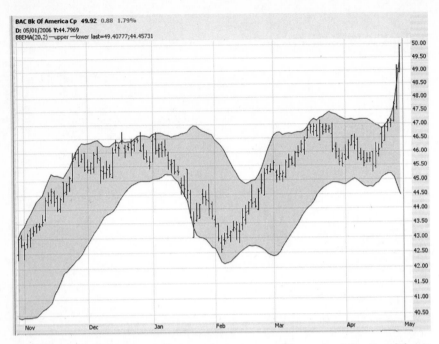

FIGURE 6.9   Sometimes a price movement is so sudden and unidirectional that it stretches the Bollinger Band in the extreme.

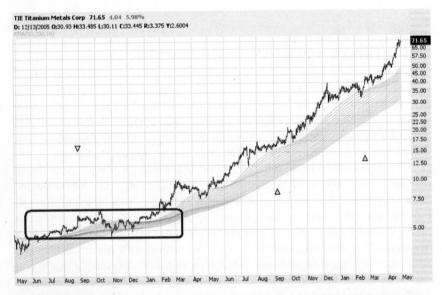

FIGURE 6.10   The ribbons were tightly wound here, preceding the major movement of this stock.

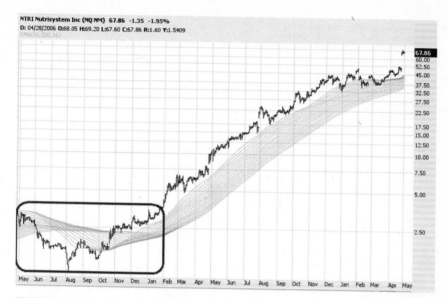

NTRI Nutrisystem Inc (NQ NM) 67.86 -1.35 -1.95%
D: 04/28/2006 O:68.05 H:69.20 L:67.60 C:67.86 R:1.60 Y:1.5409
RMA(50, 200, 16)

FIGURE 6.11 The ribbon study can often take on a three-dimensional effect, as shown here, as the ribbons twist into a new direction.

Figure 6.12 shows a close-up view of the area called out from Figure 6.11. This stock, NutriSystem (symbol NTRI) made an incredible upward move from $1.50 to about $70 in just a couple of years. The individual strands of the ribbon were moving up together, then started heading down, and then twisted back up again. This twist of the ribbon preceded an astonishing move higher, and the twisting of this study demonstrated that although the prices were basing for a short period, the core direction of the stock was up, and the energy released after this coiling was sufficient to propel NTRI far higher.

The Ribbon Study is just noise for a stock that isn't heading in any particular direction (Figure 6.13). The threads of the study remain compressed, twisting this way and that, indicating no plain movement.

The Ribbon Study is most useful for a stock that is about to commence a broad move up or down, as shown in Figure 6.14. These moves are usually preceded by a compressing of the threads. The more compressed the study, the more powerful the subsequent move, particularly if the ribbon twists and changes direction. The application of this indicator is very similar to that of the moving average except that, because there are many moving averages involved, you have the added benefit of seeing multiple time periods represented all at once.

FIGURE 6.12 This close-up of the symbol NTRI illustrates the detail of how the ribbons twist to change direction.

FIGURE 6.13 A stock stuck in a trading range, such as YHOO during the time shown here, results in a ribbon study that remains relatively compressed.

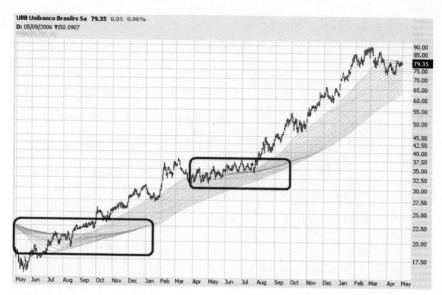

UBB Unibanco Brasilrs Sa 79.35 0.05 0.06%
D: 05/09/2006 Y:50.0907
RMA(50, 200, 18)

FIGURE 6.14 When a stock price is moving sideways, the ribbons will become denser.

LINEAR REGRESSION CHANNEL

One study, which is somewhat like Bollinger Bands in its application, is the Linear Regression Channel. There are actually a variety of Linear Regression studies, but they all are based on the same principle: a trend line is laid down that corresponds to an equilibrium in price. That is, a line is drawn that is the best fit based on past price activity. Two other lines are then laid down—one above and one below—that are the same distance from the equilibrium line, with distance based on past price volatility.

What this results in is a channel with an upper half and a lower half. Some Linear Regression studies have straight lines, and others are curved. Figure 6.15 shows one style of Linear Regression Channel with curved lines. The prices are generally bound by the lines, bouncing between the upper and lower boundaries and hugging the center line. As the area with the rounded rectangle illustrates, the prices sometimes do go outside their boundaries. These extremes are usually corrected, however, which means that these outlier prices can be viewed as special buying or selling opportunities.

While the prior figure shows price action that had dipped beneath the lower boundary, Figure 6.16 shows a stock whose upward movement was so swift and strong that it moved above its upper boundary.

FIGURE 6.15 A linear regression study will typically keep a boundary on prices, but sometimes price movement is so extreme it goes outside the lines.

FIGURE 6.16 Another example of the price movement being so extreme that it moves outside the normal range of the linear regression channel.

Events like this can sometimes be exploited for quick trading profits, since the stock has moved to an extreme level based on its past price behavior.

PARABOLIC STOP AND REVERSAL (PSAR)

The Parabolic Stop And Reversal (PSAR for short) was developed by famed technician Welles Wilder in 1978. The PSAR is a wonderfully simple indicator to use, and its express purpose is to provide a stop price for a given position. The PSAR provides a trailing stop so that a person knows when to get out of (and, if he is a particularly aggressive trader, even reverse) a position.

Unlike most other indicators, the PSAR is drawn using not lines but dots. If the dots are below the prices, it indicates the stock is moving upward. If the dots are above the prices, it indicates the stock is moving downward. If the price touches or goes beyond its dot for a current day, the PSAR flips and moves to the other side of the price movement (Figure 6.17).

So, at any given time, the current PSAR dot will be either above or below the current day's price bar. Strictly speaking, you would reset your stop

FIGURE 6.17 The PSAR indicator is very easy to use: be long if the price is above the PSAR and short if the price is below it.

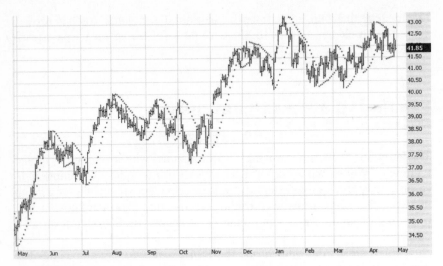

FIGURE 6.18 When a price bar pushes through a PSAR level, the PSAR flips from either bullish to bearish or vice versa.

price every day based on the PSAR value, if you were using this indicator devoutly. Take a look at the chart of symbol HANS in Figure 6.18. The activity for most of April had prices moving higher, and the PSAR was below the prices. The last two price bars on the graph, however, have the PSAR above instead of below the prices. The reason is that the second-to-last price bar touched the PSAR dot, flipping this dot's location from beneath the price bar to above it. Until such time as the prices touch a PSAR dot, the PSAR will remain in this bearish position.

MACD INDICATOR

So far in this chapter, the indicators discussed have been overlays. The Moving Average Convergence Divergence (MACD) indicator is an independent study, since it is displayed in its own graph pane instead of being put on top of the price chart.

As the name suggests, the MACD is based on moving averages. There are three moving averages involved:

1. A fast-moving one.
2. A slow-moving one.
3. A trigger.

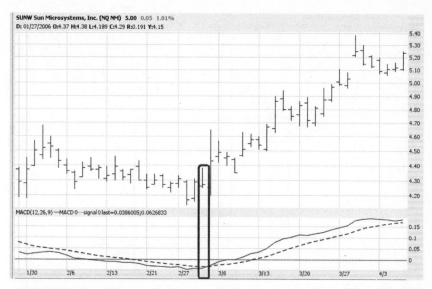

FIGURE 6.19 The MACD provides a good signal to buy SUNW before the stock began its move upward.

The most common figures are to have a 26-day exponential moving average (EMA) as the slow one, a 12-day EMA as the fast one, and a 9-day as the crossover. ProphetCharts calculates the difference between the 26-day and 12-day EMAs and plots this final value. This value moves above and below a flat plot line, and there is no preestablished upper or lower limit to this value, since the difference between these moving averages will be different for every security examined.

Figure 6.19 shows the two-line MACD study: the black line is the difference between the 26-day and 12-day EMA; the dashed line is the 9-day EMA. A signal takes place when the black line crosses above the dashed line (bullish) or below the dashed line (bearish). The MACD's purpose is to plot the underlying momentum of a security and to offer crossover points as a basis for trade decisions. In this example, the MACD provided a buy signal just before Sun Microsystems (symbol SUNW) started a healthy move upward.

There are actually two different ways of making use of the MACD: crossovers and divergences. A crossover is the plainest, because you simply need to watch for the black line to cross above or below the dashed line. A divergence takes place when the general direction of an indicator is the opposite of the general direction of the security. For example, if a particular stock seemed to be in a downtrend, yet its MACD was firm and heading up at the same time, that is a divergent indicator as to where the

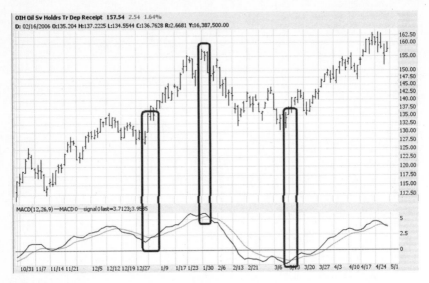

FIGURE 6.20 Three signals in a relatively short period—first a buy, then a sell, then another buy.

price is going to move next. A person using the MACD in this way would acquire the stock, trusting the MACD to be providing a buy signal prior to the stock following suit and moving higher.

As with any other crossover signal, the MACD is prone to providing multiple signals. The more volatile a security, the more frequent (and less reliable) these signals will be. If you are a very active trader, you can use multiple signals as an opportunity to trade the stock more frequently and in both directions (that is, both the long side and the short side). The symbol OIH (Figure 6.20) provides an illustration of this, since there were three signals given in a relatively short period: first a buy, then a sell, then another buy.

The most powerful MACD signals are preceded by relatively quiet price activity. If a stock is moving along in a relatively tight channel and then gives a clear MACD signal, it is often an indicator of an important price change. For example, A G Edwards (symbol AGE) was trading for months in a tight range of just a few dollars (Figure 6.21). In mid-March, even though the prices did not seem to be doing anything particularly unusual, an MACD signal was generated to buy the stock. Although it took a couple of weeks before any breakout occurred, the subsequent movement was significant, and the MACD gave warning far in advance of the actual price move.

Indicators can sometimes take on an almost clairvoyant quality about them. The reason is that indicators provide a different insight and

AGE A G Edwards Holding 52.84 -0.43 -0.81%
D: 03/07/2006 O:43.5488 H:43.6483 L:42.9714 C:43.3198 R:0.6769 Y:825,122.50

MACD(12,26,9)—MACD 0—signal 0 last=1.59005;1.67358

FIGURE 6.21 The MACD shown here signaled a substantial move in A G Edwards stock.

representation of the underlying price movement that is not visible by simply looking at the price chart. In Figure 6.22, the stock of the Chicago Mercantile Exchange (symbol CME) had been steady in July and August, drifting downward late in August. In spite of this anemic behavior, the MACD provided a crossover to the upside. This crossover preceded not just a very large up movement, but it specifically preceded a single-day movement of 20 points.

There is another way you can view MACD information, and that is by the use of a histogram. The MACD histogram is computed in the same way, but instead of providing two lines, it illustrates the difference between the two lines with positive bars (above the 0.00 line) or negative bars (below the 0.00 line).

Figure 6.23 shows an example of an MACD histogram. Because the bars are different and the transition from positive to negative (or vice versa) is so obvious, this representation of MACD movement makes it much easier to spot crossovers.

Figure 6.24 shows the analysis of a stock with an MACD histogram and a two-line MACD stacked on top of one another. This makes it easier to understand how these two studies correlate. In the two-line study, when the black line is beneath the dashed trigger line, there are negative bars in the histogram. When the black line is above the dashed trigger line, there are positive bars in the histogram. As you can see, the trigger points

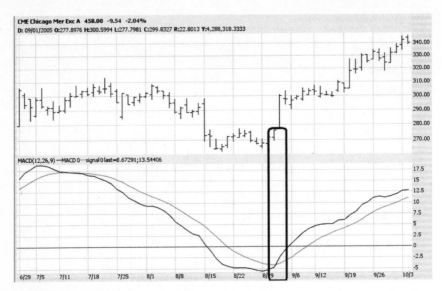

FIGURE 6.22 This MACD not only preceded a big move up by the stock CME but also was a day in advance of the 20-point move made in a single day.

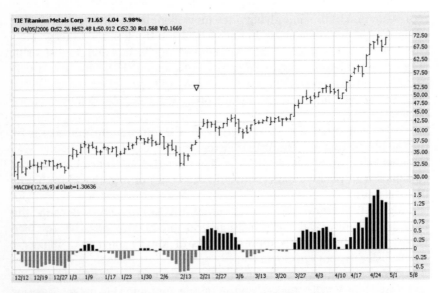

FIGURE 6.23 The MACD can also be viewed as a histogram.

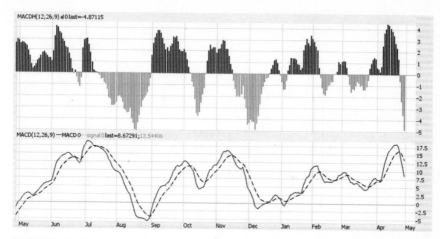

FIGURE 6.24 The differences between the MACD histogram and the two-line indicator.

are identical for both studies, and which study you elect to use is strictly personal preference.

RELATIVE STRENGTH INDEX (RSI)

The Relative Strength Index, often shortened to simply RSI, is a study that compares the magnitude of a stock's recent gains to recent losses. The study itself is a single line that is in its own pane, moving up and down between the ranges of 0 (at the bottom) to 100 (at the top). The RSI (Figure 6.25) is very simple to interpret and use: if it drops below 70 (which is marked with a horizontal dashed line), there is a sell signal; if it goes above 30 (also marked with a dashed horizontal line), there is a buy signal.

The path the RSI takes depends completely on the direction and momentum of the security's price. It may bob up and down between the 30 and 70 levels, generating no signals for quite some time. The best RSI indications happen when the study is plainly above or below one of the horizontal lines (Figure 6.26) and makes a decisive move back into the middle range.

Unlike slower-moving studies, the RSI is prone to generating many buy and sell signals. In Chapter 7, you will learn how to use multiple studies together so they can essentially vote on the predicted direction of a stock. Figure 6.27 shows the popular NASDAQ exchange-traded fund (ETF; symbol QQQQ) with four different RSI signals: three of them sells, and one of

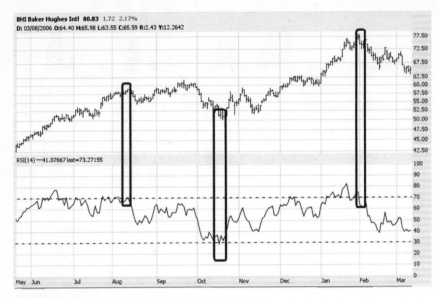

FIGURE 6.25 Three RSI signals on symbol BHI—first a sell, then a buy, then another sell.

FIGURE 6.26 A very clean RSI buy signal, since the RSI line went plainly below—and then above—the 30 mark.

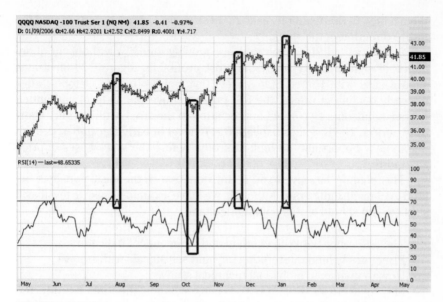

FIGURE 6.27 Some securities are so volatile that they provide multiple entry and exit points in a relatively short time frame.

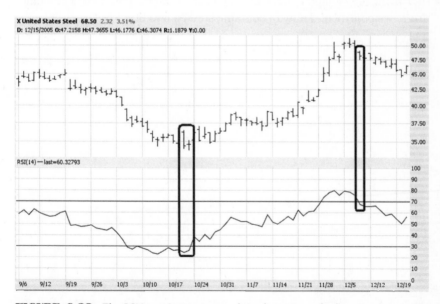

FIGURE 6.28 The RSI is easiest to use on broad, more gradual movements, such as are shown here for United States Steel.

them a buy. In this example, each of these signals correctly anticipated the future direction of the stock.

Stocks with RSI studies that are moving steadily without an abundance of signals are typically the most profitable. Figure 6.28 illustrates such a case with United States Steel (symbol X). In late October, after a steady decline in prices, the RSI pushes above the 30 level and anticipates a handsome 40 percent appreciation in the stock within a very short time period. The RSI slips beneath the 70 level in early December, providing an easy opportunity to lock in profits before the stock eases in price any more.

This chapter has given you an introduction to the basic concepts behind technical indicators. Although we have examined just a few basic studies, you should at this point understand:

- The difference between overlaid and independent indicators.
- Principles behind interpreting buy and sell signals with studies.
- How to invoke an individual technical study.
- Moving averages, RSI, MACD, Bollinger Bands, the Ribbon Study, the Linear Regression Channel, and PSAR studies.

In the next chapter, you will learn how to edit the parameters of studies for more control and how to combine studies into Study Sets.

CHAPTER 7

Multiple Studies and Comparisons

In Chapter 6, we learned how the application of technical studies (also known as indicators) can provide new insights into a chart's price action, including providing explicit buy and sell signals. However, you may find there is value in applying more than just one study at a time.

In ProphetCharts, the price graph and any overlay studies are in a single charting pane. The volume, if displayed, is in a separate pane and any other independent technical indicator each has its own pane (Figure 7.1). The value of having separate panes is that you can rearrange the order and size of each of those panes. Panes in ProphetCharts have a number of powerful properties:

- They can be arranged in any order you like.
- They can each be as tall or short as you like.
- The volume pane can be suppressed or revealed at any time.
- You can apply technical studies to virtually any pane.

That last point is particularly important. There is no reason, for instance, that a Simple Moving Average cannot be applied to the Volume pane as easily as it could be applied to the Price pane. The flexibility in ProphetCharts provides a virtually unlimited palette for crafting technical studies to help you make better trading decisions.

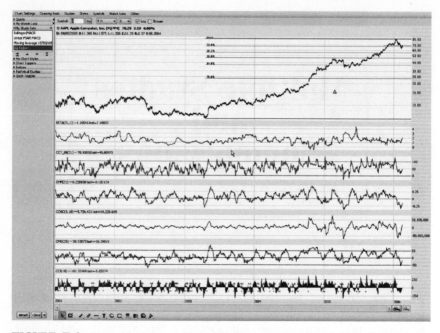

FIGURE 7.1   Many studies can be applied at once to assist in the analysis of a chart, and each study can be in its own individual pane.

THE TECHNICAL STUDIES EDITOR

One of ProphetCharts' most powerful features is its technical studies editor, which allows you to apply, arrange, and adjust any of the nearly 200 different studies available in the program. This section will introduce you to the editor and how to use it.

Applying a single study is something you learned about in Chapter 6. The easiest way to apply one study is from the Technical Studies module (Figure 7.2), which has an alphabetical listing of all the selections. Double-click on any study to apply it to the current chart, or drag-and-drop the study onto the chart. Once the study is applied, it will remain there until you choose Clear Studies from the Studies menu. So even if you enter many other stock symbols, you will see the study applied to each one of them.

The Technical Studies module limits you to applying just one indicator at a time. If you are using one study and double-click on another, the original study will be replaced by the new one. If you want to apply multiple studies, or if you want to fine-tune the settings of one or more of the indicators, you will need to use the technical studies editor. To get to this editor, choose the Apply Studies item from the Studies menu (Figure 7.3).

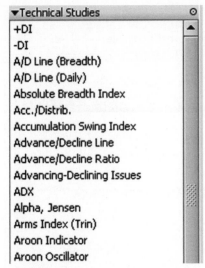

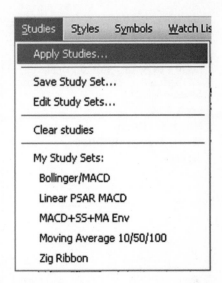

FIGURE 7.2 A list of all the studies is shown in the Technical Studies module. You can drag-and-drop or double click any of these to apply them.

FIGURE 7.3 To access the technical studies editor, click Apply Studies from the Studies menu.

When you choose Apply Studies, a dialog box like the one in Figure 7.4 appears. This is the technical studies editor, and it has four main components:

1. *Studies tab.* Notice on the left side of the editor there are two tabs—Studies and My Study Sets. The leftmost one, Studies, is selected by default. This gives you access to the same list of technical studies as is available in the Technical Studies module. You can add a study in any of three ways—by double clicking it, by clicking it once and then clicking Apply Study, or by dragging-and-dropping the study into the pane of your choice.

2. *My Study Sets tab.* The content here is identical to the My Study Sets module. You can choose this tab by clicking on the tab, and by clicking on any of the study sets, you can examine or edit the components of that study set. You will learn later in this chapter exactly how to make and name a study set.

3. *Panes.* Most of the right side of this dialog box is devoted to the placement of the panes that make up the entire chart. Each small rectangle represents a pane, and they are in the same order as they would be displayed on the chart itself. You can grab the upper portion of any of

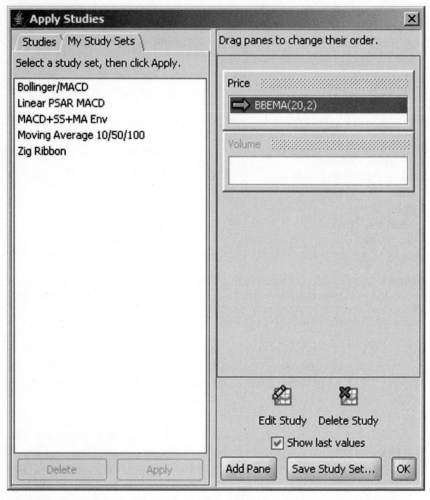

FIGURE 7.4 When you apply a technical study to the price, a shorthand abbreviation for that study will appear in the price pane.

these panes and drag it up or down in order to rearrange the order of the panes. You can also drag a study from the Studies tab into any of the panes in order to apply that study to that pane. For example, if you dragged Simple Moving Average into the Volume pane, it would apply that study to the volume.

4. *Buttons.* There are eight other elements to this editor, seven of which are buttons and one of which is a checkbox. These are each described next.

The buttons in the studies editor perform the following functions:

- *Apply Study*. Clicking this is the equivalent of double-clicking a study. You have to click a particular study first before this button.
- *Edit Study*. Clicking this brings up a dialog box to let you edit any study you have applied to the chart. You must click any of the studies on the right side of the screen before clicking Edit Study. The dialog box you see will depend on the study selected. A shortcut to get to the same place is to double-click the study within the pane.
- *Delete Study*. This deletes a study you have applied to the chart. As with Edit Study, you have to choose one of the studies in one of the panes for this to do anything.
- *Show Last Values*. This is a checkbox, not a button, but it has one simple function: to display the most recent values for each of the studies you have applied to the chart. If this is checked, the most recent values for each study will appear in the upper-left corner of each pane.
- *Add Pane*. This adds a blank pane to your chart. The purpose of a pane is to put studies within it. You probably will not need to use this button very often, because when you add a study to a chart, it is given a new pane for itself, anyway.
- *Save Study Set*. Clicking this button lets you preserve all the studies and their settings into a study set which you can later access by just double-clicking the name of the study set.
- *OK*. This accepts all the changes you have made and closes the editor.

EDITING A STUDY

Whether you are applying one study or a multitude of them to a chart, you can edit any study to change its settings and appearance. Although you probably will be satisfied with the default settings provided with any given study, you might want to change the appearance settings to your liking. Plus, if you are particularly sophisticated with a given technical indicator, you may have your own settings you want to apply instead.

Generally speaking, what you are able to edit for any given study falls into three general categories: (1) the source of the data; that is, the numbers upon which the resulting technical indicator is based; (2) other numeric parameters used to compute the study, such as the number of time periods to use; (3) the presentation of the study, such as its color, opacity, line style, and so forth.

It should also be noted that the concept of time periods strictly depends on the frequency of the bars being shown in your chart. If you are looking at a daily graph, then a "period" is a day. So a 20-period moving average is a 20-day moving average. If you are instead looking at the past five days of trading activity on an hour-by-hour basis, each bar represents one hour of time, so the same moving average study would be a 20-hour moving average.

For the sake of simplicity, we will assume you are looking at a daily chart, so we will use terms such as "50-day moving average" instead of the more precise and accurate "50-period moving average."

To edit a study, all you need to do is double-click the study that has been applied and appears on the right side of the technical studies editor. You can also click the study once and then click the Edit Study button. When you do this, a Study Editor for that particular study will appear (Figure 7.5) and will contain the various controls germane to that study as well as the settings that are being used for it (which will typically be the default settings, unless you have changed them).

Although every dialog box will be a little different, based on the study, the one shown in Figure 7.5 (which is for Bollinger Bands) is representative of the general components you will see for a Study Editor. These are:

- *Data source.* This dropdown lets you choose which element of the price should be used as the basis for computing the study. Most people want to use the closing price for their studies. But perhaps you'd rather use the high price. Or the low price. You can click on this dropdown and choose any of the available price fields. The fields available to you depend on the study and how it is being used.
- *Bar period and standard deviations.* These two fields are specific to the Bollinger Bands study, but they are a good example of the kind of fine-tuning you can do with a technical study. You should have a deep understanding of the study in question before adjusting the default parameters, however. One exception is the Moving Average, whose principal parameter (the number of periods to use) is simple enough for anyone to understand.
- *Fill, upper, and lower buttons.* These three graphical buttons control the color, upper-line appearance, and lower-line appearance, respectively. Again, these are specific to Bollinger Bands but are good general examples of the kinds of controls you will see on a Study Editor.

Clicking on any of the appearance control buttons yields other dialog boxes. For example, clicking the Fill button (which has a colored square in it) opens a Color dialog box (Figure 7.6) that gives you control over the color and opacity of the study. Choosing the color is simple enough—you

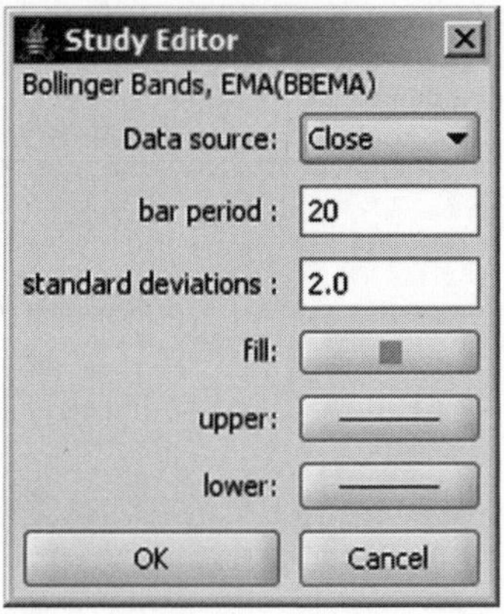

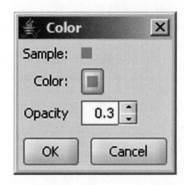

FIGURE 7.5 You have a lot of control over each technical study, since virtually any aspect of its computation or appearance can be adjusted.

FIGURE 7.6 The color of a particular study makes it easy to read. You can adjust the color and opacity of any study to your preference.

are provided a palette of colors from which to choose—but you might not be acquainted with the term "opacity."

The opacity of an object controls how much you can see through it, if at all. You can change this setting from as little as 0.1 (as see-through as possible) up to 1.0 (solid). This is valuable because you will quickly find that studies can clutter your chart. You want them to enhance your charting experience, not get in the way of it. One effective way to do this is to tone down the appearance of a study (particularly overlaid studies) so that they are more subtle. Your principal focus should always be on the price action, with the studies providing you different insights into the general trend of the price.

Clicking either the "upper" or "lower" button produces a special dialog box to control the style of each line (Figure 7.7). As with the prior dialog box, you have control over the color and opacity. You also have two new controls: Weight (wherein the selection from the dropdown menu lets you select how thick the line should be) and Pattern (wherein the selection lets you choose if the line is solid, dashed, dotted, or some other style). It bears repeating that all the studies will have different controls, but these controls will be self-explanatory. You will also see the effects on the chart immediately, so you can continue to make adjustments before committing the changes with an OK.

As another illustration of how each Study Editor is different, Figure 7.8 shows the dialog box for the MACD technical indicator. It has the Data Source dropdown, as the other one did, but its numeric input is

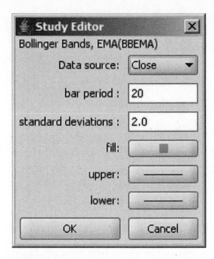

FIGURE 7.7 Use the line style editor to change the color, opacity, weight, and pattern of each line in a study.

FIGURE 7.8 You can edit any study. In this case, you can alter the data used as the basis for the MACD as well as its three moving average periods and the appearance of both the MACD and signal lines.

different, since the MACD calls for different parameters (in this case, fast period, slow period, and signal period). Whereas the Bollinger Bands had an upper line and a lower line, the MACD has a MACD line and a Signal line. As with the numeric parameters, these appearance settings are given default values, which suit the majority of users.

WORKING WITH PANES

The ability to size and arrange the panes which comprise the entire chart is one of ProphetCharts' most powerful features. Manipulating the panes is quite intuitive, since it merely involves dragging-and-dropping the panes in the order you want. First, it helps to fully understand the nature of panes.

In ProphetCharts, a pane can either be (a) the Price pane, (b) the Volume pane, or (c) a study pane. Any of these panes can contain technical indicators, and the item affected depends on where those indicators are placed. If a Moving Average is in the Price pane, that study will show up overlaid with the prices. If it is in the Volume pane, it will show up overlaid with volume. If it is in its own pane, it will be the same shape as if it were in the Price pane, but it will be by itself.

FIGURE 7.9 Independent indicators are provided with their own pane.

You can also edit any given study within its pane. The editing you do in one pane does not affect the other panes. So if you had three moving averages in the Price pane (a 30-, 50-, and 100-day moving average) and a single moving average in the Volume pane, editing the moving average in the Volume pane would not alter the other three moving averages. The only "tie that binds" the panes together is the x-axis, which is time. All the panes will line up with respect to time, because the chart would be meaningless otherwise.

You typically needn't worry about the creation and management of panes, except insofar as you want to change their order. When you apply a study, that study will go into the most common place, and if it calls for the creation of a new pane, such a pane will be created. Figure 7.9 illustrates how the Price pane has its own indicator (BBEMA, which is the abbreviation for Bollinger Band Exponential Moving Average) while the MACD indicator is in its own pane.

You may have reason for the panes to be in a different vertical order than is provided. It is completely up to you how you want these to appear. Typically, the volume for a price chart appears beneath the price. Perhaps you'd prefer the volume to be on top. All you need do is click on the Volume pane, hold down the mouse button, and drag the pane to be above the Price

FIGURE 7.10 This chart shows the result of dragging the volume pane above the price pane.

pane. As shown in Figure 7.10, your chart will then have these panes in the order you have stated.

As you are dragging objects around the technical study editor, a ghost image of what is being dragged appears so you can accurately place it, whether it's a pane or a study. Figure 7.11 shows the Simple Moving Average study being dragged from the Studies list over to the Price pane. It will have its default setting (a 30-period moving average), which can be changed once the drag-and-drop operation is complete. As you can see, there are three panes on this chart—a pane for the MACD study, a Price pane with two studies, and a Volume pane (which is grayed-out, since the volume is being hidden on this chart based on the Quick Toggles).

And, as always, once you finish dropping a study to its location, you can double-click on that study to adjust its settings (Figure 7.12). You will certainly do this with moving averages if you use more than one moving average, since they will otherwise all have the same periods.

DELETING STUDIES AND PANES

If you want to remove a study, just click on it and then click on Delete Study. It will be removed at once.

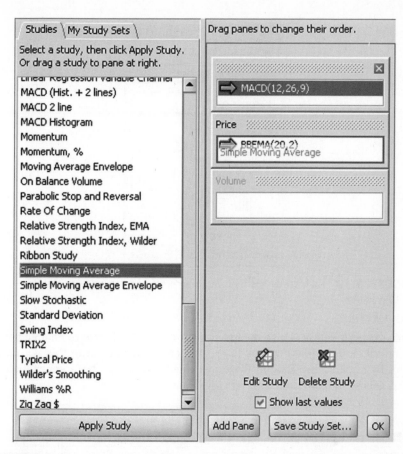

FIGURE 7.11 You can drag-and-drop a study from the left side to the right, and when you do so, a ghost image of what you are dragging appears so you can place it in the correct pane.

If the study you are deleting is the only thing in its pane, and the pane is not Price or Volume, ProphetCharts will ask you if you would like to go ahead and delete the pane at the same time. After all, there is not much value in having an empty pane unless you intend to put something else there. If you want the pane removed, click on Yes. You can save yourself time by checking the "Don't warn me" checkbox before clicking Yes so that ProphetCharts does not need to ask you anymore.

A more direct way to delete both the pane and all the studies within it is to click the close box in the upper-right corner of any pane. When you do, a dialog box like the one in Figure 7.13 appears, verifying you want to make this deletion. You can click OK to proceed and, as before, you can click the "Don't warn me" checkbox in order not to be advised in the future.

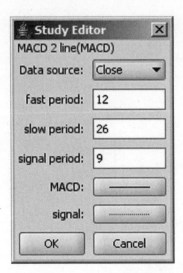

FIGURE 7.12 Each study has its own parameters and settings you can fine-tune to your liking.

This saves time, but it also means you won't have a chance to change your mind when you delete panes later (you can also reactivate this warning later by clicking the Enable Warnings checkbox in the Preferences dialog box, accessed from the Chart Settings menu).

CROSSOVERS AND MULTIPLE STUDIES

Many indicators offer buy or sell signals based on a specific rule. For instance, as you learned in Chapter 6, the RSI indicator issues a buy signal when it crosses above the 30 line and a sell signal when it crosses below

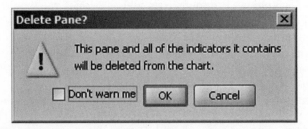

FIGURE 7.13 Any time you delete a pane in the technical studies editor, this warning box will appear. You can click "Don't warn me" and then OK if you do not want to see this anymore.

FIGURE 7.14 If you want to see when crossovers take place on a particular technical indicator, check the Show Trade Signals checkbox in the Study Editor.

the 70 line. The MACD provides signals when the MACD line crosses the trigger line either upward (buy) or downward (sell).

ProphetCharts can make it easier for you to see these crossover points by providing upward-pointing arrows ("buy") and downward-pointing arrows ("sell") to show where these signals take place. It is very important to take note that these are *not* explicit trading recommendations. They simply indicate when a given indicator has crossed a certain threshold or otherwise achieved a predefined parameter. Any application of real money in the world of investments must involve your own judgment and decision making.

To make these up and down arrows appear, click on the Show Trade Signals checkbox (Figure 7.14) in the technical study in which you want arrows to appear.

If you activate these crossover arrows, you will see the crossovers plainly marked, as illustrated in Figure 7.15.

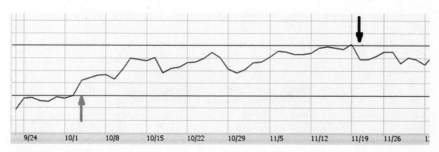

FIGURE 7.15 Buy and sell arrows are displayed on the study if the Show Trade Signals checkbox is checked.

Before moving on to comparison charts, we will revisit the subject of putting multiple studies in a single pane. This is most valuable in the Price pane, because independent studies (such as MACD and the Fast Stochastic) typically get too crowded and confusing when clustered into the same pane.

Assume you wanted to apply three different exponential moving averages to the price chart. The steps to do this would be:

1. Pull up the price chart of any financial instrument.
2. Choose Apply Studies from the Studies menu.
3. Find "Exponential Moving Average" from the Studies list, and double-click on it three times. This makes three identical studies go into the Price pane. These are all marked EMA(30), indicating in short-hand that three 30-period Exponential Moving Averages have been added.
4. Double-click on the first EMA(30) and change the value in the period box to 10, then click OK. That will make it a 10-day moving average.
5. Double-click on the second EMA(30) and change its period value to 50, then click OK. Change the third EMA to 100 in the same manner. The Price pane will resemble Figure 7.16.
6. Click the OK button to finish.

The result is shown in Figure 7.17, with three moving averages overlaid on the price chart. A legend of the studies appears just beneath the data line, showing each of the studies followed by (1) its current numeric value, based on where you are pointing on the chart; and (2) its last, most recent value from the chart, since the "Show Last Value" checkbox was checked on the technical studies editor.

Now that you understand how to combine technical studies, you can use the time-saving Study Sets feature.

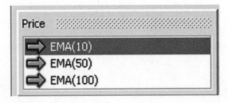

FIGURE 7.16 Three exponential moving averages being applied to the Price pane in the technical studies editor.

FIGURE 7.17 Three moving averages on one chart, each of which has its color and value display in the legend just under the data line.

SAVING STUDY SETS

As you become more expert with various studies, you will find certain ones that you especially like to use. You will also find that some combinations of these studies work well together, since they can be used to help you weigh your trading decisions and, in a way, vote on whether you are going to buy a stock or not. You may even find yourself so adept with some indicators that you adjust their parameters (certainly those involving appearance) to your liking.

It becomes time-consuming and tedious to go through the process of applying and adjusting these studies every time. For this reason, ProphetCharts provides for study sets. A study set is simply a collection of technical studies (including all of its computation and appearance parameters) housed under a name that you assign.

You may, for example, create a study set named "Three Moving Averages," and another one called "Bullish Breakout System," and another called "Bollingers with PSAR and MACD." What's important is that the names are distinct and meaningful to you, since study sets are your shortcut to applying what might otherwise be a very tedious application of settings.

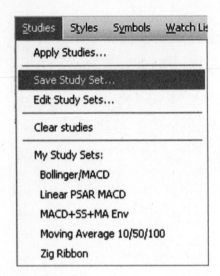

FIGURE 7.18 To preserve the technical studies you have used into a single set, choose Save Study Set from the Studies menu.

FIGURE 7.19 When you save a study set, you can either enter a new name to save a new set or update a set you made earlier.

Creating a study set is done from either the Studies menu or the technical studies editor. In either case all you do, once you have set up the technical studies to your liking, is click Save Study Set (Figure 7.18).

After you choose this option, a dialog box is presented (Figure 7.19) that lets you either enter a new name or save the set onto an existing name. The radio buttons in this dialog box control whether or not you are going to create a new study set with a new name (the default choice) or if you want to overwrite a previously created study set (the second choice), in which case you'll need to choose the study set that you want to replace from the dropdown menu. Once you are done, you can click OK to save your study set.

If you decide to edit a study set later, you can do so from within the technical studies editor. Just click on the name of the study set in the My Study Sets tab, and the definition of that set will appear on the right side (Figure 7.20) for you to examine or modify.

After you have created your study set, you can apply it by choosing it from the Studies menu or by double-clicking it from the My Studies module (Figure 7.21). Generally speaking, the more you use ProphetCharts, the more customized it becomes, and the study sets are one important aspect of this customization.

The convenience of being able to simply choose a study set and have all the customized studies applied instantly (Figure 7.22) will allow you to

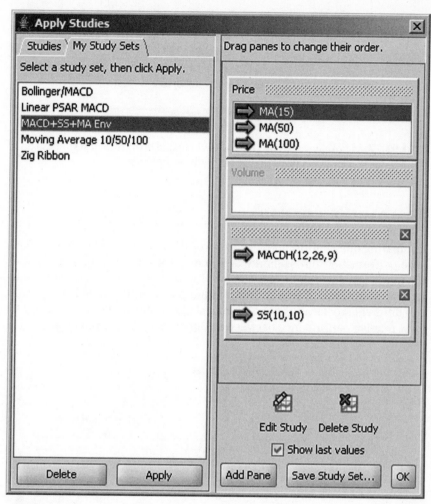

FIGURE 7.20 When a study set is selected, all the components and settings of that set are displayed on the right side of the dialog box.

focus more on your trading decisions instead of the adjustment of menus and numbers.

Once again, the "Show Last Values" checkbox was checked in the creation of the study set in Figure 7.22, so the most recent values of every study appear at the top-left of every pane. Figure 7.23 shows the detail from the prior chart, illustrating how the precise value (in this case, from the 15-day moving average) is provided just beneath the data line.

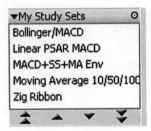

FIGURE 7.21 Whatever study sets you have created in the technical studies editor will also show up alphabetically in the My Study Sets module.

COMPARING CHARTS

Comparing one chart to another is one of the most valuable ways to compare performance across markets. You might want to compare a stock to the market in general, or one commodity to another, or a mutual fund to a broad stock market index, or even multiple securities together (such as five different stocks all at once). Being able to compare gives you a way to view relative performance between different financial instruments.

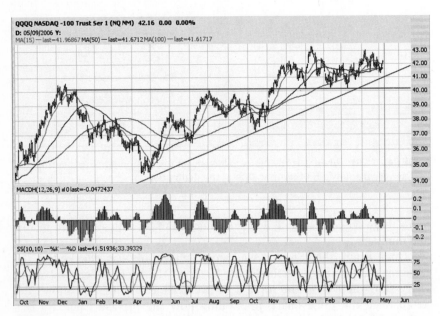

FIGURE 7.22 This chart has three overlaid studies and two independent studies, and in the upper-left corner of each pane is a legend showing the values.

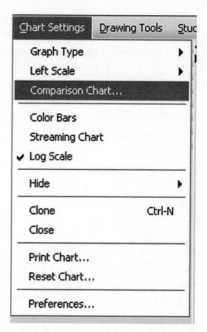

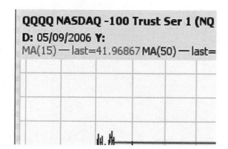

FIGURE 7.23 If you have selected Show Last Value from the Technical Studies dialog box, then the most recent value for each study you are using will be shown in the legend.

FIGURE 7.24 To compare the current chart to another security, select Comparison Chart from the Chart Settings menu.

There are two basic kinds of comparison: price and percentage. A price comparison plots two or more securities into a price pane, showing their actual prices over the requested period of time. Because the prices might be very different (for example, comparing a stock of about $3 to another of about $80), this can often yield a graph that is not very useful. The other kind of comparison is a percentage comparison, which is much more common, since it illustrates the percentage change in price over a certain period of time, irrespective of the price of the securities.

Once you have a single security chart, you can compare this security to one or more others by choosing Comparison Chart from the Chart Settings menu (Figure 7.24).

When you do this, the Comparison Chart dialog box appears (Figure 7.25). In it are these controls:

- *Index selection.* A list of major U.S. indexes is presented. You can double-click any one of these to add it to the list of items that should be compared. Index symbols are often strange and hard to remember, so this list makes it convenient to choose an index.

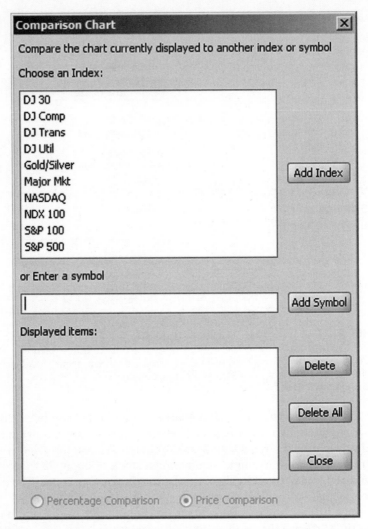

FIGURE 7.25 When using the Comparison Chart function, choose from a list of Indexes or enter your own symbols for the comparison.

- *Enter a symbol entry box.* This is where you can enter any valid symbol that you want. It can be anything chartable—an index, a stock, a mutual fund, a commodity, an option—just type in the symbol and click Add Symbol, and it will be added to the Displayed Items list.
- *Displayed items.* These are the items which will be compared to the original security charted. There may be anywhere from zero items (normal chart, no comparisons) to multiple items in this box. You can

erase everything to start over by clicking Delete All, or if you want to get rid of just one item, click on it and click Delete.

- *Comparison type.* The radio buttons, Percentage Comparison and Price Comparison, control what kind of comparison will be done. Percentage is the default, since that is usually more useful.

Figure 7.26 shows that the S&P 100 has been added, as well as the symbol IWM. The list of symbols in the lower portion of the dialog box

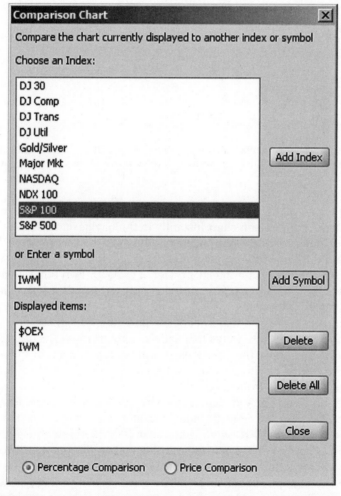

FIGURE 7.26 The Comparison Chart dialog box lets you enter multiple items so that you can compare many other securities to the original one charted.

FIGURE 7.27 A Percentage Comparison is the default for the Comparison function, since it's typically the most useful way to compare various securities, irrespective of their prices.

will appear in alphabetical order, and as you add symbols, you will see the resulting comparison chart instantly in the background. When you are done, you can click the Close button.

Figure 7.27 illustrates a percentage comparison. The original security plotted was the NASDAQ 100 ETF (symbol QQQQ). Two other items were added via the Comparison function: the S&P 100 (symbol $OEX) and the Russell 2000 ETF (symbol IWM). These symbols and their most recent price values appear just underneath the data line. The chart clearly illustrates how one of these items has widely outperformed the others (as in the rest of this book, the colors used are not reproduced in these black and white charts, but ProphetCharts does make ample use of color to help distinguish one item from another).

The same comparison chart done with a Price comparison looks very different. Because the S&P 100 index was at a value of about 600, whereas both the IWM and QQQQ were well under 100, the three graphs get very flattened (Figure 7.28), since they are scaled based on the lowest and highest values among all three securities. This kind of chart distortion makes such a graph almost useless. There are certainly examples where a Price comparison would be useful, but those would almost always involve similarly-priced instruments.

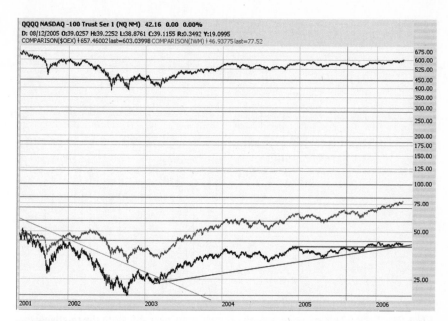

FIGURE 7.28 Unless the securities you are comparing have similar prices, it probably doesn't make sense to do a Price Comparison, since the scales will be very distorted.

THE LEFT-SCALE AXIS

There is one other way to compare securities that is in many ways more useful and powerful than using prices or percentages. Very few charting systems in the world do it, and it is called Left Scale charting.

What that means is that two securities are compared, and one of them is based on a price axis on the right side of the chart and the second is based on a price axis on the left side of the chart. These scales are custom-fitted to their respective securities, which means that even if the prices are extremely different, the resulting chart is readable and undistorted by price disparity.

As an example of this, consider the comparison between the NASDAQ 100 ETF (symbol QQQQ) and one of its put options. For the sake of this example, assume the QQQQ is priced at about $41 and that one of its put options (Figure 7.29) is priced in the $1 to $2 range.

If you wanted to compare the graph of this put option to the graph of the underlying security, the most effective way to do it would be with the Left Price Scale Chart option in Chart Settings (Figure 7.30). Unlike normal

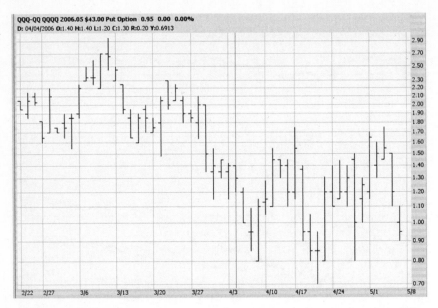

QQQ-QQ QQQQ 2006.05 $43.00 Put Option 0.95 0.00 0.00%
D: 04/04/2006 O:1.40 H:1.40 L:1.20 C:1.30 R:0.20 Y:0.6913

FIGURE 7.29   This graph shows an options chart by itself. Note the relatively low price on the y-axis.

Comparison charting, you may compare only two securities at a time with this function.

All you need to do at this point is enter the symbol (Figure 7.31) that should be plotted on the left scale. You do not have to compare similar instruments (such as a stock versus a stock). The two securities can be anything that is otherwise chartable.

Before examining the result, let us see what a similar comparison would yield with the normal Comparison function to understand the benefits of this feature. Figure 7.32 shows a percentage comparison of QQQQ versus the put option. As you can see, the put option is far more volatile

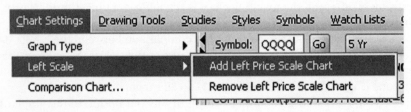

FIGURE 7.30   To add another financial instrument and have its own y-axis applied, select Add Left Price Scale Chart from the Chart Settings menu.

FIGURE 7.31 You can enter any kind of symbol into the Left-Axis chart, such as an option, an index, a commodity, or a stock.

(with a range of from minus 55 percent to plus 30 percent in this short time range), whereas the QQQQ only budges a percent or two. It's a somewhat interesting chart only in the respect that it shows how much more volatile an option is than its underlying stock, but you aren't going to learn much more from such a chart.

The same comparison done based on price is even less useful (Figure 7.33). The QQQQ is at the very top of the chart, clinging close to the $42.50 price, while the option bounces along at the bottom of the chart in the $1 to $2 range. Because the scale is so distorted, both graphs are rendered virtually meaningless.

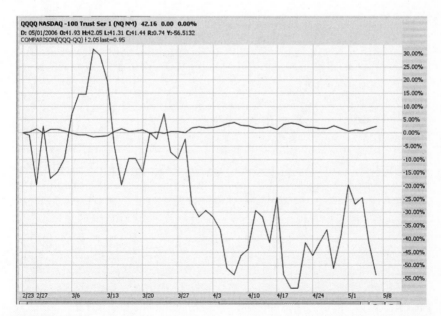

FIGURE 7.32 Comparing an option to its underlying security with a percentage comparison is not useful, since the option is almost certainly going to be dramatic.

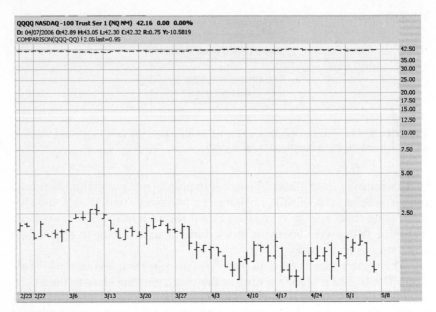

FIGURE 7.33 A comparison graph based on price of two very differently-priced securities yields a graph which is not at all useful.

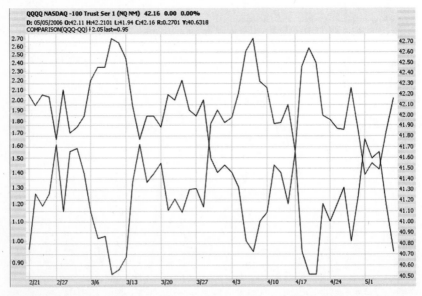

FIGURE 7.34 By using two different y-axis scales, ProphetCharts is able to display two disparate kinds of financial instruments in a form that is still useful in spite of their different prices.

But the Left Scale graph (Figure 7.34) does away with the price disparity by having each security depend on its own, independent scale. The price range on the left (from 80 cents to nearly $2.70) and the price range on the right (from $40.50 to $42.70) give both graphs the room they need to present themselves and, to no surprise, the graphs are inversely related (one graph being a put option, in this case). Note that in the Option Controls module, the Compare with Stock checkbox automatically loads the stock chart corresponding to an option chart. It does this by taking advantage of the Left Scale feature.

SUMMARY

Both Chapters 6 and 7 have been devoted to mathematical studies and chart comparison, and you are now equipped to do some extremely sophisticated charts. As we head into Chapter 8, we will refocus on drawn objects, with our initial concentration being on trendlines, one of the most basic but essential tools of securities charting.

Trendlines and Reversals

T rendlines are very basic—but very powerful—drawn objects that can be placed onto a chart. In the context of ProphetCharts, a drawn object is an item that is added to a chart to provide insight into likely future price behavior, usually by indicating support or resistance levels. You will explore a variety of drawn objects in this and coming chapters, but a solid knowledge of the use and interpretation of trendlines is essential to your success as a technical analyst.

The properties of a well-drawn trendline are as follows:

- It connects at least two points of a graph (with high points or low points), and the more points it touches, the more valid and useful the line is.
- It is never violated by prices between the starting and ending points; in other words, all of the stock prices are either below the trendline (in which case the line is resistance) or above the trendline (in which case the line is support).

A trendline's purpose depends on your position with a particular stock. If you have a position in a stock, the trendline's value is to ensure that the trend of the stock is intact (Figure 8.1), so that when the trend is violated, you exit your position as profitably as possible. If you do not have a position in a stock, the purpose of a trendline is to show you when a possible trend change has taken place so that you can consider taking a position in the stock.

FIGURE 8.1 This trendline, going back for years, is intact for this stock during its climb from $27.50 to over $100.

Drawing a trendline is very simple for most people, since laying down a straight line to "bound" the uptrend or downtrend of a stock makes intuitive sense. The art, however, is discerning when to redraw a trendline, because as a stock moves, it may become appropriate to redraw a trendline to take into account the more complete price data. The danger, of course, is that you can wind up fooling yourself. If your trendlines become so elastic that they bend and move no matter which direction prices are heading, then you have eliminated their value.

Figure 8.2 illustrates this point. It shows the astonishing climb of Hansen Natural (HANS) from $2 to more than 100 times that amount. The trendline on this chart looks extremely clean, because the price stayed above it at all times and, indeed, usually was well above it except for the two "touchpoints" at the beginning of the graph and about two-thirds of the way from the left side. But as you can see, until the second touchpoint was established, the trendline would have been steeper, so the original trendline would have been crossed to the downside, indicating a possible trend change. In retrospect we can see that the trend certainly did not change, as the stock continued to soar hundreds of percent.

FIGURE 8.2 Hansen Natural climbed from $2 to over $200 over the course of a couple of years, and it never violated its ascending trendline.

When prices violate a trendline, however, it should normally be heeded. To illustrate this point, imagine yourself driving a car down a deserted highway. Since you want to understand the concept of trendlines well, you decide to not look at the road ahead but simply open your door and keep your eye on the median line. You have no idea how the road will twist or turn or whether it will continue straight.

For a while, the yellow line whizzes by more or less in the same place. It sometimes moves a little away from the car, but it soon returns to be just outside the driver's door. Suddenly, the median line moves underneath your car, disappearing from sight. You'd better look up quickly to see what's happening, because the road must be turning!

That's sort of what trendlines are like (although not nearly as dangerous—at least in the physical sense). They provide a line that prices should stay above (if the line is support) or below (if resistance), and if prices should stray across the trendline, something has changed. As with your car, it doesn't necessarily mean a crash is ahead, but you'd better start paying better attention.

One instance where a crash certainly did happen is Yahoo! in early 2000. Yahoo! had soared hundreds of percent during the Internet bubble

FIGURE 8.3 As the Internet bubble of the late 1990s ended, Yahoo! violated its ascending trendline early in April 2000. It tried to recover, but once the trend was broken, the damage was done.

of the late 1990s. Figure 8.3 shows how Yahoo! peaked at about $125 on the first day of the 2000 trading year, then it starting softening. After losing about 40 percent of its value, it started firming up again, making a small saucer pattern, then it reweakened.

On the first trading day of April, 2000, the price briefly pierced the long-term trendline, only to recover. A few days later, prices clearly slipped beneath the trendline. *At this point, the line which formerly had been support now had become resistance.* This is a vital concept, since the "turncoat" nature of trendlines is a key part of their value.

Just because the trendline was broken doesn't mean Yahoo! immediately collapsed. But it did mean that the stock was no longer in a defined up-trend. Paradoxically, stocks that break their uptrends can still move higher in price, as you will learn later in this chapter. In Yahoo!'s case (Figure 8.4), the price firmed up for a couple of months and then started falling even more. Before it was all over, Yahoo! had lost more than 97 percent of its peak value.

A similar chart during the same time period can be seen in Figure 8.5, which shows the S&P 500 exchange-traded fund (symbol SPY, commonly

FIGURE 8.4 Following the violation of its trendline, Yahoo! collapsed, losing almost its entire value.

FIGURE 8.5 Here is the SPY over a period close to a decade. Its ascending trendline was intact from 1994 through 2000, but once it was violated, the fall that followed was severe.

known as the "spiders"). The ascending trendline is quite long, beginning in late 1994 and being violated in the autumn of 2000. After prices cracked below the trendline, the decline was swift and terrible. This illustrates an important principle with trendlines: *the length of the trendline is a strong indicator of how meaningful the trend change will be once that line has been crossed.* A trendline spanning 10 days is probably meaningless, whereas a trendline spanning ten years is terribly important.

You certainly don't have to look just at the Internet bubble to find examples of trendline violations and their aftermath. Krispy Kreme (Figure 8.6), the makers of incredibly delicious (particularly when fresh) doughnuts was the darling of 2000 and 2001. It held onto that distinction since virtually every other stock was getting clobbered. Perhaps people were gobbling down doughnuts to distract themselves from their sorrows of this major bear market. In any event, as the Atkins diet craze started gathering momentum, Krispy starting to weaken.

Late in 2003, KKD broke below its trendline. Had you been long this stock, you would have already suffered a 20 percent loss from the stock's peak. But the value of trendlines isn't that they guarantee you will make as

FIGURE 8.6 Krispy Kreme was one of the very few stocks that went up during 2000 and 2001. It violated its trendline late in 2003 and quickly lost most of its value.

much profit as possible. Instead, they try to give you as much time as possible to remain in a position before being given evidence that you should get out. So in this case, even though the stock had already fallen from $50 to $40 before you were warned, this warning at least would have prevented you from holding on to the later price of $4, a 90 percent drop from the trendline violation.

As mentioned earlier in this chapter, a stock doesn't necessarily collapse because it has broken below its trendline (keep in mind prices can break above trendlines as well, but for this introduction, we will focus on breakdowns). After a price crosses below a trendline, the price can (a) go up, (b) go down, or (c) go sideways. There's really no way to know for sure! But the trendline at least provides a likely indication of what the stock will do next.

Take Diebold, for instance (Figure 8.7), which fell below its trendline in early 1984. Had you sold right away, you would have received about $6.50 per share for your stock. However, it slowly climbed its way to $8, more than a 20 percent increase in value. But this is the important point: The stock did not cross above its trendline again. It clung to it, inching higher, staying just beneath its newfound resistance level. It finally

FIGURE 8.7 A stock can break its trendline and still go up in price. Diebold fell below its trendline early in 1984, then it climbed higher for the first half of the year. It failed to cross back over its trendline, however, and subsequently fell hard.

FIGURE 8.8 A trendline break can precede the creation of a different pattern. In this case, after Cleveland Cliffs broke its trendline, it formed a head and shoulders pattern, which strengthened the bearish case.

succumbed and fell over the next year to $4.50, losing about half its peak value.

As you learn about other drawn objects (such as channels, retracements, horizontal lines, and so on), you will see how to combine them to perform more complex analyses. Figure 8.8 shows Cleveland Cliffs (CLF) dipping beneath its trendline. In retrospect, when it did this, it was about halfway through the job of creating what is known as a head and shoulders pattern, highlighted here by the use of a horizontal line.

Now that you have the general idea as to what constitutes a trendline and why it is useful, it's time to learn how to make them in ProphetCharts.

USING THE TOOL

Using any drawn object in ProphetCharts begins with the selection of the tool you want from the toolbar (Figure 8.9). The toolbar's default location is in the lower-left portion of the price pane, although you can drag-and-drop the toolbar to any other side or even have it "float" separate from the chart area.

FIGURE 8.9 The toolbar contains all the drawing tools, including the trendline, which is the third from the left.

The tools are, from left to right: pointer, expansion, trendline, channels, horizontal line, text, oval highlight, rectangle highlight, Fibonacci retracements, Fibonacci time series, Fibonacci arcs, and Fibonacci fans. The trendline tool, the third from the left, is the one you want to click.

Once you have selected the trendline tool, all you need to do to draw a trendline is (1) click on the point where you want the line to begin, (2) drag the mouse, during which time the line will be displayed, no matter where you move the mouse, and (3) click a second time, which completes the creation of the line.

Any trendline you draw has a number of properties, any one of which can be changed: color, style, and extension. You will learn how to alter the color and style later in this chapter, but let us take a moment to understand the concept of trendline extension.

You may recall from geometry the distinction between a line segment and a ray. A line segment is a finite line that has two endpoints. A ray has one endpoint and continues into infinity. And a line, just to complete the review, goes infinitely in both directions.

In the case of trendlines, you will apply either a line segment or a ray. Using a ray is more common, since you are watching prices on an ongoing basis, and the trend will extend off the right edge of the chart. Using a line segment is more appropriate in the case of prior trends, since the trend has already changed and there is no reason to clutter your chart with a line that continues going past the trend's end.

In order to choose whether you want to extend the line or not, you use the Extend option. This option is available for a number of drawn objects, but the principle is the same for all of them: Extend makes the drawn object continue forward in time, all the way to the rightmost edge of the chart.

Notice how the pointer changes into a hand when you move the mouse over the drawn object. This is the signal that you can right-click to modify that particular object. To access Extend, right-click on any trendline, which creates the popup menu shown in Figure 8.10, and choose Extend. If it is checked, the line will be extended into a ray. If it is unchecked, the line will exist only between its two endpoints. You can toggle back and forth between these settings for any given trendline (it does not affect any others elsewhere).

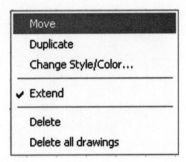

FIGURE 8.10 Right-clicking on a trendline yields a popup menu with a number of command choices.

Let us take an opportunity to consider several important properties of the popup menu. These four general rules are important to effective and efficient use of any of the drawn objects.

1. To access the popup menu that controls one particular drawn object, right-click on that object.

2. Changes made to that object affect that object and no others. You therefore need not be concerned that you will alter any of the other trendlines (or any other kind of object, for that matter) by altering one of them.

3. However, when you draw another drawn object—in this case, a trendline—ProphetCharts will use the most recent settings since it assumes that is what you want to use. So whatever color, style, and extension choice you last made will be applied to all subsequent trendlines until you change those settings again.

4. Every single object on a chart can be completely unique. Each and every object can be colored differently, styled differently, and extended differently. Although you can preserve the settings you have chosen to save yourself time when drawing additional objects, it is useful to keep in mind the uniqueness of every drawn object, since those distinctions can help make a chart easier to read and interpret.

Another selection on the popup menu is Move. The Move function reveals the two handles on the trendline, thus allowing you to change the location of the trendline. The existence of these handles is probably the single most powerful and useful feature of all the drawn objects, so it is crucial to understand their purpose.

FIGURE 8.11 Double-clicking on a trendline gives you access to the two handles, which allow for careful placement of the line.

The handles of any drawn object are the places where the endpoints were established. Once you draw a trendline, only the line is shown, and no special mark is given to the endpoints. However, once you select Move from the popup menu (or once you double-click on the trendline, which is actually a faster way to achieve the same thing), the two handles will appear as small squares (Figure 8.11).

When you point your mouse to a handle, the mouse pointer changes from an arrow to a hand, indicating it is ready for you to move the handle. You can drag the handle anywhere in the chart that you like. One of the reasons this is so useful is that you can create very precisely laid trendlines, which is important to good charting (Figure 8.12). You might want to make sure that the "Snap to OHLC values during drawing" checkbox is checked in the preferences menu (see Figure 3.18 back in Chapter 3) to make precise placement of handles easier.

If you point at the trendline but do not click any button (this is known as a "mouseover"), then information about the trendline will appear as a tool tip (Figure 8.13). This tool tip will identify the object (in this case, "Trendline") as well as the starting and ending values of the endpoints in terms of both price and date.

There is usually a variety of ways to get to the same function, in order to save time. The ability to alter a trendline's style, color, or extension is

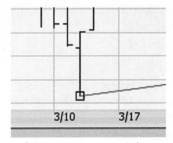

FIGURE 8.12 You can zoom in to the handle of a trendline to ensure precise placement.

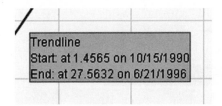

FIGURE 8.13 When you mouseover a trendline, a tool tip will appear identifying the object as well as its starting and ending points.

FIGURE 8.14 By clicking on the small triangle in the trendline tool you can access the features of the tool.

available through right-clicking the line as well as clicking the trendline tool itself (Figure 8.14). There are two ways to access the popup menu using the trendline tool: You can either hold down the mouse button on the tool for a few moments, or you can click the small triangle in the tool's lower-right corner to get instant access.

You can also access many of the functions of the toolbar through the Drawing Tools menu itself (Figure 8.15). The choices on this menu provide the functions shown in Table 8.1.

CHANGING COLOR AND STYLE

Flexibility is one of ProphetCharts' main advantages, and one example of this is that you can alter the color and style of any individual object on any chart. As you are applying drawn objects, whatever settings you most recently used for that tool will be applied until such time as you either customize that tool or modify an individual object that you drew earlier.

To alter the color or style of a trendline you've already drawn, right-click on the trendline and choose "Change Style/Color" from the

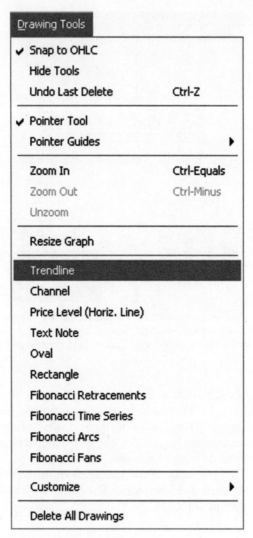

FIGURE 8.15 The Drawing Tools menu also provides access to any of the drawn objects and their settings.

popup menu. A dialog box (Figure 8.16) will appear with the following elements:

- *Sample*—This shows what the trendline will look like based on the settings. As you change settings, this sample will update to reflect those changes. Think of it as a preview of what your trendline will look like.

TABLE 8.1	Drawing Tools Functions
Snap to	This is either checked or unchecked, which indicates whether or not handles will snap to OHLC (open, high, low, or close) values. You alter this setting either here or through the Preferences menu. It is recommended that you leave this checked, since doing so makes laying down precise trendlines much easier. If you would prefer to have total free-form control over the placement of trendlines, you should uncheck this box. Otherwise, price points in bars will attract the handles of your trendlines like magnets.
Hide Tools	If you do not want to see the toolbar, you can choose this setting, which will put a checkmark next to it. The only reason you would want to do so would be to free up a little more space for the chart. Keep in mind you do not necessarily have to leave the toolbar where it is. You can click on the handle of the toolbar, located on its left edge, and drag the toolbar to any edge of the chart or have it free-floating for quick access.
Undo	ProphetCharts provides the ability to undo your last action (and that action will alter the exact wording of this menu item; for instance, it might read Undo Last Deletion if you most recently deleted an object). There will be many times that you accidentally do something that you realize was a mistake, and by selecting Undo or its keyboard equivalent, Ctrl-Z, ProphetCharts will undo the action.
Pointer Tool	This is the default tool, which is just the mouse cursor. The Pointer doesn't alter the graph in any way; it simply lets you move the mouse around and take actions. The Pointer is by default the selection, and choosing any other tool (such as Trendline) temporarily deselects this choice. Once you have finished drawing your object, the Pointer will be selected once again.
Pointer Guides	You have four choices for what appears wherever the cursor goes: None, Vertical, Horizontal, or Crosshair. You can therefore have a horizontal line only, a vertical line only, both, or neither as you move your mouse around. Most people leave the vertical line on, using the crosshair choice when they are trying to make a very precise judgment on both time and price. If you find the lines bothersome or annoying, you change this to None.
Zoom In	This zooms in on the rightmost 50 percent of the chart. The keyboard equivalent is Ctrl-Plus. If you want to zoom in on a precise part of the chart, just click-and-drag with the mouse. Using Zoom In repeatedly will home in closer and closer to the most recent data.

(Continued)

TABLE 8.1	*(Continued)*
Zoom Out	This does the opposite of Zoom In, since it doubles the amount of time you are viewing (until you see all the data that you fetched in the first place, at which time this menu choice becomes grayed out). The keyboard equivalent is Ctrl-Minus.
Unzoom	To unzoom all the way and see all of the data you have fetched for the chart, you can choose this function or, for the same result, double-click anywhere inside the chart.
Resize Graph	This allows you to change how much of the chart space is dedicated to the chart itself. This function is covered in detail in Chapter 9.
Various tools	There are 10 different tool choices, the first of which is Trendline. Choosing any of these selections is the equivalent of choosing the tool icon within the toolbar. A checkmark will appear next to whatever tool is currently selected (which may be the Pointer Guides, previously described).
Customize	This brings up a submenu of the same 10 tools so that you can select the tool whose settings you want to customize. The equivalent action can be performed by holding down the mouse button on top of the tool you want to customize or clicking on the small triangle in the lower-right corner of any of the tool icon squares.
Delete All Drawings	This deletes all of the drawn objects on the currently displayed graph. It will not affect the drawn objects on any other charts. If you use this accidentally, you can reverse the damage by choosing the Undo command. Take note that when you right-click on any drawn object, this command is also available in the popup menu, as well as another command—Delete—which will delete only the currently selected object.

- *Color*—This shows the color you have selected. By clicking this small box, a palette of 15 color choices will appear. You can click on any of these color choices to change the color of the selected trendline.
- *Opacity*—This is a number ranging from 0.1 to 1 that dictates how transparent or not the trendline is. An opacity setting of 1 means the trendline will be a solid line and nothing can be seen through it. At the other extreme, an opacity setting of .1 would result in an extremely faint line through which other objects can be seen. As you become an expert user of ProphetCharts, you will develop your own preferences for how bold certain objects appear.

FIGURE 8.16 Changing the color and style of a trendline can be done with this dialog box.

FIGURE 8.17 Clicking on the Pattern dropdown shows the patterns available for the trendline selected.

- *Weight*—This controls how thick the line is. Clicking on this lets you choose from a dropdown menu of five different weights. If you want lines to be heavy and easy to see, choose a heavier weight.
- *Pattern*—Clicking on this (Figure 8.17) yields a dropdown of three different pattern styles (solid, dotted, and dashed). Most people use solid trendlines, but you may want to use different line styles to indicate different meanings of lines on the chart.

There also is a checkbox at the bottom of the dialog box that reads, "Save as default trendline style." If you check this, all the future trendlines you draw with ProphetCharts will use these same settings unless you alter them later.

HISTORICAL CHART EXAMPLES

Understanding the mechanics of creating trendlines is important, but more important is the knowledge of how to apply trendlines well. Part of this comes from taking care to follow the rules cited earlier in this chapter about the properties of trendlines. But most of it comes from experience, and you can gain experience yourself or by learning about the experiences of others. This chapter seeks to help you with the latter.

There is an adage about how a person can never step into the same stream twice, and the reason is that the stream is constantly changing. The markets are like that, which is why it is not possible to describe precisely what rules to follow when embellishing charts with drawn objects

FIGURE 8.18 Multiple trendlines can work together to identify directional changes in a stock.

under all circumstances. You will gain proficiency—some may even say artistry—about how you mark up your charts only through trial, error, and experience.

This book has hundreds of different charts from actual market history to help save you some of the challenges of learning through only your experience. Study these charts and their commentary, not to seek unbendable rules about how trendlines are laid down, but to understand the different circumstances and nuances to charts and what they demand of your analytical skills.

Figure 8.18 illustrates how charts are certainly not limited to one trendline. In this case, two are used, and you could just as easily have three, four, or more. You want to avoid what some call the "pick-up sticks effect" of having lines scattered all over the chart, because that just creates noise, and what you seek is clarity. The old saw that "less is more" certainly applies to good charting.

The reasons for having multiple trendlines fall into two camps: to show contrary trends (as was the case with Figure 8.18, which showed a general uptrend and a shorter-lived downtrend) or to show varying degrees of momentum for a single trend, such as with Figure 8.19. In this instance, which is a chart of the crude oil commodity market from 2001

FIGURE 8.19 Multiple trendlines can also help trace movements of different strength and length.

through 2006, the lower trendline shows a decisive uptrend that spans virtually the entire graph, and the higher trendline shows how, starting late in 2003, the market accelerated even faster, resulting in a steeper trendline. Both trendlines are valid, and both are useful. If the prices violated the medium-term trendline, that would negate the faster uptrend, but it would not negate the broader, larger uptrend until such time as that trendline was itself crossed.

A similar graph is shown in Figure 8.20, which is the Dow Jones Industrial Average over a four-year period. The uptrend is firmly intact, even with smaller ups and downs, and beginning in the autumn of 2005, the market picks up even more steam.

As you learn about other drawn objects, you will learn to apply different objects to the same chart to deepen your analysis, since chart action is certainly more complex than "it's going up" or "it's going down." Figure 8.21 shows that after an ascending trendline was violated, the prices actually moved higher quite substantially. In the course of doing so, they hammered out a small head and shoulders pattern, thus providing two reasons to sell the stock: (1) that it had broken beneath its ascending trend;

FIGURE 8.20 This chart of the Dow 30 shows the long-term trendline and the medium term trendline, the latter showing an increase in upward momentum.

(2) it had formed a bearish pattern. Following this confirmation, the stock lost about 25 percent of its value in just a few weeks.

A more sophisticated example of the same concept is shown in Figure 8.22, which is a chart of the Dow Jones Utilities ETF (symbol UTH). The uptrend lasted many years, but when prices broke the trendline, a new pattern began to form.

A close-up of this graph (Figure 8.23) gives you more detail as to how the prices shaped their new post-uptrend pattern. The first thing you notice is how the trendline did the classic "support to resistance" metamorphosis. Even though the fall through the trendline swiftly sent the stock to $107, it recovered and climbed to about $120, nearly a new record high. But by then it had already formed the left shoulder and the head of a classic head

FIGURE 8.21 A variety of drawn objects can be used to identify the complex mechanics of a stock's price action.

FIGURE 8.22 This illustrates how the price clung to the trendline even after support had been violated.

FIGURE 8.23 This close-up view shows how the trendline changed its nature from support to resistance.

and shoulders pattern. It went on to form the right shoulder (two, actually) and broke down. Simply stated, the price action was very messy after the trendline was broken, and a holder of UTH would have been wise to have quickly closed the position and taken profits on the day the trendline was violated.

Some more recent examples—Figures 8.24 through 8.29—further illustrate what an important role support and resistance play in price movement.

As you know, trendlines come in only two forms: resistance and support. We will now focus on resistance trendlines and their application.

RESISTANCE

For a trendline to represent resistance, it simply has to be above the prices. It doesn't matter if the stock is going up or down (although resistance during a downtrend is more useful from a chartist's perspective). So long as the prices are trapped underneath the trendline, that trendline represents

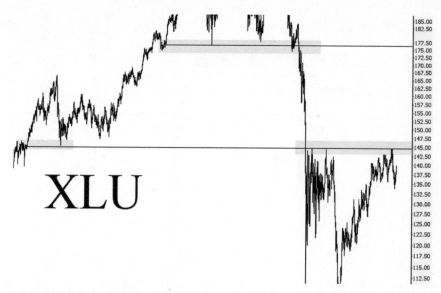

FIGURE 8.24 The Utilities index, XLU, fell hard after violating support (the upper line) and, once it started to establish a base and tried to recover, had trouble pushing above resistance (the lower line).

resistance, meaning that buyers do not have the strength to push it above the line.

Figure 8.30 offers a superb example of resistance with a downtrending market. This is the USD/CAD (that is, the foreign exchange market of the U.S. dollar and Canadian dollar pair). At the beginning of the graph, a Canadian dollar was worth about $1.58 in U.S. dollars. The downtrend shown here was in place for years, erasing over a third of Canadian purchasing power versus the U.S. Again and again, the prices made a move toward the resistance level, sometimes getting close to crossing it, but they failed each time. This graph represents a staggering loss in currency value, and a person short this position would have enjoyed steadily mounting profits, knowing to get out only when the trend was broken.

A trader positioned in a security can use trendlines for just such a purpose—that is, "as long as the price is on the correct side of the line, I'm fine." Imagine having a short position in Express Scripts (ESRX) during the time shown in Figure 8.31. Suppose you shorted the stock on March 27 at about $88 per share. Using the descending trendline shown in the upper-right of the chart, you would be assured that your position was safely intact as long as the prices remained below the line. You might have had a close scare in mid-April when prices got close to the line, but they did not violate

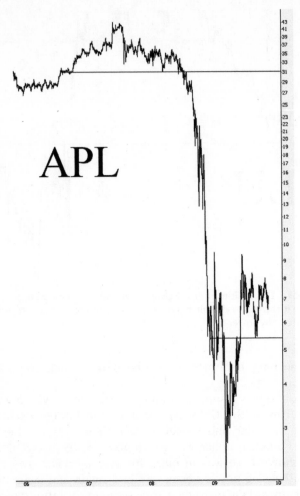

FIGURE 8.25 Symbol APL succumbed to price failure at the high horizontal support line and later stabilized at a lower level which became a new support level.

it. Afterwards, they eased back a few dollars, finally tumbling significantly and providing an excellent profit on the trade. One simple trendline was all it took to know that the position was still prudent.

When prices do violate the resistance line—and they almost certainly will, sooner or later—it informs you based on your position with the stock. If you have a position, it tells you to get out. And if you do not have a position, it tells you that you might want to take advantage of what might be a trend change.

FIGURE 8.26 Honeywell, symbol HON, had its prices bounded by both support and resistance levels. The lower horizontal line illustrates how resistance eventually changed its role into support, once the price finally pushed higher.

A typical example of an upside break through resistance is shown in Figure 8.32, where the prices bumped up repeatedly against the trendline. Finally, in one decisive trading session, prices blasted through the trendline and stayed consistently higher.

The real power of this is shown in Figure 8.33, which is a much longer-range view of the same security. What was shown in Figure 8.32 was only the rightmost portion of this graph. The push above the resistance line was very significant, because resistance went back for years. This signal would have provided an excellent indication that the trend had reversed and would have provided a great opportunity to take advantage of the big upsurge in the NASDAQ market in 2003 and 2004. As usual, the trend reversal didn't pinpoint the exact bottom, but it certainly allowed for tremendous profit opportunity in spite of the market's modest rise that had already taken place.

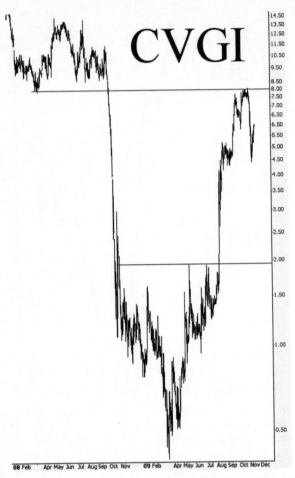

FIGURE 8.27 A stock's "memory" about support and resistance levels can be long-lived. Note how the important support level, the upper horizontal line, represented resistance over a year later as prices tried to recover their old levels.

A similar graph, with extremely dramatic positive results, is Primus Telecommunications Group (Figure 8.34). The stock had suffered a terrible downtrend, dropping from $52 to the realm of penny stocks. You can see here that prices finally pushed above resistance. But note this well: prices continued to drop. If you had bought this stock, you may have been disappointed that trendlines don't work so well after all.

The seasoned chartist, however, would be watching the trendline closely, even after it had been crossed, because the trendline now represented support, since the prices were higher than the line, not lower. What is painful about this, of course, is that it sets no lower limit on how long

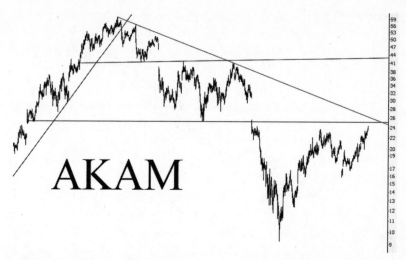

FIGURE 8.28 Akamai's relationship with trendlines is complex. Here we see a descending trendline creating a formidable resistance zone, whereas the two horizontal lines are demarcation levels for descending price ranges.

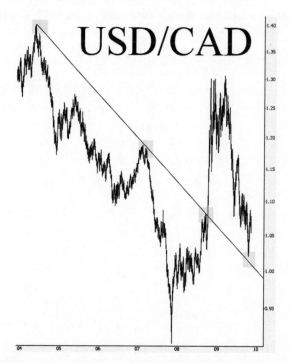

FIGURE 8.29 The ratio of the U.S. dollar to the Canadian dollar—a longer-term version of which is shown in Figure 8.30—had an explosive move higher, but when it fell, the price stopped short at the former resistance trendline.

FIGURE 8.30 The Canadian dollar's long slide versus the U.S. dollar is shown here, with the resisting trendline never being overcome.

FIGURE 8.31 Resistance trendlines can be invaluable in minimizing risk and maximizing reward with your trading.

FIGURE 8.32 When a price breaks through a descending trendline, the change in direction can be fast and powerful.

to hold on to the stock. Prices can remain above the trendline all the way to $0, so you might want to apply other criteria to how long you would hang on to the trade (in this instance, you may have put in a stop-loss order just below the lifetime low of the stock, at least assuring you would get something back and not ride the stock all the way to bankruptcy).

In fact, such a strategy would have worked well. As you can see, even though the stock continued to fall for a few months after crossing above the trendline, it began to compose itself and started a rise well over 1,000 percent. The patient chartist would have been handsomely rewarded with this position.

The importance of how trendlines act as a "turncoat" (reversing roles) cannot be over-emphasized. A fine example is Figure 8.35, which is the Ultra Short OTC Fund from ProFunds. This is a really interesting mutual

FIGURE 8.33 This shows the NASDAQ bottoming in late 2002, at which time the index pushed its way above its very long descending trendline.

FIGURE 8.34 This stock went up well over 1,000 percent after it pushed its way through resistance.

FIGURE 8.35   A security can continue to decline, even when its trendline changes from resistance to support.

fund, because it is a double-inverse index fund. What that means is that if a particular market (in this case, the NASDAQ 100) goes down 1 percent, the value of the fund goes twice as far the opposite direction (up 2 percent). So in a bear market, a fund like this provides an opportunity for people to still increase their portfolio's value.

This graph shows the fund during a relatively bullish phase of the stock market, when the fund's value declined from \$97.50 to below \$15. Notice how on three separate occasions the prices just barely "kissed" the trend-line, only to be repelled each time. After the third kiss, prices got enough strength to push through to the other side, allowing the fund to form a basing pattern and stabilize at about \$15.

Now let's examine the opposite effect—a stock in an uptrend that breaks beneath it.

BREAKS TO THE DOWNSIDE

Stocks in an uptrend that violate that trend provide a signal for bulls to get out of the stock and for bears to consider selling the stock short. All the rules cited for breaking through upside resistance apply, only in reverse.

FIGURE 8.36 The shorter trendline on the right helps gauge a resistance level after the larger trendline has been violated.

The Dow Jones Utilities enjoyed a multi-year bull market in the early part of the twenty-first century, mainly due to declining interest rates (Figure 8.36). As interest rates started increasing, this uptrend was quickly stopped, and in a matter of a couple of weeks, the $UTIL went from a lifetime high to a clear break in its uptrend.

When a stock breaks its support line, it is prone to weakness, because the faith in the stock's bulls is going to be badly shaken. Figure 8.37 illustrates this with Autodesk (symbol ADSK), which had climbed from $7 to $47, often priced far above its support line. Late in 2005, the stock gapped down, and the prices never crossed above the trendline again. Although the price recovered over the next few weeks, nearly marking a new lifetime high, the trend change was already in place: The stock succumbed to the loss of momentum and lost about a quarter of its value. The multiple trendlines in the chart illustrate how shorter-term trendlines can be helpful in seeing the new direction a stock is taking, since that is prone to change in the early stages of a trend reversal.

A closer view of ADSK's change from bullish to bearish (Figure 8.38) highlights the fascinating ability of stock prices to have a sixth sense about their former trendline, sometimes touching it to the penny, but not going

FIGURE 8.37 A stock's failure to hold above its trendline usually precedes major changes in direction.

FIGURE 8.38 This is a close-up view of AutoDesk as it changed from bullish to bearish.

FIGURE 8.39 Cleveland Cliffs lost momentum just before falling through its trendline.

above it again. The middle of the graph shows the price's failed attempt to get above the long-term trendline, and from February through May, the prices had an even lower level of resistance they were not able to mount.

The psychology behind these trend shifts is important to understand. If a stock has been in an uptrend for years, once it loses momentum, the holders of that stock are going to be frustrated and disappointed (Figure 8.39).

But after the initial shock, they will try to reestablish the stock to its old bullish ways. Figure 8.40 shows that after Cleveland Cliffs fell to $81, the bulls wrested control from the bears and were able to add about 25 percent to the stock in a matter of days. But the uptrend was over, in spite of the bulls' efforts. After this final run-up into the triple digits, the stock fell yet again below the $81 low it had so recently established.

Lastly, Figures 8.41–8.47 offer excellent examples of price failure from the financial crisis of 2008 and 2009.

SUPPORT BECOMES RESISTANCE

Knowing that support become resistance (and vice versa), and understanding how prices can cling to trendlines is powerful knowledge that you can

FIGURE 8.40 A close-up of Cleveland Cliffs shows the stock attempting to regain its former bullish self, which ultimately failed.

turn into profitable opportunities. Knowing how to use trendlines well can help you minimize your risk at the same time.

When prices fall beneath support and try to get back to the trendline, it's as if the prices are kissing the underbelly of the line. Keep in mind very few people know how to use trendlines (and even fewer know how to use them well), so it's not as if the markets are zealously following one agreed-upon line and marking prices along it. But the mass psychology driving millions of individuals to do what they do in the markets helps create these phenomenon and those practiced in charting can exploit them.

Imagine you had watched Allegheny Technology climb from $2 to thousands of percent above that level, and you wanted to short the stock. But because the stock was so strong, you didn't know where to enter the trade. The trendline for the stock (Figure 8.48) was broken when the stock was about $22, and the stock kept climbing. Shorting the stock in the subsequent months would have been a very unprofitable decision, since the stock climbed hundreds of percent more. Waiting until the price finally mustered enough strength to touch the underside of the trendline at $77.50 would have created a much safer opportunity for the short sale.

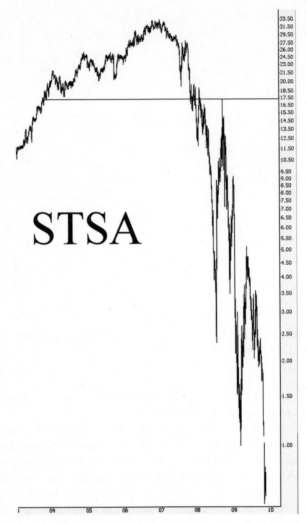

FIGURE 8.41 Sterling Financial lost virtually its entire value after breaking important support at the $17.50 level.

The typical action after a price break usually does not take as long as that, however. Figure 8.49 shows a more common pattern of the price quickly moving down after the price break, regaining its strength, and then pushing back up to touch the underside of its former support line.

The danger of shorting a stock merely because it has broken support is highlighted in Figure 8.50. After the initial break, the stock (Hilton) did indeed fall badly. But it didn't take long for it to recover and make a series

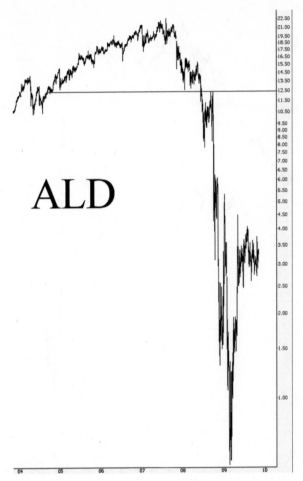

FIGURE 8.42 Allied Capital perfectly retracted its price drop in September 2008, only to rapidly resume its fall.

of new lifetime highs. A person bearish on this stock would have been wise to wait until the price was just barely underneath the former support level before placing the short. That way, if the price does manage to cross above the line, you can close the position quickly with a relatively small loss.

This kind of thinking applies not just to individual securities but to entire markets as well. The NASDAQ Composite (Figure 8.51) broke its support line and, similar to Hilton, initially fell swiftly, gathered its strength, and began moving substantially higher. The market eventually got extraordinarily close to the trendline, which would have represented a very low-risk price level to short the market. Of course, there's no

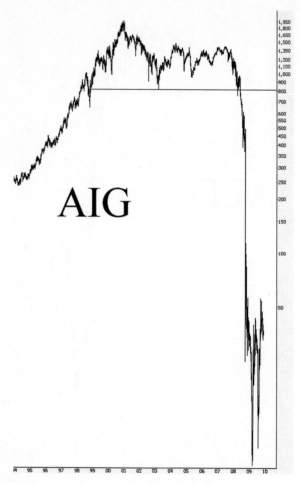

FIGURE 8.43 Former giant AIG stayed above the horizontal line shown here for an entire decade. Once that level was breached, it only took a few months for the stock's price to approach zero.

guarantee a stock or index will have enough strength to get close to its former support level—it may simply fall away. But it is definitely safer to wait for the possibility that it does so.

It takes a lot of buying power to overcome the disappointment of a trendline break. Figure 8.52 shows a closer view of the NASDAQ's attempt to get back above its trendline. It took about four months to do so, and in the end, it failed, because the uptrend was simply no longer valid.

Continued strong volume can push a stock in an uptrend, even if a former trend has been damaged. One of the most amazing stocks of 2005

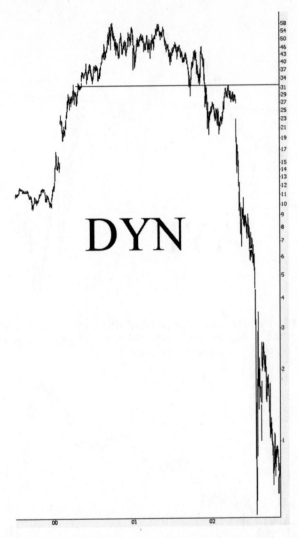

FIGURE 8.44 Not all price falls are rapid. Dynegy broke its support in November 2001 and lingered just beneath it for five months. But in the next few months following that, the price went from $27 to about fifty cents.

and 2006 was NutriSystem (symbol NTRI), shown in Figure 8.53. Bears would have had a number of opportunities to short the stock at relatively safe levels, but in this graph, they would have lost money each time. The techniques being illustrated here are certainly no guarantee of profit. But they do provide a measuring tool to know when you are wrong with your speculation.

FIGURE 8.45 Trendlines are often retraced after they are broken. Acuity Brands broke its trendline in October 2007 and tried to recapture the same line through June 2008, at which time it started to fall hard.

FIGURE 8.46 Insurance firm Aflac had a burst in September 2008, but the next month, it broke its long-term trendline and lost about 80 percent of its value.

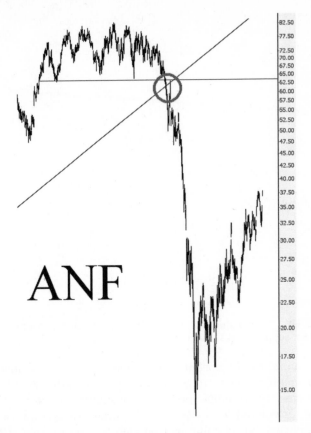

FIGURE 8.47 Clothes retailer Abercrombie & Fitch held above its long-term trendline until the summer of 2008. Once the trendline was broken, ANF lost over 80 percent of its value as measured from its lifetime high.

One success story with this technique was Safeway Stores (symbol SWY), shown in Figure 8.54. After a staggering rise in value, the stock started softening, and it fell beneath support in the first half of 1999. In a few months, it had recovered some and was pushed up against the underside of its trendline. A short sale at that point would have yielded marvelous profits, since the stock was exhausted and didn't attempt such an assault on its trendline again.

A close-up view of this event is shown in Figure 8.55, which also highlights how one must be somewhat discerning when watching price action around trendlines. On the very first day of August, prices just barely peeked above the trendline. This did not mean that suddenly a new bull market was in place for the stock. Once the ascending trendline is

FIGURE 8.48 This gigantic push upward was in the context of a major trendline changing from support to resistance.

broken, it cannot regain its stature as a reliable measure of upward price movement simply because prices manage to sneak to the other side.

In this case, the trendline provided a valuable "line in the sand" that prices were prohibited from crossing. The prices did get across this line by a few pennies, but certainly not enough to stop looking at the short opportunity. This day in August established the high-water mark for the

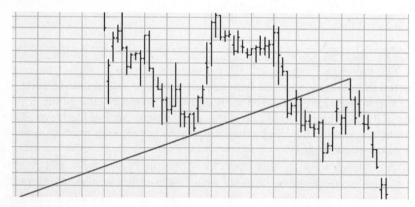

FIGURE 8.49 This is typical price action following a trendline break, as prices push up against the former supporting trendline.

FIGURE 8.50 In a strong market, it is typical for a stock to continue to push higher, even though it is underneath resistance.

FIGURE 8.51 The safest place to short a market after a trendline break is when it is up against the resistance line.

FIGURE 8.52 This illustrates how much strength is required for a stock to make an assault on its former trendline.

stock after its trendline break, and it went on to a substantial loss in value afterward.

Figures 8.56–8.61 provide a few more examples, all from recent history, of resistance and support changing their roles.

As stated earlier in this chapter, the more experience you gain with drawing, interpreting, and trading based on trendlines, the better you will become. The markets are always changing, and you will learn many of the subtleties in applying drawn objects well and profitably.

PARALLEL TRENDLINES

There are some instances—relatively rare—when price action is bound by two parallel trendlines: one below as support, and the other above as resistance. We will explore these "channels" in Chapter 9, but for now, let us see how to use the Trendline tool to track these channels.

FIGURE 8.53 NutriSystem provided many shorting opportunities during its rise, but its strength kept the bears at bay.

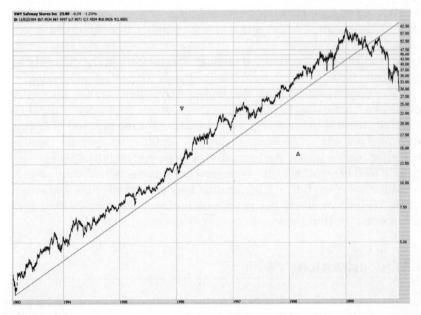

FIGURE 8.54 Safeway Stores provides a classic example of a stock trying to get above its trendline only to exhaust itself and fall in earnest.

FIGURE 8.55 This close-up of Safeway illustrates what an excellent short sale this stock presented.

When you right-click on a trendline, one of the choices in the popup menu is Duplicate. Choosing this creates another trendline right next to the selected one (Figure 8.62), and the trendline will be the same length, color, and angle as the selected original. The handles of the duplicate will be preselected so you can move it immediately to the desired location.

You do not have to leave the duplicate trendline parallel, since either of the two handles can be moved. But the most practical value of the Duplicate command is to create a parallel trendline for the purpose of drawing a channel pattern. As shown in Figure 8.63, dragging the parallel trendline to its destination makes the formation of a channel pattern simple.

Up to this point, we have examined price patterns that were ideal for trendline analysis. But real-life trading isn't always so clean and easy to track. We will complete our examination of trendlines by looking at the times when the price action isn't so predictable and apparent.

FALSE BREAKOUTS

As discussed earlier in this chapter, the violation of a trendline by price action can be a meaningful signal that the current trend has ended and is possibly even reversing. This is absolutely not a hard and fast rule, and with

FIGURE 8.56 The Morgan Stanley High-Tech Index shows two examples of price levels fighting back toward broken support. The first support was broken in January 2008, and that line was almost recovered by May. By September of that year, the lower support line was broken, and it took over a year to re-approach the same line.

any chart, only time will tell the ultimate destination of the prices. It is your task to make a prediction of future price action with enough statistical likelihood that your odds of winning are better than your odds of being wrong.

For one thing, trendlines represent very potent boundary lines, and prices piercing a trendline do not necessarily make that trend moot. Figure 8.64 shows the S&P 100 index moving sharply higher and piercing the upper trendline, representing resistance. One might conclude that the index should push above the resistance line and henceforth treat it as support. In this case, prices simply got ahead of themselves and were pushed back well underneath the resistance line in just a couple of trading sessions.

Another interesting example is that of MicroStrategy (Figure 8.65), which was enjoying a very healthy uptrend in price. Late in April, during two trading sessions, the stock lost about 10 percent of its value, and in

FIGURE 8.57 The Dow Transports has an entire series of lines which, in turns, represented support and resistance. Both the horizontal levels, tinted in green, and the angled levels, shown with red lines, have a powerful effect on the prices.

doing so it crossed plainly beneath the ascending, supporting trendline. Those long the stock may have made a swift exit. Even more aggressive traders might have decided the stock was ready for a big tumble and entered a short position on the stock. This would have been a costly mistake, as the stock quickly recovered and nearly matched its all-time high within a few days.

In retrospect, were holders of this stock wrong to sell it? And were those bearish on this stock wrong to sell it short? As of this writing, it is impossible to know whether this stock will be $200 in a year, or $50, or anywhere in between. In the very short-term analysis, two things can be said: First, those long the stock were probably wise to close (or at least reduce) their positions in the stock since the uptrend was violated. It is very hazardous to speculate what the meaning of a trendline break is. If one is to ignore it and see what happens, there is much less value in even

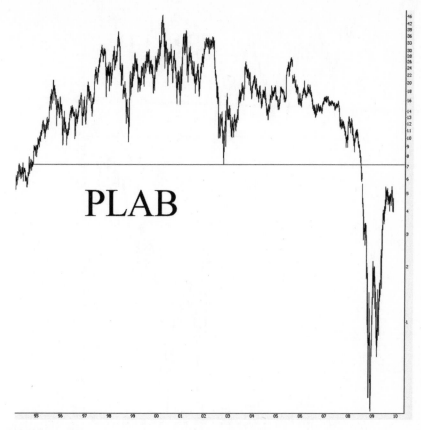

FIGURE 8.58 It took nearly a year, but Photronics staged a 1500 percent price recovery to try to get back to its former support zone.

bothering to watch a trendline in the first place. So the disciplined trader would have been wise to take the trendline break seriously.

A less generous analysis could be made of the people selling the stock short. A more careful approach would have been to wait for a few days to see if the stock consolidated and touched the underside of the trendline, demonstrating that it was "respecting" the former support line as its new resistance line. By waiting, the potential short seller would have seen prices blast right back above the trendline, indicating not only that the line didn't represent resistance, but that it probably didn't have much meaning at all. The more times a former trendline is penetrated from either direction, the less meaningful it is. Simply stated, it has worn out its usefulness as an observational tool.

A similar example of a security that broke below—and then above—a trendline is shown with the S&P 400 MidCap index in Figure 8.66. In this

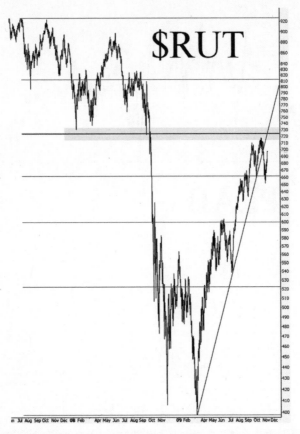

FIGURE 8.59 The Russell 2000 index had a support level going back over four years. Once it was broken, the fall was swift and brutal. Prices approached the underside of former support almost exactly a year later.

case, prices broke below the trendline and stayed there for a full month before breaking above the former support line again. From there, it regained its former bullish disposition and soared another 20 percent. Interestingly, in spite of the damage caused to the support line by the price action being beneath it for a full month, the prices still seemed to have a healthy respect for this as a support line once it regained its composure.

A close-up view of this month-long hiatus from support levels is illustrated with Figure 8.67. It is interesting to see how, on a day-by-day basis, price actions behave with respect to the supporting trendline.

More often than not, trendline breaks do indicate directional change, so let us turn our attention to some chart examples that show this concept in action.

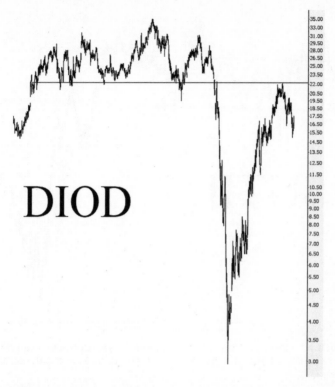

FIGURE 8.60 Typically, the longer a support level is in place, the more formidable it will be as resistance later. Diodes' stock enjoyed years of support at about $22. After plunging to $3, it soared much higher, only to be stopped by its former support level.

MULTIPLE TRENDLINES OVER THE LONG HAUL

The chart in Figure 8.68 is worth careful study. On the chart, five separate trendlines are shown, each of which lasts a significant period—in some cases, many years. There are a couple of fascinating things about this graph, which help drive home the power of trendline analysis. First, there are five clear directional trends, and they toggle to a different direction each time: up, down, up, down, and then up again (although this last uptrend is violated on the extreme right portion of the graph, suggesting that perhaps even a sixth line is in the process of being formed).

Second, each trendline has multiple "touch points" on the price data. In spite of all of the events that happened during the 11 years of this

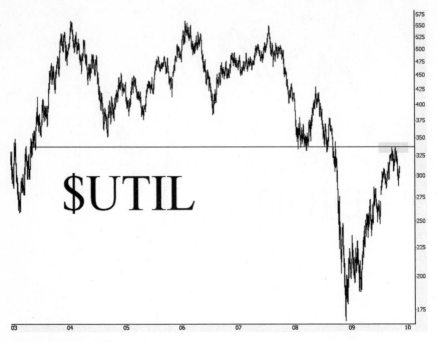

FIGURE 8.61 Relatively low-risk entry points for short positions can be enjoyed when a price pushes back up to its former support, as illustrated with the Dow Jones Utility Index.

FIGURE 8.62 Choosing the Duplicate function creates a parallel trendline of the same length and style with its handles preselected.

FIGURE 8.63 Drag the parallel trendline to an appropriate location to form a channel pattern, which consists of two trendlines.

graph—economic booms and busts, changes in Presidential administrations, dozens of earnings releases for this stock, hundreds of news releases, and all the ups and downs of the stock market in general—the price action can still be clearly bounded by a series of simple, straight lines.

Harrah's Entertainment had a similar situation of multiple trend changes, although the chart in Figure 8.69 shows three trendlines as opposed to five. It's important to notice that even though it would not have been apparent in 1999, the descending trend was in the process of ending just as the ascending trend was in the process of being formed. Trends rarely change instantly; it takes time, sometimes measured in many months. This explains why, when drawn with the benefit of hindsight, trendlines often overlap with respect to time.

Take a closer look at this trend change with a zoomed-in view of the same graph (Figure 8.70). As the stock is downtrending, it starts to make a move up and tries to push above the descending trendline, but it fails. It falls hard and fast, making a low in October, and then again makes an assault on the descending trendline. This time, it succeeds, and you can plainly see how, after it pushes its way above the trendline, it finds support on the same line, bouncing off it several times. Even though the stock once

FIGURE 8.64 The S&P 100 just barely pushed above its resistance line before succumbing.

FIGURE 8.65 MicroStrategy appeared to be breaking down, but it quickly recovered.

FIGURE 8.66 The S&P 400 MidCap seemed to be seriously breaking down, but it composed itself and pushed on to new highs.

FIGURE 8.67 This close-up of the S&P 400 shows the brief period it was below its support line.

FIGURE 8.68 This chart illustrates five distinct trend changes for symbol KMI.

FIGURE 8.69 Trendlines working together are invaluable in identifying core trend changes in a stock.

FIGURE 8.70 Harrah's clearly shifted from a downtrend to an uptrend during this time period.

again falls very badly, it does not fall below its new support level, and this lends credence to the idea that the trend has changed. From this point, it enjoyed a 400 percent price increase.

Knowing when a trend changes is not easy, but it is made possible with experience and well-placed lines. But even a beginning chartist can gain value from the signals trendlines provide, both when they are obeyed and when they are violated.

INTERPRETING AMBIGUITY

Using trendlines when the price action is neat and well-defined is pretty simple. When prices don't bounce precisely off trendlines and the price behavior is "mushy" with respect to support and resistance levels, it is far more challenging. Although, by definition, there aren't any absolute rules when dealing with this ambiguous behavior, it is still helpful to look at some past, real-life examples to see how they played out.

The S&P 600, showed in Figure 8.71, enjoyed a long, persistent uptrend. There are two trendlines shown, both of them ascending. The

FIGURE 8.71 Although the trendline has been violated, the basic direction remains intact.

higher trendline was violated about halfway along the graph, and although it briefly moved above this line later, it fell once more, clearly showing this uptrend was history.

The line beneath it had a similar result, although in the opposite sense. In this instance, support held for virtually the entire graph, although it was briefly violated. But both of these trendlines tell the same story: Even though price action can move to the other side of a line, so long as this violation is brief, and provided that the prices resume "obeying" the trendline afterward, the trendline still does have meaning. There's no doubt that the validity of the trendline is diminished with any violation, but it is not eliminated completely.

An extremely interesting example of this is shown with Raven Industries (Figure 8.72). From 2000 through 2004, five whole years, the prices steadily climbed, never piercing the ascending support line. Early in 2005, when the prices broke the trendline, they did not signal a trend change. Instead, the trend continued upward, simply shifted downward several price points. What's remarkable about this graph is how the prices clung to the former support line, crossing above and below it many times, but generally sticking rigidly to the line as if it were a magnet.

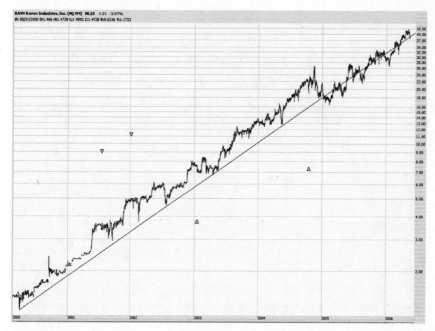

FIGURE 8.72 After RAVN breaks through its trendline, the price seems to cling to the line as a median instead of either support or resistance.

The softening of a trend's direction can take the form of a price reduction, as with Raven Industries, or the form of a reduction in the steepness of a trend, such as with Figure 8.73. In this case, the NASDAQ 100 market violated its major ascending trendline, but over time it continued a softer uptrend. Compare the medium-length trendline, shown on the right side of the graph, with the longer trendline that spans virtually the entire graph. As you can see, the medium-term line has a reduced slope, indicating that even though the uptrend is continuing, it is doing so with less potency.

A close-up of this graph (Figure 8.74) highlights the breakdown from the long-term trendline, the establishment of the medium-term trendline, and—in the end—the violation of this trendline as well. Another element at play here is the horizontal line at the 1,760 price level. If the market had been stronger, the prices would have pierced above this horizontal line, completing a small saucer-shaped pattern. Instead, in spite of an attempt to reach this line, the market didn't have enough power, and it quickly fell away from this line and instead pierced beneath the medium-term trendline.

The main lesson with all of these graphs is that price charts are, in a sense, living creatures, and you need to keep them updated with

FIGURE 8.73 Multiple trendlines can work together to show the softening of a market, as shown here with the NASDAQ 100 index.

FIGURE 8.74 This close-up of the NASDAQ 100 shows its value pushing above its horizontal resistance as well as its subsequent trendline failure.

AIG Amer Intl Group Inc 63.15 0.00 0.00%
Dt 01/05/2001 O:87.387 H:87.9922 L:84.5427 C:85.0673 R:3.4495 Y:99.9191

FIGURE 8.75 American International Group provides a beautiful example of resistance changing to support as well as the creation of a new resistance line.

appropriate drawn objects in order to interpret their action and have your attention drawn to meaningful price events. You should treat your trendlines seriously—certainly not moving them here and there each day in order to falsely bound price action that has no business being bounded—but you also need to be open to the creation of new trendlines (and other drawn objects) as the price action gets hammered out, day by day, one bar at a time.

American International Group (Figure 8.75) gives us another fine example of a graph whose price momentum changed both direction and angle. Notice how the prices fell steadily from 2000 to 2003. Late in 2003, prices pushed above the descending resistance line. Notice the exceptional behavior of the prices after this—in two instances (late in 2004 and early in 2005) prices fell swiftly and perfectly touched the support line (the still-intact trendline that had been resistance before). Afterwards, prices started moving up. In retrospect, we can see three exceptionally well-formed trendlines: the large one (representing resistance and, later, support); the other descending line above it (representing resistance); and the ascending trendline, illustrating the rapid recovery of the stock along this support level. It is easy to see what an

FIGURE 8.76   It is helpful to leave older trendlines in place, as they can help illustrate the general strength or weakness of a stock historically.

advantage a trader has if he has equipped himself with information such as this.

Even when trendlines have been violated, it is worthwhile to leave them in place unless the price action around them becomes so noisy as to render them meaningless. An old trendline may yield new insight later in the graph, since price levels may ultimately push up against that line again. Or, as in the graph shown in Figure 8.76, older trendlines can help you see broad market changes, such as the softening of ascending prices when comparing the first trendline here with the second.

SUMMARY

We have covered a tremendous amount of ground in this chapter. We've learned how to construct and interpret trendlines in many different circumstances. We can see how to make use of them to measure resistance and support levels and to judge when a trend has changed. Now we will add to this knowledge in the next chapter by learning about trendline pairs that make up the much rarer, but still very useful, channel pattern.

CHAPTER 9

Expansion and Channels

I n this chapter we are going to undertake two different but related subjects: chart resizing and drawn channels. A channel is a drawn object that consists of two parallel trendlines, so many of the same principles you learned in Chapter 8 apply. First, though, we will examine charting resizing since it is relevant not just to channels but to almost all drawn objects.

RESIZING AND EXPANSION

The ability to resize the space allocated to a chart is one of the most unique and vital features in ProphetCharts. To understand this concept, think about what the right side of virtually all charts looks like, ending with the most recent data point and the most recently available date. This makes sense, because charts are read from left (earliest date) to right (latest date), and it seems logical for the chart to end wherever the data end.

In addition, it makes sense for a chart's upper and lower extremes to be bounded by extremes in price. If you are charting a stock that, during the time period shown, ranges in price from $5 to $10, it would unnecessarily flatten the chart if the price range available on the y-axis started at $0 and ended at $500.

However, there is real value in being able to modify how much empty space is above, below, and to the right of a chart. To make this easier to understand, think of the entire area available (the entire y-axis, which is vertical, and the entire x-axis, which is horizontal) as the "chart area" and think of the area in which prices are actually displayed as the "price area."

Usually, the price area and the chart area are one and the same. This is certainly the case with most printed and electronic charts. In ProphetCharts, however, you can create empty space in the upper, lower, and right portions of the chart with pixel-by-pixel flexibility, which means the price area can be smaller—even much smaller—than the chart area.

WHY RESIZE?

Those relatively new to ProphetCharts may wonder what value there is in resizing. After all, it is simply going to create empty space without any price data. You will be adding either dollar values that are higher or lower than the stock's historical range, or you will be adding dates in the calendar that have not occurred yet.

The reason this has value is because, as you examine charts, you will find it helpful to be able to picture what may be in store for the stock you are charting in the future. When you are using drawn objects or trying to recognize certain chart patterns, it is invaluable to look using your mind's eye into the future to predict the most likely direction of a stock's price and how high or low the stock will go during that movement.

You will see some examples of this soon, but as a start, it is valuable to know how to expand a chart in the first place. This is accomplished with the item in the toolbar second from the left (or, from the menu, the item Resize Graph). Clicking the resize tool (Figure 9.1) instantly allows you to reshape the price area to any rectangular shape within the chart area.

The moment you click on the Resize tool, the entire chart area becomes grey, and a message appears in the center of the chart: "Drag the graph's corner or edge handles to resize. Click inside the graph when finished." (See Figure 9.2.) And that really tells you everything you need to know.

There are five handles you can grab—one on the top, one on the bottom, one on the right, and one on both the upper-right and lower-left corners (Figure 9.3). You can click on any of these and drag to resize the chart to your liking. It is more common to create x-axis (time-based) space as

FIGURE 9.1 Clicking the resize tool lets you change the height and width of the area allocated to the chart data.

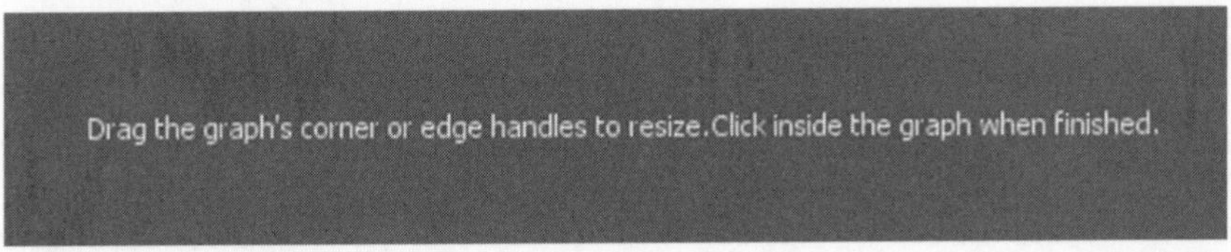

Drag the graph's corner or edge handles to resize. Click inside the graph when finished.

FIGURE 9.2 When you click Resize, ProphetCharts gives you basic instructions about what to do next.

opposed to y-axis (price-based) space, but the extra blank space you form is totally up to you, and of course it can be changed at any time. Once you are satisfied with the new size of your chart, you can click anywhere within the chart to set that size.

Let's look at a simple example of how a resized chart might be useful. Figure 9.4 shows a graph of the S&P 500 index over the span of a couple of years, and it has a channel (with a median line) drawn on top of it. The graph shows that the market fell quickly from about 1,330 to about 1,255. Suppose you were interested in shorting this market, but you wanted to wait until the price had climbed back to the median line in order to reduce the risk of the trade. If you had a normal graph, it would not be possible to judge this accurately. However, by being able to see six weeks into the future (albeit without price data), you can easily picture how a retracement might take place, and, using your cursor and the data line, you could point at the likely "touch point" on the median and get an accurate estimate as to the price the S&P needs to hit before you place your trade.

To take a far more dramatic example, suppose you were taking an extremely long-range view of the market, and you used the Fibonacci time series study (which you will read about in Chapter 15) to project when the next major market top might take place. It would be entirely impractical to do this without being able to resize the chart. But as Figure 9.5 shows,

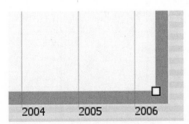

FIGURE 9.3 Five handles appear on the chart area, any one of which can be dragged to reshape the chart. One of the handles is shown here.

FIGURE 9.4 This graph shows a small amount of expansion, allowing you to see about six weeks into the future.

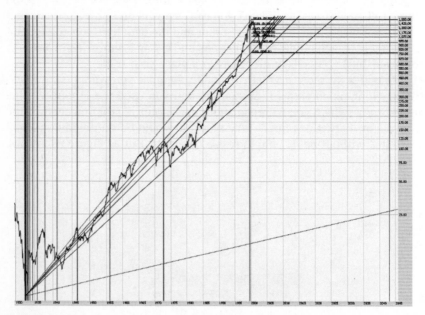

FIGURE 9.5 This is a more extreme example of showing the future, since this Fibonacci time series has its next data point decades away.

this analysis is possible, even though the next line in the series is decades in the future, in approximately 2043.

As a practical matter, it is useful to leave the chart permanently expanded, and although the amount of expansion is up to you, allocating approximately the rightmost 10 percent and the uppermost 5 percent of the chart to a "price-free" chart area is usually enough. You will find it invaluable in being able to speculate on future price movement, particularly since all the objects you have drawn (such as trendlines, Fibonacci studies, and so forth) will project into the future. You can use those as guides to predict future support and resistance levels, and when combined with the data line, you can pinpoint those predicted dates and prices.

PARALLEL LINES

In Chapter 8, you learned how to use and draw trendlines. The tool next to the trendline tool, which is the channel tool (Figure 9.6), lets you draw two parallel trendlines easily in order to bound price data in a channel pattern.

Channel patterns are rarer than trendline patterns, simply because it is much easier to find prices bouncing off a consistent support or resistance level than it is to find prices bouncing within *both* support and resistance in a parallel fashion. In the case of a supporting trendline, you will probably see prices touching the trendline below and not having any particular pattern above it, and with a resisting trendline, you will see prices touching the trendline above and not having any meaningful shape below. In other words, trendlines bounce off either the upper or lower price action, and otherwise the price action may be just noise.

With a channel, however, prices are confined within parallel trendlines. Because this pattern is much more unusual, it is also much more meaningful. The prices are obeying more complex mechanics, and thus when prices exit that channel in either direction, the move up or down will likely be more potent. As always, the longer the pattern, the more meaningful the breakout from the pattern, and a breakout from a channel is usually more significant than a breakout from a single trendline.

FIGURE 9.6 The channel tool is represented by two small parallel trendlines.

Drawing a channel is very similar to drawing a trendline. You follow these steps:

1. Click on the channel tool.
2. Click in the chart area where you want to begin your first trendline.
3. Drag the mouse to where you want this trendline to end and click once more.
4. At this point, another parallel line will appear. As you move the mouse up and down, this parallel line will follow your mouse movement.
5. Place the line at its destination and click the mouse button to complete the drawing. You will now have a drawn channel.

As with the trendline, you can right-click on a drawn channel (Figure 9.7) to make use of other features, one of which is unique to the channel. Here is what each item from the menu does:

Move: Allows you to move the channel or change its angle. When you select this, three handles appear: one at the start point of the first trendline, another on the end point of the first trendline, and another on the end point of the second trendline. You can drag any of these handles to change the angle of the channel (the full 360 degrees of a circle are available) or to adjust the distance of the second trendline from the first.

Duplicate: This creates an identical channel (same size, angle, color) near the first one, and this duplicate channel will have all three handles preselected so you can immediately move it to the desired location.

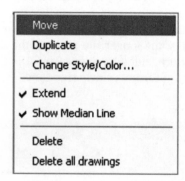

FIGURE 9.7 When you right-click on a channel, this popup menu appears.

Change Style/Color: Brings up the same dialog box as was shown in Figure 8.16, allowing you to change the color, opacity, weight, and pattern of the channel. You can also preserve these settings so they are used as the default for all future channel drawings.

Extend: As with the same option for trendlines, the Extend function makes the trendlines (and the median line, if selected) extend infinitely into the future. This is especially useful if you are using an expanded chart, as described earlier in this chapter.

Show Median Line: This option is unique to the channel tool. It creates another parallel trendline exactly between the upper and lower trendlines of the channel. There are instances (such as with Figure 9.4) in which not only the prices are bounded by a channel but also tend to cling to the middle line between the upper and lower trendlines. This can make for more insightful and precise analysis.

Delete: Choosing this deletes the selected channel. If you make a mistake, you can always undo your decision with the Undo command (Ctrl-Z).

Delete All Drawings: Choosing this deletes all the drawn objects on the current chart. If you make a mistake, you can always undo your decision with the Undo command (Ctrl-Z).

Being able to spot channels on a chart can be challenging, because you have to ascertain whether price action is intended to fit a uniform, parallel pattern. Experimentation with drawings is the best approach when you are learning, since there is no harm in creating and deleting channels if you find that you were wrong. And if your drawing doesn't quite conform to the price action, you can also use the Move command to adjust the position of the channel so prices line up within the boundaries.

The application of channels is very similar to that of trendlines. If you are in a position, you should stay in that position so long as the prices stay within the boundaries (Figure 9.8). And if you are not in a position, you may want to wait until the price breaks above (bullish) or below (bearish) the channel before taking action. You should also keep in mind that breakouts are more potent if they are contrary to the primary trend of the channel. In other words, a breakout above a descending channel is especially bullish, and a breakdown below an ascending channel is especially bearish, because in each case, the breakout is in opposition to the former trend.

As mentioned before, channel patterns are unusual, but they do happen, and the longer they last, the more meaningful they are. Any price trend will eventually change, so as a channel gets progressively old, the likelihood of its staying within that channel diminishes, and the potency of the move once it escapes that channel increases. As Figure 9.9 shows, it is

FIGURE 9.8 An open position can be held as long as the price action remains bounded by the support and resistance levels.

FIGURE 9.9 Prices can remain within channels for many months, or even years.

hazardous to try to anticipate the breakout from a channel until is actually happens, since prices can stay within the confines of a channel for months or even years.

BREAKDOWNS AND BREAKOUTS

When prices do finally leave their channels—and they always will, eventually—those holding positions in those securities are wise to close them out, and those looking for an entry point should examine the chart as an opportunity. Figure 9.10 illustrates typical action after a channel is broken. In this instance, prices were trending slowly lower, making a series of lower highs and lower lows. A person exploiting this channel may have seized on opportunities to buy the stock when it was at the lower support line and sell the stock short when it was at the upper resistance line. But as the chart shows, the fourth time it touched the support line, it subsequently broke it, and the downfall in price from there was fast and powerful.

FIGURE 9.10 This channel shows how swiftly prices fell after prices violated the lower support line.

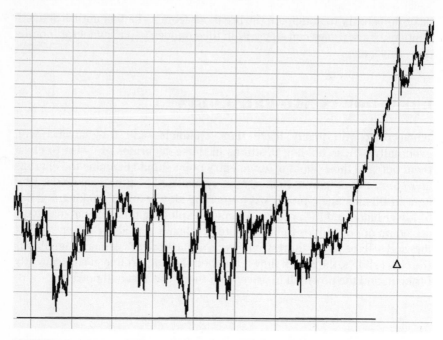

FIGURE 9.11 In a bullish move, prices pushed above support in this chart and moved significantly higher.

Prices can move out of a channel in either direction, of course. Figure 9.11 shows a channel made of two horizontal, parallel trendlines. This also happens to be an inverted head and shoulders pattern, which you will read about in Chapter 13. After prices moved above resistance, they swiftly more than doubled, and a person purchasing this stock after the breakout would have had a profit almost immediately after the trade since prices never dipped beneath the former resistance line.

Channels appear in three different forms: ascending (a series of higher highs and higher lows), descending (lower highs and lower lows), and horizontal (equal highs and equal lows). A stock breaking above its ascending channel or breaking below its descending channel isn't usually a good trade, because it is simply moving in the same direction at a faster rate. The better trades are those where a reversal pattern takes place.

Figure 9.12, for example, shows a stock that was moving higher within an ascending channel. When it finally broke beneath support late in October, it lost about 20 percent of its value, and the stock was clearly in a downtrend versus its prior uptrend.

Because channels are made of a trendline pair, the same guidelines can apply. The idea of prices moving back toward the trendline after a breakout

FIGURE 9.12 Channels do not have to be horizontal to be effective. Breakouts contrary to the prior trend are often the most potent.

is still true. For example, when prices break beneath a channel's support-ing line, they can move higher (in spite of the bearish signal) and touch the line that used to represent support (Figure 9.13). It is also helpful, af-ter a channel violation, to watch for the formation of new patterns, since the channel by definition has become a pattern of the past. Looking at Fig-ure 9.13 once again, the prices formed a clear topping pattern spanning nearly a year once prices cut beneath support in October. In addition, you can see prices moving from $36 to $46 even after this pattern failure, since prices were clinging to the underside of the former support line before they succumbed to the new pattern's direction.

Another interesting thing about channels is that they often represent temporary changes in trend. Figure 9.14 offers a real-life example. At the beginning of the chart, the stock was moving down badly, descending from $15 to $8.50 per share. Following this weakness, the stock began a coun-termove lasting nearly two years, and the prices nearly tripled. Once the channel was broken, the descent in prices began anew. What's particularly interesting about this channel is that the channel itself was defined early

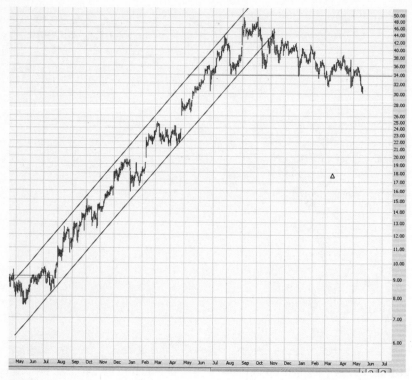

FIGURE 9.13 After prices fell below support, they gradually weakened over the months ahead.

on: The price points established in the first few months of the channel accurately predicted the entire move. Had a trader made use of this channel, he would have benefited from virtually the entirety of the price move, since by and large the stock went up until it broke beneath the support line.

The very best channel-based trades are those where prices break out in the direction opposite the channel. Figure 9.15 provides a fitting example. Prices had been moving steadily lower, bottoming at less than $2.50. When prices more than doubled after that, they were up against the upper resistance line. Once they broke above that line, however, the subsequent move nearly quadrupled prices from that level. Although a person entering this trade might begrudge the fact that they had already missed a 100 percent move (from $2.50 to $5.00), the fact is that until the prices are outside the channel, there is no basis for that trade. There were many other occasions when the price was at resistance and could have broken out, but it did not. Only until the reversal is confirmed with a breakout is there a rational reason to place the trade.

FIGURE 9.14 This channel was entered into when the stock was much weaker. The channel represents a time of consistent strength.

FIGURE 9.15 Breaking above a descending channel usually precedes significant upward moves.

FIGURE 9.16 Other patterns may form within channels, which can offer more thorough insight into a stock's future behavior.

Just because prices are bound by a channel does not mean that a channel is the only pattern that can take place during that timespan, especially if a channel is somewhat lengthy. There are many instances where patterns can appear within other patterns, and having an awareness of those can yield fresh insight into the stock's future behavior.

In Figure 9.16, the price of the Russell 2000 index moved within the confines of a very large channel for many months. But inside the channel, a series of different patterns appears: The three horizontal lines indicate breakouts from smaller bullish patterns. By having an awareness of these smaller patterns, you could look for repeated behavior. So not only would you be aware of a broad-based uptrend, but you could make predictions based on the smaller patterns—in this case, bullish patterns within a much larger bullish pattern, which made the case especially strong for holding onto this winning position.

SUMMARY

In this chapter and the prior one, you have studied line-based patterns: that is, trendlines and channels. Understanding and using these are essential to good charting. But these straight-line patterns are relatively easy to find, and there are many other kinds of patterns that are important to your knowledge of technical analysis but may not be so obvious.

In the next chapter, we will begin this journey into more ambiguous patterns by studying rounded tops and rounded bottoms. These are patterns which can help you predict reversals of a security from which you can profit.

CHAPTER 10

Rounded Tops and Saucers

T wo of the most important events that occur repeatedly in technical analysis are breakouts and reversals. A breakout is the act of a price escaping from a relatively tight price range, either to the upside (a breakout above resistance) or the downside (a failure below support). A reversal is the act of a price changing directly either from (1) up to down or (2) from down to up. What is going on in each case is the same—an escape from a price range. The terminology differs only to state what has happened prior to that escape.

Breakouts and reversals are crucial events to discern on a chart since they can make you money, and two of the most common patterns found on charts that relate to these events are rounded tops (at the peak of a chart) and saucers (at the bottom). There are many terms used for this phenomenon. A rounded top, as the name suggests, is price action at the upper end of a chart, and it is sometimes called a distribution top or an inverted saucer. A saucer, which is typically at the low end of a chart's recent price range, is also referred to as a rounded bottom, a basing pattern, or a dish pattern.

Tops and bottoms are not always as clean and neat as saucers and tops, so we will begin by examining the more fundamental price breakouts, which are the progenitors of saucers and tops. A breakout is the escape from a price range bounded by a lower line (support) and an upper line (resistance). Figure 10.1 illustrates a breakout pattern in which the price action had been around $7 to $9 for many months. When prices broke above the resistance line in mid-June, the stock swiftly moved up several hundred percent.

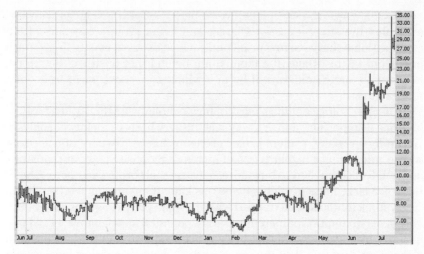

FIGURE 10.1 This stock bounced between $7 and $9 for a year before finally breaking above its resistance level. Notice the pullback to the former resistance level after the breakout, after which the price soared.

A longer-term chart is provided by Owens Illinois (Figure 10.2), whose stock was forming a base from 1992 through 1996. Traders sometimes refer to this price action as hammering out a base, because there is a tug-of-war happening between buyers and sellers as they try to establish a fair price for the stock. This is a search for equilibrium or price discovery, since the market is working at discovering what the proper price is for the security.

FIGURE 10.2 Owens Illinois (symbol OI) tripled after it broke above this breakout pattern.

As this goes on—especially over a period of years, such as with this example—the stock amasses a larger and larger group of owners of the stock within a fairly narrow price range. Once external events finally push prices out of this range, the momentum behind that push will be strong, because so many holders will be in a winning position, eager to acquire more shares.

The psychology behind a mass of buyers holding a security at a particular price is important, and in a way it is the very basis of technical analysis. Generally speaking, traders prefer profits to losses. Owners of a security whose price moves higher will feel increasingly positive about that stock and will feel compelled to buy more, because their profits are increasing. If there is a large mass of such buyers, this kind of buying can feed on itself.

A stock that has been trapped within a small price range for a long term will have two important ingredients for a potential upside move: (1) a large quantity of buyers within that price range, eager to add to their position if the stock breaks out of the range, and (2) a strong support level at that price range, which will create a firm floor for prices if an initial breakout weakens. If a stock breaks above its price range and then starts sinking, that same mass of owners of the stock is going to be reluctant to sell their holdings as the price softens, which will cause the price to firm as sellers dry up. This army of security owners within that price range is a potent force, both for pushing the stock higher and for protecting the stock from falling through the well-established price range.

An extraordinary example of the power of a long-term base is shown with Newport Corporation in Figure 10.3. The stock hammered out a

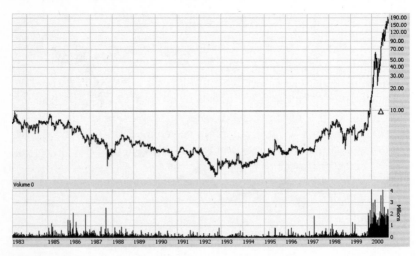

FIGURE 10.3 Newport Corporation (symbol NEWP) exploded in both price and volume in 2000, going up almost twentyfold in a very short time.

gargantuan base over nearly two decades, from 1983 to 1999. When it finally broke above $10, the ascent was fast and furious, with a nearly twentyfold increase in value within just over a year. Notice also the gigantic increase in volume during this time, which is illustrative of the ascent feeding on itself. Having waited so many years for the stock to finally wake up and do something, buyers were falling all over themselves to acquire more shares once it finally did burst above its well-established resistance level.

PRICE PULLBACKS

One nice feature of breakouts is that they often give traders a second chance to get in after the breakout. This temporary softening in prices after the breakout is known as a pullback, and it is caused by a portion of the owners of the stock anxious to bank their profits on their stock's newfound price activity.

Imagine a hypothetical group of 1,000 people, each of whom owns shares in a company that has been trading between $10 and $12 for years. If the stock finally breaks out and hits $15, you can understand the excitement of these owners, since they have been holding a do-nothing stock for years and it is finally showing signs of life.

Although most of these owners may be patient enough to let their profits build, a subset of this group is going to want to get out of the stock immediately and take their profits. The psychology behind this group is understandable, too—after all, their stock has done absolutely nothing, and now it is giving them an opportunity to get out with some extra cash. So some people—let's say 100 of the group of 1,000—immediately place orders to sell the stock at the current market price.

This influx of selling is going to cause the price to soften, at least temporarily. It usually will head back to the upper end of its former trading range, at which point selling will dry up since any newfound profits the group enjoyed have now vanished, eliminating the compulsion to sell the stock for a quick profit. This temporary softening of prices is the pullback, and those people watching the stock chart closely can take advantage of this by acquiring the stock at the prebreakout price. It is an especially attractive opportunity because the stock has, in a manner of speaking, tipped its hand about its price direction since it has finally broken out of its price range.

The stock of the company Potash, shown in Figure 10.4, broke above the upper end of its price range and swiftly moved from $38 to $44. It then started slipping back to $38, and for the first few months of 2004, the stock bobbled between a miniature price zone of $38 to $44 before doubling in

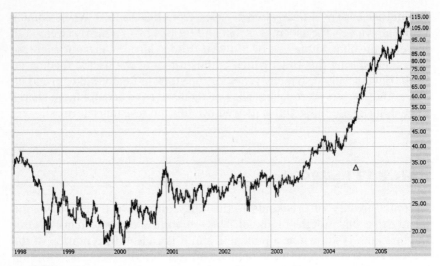

FIGURE 10.4   Potash (symbol POT) more than doubled after this beautiful saucer breakout.

value. This pullback created a great opportunity for getting into the stock at a relatively low-risk price. After the breakout, the saucer's price range of $18 to $38 was a thing of the past. The stock was now trading above $38. It took a few months to get the strength and confidence to soar over 100 percent, but during that period, a savvy trader could have acquired the stock at a price very close to the initial breakout level (without the misery of holding a do-nothing stock for many years beforehand).

Some of the most exceptional market gains in history have been enjoyed following the decisive breakout of a stock above a long-established price range. The more defined and longer the chart pattern, the better it is for owners of that stock. An extraordinary instance of this is shown in Figure 10.5 with 3M. (At the time of the breakout, the company was called Minnesota Mining & Manufacturing.) The age of the price range was substantial, spanning from 1973 to 1986. Once the stock broke above resistance, it hardly ever looked back (except for the crash of 1987, which, interestingly, pushed the stock back to the top of its former trading range and no lower). The stock moved literally thousands of percent higher after this breakout.

It is easy to see in retrospect how obvious these patterns are. It seems that, armed with this knowledge, people would know exactly what to do. But this is not the case, and it again goes back to human psychology.

When a breakout occurs, a person examining the stock doesn't have the benefit of the next 20 years of price history. They can see only what

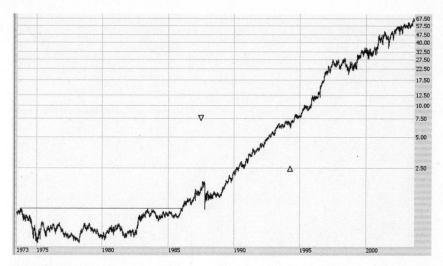

FIGURE 10.5 The benefits after a breakout can last decades. This shows 3M Corporation (symbol MMM) moving thousands of percent higher after a handsome breakout.

has happened so far. Imagine yourself looking at 3M in 1986 just after it broke above its former resistance level. You would be confronted with a stock that (1) had done very little for more than a decade and (2) was at a higher price than anyone had ever paid for it. You might feel foolish to consider paying a premium price for a do-nothing stock. Those already owning the stock might feel compelled to increase their holdings and add to their profits, but for newcomers, a stock that has just made a new high price is seldom tempting because everyone else was able to get the stock before, when it was cheap.

In retrospect, of course, a person buying 3M in 1986 would indeed be getting it cheap, because once the stock has moved up thousands of percent, whether you paid $1.25 a share or $1.10 a share doesn't make much difference. But at the time, few people want to pay what they see as top dollar for a stock, and they prefer to wait until the stock gets cheap again. The fact is, sometimes that second opportunity will never come along.

This, again, is where pullbacks represent a possible entry point for newcomers to a stock. There is absolutely no guarantee that a stock breaking above its base will provide such an opportunity. The momentum may simply carry it skyward, giving no one a second chance to get in cheaply. But if you have a lower tolerance for risk, you may want to acquire only during a pullback. Using 3M again as an example (Figure 10.6), the pullback took over a year to happen (and then only because there was a major market crash to provide such a pullback), but the arrow illustrates where

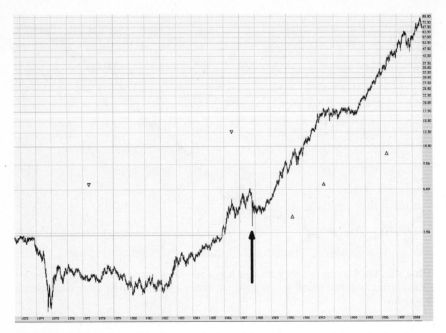

FIGURE 10.6 This pullback erased most of the gains enjoyed since the breakout, but it did not violate the pattern.

more cautious buyers could have acquired the stock at a relatively modest price as weaker holders of the stock sold it off to prebreakout levels.

PRICE FAILURE

The opposite of a price breakout is a price failure, or breakdown. The rules are very similar to what you've learned about price breakouts, except that instead of prices moving above resistance, prices are moving below support. If they do so, it is likely they will continue moving substantially lower as the mass of buyers at the former price range loses hope and sells off the stock.

Monsanto (Figure 10.7) provides a clear example of this. The price of the stock had a range of about $27 to $36. Holders of the stock were surely getting anxious and frustrated that their investment wasn't really doing anything. The psychology of stockholders when a stock dips below support is quite different from when it pushes above resistance; instead of greed and excitement (which drives more buying and higher prices), there is fear and panic (which compels selling and lower prices). Just as buying at higher prices can feed on itself, selling at lower prices can, too.

FIGURE 10.7 Monsanto Corporation (symbol MON) lost about half its value following this fall beneath support.

As with price breakouts, the power of a price breakdown is partly based on the amount of time that the stock has been trapped within a certain range. If a person has been holding onto a security for years, and when that security finally does make a move, it's a losing move, the typical holder will vow "Enough is enough" and simply sell the stock out of frustration and despair. Figure 10.8 shows the chart of a company called Hop-In,

FIGURE 10.8 Hop-In Inc. (symbol HPNN) lost almost 100 percent of its value following this huge top.

which, after falling below its support level, lost virtually all of its value. Clearly, there are fundamentals at play here, too—any company whose price could get this ruined had some core problems in its business. But stock price action often precedes public knowledge of fundamental issues. The stock action didn't cause the company's collapse, but it certainly saw it coming.

SAUCER BOTTOMS

Let us turn our attention now to saucers, which are the clean, well-formed version of breakout patterns. It takes years of experience to be able to swiftly go through charts and spot patterns, but, to use an astronomical metaphor, the saucer is the Big Dipper of chart patterns—so easy to spot that just about anyone can do it.

Figure 10.9 shows an actual price chart with a saucer shape drawn below it to emphasize the pattern's presence. This is about as ideal a saucer as you will see in the real world. Keep in mind there is no crew of stockholders whose purpose it is to hammer out a well-defined shape on a chart. These patterns are formed as a consequence of thousands of people pushing millions of dollars around. It is only when mass psychology on a stock is behaving in such a way as to form a clean pattern that these become evident.

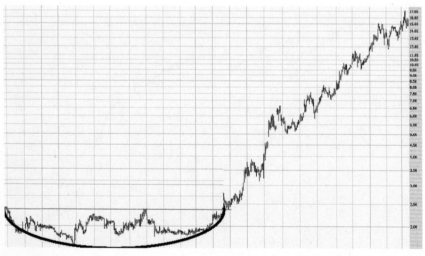

FIGURE 10.9 The basic saucer formation is illustrated here with the semi-oval drawn beneath the chart.

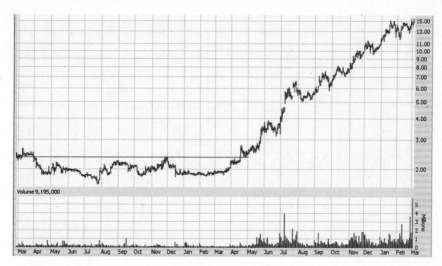

FIGURE 10.10 Alvarian (symbol ALVR) looked like it would break out of its saucer pattern in December, but it took several more months before the stock was actually ready to move higher.

The ingredients for a potent saucer breakout are:

- A clean pattern—the cleaner and more defined, the better.
- Longevity—the longer the pattern, the better.
- Volume increase after the breakout—the bigger, the better.

A beautiful example of this is Figure 10.10, which is the chart of Alvarian. The horizontal line shows the resistance level. For about the first half of the chart, the price meanders between about $1.80 and $2.50. The pattern formed isn't an absolutely perfect saucer, but it is fairly clean. The length of the pattern is impressive—more than a year. And best of all, the pickup in volume after the breakout is superb. You can see on the lower graph (which shows the volume bars) that volume increases more and more as the price launches from $2.50 to $15 in less than one year.

An even more impressive example is shown with Figure 10.11, which had a chart pattern spanning not just one year but more than two. The volume was terrifically higher after the breakout than before. Another interesting aspect of this chart is that after the saucer breakout, an entirely new pattern took hold—a channel, illustrated by the ascending parallel lines that bound the stock price as it moved from $10 to five times that amount.

The importance of strong volume after a breakout cannot be overstated. Volume is the fuel that drives prices higher, as it was with the

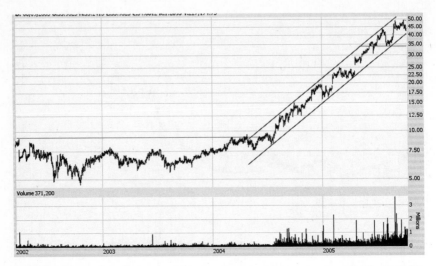

FIGURE 10.11 Building Materials (symbol BMHC) saw its volume explode and its price go into a steady channel after moving above its saucer breakout.

astonishing ascent of Hansen Natural's price, shown in Figure 10.12. When volume is going up at the same time as a price is going up, the market is saying that more and more people are willing to pay increasingly higher prices. As it does this, media and other attention is focused on the stock.

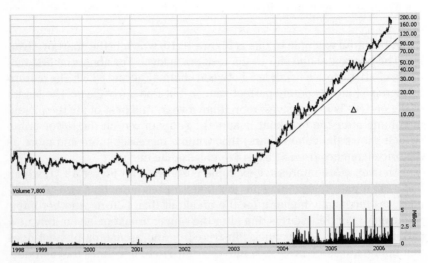

FIGURE 10.12 Strong volume is key to a steady ascent in prices, as Hansen (symbol HANS) shows here.

FIGURE 10.13 This close-up of Hansen Natural illustrates that although it took a few months after the breakout, volume exploded higher once the price ascent was underway.

In some cases, just as some people are famous for being famous, some stocks go higher simply because they are known for going higher. This is sometimes called the greater fool theory, meaning that buyers of the stock realize they are paying an exorbitant price for it, but they are confident a fool greater than themselves will be willing to pay an even higher price, as so many have done before them.

The increase in the price of Hansen Natural Corporation (symbol HANS) was so amazing that it warrants a closer examination with respect to the volume change. Looking at Figure 10.13, you can see that the price broke above its former resistance level of $3.50 after having traded below that price for many years. Notice that volume did not instantly explode higher. After a breakout, sometimes the volume soars, and sometimes it doesn't. The market may be acting with caution toward a stock such as this, even after a breakout, simply because it has been so inactive and un-exciting for so many years.

The area highlighted with an oval shows when volume of the stock did finally pick up. There could be many reasons for this—the recommendation of a popular newsletter or the buy rating of a major analyst who initiates coverage of the stock. No matter what the reason, the explosion in volume is going to get just as much attention as the increase in price, since this is the market's affirmation that it believes in the new direction of the stock and is willing to put its dollars behind the movement.

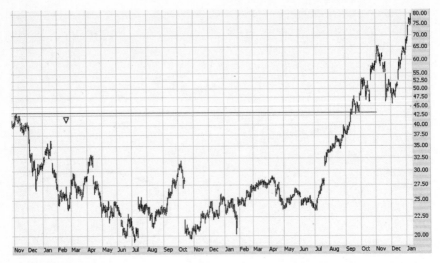

FIGURE 10.14 When saucer patterns first break out, they are not always as obvious as they are on a long-term chart.

One of the real tricks to recognizing patterns is to be able to do so before you have much perspective. In other words, looking at a multiyear chart, most people can easily spot patterns that took place long ago. But being able to discern a pattern when it actually completes is much more difficult, because often the scale of the chart makes the pattern not very obvious. Look at Figure 10.14 and notice that the price action is relatively messy (and it's even messier without the clarity that the horizontal line helps bring to it). In retrospect, one would see this was a rather clean breakout from a saucer pattern, but at the time this breakout took place, it would not have been nearly as easy to discern.

The other challenge with buying breakouts is that once the pattern completes, the stock might seem too expensive. Figure 10.15 provides a nice illustration of this. In this instance, the stock struggled for years, finally pushing its way from $7 to $22 before it finally broke above a very well-formed saucer. Many people at the time would think twice about buying such a stock, since it had already moved up over 200 percent. The paradox is that this is in fact the ideal time to purchase the stock, since it has already proven itself with the pattern breakout. As is so often the case, it went on to much higher prices once the pattern completed.

The old saying that history repeats itself is true for technical analysis (indeed, it's a significant part of the basis for technical analysis). This applies to patterns as well, particularly within the same stock. If you notice a particular stock is prone to a certain pattern (be it a saucer, head and

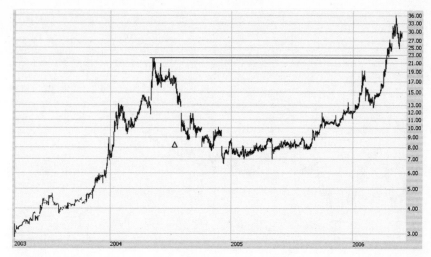

FIGURE 10.15 This stock consolidated for almost two years before pushing higher, and it had already tripled in price by the time it broke out.

shoulders, or what have you), it is likely you'll see more than one instance of that pattern for that stock.

This can be helpful, since as you become acquainted with the price behavior of a particular stock, you can better anticipate its next move. The pattern isn't always the same length each time, as Figure 10.16 shows, but

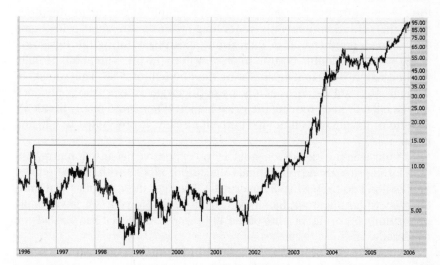

FIGURE 10.16 Saucer patterns can repeat themselves in the same chart. Here we see a nearly seven-year saucer breakout, followed by a much smaller one-year saucer during more recent history.

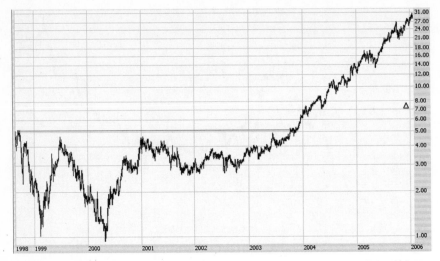

FIGURE 10.17 This stock had a major double bottom before consolidating into a saucer formation.

its shape and consequences tend to be similar. The longer the pattern, the more pronounced the consequences.

Let's take a look at a few more saucers to complete the picture. As stated earlier, the length of the pattern has a lot to do with how much force comes afterward. Figure 10.17 has a couple of interesting features. First, the pattern is nearly six years long (with the breakout price being $5). Second, another bullish indication takes place during the formation of the pattern: a double bottom in price, where the price hit about $1.00 in the first half of 1999 and again during the first half of 2000. This refusal of the market to sell the stock at any lower prices gave buyers the confidence they needed to keep moving the price higher. When it did finally break $5, in spite of having moved up 400 percent already, it proceeded to $30 and beyond.

Dismissing the idea that a stock is too expensive because it has moved up a lot in price already is critical to acquiring stocks with major returns. Stocks don't go from $1 to $5 overnight. They get there a dollar at a time. So even when the stock has moved from $1 to $5, you still have ample opportunity for profit, in spite of the 400 percent move that has passed you by already.

Whole Foods, for instance (Figure 10.18), was a stock powerhouse for years. From 1998 through 2001, the stock hammered out a pattern ranging from about $7.50 to $17.50. In late 2001 and early 2002, Whole Foods pushed away from its basing pattern, only to subsequently ease back to

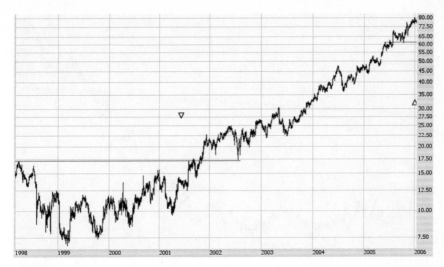

FIGURE 10.18 Popular grocer Whole Foods (symbol WFMI) formed a beautiful saucer from 1998 through 2001 before breaking out, pulling back, and then finally moving significantly higher in price.

the $17.50 price level. As you know, this presented an ideal opportunity to acquire the stock. The time-consuming and nail-biting pullback was already finished, and you could purchase the stock knowing that any meaningful descent was less likely since it was once again at a support level. Sure enough, the stock marched from $17.50 up into the $80 range within a few years.

A similar example with a very different kind of retailer can be seen with Wal-Mart (Figure 10.19). Here again we see the laborious, multiyear process of the saucer being formed (1993 through 1997), followed by a breakout, a pullback, and a subsequent ascent. WMT pushed from its proven support level of $15 to a handsome price of $65 in just a couple of years.

You've seen many examples of multihundred-percent profits that are possible with saucer patterns. Equally exciting profits can be enjoyed if we turn this concept upside down and look for topping patterns instead of basing ones.

ROUNDED TOP PATTERNS

When you are a skilled technician, you can make money in both bull and bear markets. When the market is going down, most of the investing public

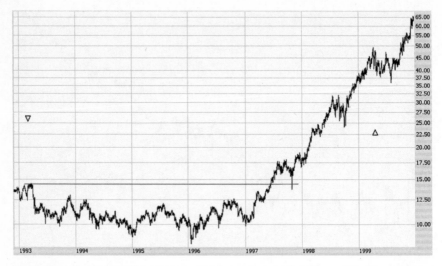

FIGURE 10.19   Retail powerhouse Wal-Mart (symbol WMT) exploded higher after this five-year saucer pattern was finished.

is frustrated at not being able to make money. Typically, they stick with stocks as their values decrease. The skilled use of technical analysis allows you to avoid these losses and actually make profits from the declining values of stocks.

In the context of this chapter, the pattern most indicative of a looming price decrease is the rounded top. This is exactly the same in appearance as the saucer, except that it is turned upside down. In a way, the rules are turned upside down as well.

With a saucer (or basing) pattern, the buying public is trying to push prices past a certain level of resistance. Over the course of time—years, sometimes—a mass of owners are accumulated at a relatively similar price level, and this creates a floor of support for the price from which it can move higher.

With a rounded top, a similar situation takes place, but the price falls below the mass of owners instead of above it. What this means is that as the price attempts to move higher again, it will be met with a wall of sellers. Figure 10.20 shows how Terra Industries traded for years just above the $10 level. Once the selling began, there was no turning back. Even though people were buying the stock, they were doing so at lower and lower prices. The desire of the owners between $10 and $12 to get out of the stock and cut their losses was simply too strong.

Rounded tops are even more potent when the break below the support level begins with a gap down. Take the case of Jacuzzi (Figure 10.21). The

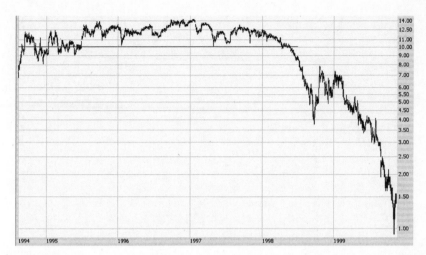

FIGURE 10.20 Terra Industries (symbol TRA) was steadily trading at about $10 for many years, but once it cracked beneath support, it had a 90 percent loss in just 18 months.

support price was about $25. In mid-1998, the stock started its trading day at $20, leaving a $5 gap in price between its last close and its next open. This would have been terribly demoralizing to all owners of the stock, and the sell-off was strong. Even if the company had a major turnaround later, it would have been difficult to overcome the wall of stock owners eager to get out of the stock at the best price possible. Once a mass of owners has

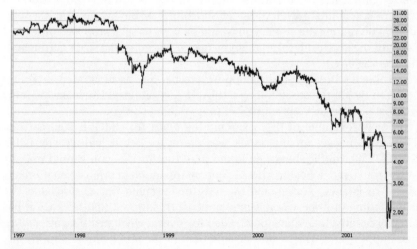

FIGURE 10.21 Jacuzzi (symbol JJZ) fell from $25 to $2 after it gapped down beneath a rounded top in mid-1998.

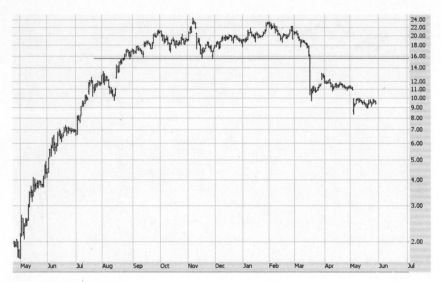

FIGURE 10.22   This is what a rounded top looks like shortly after the initial break.

been hit with a loss, you can expect many of them to be thinking the same thing: "If I can just get out of this at breakeven, I'll be happy." So the sellers are lined up, ready to pounce.

Price movement after a stock sinks beneath a rounded top can be devastating. This can be good for you in two ways: if you are long the stock, it's a strong indication that you had better get out; if you have no position in the stock, you might even consider shorting it or buying puts on it. (Actually, if you're long the stock, you would be wise to set a stop-loss order just beneath the support level so that you needn't monitor the stock throughout the trading day.)

A stock's break beneath support can be fast, as illustrated in Figure 10.22, in which the stock fell by a third in just one day. However, piercing support is often just a precursor of more declines to come.

For an example of this, examine the chart for OMG in Figure 10.23. The support level for this stock was about $42.50. It had already fallen from $72.50 (and it should be noted here that just as you should not shy away from a stock because it has gone up too much in price when it breaks above resistance, you should likewise not assume that a stock has finished falling in price when it breaks beneath support, just because it has already fallen a lot). The stock traded for over a week just beneath its former support line. This would give owners of the stock ample opportunity to get out, as well as give newcomers to the stock an opportunity to sell it short.

FIGURE 10.23 OM Group (symbol OMG) fell so swiftly after this rounded top that some might think the symbol stood for Oh My God.

When the stock started to collapse, it didn't take long to lose virtually all of its value. Support had been broken, and there was no turning back. The selling kept feeding on itself, and what used to be a $70 stock was now a $4 stock. Those who recognized the rounded top formation would have had plenty of opportunity to spare themselves losses (had they been long) and even make money (had they been short) with this insight.

You'll recall that when a stock pushes above its saucer pattern, it sometimes gives people a second opportunity to buy into the stock at attractive prices by pulling back in price. The rounded top has this property as well (but, again, in reverse). Let's take a moment to think about the psychology behind this phenomenon.

Look at Figure 10.24 and imagine the point of view of the people who purchased Solectron (symbol SLR) in 1999 and 2000. The stock was bouncing between $30 and $50. Within this range, some people had profits (such as those who bought at around $30), and others had losses (like those who acquired it at $50). So there was a mixed bag of winners and losers at these price levels. Everyone wants a profit, and nobody wants a loss.

Now imagine the situation in March 2001 as the stock sank beneath its $30 support level. Some people started to panic and the selling mounted, because at this point all the buyers from $30 to $50 had lost money. The stock rapidly lost half of its value, and the selling finally abated at $15.

This is when the pullback begins. Others begin to take an interest in this stock, which is having a half-off sale (it used to be $30, and now it is

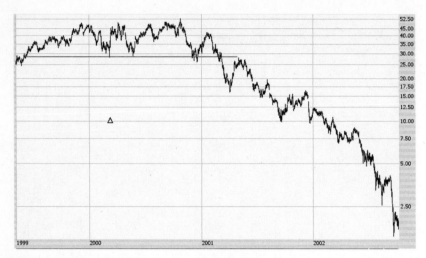

FIGURE 10.24 Solectron (symbol SLR) fell from $30 to $2 once it failed to hold above its support level.

only $15), so buyers start to nibble at it. As the stock begins to recover to $20 and then to $25, interest in the stock increases. But the balance between sellers and buyers starts to equalize as the stock approaches $30, and as technicians we know the reason why: because we are now at the lower boundary of that mass of buyers who purchased in the $30 to $50 price range. All those people who bought at about $30 now see a reprieve from their misfortune of having a losing stock (keep in mind, they were staring at a 50 percent loss only weeks before), and they rush to push the Sell button on their browsers. The selling starts anew.

As you can tell from the graph, the waves of selling and buying continue until the stock is virtually worthless. The sell-offs indicate when the sellers are overwhelming the buyers, and the recovery periods show when buyers believe they are getting a bargain on a stock that has bottomed out. This plays itself out until all the selling is completely exhausted.

A very similar story happened to Lucent Technologies (symbol LU), which benefited from the Internet mania of the late 1990s by being a provider of network and communications products (Figure 10.25). The stock got up to about $85 with a huge mass of buyers between $50 and $85. In the summer of 2000, all networking stocks weakened, and LU fell underneath its $50 support level. One thing to note in this graph is that stocks do not collapse instantly: it took a full two years for LU to fully unwind and fall, ultimately, to about 55 cents. There was plenty of time to profit from selling this stock short or owning puts on it.

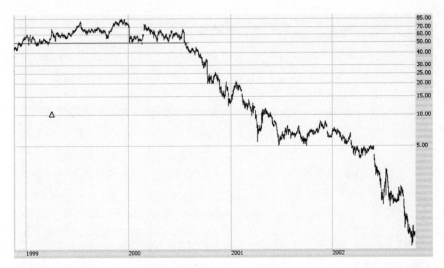

FIGURE 10.25 One of the big winners of the telecom bubble of 1999/2000 was Lucent (symbol LU). Once the bubble burst, heralded by the rounded top, LU descended from $50 to nearly $0.

Every stock chart tells a different story, and even though patterns often play out with similar directional movements, the speed of those movements varies quite a bit. Figure 10.26 provides a nice contrast to the LU graph. We see the classic signs of a rounded top: the well-defined support line, the break beneath support, and the subsequent recovery up to the former support level. Unlike Lucent, however, this stock subsequently took only about a week to wipe out virtually all of its equity value. Those who entered short positions at the recovery level of about $7 would have enjoyed very rapid profits in this case.

Another crucial aspect of rounded tops is that, to be profitable, they need to be preceded by a meaningful ascent in price. If a stock has traded between $10 and $12 for years, and then it creates a rounded top between $12 and $13, it's not going to matter very much if it falls beneath its support level. The reason is that there is already a huge mass of buyers from $10 to $12 to support it. A more exciting pattern would be for a stock that has gone from $1 to $80 and forms a rounded top between $80 and $90. In that instance, the stock has plenty of room to fall.

Take Ipsco (symbol IPS) as an example, shown in Figure 10.27. There is a rounded top over the span of about two and a half months starting in March and ending in mid-May. In less than a year, the stock has risen from $42.50 to $110, thus providing plenty of empty air for the stock to

FIGURE 10.26 A failure following a rounded top can be extremely swift. It took only a few trading sessions to wipe out virtually the entire value of this security.

start falling. A rounded top, therefore, has to be at the top of something. It cannot simply be a curvature in a graph that hasn't moved up much in the first place.

A more dramatic example of this concept is shown with Coventry Health (Figure 10.28), which also points out how multiple patterns or techniques can be used together. Coventry Health had climbed from $2 to

FIGURE 10.27 This is what a reversal formation in the form of a rounded top looks like. In this instance, the security is Ipsco (symbol IPS).

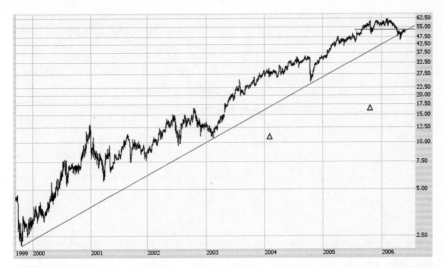

FIGURE 10.28 This rounded top for Coventry Health (CVH) took place at the end of a major ascending trend line.

$62 in about six years. Three things happened, however, to indicate this would be a good stock to sell or even sell short. First, the ascending trend line spanning back to 1999 had been broken; second, a rounded top had formed over the span of about half a year; and third, the price had subsequently climbed back both to the rounded top's former support level and to the trendline itself, indicating a low-risk/high-return place to short the security.

The more rapid the ascent, the more rapid the subsequent fall. This is not true every single time, but it's a good general rule to remember. The NASDAQ Corporation (Figure 10.29) enjoyed an almost 10-fold increase in just over a year. Once the support level at $35 was broken, however, the move down did not take long. This graph illustrates just the beginning of the fall, but prices lower than this happened soon, simply because there were not many owners of the stock at these levels. If a price is falling on a stock whose ascent was swift, the downward fall can resemble a hot knife through butter.

Although support lines are easiest to perceive if they are perfectly horizontal, there are times when this isn't the case. The support line has to be straight, but it can be at a slight angle, such as is illustrated by Figure 10.30. Psychologically, it's clearest if the line is horizontal, because everyone shares a similar panic price. But from a chartist's perspective, a slightly angled line (either upward or downward) is acceptable.

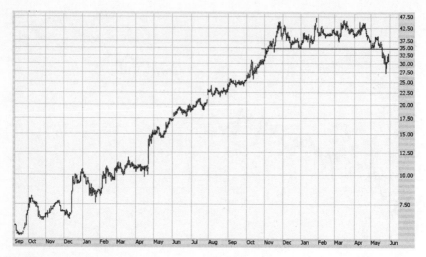

FIGURE 10.29 The NASDAQ (symbol NDAQ) Corporation went through a major reversal that culminated in this rounded top.

PATTERN FAILURES AND BREAKDOWNS

It can be very tempting, having seen the charts in this chapter that show subsequent explosions (or collapses) in price, to rush out and try to find every saucer pattern and rounded top you can locate. Keep in mind that these charts are particularly good examples of such patterns, and it is absolutely

FIGURE 10.30 Not all tops have to be perfectly horizontal. This rounded top shows that the pullback was based on a tilted support/resistance line.

not the case that a price will behave as it is supposed to behave once a particular pattern is completed. Let us examine some charts where just about everything seemed perfect, but the price action contradicted the prediction. It is important to see these examples to understand how the predictive power of patterns is limited and to understand what to watch out for so you don't hold a position that isn't working out the way you anticipated.

Figure 10.31 provides an extraordinary example. Notice first the basing action in the left three-quarters of the chart. The resistance line is very well defined at $10, and when the price does push past this line, it explodes higher. Indeed, the stock rises almost 20-fold, so savvy owners of this stock would indeed have benefited from recognizing the saucer and the importance of moving above $10. However, the stock's rise was short-lived, and the price fell so hard and fast it even dipped briefly below $10 again. Patient owners of this stock would have been profoundly frustrated that their 1,900 percent gains had withered away to 50 percent.

Far worse than having profits attenuated is to wind up with an outright loss. Bookham Technologies (symbol BKHM) had formed a magnificent pattern between about $7 and $30 (Figure 10.32). It broke cleanly above $30, and savvy buyers at this level surely must have had hopes that the stock would reach $100, $150, or even beyond. The breakout faltered, however, and the fact that the price sank beneath its former support level should have set off alarm bells for experienced chartists.

If a stock moves above its resistance level, it's perfectly acceptable for it to tumble back to that level after its initial rise. But if it clearly moves beneath that level, then the breakout has virtually no value. For our

FIGURE 10.31 In spite of the explosive rise of this stock, in the long term, the price wound up little changed.

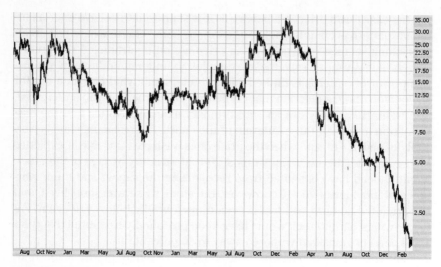

FIGURE 10.32 Bookham (symbol BKHM) broke above a nicely-formed saucer, but after failing to follow through, it lost virtually its entire value.

purposes, the breakout no longer exists, because the price couldn't sustain its new level. In the case of BKHM, the stock slipped to $25, then to $20, and ultimately collapsed to near $0. You can plainly see how it is a mistake to hold onto a stock once its pattern breakout has been neutralized by subsequent price failure.

Arbinet (symbol ARBX, shown in Figure 10.33) buyers experienced a similar disappointment. For nearly a year, the stock had moved between $6 and $8, accumulating buyers and interest at those price levels. At last, late in April, the stock pushed above $8, and it spent several sessions above that price, appearing to ready itself for a much higher price level. But in one trading session early in May, the price moved to the other side of the former resistance line. Knowledgeable chartists would have seen this as an opportunity to exit the position immediately. Indeed, it would be wise for buyers of this stock to have placed stop-loss orders at the $7.99 level (or somewhat lower to allow for market noise) to protect their positions.

The chart for 7/24 Solutions (Figure 10.34, symbol SVNX) is especially interesting since it has not one but two resistance lines. The stock had fallen terrifically from 2000 to 2002, losing virtually all of its value. In 2003 and 2004, the price steadied, and a near textbook-quality saucer pattern was hammered out, illustrated by the lower horizontal line representing resistance. It moved above this level and made an assault on the higher horizontal line, representing the next level of resistance. This,

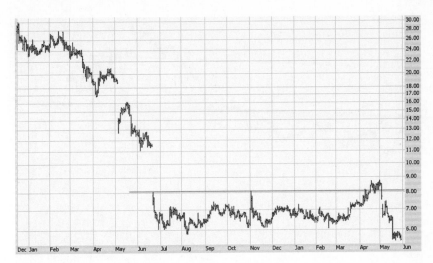

FIGURE 10.33 Arbinet (symbol ARBX) pushed above a nearly year-long resistance line only to quickly fall back beneath it.

too, was pierced, indicating what seemed like a great future for this stock.

Sadly, the price faltered. It fell beneath the upper horizontal line, and it wasn't long before it was below even the lower horizontal line. The stock was back to its old ways, floundering at a very low price level, the disheartened buyers of the stock having given up on it. Skilled chartists would have

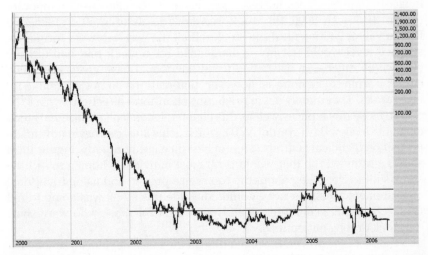

FIGURE 10.34 7/24 Solutions (symbol SVNX) had a textbook-quality saucer pattern, but the stock swiftly weakened and plunged back to its historic lows.

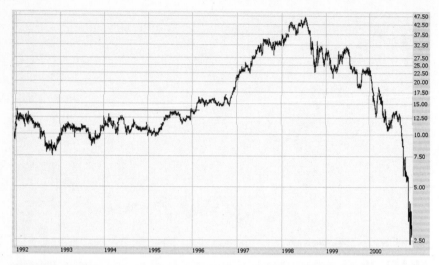

FIGURE 10.35 Compare this chart of Owens Illinois to Figure 10.2. In spite of the initial gains, the stock eventually weakened and went on to a substantial loss.

saved themselves much of this pain by recognizing that they should get out immediately when the higher line was violated.

A stock can be very successful for you but then turn sour. Much earlier in this chapter, Figure 10.2 showed how Owens Illinois enjoyed multihundred percent gains from 1996 through mid-1998. Taking the longer-term perspective, however, we can see these gains were temporary (Figure 10.35). By 2000, the stock was down to about $2.50, a staggering loss in value. Waiting until the stock fell all the way below its former resistance level would not be recommended for a stock that had already climbed so much—an ascending trend line would have given you much earlier warning. The point is, however, that patterns do not guarantee future results. They simply aid in predicting short-term direction.

To close this topic as well as this chapter, let us look at one final stock example: Avalon Bay (symbol AVB), which helps illustrate again how much protection technical analysis can provide when used properly. Figure 10.36 shows a rounded top that would thrill most individuals hoping to sell the stock short. Everything about the top seems proper, and using traditional measurement techniques, we could conclude this stock was going to fall from $28 to $18, generating a handsome profit for those who were short the stock or long put options.

The fact is, however, that even though the stock did indeed sink below $28, it didn't stay there long. It paused there briefly and then began moving higher. That would have been the signal for bears to close their positions

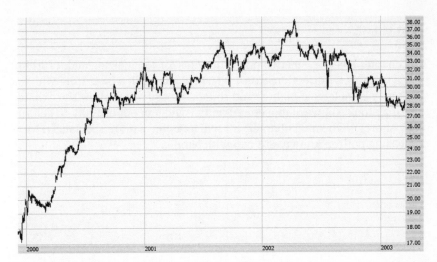

FIGURE 10.36 This chart of Avalon Bay (symbol AVB) appears to be breaking beneath support and on its way to a major fall.

at once for a very small loss. If a stock in this kind of pattern can muster the kind of strength to shake off a pattern of this size, the stock buyers are far too strong for the sellers (Figure 10.37). It is wise to move out of the way quickly. In this instance, once the stock recomposed itself, it moved higher many hundreds of percent. Those short the stock who refused to cover their positions would have been wiped out.

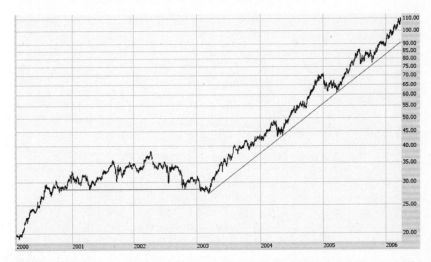

FIGURE 10.37 The longer-term chart of AVB, as compared with Figure 10.36, shows that the stock recovered quickly from its weakness and went on to a multi-hundred percent return.

SUMMARY

This chapter has given us two powerful tools for recognizing major turning points in a stock's direction: saucers (which establish a base from which a stock may launch itself higher) and rounded tops (which show the exhaustion of a stock's upward movement and provide an opportunity to sell the stock short). In the next chapter, we will examine a more specialized form of a basing pattern known as a cup with handle.

CHAPTER 11

Cup with Handle

In the previous chapter we learned (among other subjects) about the saucer pattern, in which prices consolidate beneath a resistance level and gradually ramp up to burst above that resistance level. The saucer pattern can be very powerful if it is at the bottom of a chart after a long descent and if it is accompanied by a substantial volume increase during the breakout.

A relative of the saucer pattern is one identified by newspaper publisher and author William O'Neil as the "cup with handle" pattern (which he introduced in his 1988 book, *How to Make Money in Stocks*). This pattern has a saucer shape, but instead of breaking above resistance, it pauses and hammers out a smaller, shallower saucer referred to as the handle. When the pattern is complete, it roughly resembles an edge-on view of a teacup. It is formed in this manner:

- Sellers are in control of the market as the stock price decreases (this is the left side of the cup).
- An equilibrium is created between buyers and sellers as the price stabilizes (this is the base of the cup).
- A rise in price takes place as buying interest and strength increase (this is the right side of the cup).
- A hesitation on the part of the market occurs as the price again moves away from resistance, but not nearly as deep as before.
- A renewed interest in the stock comes about, completed by a breakout above resistance (this completes the handle and the entire pattern).

FIGURE 11.1 This chart of Red Hat shows an almost perfect cup with handle formation: The left side is a well-formed cup, and the right side is a much smaller dip, forming the handle. The volume also increases substantially on the breakout.

Figure 11.1 shows an outstanding example of this pattern. For nearly two years, the price for Red Hat (symbol RHAT) fluctuated in what probably seemed at the time to be a relatively random fashion. In retrospect, it is easy to see the formation. This pattern has been highlighted with the straight lines on the chart to emphasize where the saucer and the handle are.

Notice also the change in volume, highlighted in the lower-right portion of the chart. Volume begins to swell as the handle completes, and when the breakout takes place, volume increases dramatically. This is an extremely bullish sign for the stock, since it affirms a significant increase in interest among buyers of the stock.

What happened following this breakout (Figure 11.2) is typical of well-formed cup with handle patterns: the stock increased in value significantly. In this case, the stock went up by 200 percent in less than one year. Carefully selected call options would have had even more sensational gains than this.

In the last chapter, we saw that saucer patterns can repeat for a stock. In fact, if you notice that a particular stock is prone to a particular pattern, it is likely that you will see that same pattern in the future with that stock.

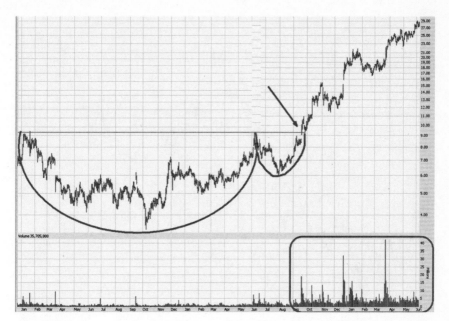

FIGURE 11.2 Following the breakout, indicated by the arrow, Red Hat tripled in price. Volume also remained strong during this period.

The same holds true for the cup with handle pattern, and Red Hat again provides us with a fitting example (Figure 11.3). After the initial pattern and 200 percent increase in price, illustrated in Figures 11.1 and 11.2, the stock price eased back significantly. It then began forming another (smaller) cup with handle pattern, and as before, the stock nearly tripled in price. Both of these breakouts are highlighted with arrows on the graph.

Before continuing, one other fact that should be pointed out is that these price charts are split-adjusted. For long-term charts, this can be extremely significant. A stock split has the effect of reducing the price of a stock in proportion to the number of the new shares issued. As a simple example, assume a stock had five million shares on the market and had a price of $100. Further assume that the board of directors for this company approved a two-for-one stock split. Assuming no further price movement in the stock, on the day of the split, the stock would be priced at $50 (half the former price) and 10 million shares would be outstanding (twice as many as before). So the value of the stock as a whole hasn't changed, although the division of the company's shares has.

When you are looking at the chart of a stock that has split a number of times, the price of the shares many years ago may seem extremely cheap. That is simply a result of the prices being adjusted to take account of the

FIGURE 11.3 Red Hat actually had two cup with handle patterns in this chart, and in each instance, the stock approximately tripled in value.

splits. If the chart showed the actual price for every day of the stock's history, the chart would be useless for a technician, because it would have huge gaps in the price every time a split took place. Using split-adjusted data is essential for analyzing the chart, which explains why a stock that traded for $75 in 1974 might show up with a price of $1 during the same time frame when you examine its graph in the present day.

As you have read earlier in this book, the length and strength of a pattern are often related. 3M Corporation provides a remarkable example of a very large cup with handle pattern and its resulting price movement. Figure 11.4 shows a cup being formed from 1974 through 1983 and a handle being formed from 1983 to 1986. Although this is an exceptionally well-formed pattern, even a pattern this good isn't smooth. We are, after all, not looking at a drawing of a physical cup. This is price movement measured over thousands of days, so you can expect a relatively high amount of noise. The experienced chartist learns to filter this out so the pattern is easy to discern. The resistance (on a split-adjusted basis) was at about $1.03, which was hit in 1974, 1983, and 1986.

Figure 11.5 shows one of those kinds of charts that make a person wish for a time machine—3M increased 85-fold in price. A $10,000 investment at the breakout in 1986 would have grown to $850,000 by 2004. There is a

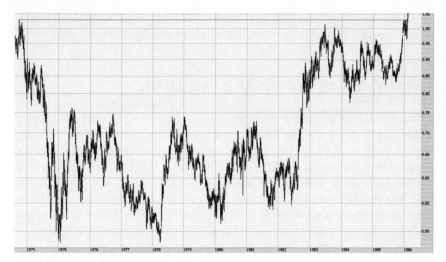

FIGURE 11.4 3M forms a massive cup with handle pattern over a 12-year period.

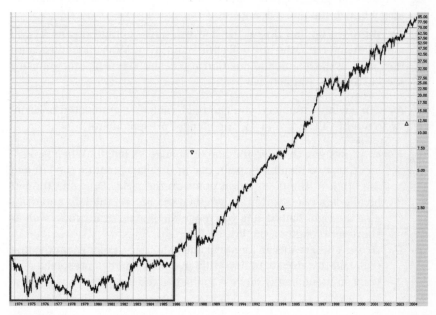

FIGURE 11.5 Following the breakout from the pattern, 3M went on to an incredible 8,500 percent gain.

rectangle drawn around the cup with handle pattern in the lower-left portion of the graph, and the rise afterward was virtually uninterrupted.

USING THE HORIZONTAL LINE TOOL

You learned how to use the trendline tool in Chapter 8 and the channel tool in Chapter 9. Now we can learn about what is the simplest (but still very useful) tool on the toolbar, the horizontal line tool (Figure 11.6). As the name states, the purpose of this tool is to draw a horizontal line. You could do the same thing with the trendline tool, but if you want a perfectly flat line, it is much easier to simply use the horizontal line tool instead. This is ideal for drawing resistance and support levels, which makes it handy for patterns such as saucers, rounded tops, and cup with handle patterns.

To put a horizontal line on your chart, do the following:

1. Click on the horizontal line tool, as shown in Figure 11.6.
2. Click on the graph approximately at the place you want to place the line; a horizontal line will appear.
3. As you move up and down, the line will move up and down. As you move left and right, the line will shrink and grow. Move the mouse until the line is at the length and position you desire, then click the mouse a second time to complete it.

As with any drawn object, you can right-click on a completed horizontal line to modify it (Figure 11.7). The choices presented are:

Move: Allows you to move the line or change its length. When you select this, two handles appear: one at the start point on the left and the other at the completion point on the right. Dragging the left handle lets you shorten or lengthen the line on the left, and dragging the right handle lets you move the line up or down as well as shorten or lengthen the line on the right.
Duplicate: This creates an identical line (same size, color) near the first one, and this duplicate line will have both handles preselected so you can immediately move it to the desired location.

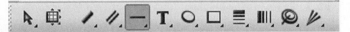

FIGURE 11.6 The horizontal tool is the fifth selection on the toolbar, located between the channel and text tools.

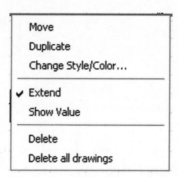

FIGURE 11.7 Right-clicking on a horizontal line produces this pop-up menu to modify the object.

Change Style/Color: Brings up the same dialog box as was shown in Figure 8.16, allowing you to change the color, opacity, weight, and pattern of the line. You can also preserve these settings so they are used as the default for all future horizontal line drawings.

Extend: As with the same option for trendlines, the Extend function makes the horizontal line extend infinitely into the future.

Show Value: Choosing this puts the price value (that is, the y-axis value) on the top left of the line so you can read what the support or resistance level is for the line you've drawn.

Delete: Choosing this deletes the selected line. If you make a mistake, you can always undo your decision with the Undo command (Ctrl-Z).

Delete All Drawings: Choosing this deletes all the drawn objects on the current chart. If you make a mistake, you can always undo your decision with the Undo command (Ctrl-Z).

MORE CUP WITH HANDLE EXAMPLES

Not all patterns are as perfect as the ones we have seen so far. Let's look at some other historical examples to help train your eyes to find these patterns in your own analysis. Figure 11.8 shows an example of a somewhat rougher cup with handle. But even though there is a lot of noise in the chart, the rules we established early in the chapter still hold here: we have a saucer (albeit a rough one) followed by a smaller, shallower saucer on the right, completed by a breakout above resistance.

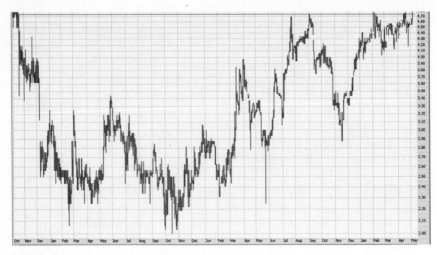

FIGURE 11.8 The stock ACMR consolidated between $2 and $4.70 over a period of several years while creating this pattern.

The arrow in Figure 11.9 shows where the stock ACMR pushed above its resistance level to enjoy a fivefold increase in price. The shape and clarity of the pattern are much easier to see on this scale. Only those who are able to discern the pattern at the time of the breakout are the ones who wind up profiting. Finding patterns in retrospect once they are much cleaner and easier to see is simply an academic exercise.

The stock CNP provides another example of a stock that increased fivefold subsequent to its pattern (Figure 11.10). This basing behavior took a while to complete, spanning 1977 to 1985.

Patient observers of this stock were rewarded, as Figure 11.11 shows. We see here another important aspect of stocks that perform well: a series of higher highs and higher lows. In 1989, 1994, 1997, and 2001, the stock sank to short-term lows. But every one of these lows was higher than the prior low, and every subsequent high was higher than the prior high. This stairstep movement can be frustrating and nerve-wracking for holders of the stock, but in the aggregate, that's where major profits are made.

The next example illustrates the largest return of any of the charts in this chapter. The stock is EMC, and Figure 11.12 shows how the stock moved between a 6-cent and 26-cent range (split-adjusted) in the late 1980s and early 1990s. Those trading the stock at the time perhaps were frustrated at its performance. During just a couple of trading sessions, the stock lost more than half its value (plunging from a split-adjusted 26 cents to 10 cents). But once the pattern was complete, an amazing thing happened.

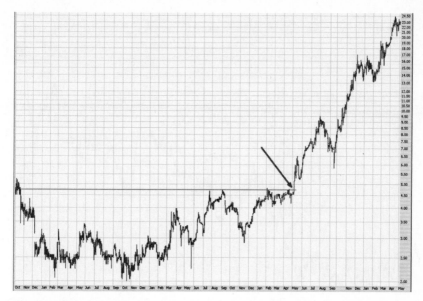

FIGURE 11.9 ACMR increased approximately fivefold after the breakout from the cup and handle pattern.

As you can see in Figure 11.13, after the stock pushed its way past the horizontal line at the 26-cent level, it ascended to above $100, which is about a 400-fold increase. Here again we could use that time machine: a $10,000 investment in 1992 would have grown to $4 million in a mere eight years. (The small arrows on the chart, remember, point out the times that the six stock splits took place).

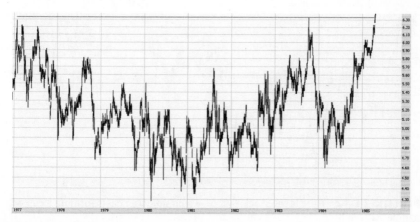

FIGURE 11.10 CNP shows an almost perfect pattern here as it creates a base beneath the $6.30 level.

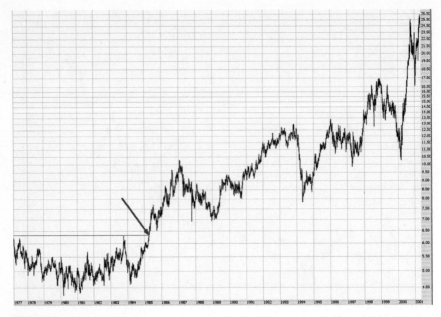

FIGURE 11.11 CNP proceeded to a nearly fivefold increase with a series of higher highs and higher lows.

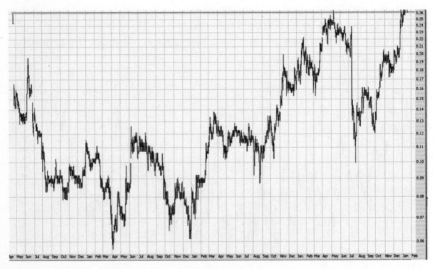

FIGURE 11.12 Here is the stock EMC on a split-adjusted basis forming a cup with handle pattern in the late 1980s and early 1990s.

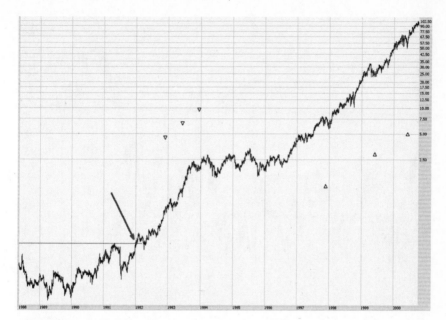

FIGURE 11.13 EMC enjoyed a spectacular 400-fold increase in value after its cup with handle pattern was complete.

Before we get too carried away with such astronomical returns, let us look at two more cup with handle examples with more typical changes in value. Figure 11.14 shows the symbol MTW sporting a cup with handle pattern that has a couple of interesting properties. First, the time length of the cup and the length of the handle are about the same. Second, if you examine the handle closely, it seems to be itself a smaller cup with handle pattern. There is nothing wrong with either of these nuances of the chart. Patterns aren't the same for every chart in every time frame. As you gain experience looking at hundreds of different charts, you will learn to be flexible (within reason) as to what constitutes a winning pattern.

Once again, the arrow highlights for us the point in time when the price pushed above resistance, eventually moving from $4 to about $57. Owners of this stock would not have suffered some of the severe ups and downs of other equities, as the ascent of MTW was relatively uninterrupted (Figure 11.15).

One final example of this pattern (before we look at some pattern failures) is stock ticker PTR, which sports a rather dainty handle on its right side (Figure 11.16). It should be pointed out once again that often the best stocks are those that already seem too expensive. When this stock made its way above resistance, you would have been fair to observe that it had

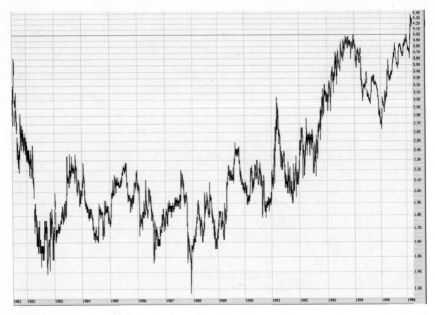

FIGURE 11.14 Here the stock MTW consolidates below the $4 resistance level before breaking above it.

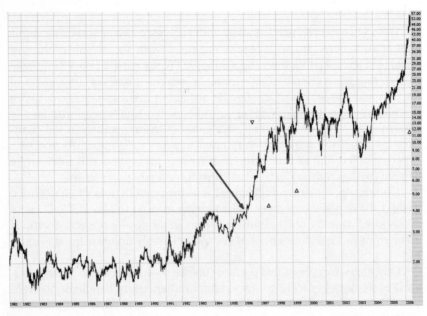

FIGURE 11.15 MTW went up virtually uninterrupted after completing the pattern, rising more than fourteenfold.

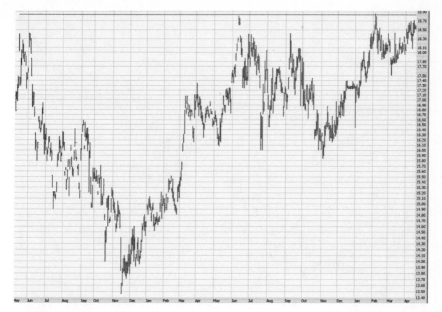

FIGURE 11.16 Here the stock PTR forms a nice pattern beneath the resistance level at $18.50.

already doubled in price in just a year. It might feel too risky to buy into the stock. The more potent fact, however, is that it was moving out of a very large, reliable pattern.

Taking the risk by buying into this expensive stock paid off remarkably for those who bought. The price increased from the breakout point (see arrow) to about $125 in only a couple of years (Figure 11.17).

These examples might seem to make it easy to get huge returns on stocks, as long as you can locate the right pattern. This is not always the case. Any pattern is prone to failure, and when a pattern fails, you should get out of the position immediately. The final portion of this chapter looks at these failures and their signs.

PATTERN FAILURES

Take a look at the chart in Figure 11.18. It seems very similar to many of the other charts shown in this chapter, and a person would be perfectly reasonable to buy into this stock and anticipate handsome gains. This is, after all, virtually a textbook example of what a cup with handle pattern should look like.

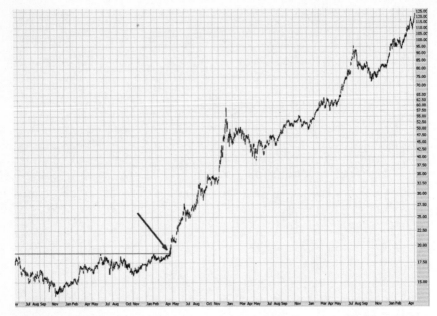

FIGURE 11.17 The stock PTR went on to a more than sixfold increase in price after the pattern was complete.

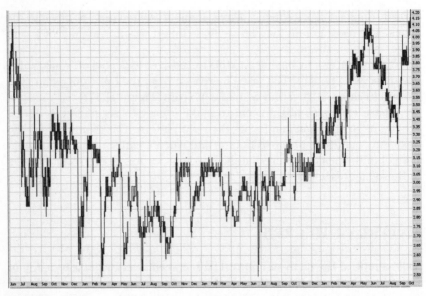

FIGURE 11.18 Here is a virtually perfect cup with handle pattern of the stock symbol SM.

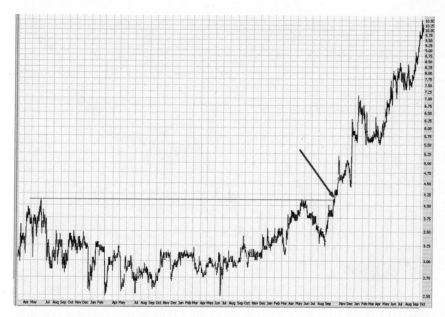

FIGURE 11.19 The break above the cup with handle by SM propelled the stock to an approximate 150 percent increase.

And in fact, buyers of this stock would have been delighted with the short-term results of their purchase. The stock, ticker symbol SM, increased in value by 150 percent in less than a year (Figure 11.19).

But there's more to the story than this. Figure 11.20 shows the initial breakout (with an arrow), the rapid increase in price, and then—surprisingly—the just as rapid decrease in price. By 1998, every bit of profit in this position would have been wiped out, and you actually would be holding onto a losing position. This would be terribly disheartening to those who had ridden the stock to a 150 percent profit only to see it disintegrate into a loss. (It should be noted, in the long term, the stock went on to fabulous gains later, but in 1998 we would not have had the benefit of a graph extending years into the future!)

How could such a loss have been avoided? How could we have at least preserved a portion of the profits after that initial 150 percent increase? Every chart is different, of course, but in this case, it probably would have been best to monitor the stock for its series of higher highs and higher lows. As long as the stock was ascending with a pattern of higher highs and higher lows, it would be a solid hold. When the price cut beneath one of the prior lows, however, it would have been a good time to get out. In this instance, it would have meant a profit of about 50 percent (instead of

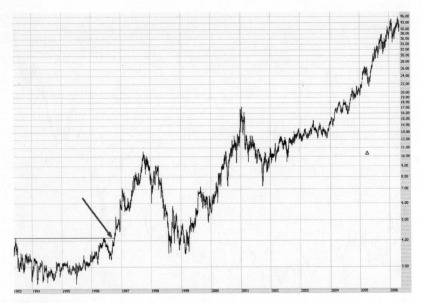

FIGURE 11.20 The price violated the support zone established by the cup with handle pattern. In spite of this, the stock ultimately went on to a more than 10-fold increase in value.

150 percent), but that's certainly a lot better than the loss that would have ensued if the position had simply been held in spite of its price action.

One of the most popular securities on the market is the QQQ, often referred to as the "cubes" and with the ticker symbol QQQQ. This ETF tracks the performance of the NASDAQ 100 stocks, and the chart in Figure 11.21 shows the QQQ with a well-formed cup with handle and a resistance level of about $40.20. At the time of this chart, the price pushed cleanly past this resistance level, portending good times for this security.

Look at the longer-term price perspective in Figure 11.22, however. The price breakout is indicated by the arrow, and as you can see, the price moved up to $42, sank back down to the former resistance level, pushed higher once again to $43.50, and sank once again to the resistance level, ascending yet again (but not as high as the last time), and then finally gave up and fell hard.

This certainly wasn't the result expected. The QQQ seemed to cling to the $40.20 line and fell to that level repeatedly. On its fourth fall down to that level, it no longer had the support from buyers that it needed, and it sank far beneath the initial breakout point. A person steadfastly holding onto this position would have had a substantial loss.

The "higher highs, higher lows" would also have been helpful here. It would not take long to see that no such pattern was forming, and the

FIGURE 11.21 Based on this pattern, it seemed that QQQQ was well-positioned for a substantial price increase.

FIGURE 11.22 In spite of the cup with handle pattern and the subsequent price action above resistance, QQQQ ultimately fell well below its former resistance level.

position could be closed. At a minimum, however, a stop price should always be set just beneath the former resistance level. In this instance, any price action below $40.20 would be cause to immediately close out the position. Even if it means sacrificing former profits, at least you keep your losses to an absolute minimum.

DIAMONDS AND DEAD-CAT BOUNCES

That is surely one of the more peculiar headings in this book, but both of these are real terms in the world of technical analysis.

A diamond pattern is formed when a stock's price swings gets increasingly wide, and then increasingly narrow, resulting in roughly a diamond shape when trendlines are applied. This pattern can be bearish or bullish, depending on whether the price breaks above or below the pattern.

Figure 11.23 shows DirectTV Group in a diamond pattern spanning from about $18.50 to $28.50. Once it broke out of this pattern to the upside, it quickly climbed to the mid 30s. The diamond pattern is worthy

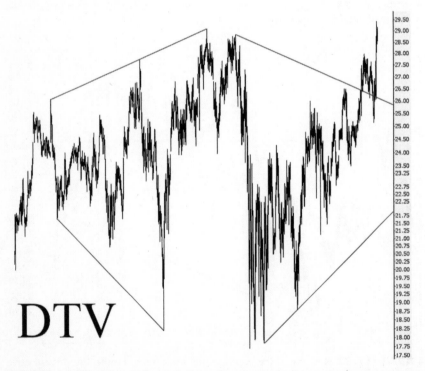

FIGURE 11.23 DirectTV's stock formed a diamond pattern that spanned three years and presaged a strong push higher in price.

of special note, not only because it is rare but also because it is one of the more reliable technical patterns.

Diamond patterns are just as potent on the bearish side. During the tremendous commodity boom in the summer of 2008, Alpha Natural Resources (ANR) spent almost that entire summer hammering out a well-formed diamond pattern. When the pattern was broken to the downside, ANR lost about 85 percent of its value in just a few months, as shown in Figure 11.24.

There is also a circumstance in technical trading known as a dead-cat bounce, which is much less well-defined than other patterns we've

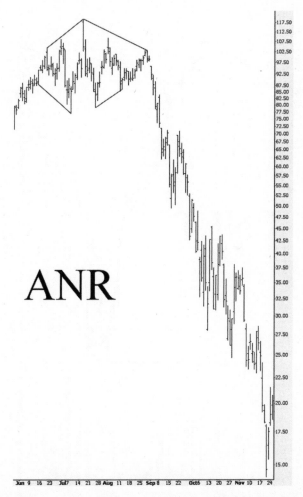

FIGURE 11.24 Between August and November 2008, ANR lost about 85 percent of its equity value, which was predicted by the preceding diamond pattern.

discussed. As the name implies, the dead-cat bounce refers to an equity that has plunged so sharply in value that, at some point, it will probably bounce up in price from a sharply oversold condition.

In the financial crisis of 2008–2009, there were hundreds of stocks that lost more than 90 percent of their peak value. In many cases, these stocks gained hundreds or even thousands of percent after they bounced off their March 2009 lows. Lodgnet Interactive, shown in Figure 11.25, climbed about 1200 percent off its March 2008 lows after having lost 98 percent of its value before.

The reason dead-cat bounces are enticing has to do with simple arithmetic: it is impossible to make anything more than 100 percent on a short

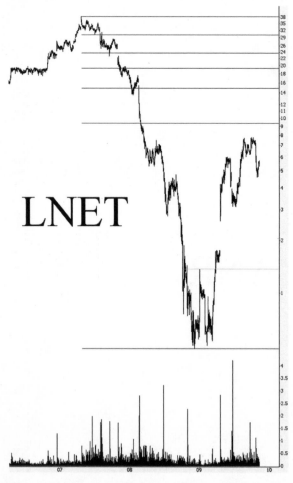

FIGURE 11.25 Lodgenet went from about $36 to 50 cents during the crisis of 2008, only to recover a portion of that loss shortly thereafter.

sale, whereas the potential profits from a long position are unlimited. If you had the impeccable timing to short LNET at its peak and cover the position at its precise bottom, you would have made a handsome 98 percent return.

However, a long position (over a much shorter time span) would have yielded 1200 percent with the dead-cat bounce. So even though the vast majority of people who had ever bought LNET were still in losing positions after this 1200 percent bounce; if you had entered anywhere near the bottom, the percentage gain would have been fantastic.

An even more remarkable example is found with Pier 1 Imports (Figure 11.26), which, having lost almost all its equity value, bounced 4300 percent. To put that in concrete terms, a $10,000 investment on March

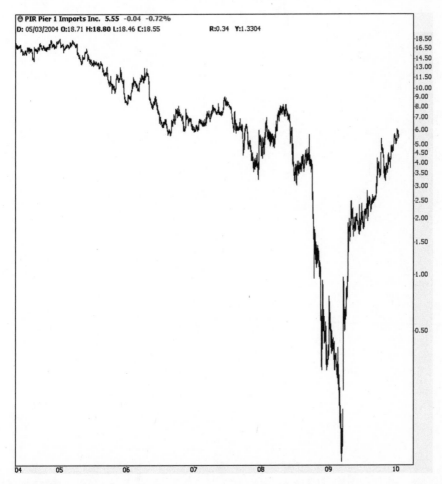

FIGURE 11.26 Pier-1 Imports fell from the lower $20s to merely a dime in price, after which it dramatically climbed 4300 percent in half a year.

13 would have been worth over half a million dollars exactly six months later. Keep in mind that such events are exceedingly rare, but this amplifies the potential of such dead-cat bounces (even though some stocks never bounce and simply drift into worthless bankruptcy).

It is all too easy to read a book like this and believe that making a fortune in the stock market is as simple as hunting down patterns similar to those found here. This is simply not the case. These patterns represent idealized examples seen with the benefit of hindsight. As you gain experience in charting, viewing thousands, tens of thousands, and ultimately hundreds of thousands of charts, you will be able to find patterns more reliably and—far more important—trade them successfully without the benefit of hindsight that is possible with historical examples.

CHAPTER 12

Multiple Tops
and Bottoms

This chapter discusses two new, related subjects: how to emphasize particular parts of a chart with highlighting and text, and how to recognize and profit from multiple tops and bottoms. When a chart is in the process of creating a multiple top or bottom, it is helpful to be able to highlight these zones as it is happening.

HIGHLIGHTING CHARTS

It is almost certain you have used a wide variety of highlighter pens. These pens allow you to draw a see-through stripe (usually in yellow) on top of text in order to call it out as important. For instance, when reading a textbook, you may highlight certain portions so that when you reread it, you can focus on just the most important parts of the text.

That is precisely the idea behind both highlighter tools in ProphetCharts. Each of them does the same thing: produces a see-through color in either an oval or rectangular shape (depending on the tool selected). You can control how transparent the color is as well as what color is used.

You may be wondering what kinds of things you would want to highlight. The answer is anything that merits attention. It could be a huge gap in a chart, a series of tops or bottoms, an area of consolidation, or an interesting price pattern. Just as with any of the other drawn objects, the principle is to embellish the chart in such a way that it is more meaningful to you both now and in the future.

FIGURE 12.1 The oval highlighting tool.

Applying a highlight to a chart is very simple:

1. Choose the tool you want; in this example, we'll use the oval tool (Figure 12.1).
2. Click on the graph in the place you want to start drawing the oval.
3. Drag the mouse until the oval is the shape and location you desire, then click the mouse once more.

An example oval is shown in Figure 12.2. Any oval has several properties: location, size, color, and opacity. (Opacity is the opposite of transparency; the more opaque something is, the more difficult it is to see through it.) This particular oval might be representing an important bottom in a stock's chart.

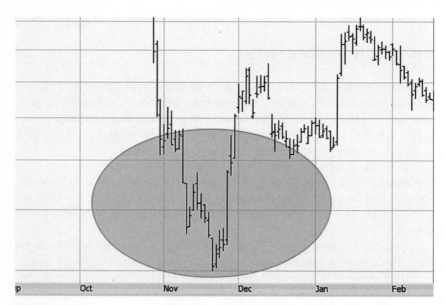

FIGURE 12.2 An oval highlight drawn on a chart to emphasize a bottom in price action.

FIGURE 12.3 The rectangle highlight tool.

Applying a rectangular highlight to a chart is achieved in the exact same manner as for an oval, with the exception that you choose the rectangle highlight tool (Figure 12.3) first.

The chart in Figure 12.4 provides an example of the effective use of a rectangular highlight. This is a chart of the Dow Jones Industrial Average spanning from about November 2005 through July 2006. The index bounced off firm support at the 10,660 level on numerous occasions. The purpose of this highlight is to show this support zone and to emphasize the consequences to the market should the zone be violated. (By the time you read this, you will be aware of how things turned out! As of this writing, the market has no such knowledge.)

Once you have put a highlight onto a chart, you can right-click on it and choose from a number of options via a pop-up menu. The first is Move, which, as with the other drawn objects, lets you reshape the object with the anchors that are displayed. The second, Duplicate, creates a copy of the object nearby the original with the anchors preselected. This is a quick way of creating multiple highlights. And the third, Change Style/Color, invokes a dialog box (Figure 12.5) so you can adjust the appearance of the highlight.

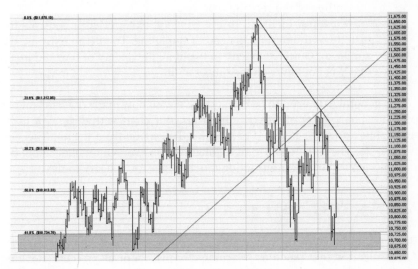

FIGURE 12.4 A rectangle highlight, which emphasizes the support zone for this index.

FIGURE 12.5　This dialog box lets you change the highlight's color and opacity.

Altering the settings from this dialog box will change the settings only for the selected object. This means you can have a variety of styles of highlight on one chart. The various elements you can alter via this dialog box are:

Color: Select from any of 15 available highlight colors

Fill Opacity: This number ranges from 0 (there is no color at all) to 1.0 (it is as dark as it can be, even though you can still see the price bars).

Outline Weight: This is a dropdown of five different selections, ranging from skinny to fat. It controls how thick the line is that constitutes the outline of the rectangle or oval.

Outline Opacity: Identical to Fill Opacity, except that it controls the opacity of the outline instead of the filling. To cite an extreme example, an Outline Opacity of 0 and a Fill Opacity of 0 would mean that you couldn't see the object at all.

In general, you want to be conservative with how many objects you put onto any chart. After all, if you clutter up your chart with dozens of lines, highlights, and other items, it becomes a distraction from the analysis you have to do. The judicious use of highlights, however, can make seeing the most germane parts of price action much easier for you day-to-day.

ADDING TEXT NOTES

ProphetCharts gives you the ability to put text onto a chart in two forms—as raw text (such as "Earnings Surprise") or as an icon (for long text notes, or in case you just don't want text all over your chart). Even

FIGURE 12.6 The text tool.

though text and a highlight color may seem very different, their purpose is similar: to call attention to something special happening at a particular point in time on a chart. In the case of text, you might describe management changes, product introductions, earnings announcements, or certain actions you took in your own trading with respect to the security being charted.

Putting a text note on a chart involves these steps:

1. Click on the text tool (Figure 12.6).
2. Click on the place on the chart where you want the text message to go.
3. A dialog box will appear. Type the text you want, and then click OK.

The text you entered now appears on the chart with a left-pointing arrow at the left side of the text. The assumption is that you'll want to point out something on the price chart, and the arrow will assist with that reference.

In step 3 of entering a text note, you are given a text note dialog box to type in the note. Besides having an area to enter the note, you are also given a radio button with two choices: Text On Chart and Icon (Figure 12.7). The default is Text On Chart. If you click on the Icon radio button, then instead

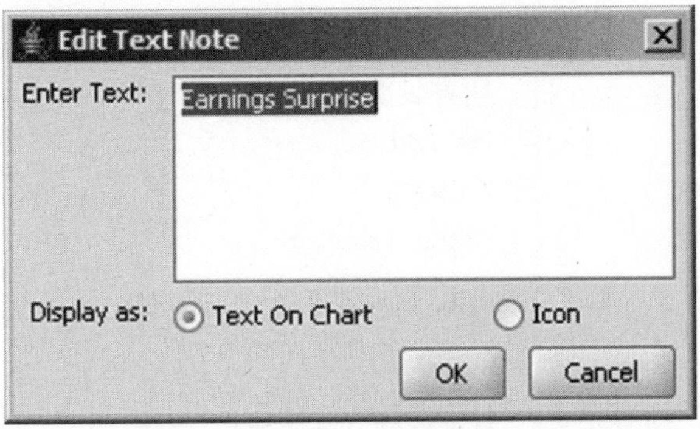

FIGURE 12.7 This dialog box lets you enter and edit a text note.

of text appearing on the chart, a small icon will be there. When you point the mouse cursor at that icon, the text note will appear in a similar fashion as a tool tip. You can put as many text icons on a chart as you like. If you intend to mark up a chart with a lot of text notes, using icons is a good way to keep the chart from being overly cluttered (unless you want all of the text visible at once).

As with the other drawn objects, text can be altered if you right-click on it. The pop-up menu (Figure 12.8) provides these choices (note that, at the bottom, Delete and Delete All Drawings have consistent functionality across all objects, so there's no need to go into that pair for every kind of object type):

Move: Clicking this lets you drag the text item anywhere you want on the chart. Unlike other objects, it does not have anchors. The entire note (or icon) can simply be dragged by clicking on it and dragging the mouse, so you can place it precisely where you like. Once you are satisfied with the new location, click anywhere else on the chart to finish with the placement.

Edit Text: This invokes the same dialog box you saw when you entered the text note in the first place. You can change the text or change from a text note to an icon (or vice versa).

Duplicate: This creates a copy of the same text note in the same style, which you can immediately move to the desired location.

Change Font/Color: This is described in detail next. Note that this feature is not relevant if you choose to show the text note as an icon.

Hide Arrow: Removes the left-pointing arrow. If you are not really pointing out something on the price chart, you might want to suppress the arrow. Note that this feature is not relevant if you choose to show the text note as an icon.

Move

Edit Text...

Duplicate

Change Font/Color

Hide Arrow

Delete

Delete All Drawings

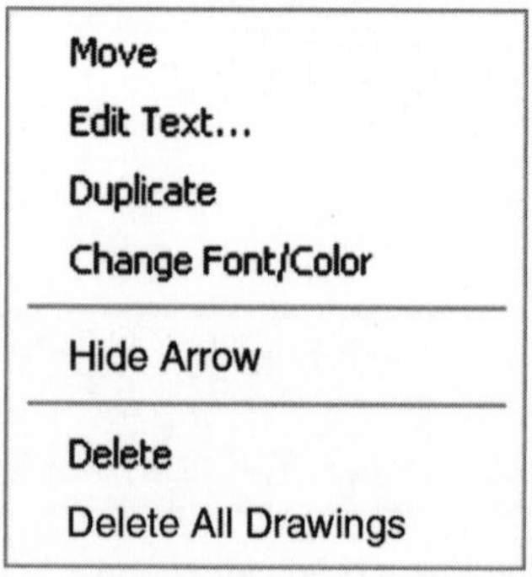

FIGURE 12.8   This pop-up menu appears when you right-click on a text object.

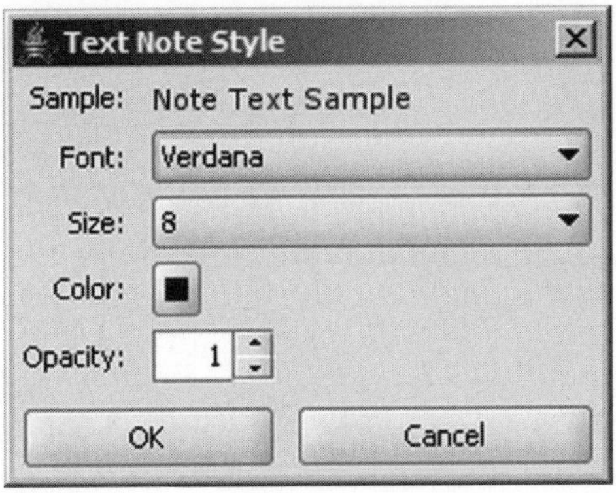

FIGURE 12.9 You can alter many aspects of the text note's appearance.

The selection Change Font/Color invokes another dialog box (Figure 12.9) that provides a number of choices. The Font dropdown lets you choose from any of the dozens of fonts available on your operating system. The Size dropdown lets you select a size ranging from tiny (8 point) to gigantic (72 point). Clicking on Color lets you choose from any of the 15 available colors. Lastly, the Opacity function lets you alter the opacity to be anywhere from 0 (invisible) to 1 (solid). As you modify Font, Color, and Opacity, the words "Note Text Sample" at the top will change to represent that font, color, and opacity. This sample will not change based on the Size, however, since it would be impractical to fit very large text in this small space.

As a final remark on text notes, making use of icons for large quantities of text information is illustrated by Figure 12.10. Notice how the rightmost text icon has the text displayed. This is because the mouse is pointing at this icon.

HIGHER HIGHS AND HIGHER LOWS

The simplest and most reliable indicator of a stock's strength can be determined by seeing if the price chart is making a consistent series of higher highs and higher lows. You may want to read and reread that sentence a dozen times, because it's crucially important and ties into so much of what technical analysis is all about. The reason this sentence is true can be illustrated with Figure 12.11, a real stock shown over a period of almost a decade.

Over this period, the stock increased nearly 10-fold in value. It didn't get there overnight, and it didn't get there in a straight line. First, it went up

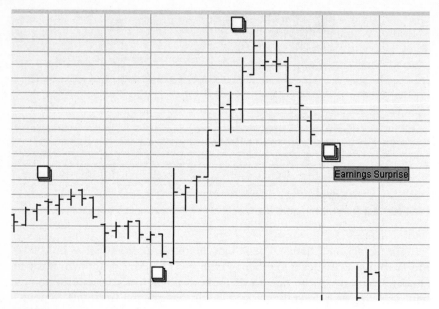

FIGURE 12.10 Multiple text notes are displayed in the form of icons.

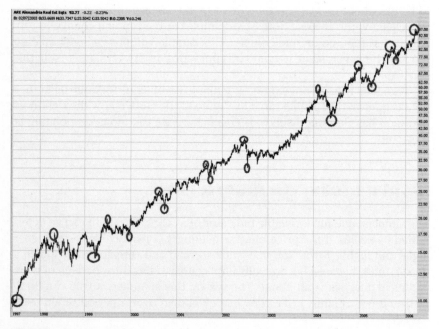

FIGURE 12.11 Alexandria Real Estate stock went up about 900 percent with a steady series of higher highs and higher lows.

a while. Then the market digested its gains and the stock decreased. Then the stock regained its strength and pushed on to a new high. Then it eased back again, not quite as low as before. Then it pushed on to yet another new lifetime high. Then it eased back once more, again, not quite so low.

This backing and filling process kept going on for years, and for the long-term investor, the results were marvelous. The core truth here, though, is that through thousands of days in both bull and bear markets, the buying interest of the stock consistently outweighed the selling interest. In other words, the bulls maintained control over the bears, because even when the stock went to a low, it was a higher low than the low before. The graph of this stock has small circles drawn on it to better illustrate this series of higher highs and higher lows.

A stock with a similar pattern is shown in Figure 12.12. The growth of this stock is even more clear, since there is an ascending trendline placed on the chart to indicate support. As with the prior chart, this one has a steady progression of higher highs and higher lows. A person owning this stock, so long as this situation does not change, will probably want to remain in the stock. If they see the next high fail to supersede the prior one, or worse, they see a low that is beneath the prior low, they may conclude the stock has run its course.

FIGURE 12.12 Avalon Bay Communities held above its ascending trendline in the course of making higher highs and higher lows.

FIGURE 12.13 Taser International was a phenomenal stock until it broke its series of higher highs and higher lows. Not long after, it started to sink badly.

Let's take a look at what happens when "higher highs, higher lows" fails. Figure 12.13 shows the chart for Taser International. From March 2003 through April 2004, it is difficult to chart the higher highs and higher lows simply because the stock seemed to do little but go straight up. The rise during this period was about 8,500 percent! Taser was the darling of the financial media, and there's no doubt someone holding this stock would have had no reason to sell it based on any lower low.

However, things started going wrong with the stock after April 2004. The next low it made was indeed a lower low, which broke the series. The stock gathered its strength again, but the next high it made before descending once more did not exceed the prior high. (Note the arrow drawn on Figure 12.13, showing the lower high.) At this point, as the saying goes, the writing was on the wall. The stock managed to push its way higher, ultimately even achieving a new lifetime high in January 2005. The damage had been done, though, and at that point, the stock lost over 80 percent of its value.

The main point of this story is to remain on the watch for a break in the "higher highs, higher lows" series, because as crude a measure as it is, it usually marks an important turning point. All of this holds true in the converse for stocks in bearish formations as well. If a stock is making a series of lower highs and lower lows, it will probably continue moving downward until that series is broken. So if you are short a stock which is making "lower highs, lower lows," it is best to hold onto it until a higher high is made. Even if you have no position in the stock, this change in trend might mark a valuable buying opportunity for a stock that has been descending for a while.

MULTIPLE TOPS

Part of the reason for discussing higher highs, higher lows is to prepare for the analysis of multiple tops and bottoms. After a stock has moved steadily higher for a while, it sometimes creates a series of similar highs, indicating a pause in that stock's upward momentum. This is a resistance level. There are really just two things a stock can do in a situation like this: finally push its way past resistance, moving on to a new high, or succumb to the resistance and fail to overcome it, often falling hard in the process.

Just as the cessation of higher highs and higher lows can mark a turning point in a stock's general direction, the establishment of a series of similar highs (that is, a multiple top) can indicate the ends of a stock's rise and, perhaps, a turning point. Let us turn our attention to Figure 12.14, which is the stock for Chesapeake Energy. As you can see, generally speaking, the stock was a fantastic performer, providing its shareholders with terrific returns for many years.

Taking a closer look at the stock's behavior in Figure 12.15, we can see that after the stock hit yet another all-time high of about $33, it eased back, moved up to about $33 again, eased back once more, pushed higher to $33, and eased back yet again. It is as if the stock had hit a wall and could not overcome this resistance level. In real-world terms, what was going on was that buyers and sellers had found a point of equilibrium at about $33. At that level, there was insufficient buying interest to propel the stock any higher, and it kept falling back.

There was a clear signal at this point that perhaps the days of a steadily ascending stock were a thing of the past. Unless the stock could gather the resolve to push past these prices, the sellers would maintain the upper hand. Indeed, the sellers started to overwhelm the buyers, and as Figure 12.16 plainly shows, this multiple top preceded an absolutely devastating loss in value in which the entirety of the gains shareholders had enjoyed were laid waste.

The best way to deepen our understanding of multiple tops is through the examination of more examples, so let's proceed with those. Figure 12.17 shows high-flier Alexion as it made its way from $5 to $120.

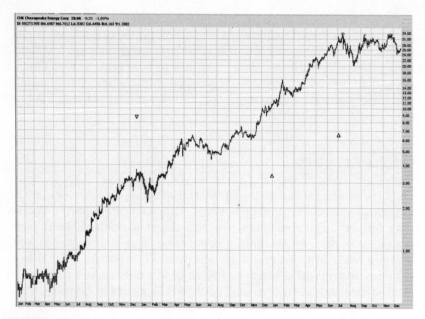

FIGURE 12.14 This stock made a consistent series of higher highs for most of this time period.

FIGURE 12.15 Here we see instance after instance of the stock hitting the $33 level and falling back due to selling pressure.

FIGURE 12.16 The triple top circled here gave a clear warning signal that preceded a complete wipeout of the stock's price.

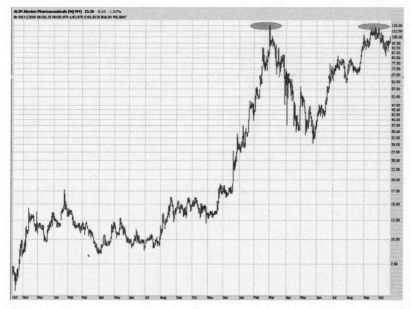

FIGURE 12.17 Alexion makes two impressive runs at the $120 price point, showing a possible double top formation.

The first highlighted oval indicates the initial peak in the stock price, and then it lost about 75 percent of its value. It subsequently regained its footing and managed to work its way back to its former peak, eliminating the entire 75 percent loss.

Think of the mind-set of the holders of this stock at about this time. Everyone who has bought this stock is in a winning position—some of them exceptionally so. Longer-term holders have held on through a breathtaking collapse in stock price, only to see the stock rally 300 percent to match its prior high. Everyone long the stock wants the same thing—for it to go higher—but owners are understandably nervous.

This is the kind of tenuous situation in which a stock can make a multiple top. It either is going to have such an exceptionally committed group of buyers that a new high price is reached, thus inciting even more interest, or people anxious to take profits overwhelm the buyers and the price simply matches the prior high.

As you can see in Figure 12.18, the latter is undoubtedly what took place with Alexion. During the second top, the price tried to push its way into a new high, day after day. After over a week of attempts, the stock finally started sinking due to selling pressure, and it really never looked

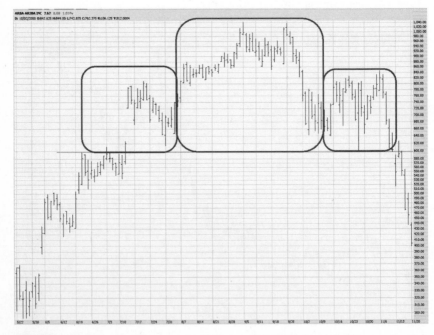

FIGURE 12.18 After the stock double-topped, ALXN lost nearly 92 percent of its peak value over the next couple of years.

back. By the time the selling was done, the stock had lost nearly 92 percent of its peak value.

The reason for the term "multiple top" is that there can be two, three, four, or even more tops. Whether the chart you are examining is forming a multiple top or is simply hitting a firm resistance level is a matter of discernment. After all, if a stock hits the same price 50 times in a row, it is not a multiple top; the stock has simply found a serious resistance level at which buyers and sellers are in a state of equal strength.

One core characteristic of a multiple top is that there is a reasonable amount of time space between the tops. Often, the longer the space between the tops, the better, because it illustrates that even under constantly changing market conditions, the stock still poops out at a certain level. A series of equal high prices over the course of a week is not a multiple top. A high price, followed by a protracted dip, followed by a roughly equal high price four weeks later would be a much better candidate for a multiple top pattern.

Figure 12.19, for instance, provides us a good example of a triple top. This is a very long-term chart, showing (on a split-adjusted basis) Huntington Bancshares (HBAN) ascending from a few pennies up to over $25.

FIGURE 12.19 Symbol HBAN started to stall at about $25, forming a series of multiple tops.

FIGURE 12.20 Multiple tops can happen many months apart from one another, as long as a consistent high price is being hit.

The three tops (not to be confused with the musical group) took place over an 18-month period. Even though the stock price fluctuated between $15 and $25—a huge range—the stock kept bumping up against the $25 price point and retreating. As you can see in Figure 12.20, by the third instance the holders of the stock had enough frustration and increased the selling pressure.

Once the triple top was in place, the price succumbed and fell from $25 to under $10 in a little over a year (Figure 12.21). Owners of this stock who were armed with this knowledge would have had ample opportunity to get out of the stock near its high.

The skill in being able to pick out a multiple top while it is happening is to be able to clearly spot the high prices among the noise of the regular ups and downs of trading activity. Take Tower Automotive, for instance (Figure 12.22). During 1998 and 1999, the stock fluctuated between about $16 and $28. If you look for the highest highs during this period, two of them stand out—one in the second quarter of 1998 and the second in the middle of 1999.

One way to visually think of this is to imagine holding a ruler horizontal at the top of the chart and slowing bringing it down the graph. Once you

FIGURE 12.21 HBAN suffered a 60 percent price decline once the triple top was in place.

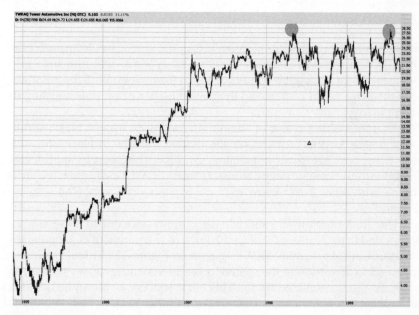

FIGURE 12.22 Tower Automotive had an impressive track record, scoring a high price in 1998 and matching that high the next year.

FIGURE 12.23   The effects of this multiple top were clear for more than six years after the pattern completed.

hit some touch points with the ruler, if they are spread out from each other by at least a few weeks and represent a fairly consistent new high price being hit, there is probably a multiple top in formation. (With the possibility that the price could push ahead to an even higher price, thus negating the multiple top.)

One interesting result of this double top was what a major turning point it was for this stock. After the double top was in place, the stock spent the next six years unraveling. By 2006, this security had disintegrated into the land of penny stocks (Figure 12.23). Once again, a chartist armed with some basic knowledge could have done very well with this insight.

One final example of a multiple top is impressive due to the quantity of tops it had in place: five of them, laid down over a period of 20 months. Dov Pharmaceuticals (symbol DOVP, shown in Figure 12.24) had risen from about $3 to about $20 in the span of a year. Over the next two years, however, the stock oscillated wildly. This chart was not a case of higher highs and higher lows. Instead, it was showing higher lows (which is good for bulls) and identical highs (which suggests a multiple top). A bull would want to see higher highs instead.

FIGURE 12.24 It is clear from this graph that $20 represented extremely strong resistance for this stock.

On five different instances, DOVP reached a price of about $20 and then softened. Note that the price does not have to be absolutely identical to create a multiple top. As long as the high prices are within a reasonable range—about 5 percent—they are close enough to qualify. As illustrated with Figure 12.25, after this quintuple multiple top was completed, the effect on the stock was horrific, destroying about 90 percent of the equity's value.

For bulls, multiple tops are an invaluable warning sign to get out and preserve profits. For bears, a multiple top can be a profitable signal to establish a short position in a stock and enjoy the ride down. Now we will turn our attention to the exact opposite pattern, the multiple bottom.

MULTIPLE BOTTOMS

Just about everything you have learned about multiple tops holds true for multiple bottoms, except that it is turned on its head. Just as the establishment of a multiple top suggests resistance, the establishment of a multiple bottom suggests support. Just as the exercise of sliding a (mental)

FIGURE 12.25 A quintuple top established by stock symbol DOVP preceded an almost complete destruction of the stock's value.

ruler from the top of a chart down until it hits similar highs can spot a multiple top in the making, so, too, can sliding the same mental ruler up from the bottom of a chart page. And just as the most valuable multiple tops are found after a prior prolonged rise in the stock's price, the most lucrative multiple bottoms can be found after an extended decline in a stock's price.

A fine example of this is Figure 12.26, which shows the price activity for Charter Communications (symbol CHTR). Over a 15-month period, the stock's price had fallen from $25 to about 70 cents. The stock then nearly tripled in price, only to sink back down again. Five months after the initial low was established, the stock hit this price once again before resuming its climb. It did not hit those lows again, and a double bottom was plainly in place, followed by a seven-fold increase in price.

The psychological value of a multiple bottom is that it helps convince the trading public that the selling is over. If a stock has been falling hard for a long time, it is comforting for the public to witness that a stock seems to be hammering out a bottom for itself and that it refuses to go any lower than a certain price point. The more times this low price point is hit without breaking, the more confident traders can be that this price level is a strong

FIGURE 12.26 This seven-fold rise in CHTR was preceded by an important double bottom price pattern.

support zone. Any stock that has been suffering a decline needs to show this line in the sand so that people aren't convinced the security is simply going to $0.

A different company (Charles & Colvard) with a nearly identical ticker symbol (CTHR) illustrates this point vividly. The stock certainly had suffered a harrowing loss, falling from $15 to about 50 cents. But on five different occasions, highlighted in Figure 12.27, the stock refused to go beneath a certain level. As is often the case, the stock was swinging wildly up and down during this time period, as buyers and sellers struggled with establishing leadership. Keep in mind also that, after such a serious decline, there would be a tremendous amount of suspicion with respect to the stock's ability to hold onto any price gains.

The time the stock spent in 2001 pushing its way between 50 cents and $1.50 was time well spent, as evidenced in Figure 12.28. The very strong multiple bottom, highlighted with an oval in this chart, gave buyers the confidence to begin reentering the stock in force, and that eventually pushed the stock toward a huge multi-thousand percentage point gain from 2002 through 2005. Incidentally, you can also see another nice bottoming pattern from 2002 through 2004 as the stock firmed up new support between

FIGURE 12.27 Here we see five separate instances of the stock hitting a low price point, firming up the importance of this support level each time.

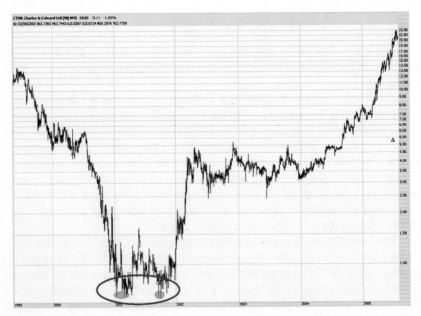

FIGURE 12.28 The support level in 2001 was hit many times before the stock finally started heading upward to a gigantic percentage gain.

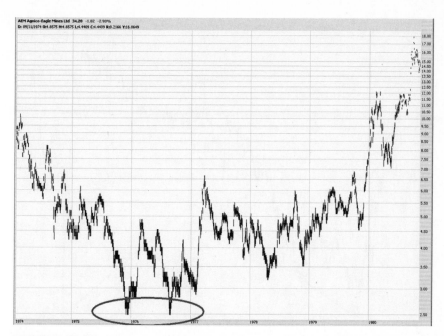

FIGURE 12.29 This is just about the ideal double bottom: Exactly the same low price was established, and a healthy amount of time—nine months—separates the two low prices.

$3 and $5. The important thing to note about this graph is how crucial the multiple bottom in 2001 was to this stock's long-term prospects.

If multiple bottoms take place over a long time frame, that is often a strong indication that the bottom is so widely respected as to be almost impenetrable. Let's turn our attention to symbol AEM, captured in Figure 12.29. The stock hit a low of $2.50 in late 1975 and the autumn of 1976. There was about a nine-month gap between these two events.

If, with all the gyrations of the stock market, a stock can hold firm at a given level after having suffered through a lot of selling pressure, prospects are good for this stock. The other benefit is that you have a very clean stop-loss point: should the stock break beneath the support zone (in this instance, $2.50), you would immediately exit the position and move on. No such stop-order would have been executed for a long position in this stock, however, which enjoyed many strong years after this double bottom was complete.

There are even a few rare instances where huge amounts of time—decades, even—can serve as affirmations of a strong support level. American Airlines, known as AMR Corporation (symbol AMR) was a

FIGURE 12.30 Even though nearly 20 years separated these two bottoms, savvy buyers in 2003 could have bought AMR shares at prices not seen since the depths of the bear market in 1974.

disastrously bad stock following the terrorist attacks in the United States in September 2001. By early 2003, the stock had lost almost its entire value, which is particularly remarkable given AMR's enormous presence in the transportation market.

A trader armed with a long-term chart, like the one shown in Figure 12.30, would have noticed something remarkable as the stock plunged from $45 to $2: a low price had been set in late 1974, after which the stock had enjoyed a huge resurgence. This is not to say that this chart represents a double bottom (unless the scale one is using to judge the chart is measured in centuries!). But, in a similar vein, this chart would be helpful to a person trying to determine how low the stock could possibly go in the worst conditions the stock had experienced before (in this case, the huge bear market in 1973 and 1974).

There is no doubt the stock could have snapped beneath its prior lifetime low and gone to $0. But in this case, a purchase of AMR at its prior low would have been extremely profitable, as the stock turned on the proverbial dime and blasted higher. It only took one insight—the recognition of the lifetime low established two decades prior—to recognize this trade.

SUMMARY

This chapter has introduced us to highlighting charts (both with ovals and rectangles), adding text notes, and identifying the higher highs, higher lows pattern. We have also learned about multiple tops and multiple bottoms, each of which can help us find important turning points in an equity's direction. We can now extend our knowledge of patterns by examining one of the most useful reversal patterns, the Head and Shoulders.

CHAPTER 13

Head and Shoulders

S o far in this book we have learned about a wide variety of analysis methods for financial charts. Saucers, multiple tops and bottoms, trendlines, and channels are just a few of the methods we have examined. After seeing so many charts with successful outcomes of applying these techniques, it can be tempting to place a trade on any chart that resembles one of the patterns shown. One might start to think that these patterns yield some kind of mystical power that can be exploited by those who understand them.

This is not the case. There is no sorcery involved with technical analysis. Any trade, after all, is a guess. It is hopefully an educated, well-informed guess with appropriate safety measures (like stop orders) in place to minimize your risk. But remember that the word "speculate" is derived from the Latin verb *speculare*, which means "to observe." It does not mean "to gamble." The object of good speculation is to observe well the information in front of you (in our case, well-drawn charts) and make a decision based on sound principles.

The patterns in this book don't always work. There are many times when there seems to be a perfect setup, and the charts go sour on you. That's okay. As long as you have a stop price in place that shields you from unreasonable losses, you can preserve the majority of your capital and move on. So if you lose 5 percent on four different trades and make 50 percent on another trade, all of which were based on the same pattern, you will still come out way ahead, because you contained your losses based on good analytics.

With this in mind, we can now turn our full attention to one of the most powerful and easy-to-recognize reversal patterns, the Head and Shoulders (and its twin, the Inverse Head and Shoulders).

THE HEAD AND SHOULDERS PATTERN

The Head and Shoulders pattern (henceforth referred to as H&S) has a funny name but a powerful purpose: to indicate the possible reversal of the security you are charting. As the name suggests, the H&S pattern looks like a head between two shoulders. It consists of these elements:

Left Shoulder: An ascent in price (ideally following a long, major ascent in the stock's value), a leveling, and then a weakening back to a certain support level known as the neckline.

Head: A further ascent in price, surpassing the high set by the left shoulder, once again leveling off and descending back to the neckline.

Right Shoulder: A final ascent in price, ideally not going as high as the left shoulder (and certainly not going as high as the head), a leveling off, and a descent back to the neckline, which it breaks beneath on strong volume.

Figure 13.1 shows an example of a very good H&S pattern exhibited by the stock Technical Olympia (symbol TOA). Lines have been drawn on top of the chart to clearly show the shoulders, the head, and the neckline. The circled part indicates where the price broke beneath the neckline, completing the pattern and sending the price sharply downward, as expected.

The H&S is a reversal pattern. It indicates that the stock is going to change direction. As such, it is most powerful when a stock has had a long, significant move higher in price. The ideal opportunity to exploit an H&S pattern is when there is a lot of air beneath the pattern—that is, a long ascent in price with very little resistance on the way down.

Take a look at Figure 13.2 for a good example of this. Here is a stock, Helen of Troy Ltd., which moved from $4 to $26 in a little over three years. The rectangle indicates a massive H&S pattern. This one is particularly good because there is an extremely clean neckline (the bottom line of the rectangle) and the right shoulder is lower than the left shoulder, indicating a diminishment in buying strength. Once the price broke beneath the neckline, notice how swiftly the price descended. It took only about a year for the stock to get to $4 again, with very few pauses along the way.

FIGURE 13.1 This is a near-perfect Head and Shoulders pattern: well-defined left shoulder, head, and right shoulder, followed by a break beneath the neckline, which is indicated here by a circle.

Think once more about the psychology behind the pattern. We return to the basic notion that bulls want to see a steady progression of higher highs and higher lows. During the formation of the left shoulder, assuming the stock has been enjoying a consistent run-up in price, the bulls are still satisfied that all is well. The peak of the left shoulder marks yet another high price in the stock.

As the head begins to form, the bulls remain satisfied, because once again they are seeing a higher high in the stock. But something is going wrong, because as the price eases back again, it returns to the same level that the left shoulder was at before (in other words, the neckline). So we no longer have a series of higher highs and higher lows. The lows are matching one another. But at least, from the bullish point of view, there is still strong support at a given price level (again, the neckline).

When the right shoulder begins to form, the bulls want to see a new high made, exceeding the price just made by the head price. (Keep in mind the vast majority of individuals watching the stock aren't even looking at a chart, let alone thinking in terms of heads and shoulders.) But not only does the price not exceed that of the head, it doesn't even match the price

FIGURE 13.2 The Head and Shoulders pattern typically precedes a major decline in price.

made by the left shoulder. So the stock is actually seen as weakening now, and the buying volume dries up as the price comes to rest, once again, at the neckline.

At this point, the market has a decision to make. It can continue to support the price at the equilibrium level it has found. Or the sellers can overcome the buyers, and the neckline will be broken. In the latter case, the H&S pattern is complete, and the stock price is probably in trouble (for the bulls, at least).

There is one more element to this story, however, and that is the retracement. Just as you saw retracements with saucer-like patterns, the H&S pattern sometimes sports a retracement as well. In this case, after a brief, quick drop in price, bargain hunters came out and temporarily provided support for the stock. If the H&S pattern holds, the price will make its way back up to the equilibrium point (the neckline), but no further. This provides a golden opportunity in the form of a second chance for those wanting to sell the stock short—because it is entirely likely once the retracement is complete, the price will begin falling again, and it will fall far past the point where it originally paused.

A CLOSE-UP VIEW OF BRCM's H&S PATTERN

One of the most remarkable examples of the H&S pattern in action in the U.S. stock market in recent years was Broadcom (BRCM) from 1998 through 2002. Looking at how this stock formed and broke down with the H&S as its reversal formation will yield insight in how to profit from this pattern.

Beginning with Figure 13.3, we can see how Broadcom, over a period of several years, had a remarkable run-up in price, moving from a single-digit stock to one priced over $180. This was during the Internet boom of the late 1990s, and Broadcom, as a major force in network-related semiconductors, was one of the hottest stocks in the United States. When the NASDAQ stock market began breaking down after March 2000, Broadcom suffered badly, falling from about $160 to about $80, a loss of 50 percent. But stocks related to networking regained their composure, and by the summer of 2000 Broadcom was reaching new lifetime highs.

FIGURE 13.3 The most lucrative H&S pattern is preceded by a long run-up in price. This chart shows BRCM starting to break after it has moved up hundreds of percent already.

FIGURE 13.4 The neckline is the key to the H&S, but there are occasions when fakeouts can occur. Here BRCM appears to break down, only to move back above its neckline. A little more than a week later, the true breakdown begins.

In retrospect, we can see something fascinating happening between July and October of 2000—the formation of a rather well-defined H&S pattern. This one is a bit unusual in the fact that it has two right shoulders. This is not unheard of, but it suggests a hesitation on the part of the market to push the stock beneath its neckline.

Looking closer at this period where the H&S formed, you can see a clear neckline at about $130. Something rather extraordinary happened on October 26, 2000: The stock pushed below the neckline on strong volume, and then returned above the neckline again! You can imagine how frustrating this was to the bears on this stock, since the widely anticipated breakdown of BRCM had finally started taking place, only to be cancelled out the very same day.

Eight sessions later, the stock gapped down beneath the neckline, but this time there was no turning back (Figure 13.4). Even more important, the breakdown in the stock was accompanied by a gigantic rise in the volume as owners of the stock rushed for the exit doors. Even though there had been a false breakdown that had faked out many investors, it seemed this second breakdown was authentic.

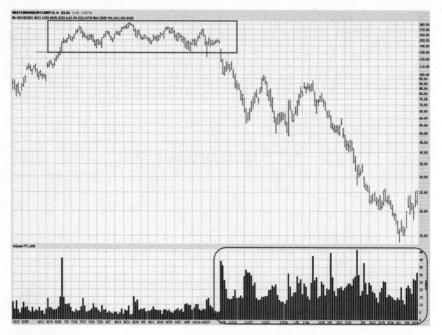

FIGURE 13.5 After BRCM snapped its neckline, the volume surged dramatically for many months afterward.

What happened following this breakdown was extraordinary. From November 7, 2000, through April 4, 2001, Broadcom lost about 90 percent of its value, all in a span of about five months. And it did so on extremely high volume (Figure 13.5). The H&S pattern, in spite of its false start, provided an astonishingly prescient prediction of this stock's direction.

After the stock reached its bottom on April 4, 2001, it spent about the next 14 months bouncing in a huge trading range between $12 and $36 (Figure 13.6). Clearly the investing public had been caught in a horrible tailspin and was trying to establish an appropriate value for the stock. After all this churning, the stock starting losing support again, and it ultimately bottomed at a little over $6 (just over 3 percent of its peak price) in October 2002.

THE IMPORTANCE OF THE NECKLINE

There is no more important feature to the H&S pattern than the neckline, because the neckline defines whether the pattern is complete and,

FIGURE 13.6 Over 96 percent of BRCM's peak value was lost during its fall, and this fall came in three large phases: the initial descent, a plateau period, and then a final collapse.

therefore, has any meaning. As with other lines in technical analysis, the neckline represents a line in the sand dividing bulls and bears. Along the line itself is a sort of equilibrium between buyers and sellers. Trading above the line represents strength and hope. Trading beneath the line represents weakness and fear.

With an ideal H&S pattern, the neckline has five unique touch points. The first is on the left side of the left shoulder; the second is at the right side of the left shoulder (which is also the left side of the head); the third is at the right side of the head; the fourth is at the right side of the right shoulder, at which point the price breaks beneath the neckline; and the fifth point (which is optional, in a sense) is when the price retraces back up to the neckline before falling hard once again.

Once the price has broken beneath the neckline, the H&S pattern has validity only if the price remains below the neckline. (When the price retraces, you may want to allow for a few pennies of "violation" before dismissing the pattern altogether.) Just because the price goes above the neckline doesn't absolutely mean the stock will not fall, but it does indicate strength that is normally not part of a good, strong H&S breakdown.

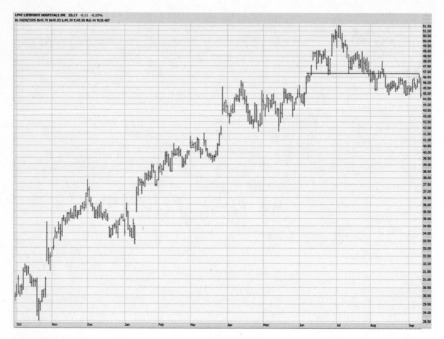

FIGURE 13.7 Sometimes the neckline is violated to the upside after it has been broken. In these instances, the pattern should be viewed with more skepticism.

Figure 13.7 shows an instance where the price broke below the neckline, went well above it again, then once more fell beneath it. A pattern with noise such as this should be viewed with more skepticism than a pattern absent such noise.

What you instead want to see is more along the lines of the chart shown in Figure 13.8, which is actually the same stock as the one in Figure 13.7 but at a different point in time. The neckline drawn on this chart clearly shows a left shoulder, a head, a right shoulder (which has a lower high than the left shoulder, always a good sign), and then a break below the neckline. When the price gains strength and retraces back to the neckline, it touches the neckline virtually to the exact penny and then swiftly falls away. This is a superb example of the H&S pattern at its best.

The aftermath of the H&S that was shown in Figure 13.7 is actually pretty impressive, in spite of the neckline violation that took place. As Figure 13.9 illustrates, the descent in price was quite rapid and relatively uninterrupted. A very clear series of lower lows and lower highs was laid out after the H&S was complete.

An even more extreme example of the H&S's ability to withstand neckline violations in shown with Figure 13.10. On the left side of this chart you

FIGURE 13.8 Here is a different H&S pattern on the same stock, which shows a cleaner pattern.

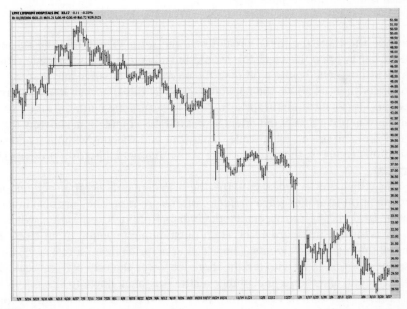

FIGURE 13.9 In spite of the imperfect behavior around the neckline, the H&S pattern performs well in this instance.

FIGURE 13.10 The price of this stock moved above the neckline but ultimately fell far below the original price target.

can see the H&S, the initial breakdown, the retracement, and the subsequent fall in price. In itself, this would have been quite a nice trade. The stock strengthened quite a bit over the subsequent months, and it spent a couple of months above the neckline price (by this time, the H&S pattern was no longer meaningful for a trade). Over the long haul, the stock fell far more in price than it did after the initial H&S completion, showing that the reversal in price took a while to play out and was not without its complications (namely, the price moving above the neckline for a protracted period).

As with many technical patterns, the H&S demands a certain amount of judgment on your part since perfect patterns are rare. They are also much easier to detect in retrospect. Authentidate Holding Corporation, whose stock is shown in Figure 13.11, is an outstanding example of an H&S. It has all the required elements: a huge run-up in price from $2 to $18.75, the formation of an H&S with a right shoulder lower than the left, a break, a retracement, and then a final plunge all the way back down to $2.

Some followers of this pattern believe you can set a price target for just how far the stock is going to fall. The calculation involves taking the difference between the peak of the stock and the value of the stock at the

FIGURE 13.11 This pattern shows the right shoulder much lower than the left shoulder, which lends credence to this H&S pattern.

neckline and then subtracting that value from the value at the neckline. For example, if a stock peaked at $40 and had a neckline at $30, the price target would be $20 (since the difference between $40 and $30 is $10 which, when subtracted from $30, yields the result of $20).

This calculation does not seem reliable. The chart in Figure 13.11, for instance, would yield a nonsensical negative value. A better approach is to judge each chart independently, looking for areas of meaningful support where the stock price might slow its descent.

USING RETRACEMENTS

The act of retracement in the world of the Head and Shoulders pattern sometimes seems like an act of generosity on the part of the stock market. When a price retraces back up to the neckline after breaking below it, two benefits are provided. First, it affirms the importance and validity of the neckline (assuming that, once the retracement is complete, the price starts to fall again). And second, for those traders who prefer less risk, it

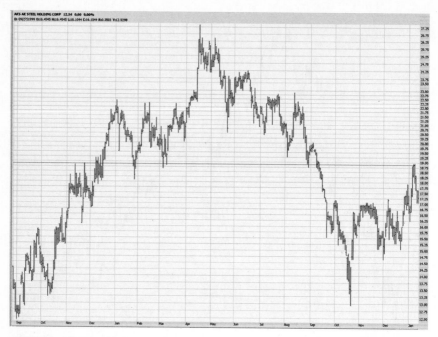

FIGURE 13.12 This is a perfect retracement, with the price moving back and touching the neckline after the break.

provides a welcome second chance to get into a position with a very clear stop price—namely, the value of the stock at the neckline.

Take AK Steel Holding, illustrated in Figure 13.12. This stock had a neckline at $19, and it cleanly broke that neckline, falling to about $13. For those people who had been bearish on this stock, it might seem that it was too late, since selling a stock short at $13 with a stop price above $19 represents an outsized risk. Getting stopped out above $19 on a position entered at $13 would represent a loss of nearly 50 percent, which most people would find unacceptable.

However, the price strengthens and makes its way back to just pennies beneath the $19 level. Now, instead of entering a short position at $13, a trader could enter it at a price just underneath the neckline and set a stop price just above the neckline. The risk in this case is pennies instead of dollars.

Such a trade would have worked out brilliantly, as shown in Figure 13.13. Once the neckline was retraced, the price fell hard, eventually descending to a price of about $2, a nearly 90 percent drop from the neckline price.

FIGURE 13.13 Shorting this stock at the retracement point would have provided the perfect low-risk/high-reward opportunity.

The problem, of course, is that not all retracements are this smooth. In fact, hardly any of them are. Perhaps the retracement will push just above the neckline for a few moments, forcing the execution of the stop-loss order. Perhaps the retracement will only be partial, not getting close to the neckline and in doing so snatching away a second chance to enter the position as the price resumes its fall. Or maybe the retracement won't happen at all, meaning the only individuals profiting from the stock's fall are those bold enough to have entered their positions immediately upon the neckline's break.

Figure 13.14, the chart of Advanced Micro Devices, shows how a stock's price can bobble around its neckline, frustrating bulls and bears simultaneously. This kind of price action indicates major uncertainty among those taking positions in the stock as they fight for direction. The stock fell below the neckline, went well above it, fell once more, went even higher above it again, and then fell a third time. This kind of cycle will shake out the weak hands trading the stock, since there is no clear direction.

Once the price fell under the neckline a third time, the bears maintained control. As the arrow in Figure 13.15 shows, the third break under the neckline led to a significant decline in price, which was then followed

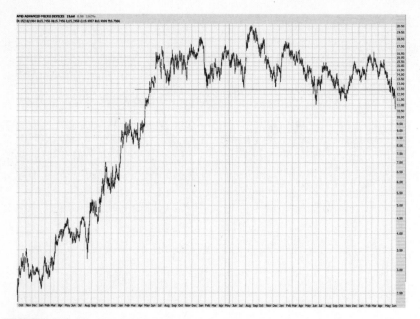

FIGURE 13.14 This break beneath the neckline is very rough, since it took three separate attempts before a true break was in place.

FIGURE 13.15 After the third break beneath the neckline, the stock began to fall badly.

FIGURE 13.16 This retracement took many months to complete, but it provided a second chance for those who had missed the short the first time.

by a retracement that took many months to complete. Those following this stock who kept the original neckline on their chart would have recognized that, finally, a clean retracement was being offered. The AMD stock was offering a second chance to those who wanted to take a bearish position, and those who did profited well from it, since the stock subsequently fell much harder.

Breaks beneath necklines can be imperfect, and retracements are all a little different. Experience as a chartist and a trader will give you the confidence required to make a sober judgment of the likely direction of a stock based on its behavior toward the neckline. After all, if a price ascends above the neckline and just keeps going higher, it should not take you long to decide that the H&S pattern no longer has any meaning for that stock at that time, and you should delete the neckline altogether.

Waiting for a retracement can take patience, but the reward for this patience is a significant reduction in risk. The chart in Figure 13.16 took many months to retrace fully to its neckline. Indeed, it could be argued on this chart that there were two necklines in place, one of which was retraced much earlier. The arrow on the chart indicates the peak of the retracement, representing the lowest-risk entry point for this security.

FIGURE 13.17   The same retracement point is marked here with an arrow.

The same point in the chart is indicated by the arrow in Figure 13.17, which shows a much longer-term perspective on this stock. The price moved in a series of lower highs and lower lows, which is the most reliable trend you want to monitor when judging when it is time to take profits and close the position. When the series of lower highs and lower lows is violated, it is probably time to close the position and bank your profits.

MORE ON THE HEAD AND SHOULDERS PATTERN

Let us reexamine the basic elements of the H&S pattern so you can more readily recognize this pattern in your own trading. Charts may not often present perfect manifestations of anything resembling two shoulders and a head. But the price movement should be close enough to warrant recognition of the pattern. Figure 13.18 shows a chart that, to most observers, would seem to be nondescript price action. The rounded rectangles drawn on top of the chart help call out the elements we seek—a left shoulder, a head, and a right shoulder. The right shoulder doesn't have

FIGURE 13.18 These rounded rectangles help more plainly show where the component parts of the H&S are.

the characteristic of being lower than the left, but this is still a perfectly reasonable H&S pattern.

Since you studied rounded tops in Chapter 10, you may wonder what distinguishes a rounded top from an H&S. The general shape and outcome of the two is similar—they both represent a loss of upward momentum in a stock's price that takes the shape of a gradual reversal. The H&S, however, does it in three stages, each of which clings to the neckline. The H&S (Figure 13.19) could even be thought of as three rounded tops, although much narrower in time scope.

The quality of the H&S is amplified when the right shoulder is lower than the left (Figure 13.20). The reason for this is that it indicates the market's ability to push the stock higher is weaker than before. It has failed to get as high as the head's peak, and it has even failed to get as high as the other shoulder's peak. Owners of the stock will begin to give up, and if the neckline is violated to the downside, the selling will rapidly intensify through a combination of stop orders being executed and owners voluntarily rushing for the exits.

One of the maxims of the stock market is that stocks fall faster than they rise. Traders not blessed with a lot of patience therefore finding

FIGURE 13.19 The difference between a rounded top and an H&S is the presence of a left and right shoulder, although the effect of both patterns is similar.

FIGURE 13.20 A lower right shoulder is a good sign of basic weakness in the stock.

FIGURE 13.21 Here is an excellent example of the price retracing to its neckline.

selling stocks short more fulfilling, since descents in price often happen at a quicker pace. Stocks usually slowly climb the fabled wall of worry, but they can swiftly slide down the slope of hope.

Figure 13.21 provides a good example of how a person selling a stock short would enjoy a relatively rapid profit. The neckline, at $31, is broken, and the stock falls to about $26. The stock then takes a few weeks to execute a nearly perfect retracement to the neckline, creating a great opportunity to enter into a short position or buy puts on this security.

As illustrated in Figure 13.22, the fall in price was fast and furious. It took this stock five years to build its equity up and only a couple of months for all that equity—and then some—to be wiped out. Those traders short this stock would have enjoyed a very fast profit, and those owning puts on this security would have enjoyed gigantic gains, all based upon the good application of an easily recognized pattern.

Holders of short positions on this stock with more patience would have seen their profits grow even more. Even though the stock had a big plunge over a two-month period, it was in a severe downtrend over the next few years (Figure 13.23). As you can see, it would have been a somewhat nerve-wracking ride, since the stock threatened to push above its neckline again

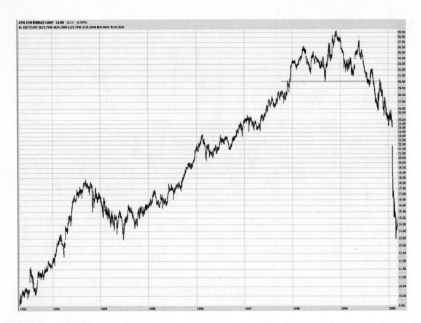

FIGURE 13.22 It took five years for the stock to climb this high in price but only a couple of months to destroy the same amount of equity.

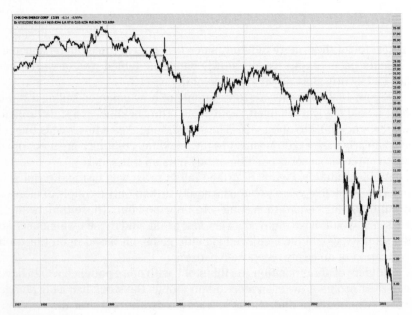

FIGURE 13.23 This retracement point, marked with an arrow, was perfect for shorting this stock.

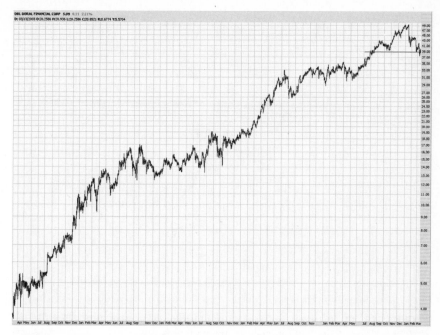

FIGURE 13.24 This H&S pattern was preceded by a more than 10-fold increase in price.

in early 2001. But by early 2003, the stock was beneath $4, a 90 percent decline from its peak four years earlier.

A vital prerequisite for fat profit potential with the H&S pattern is a major increase in price preceding the pattern. If a stock's neckline is at $20, but for years it traded in a range between $16 and $18, there is very little reason to sell the stock short since there is so much support beneath the neckline. Figure 13.24, however, shows a stock with a gigantic price increase. There is plenty of air beneath the neckline for the stock to fall. There are certainly a couple of areas with some support along the way down, but because the stock has soared many hundreds of percent, there is ample opportunity for it to fall hard.

This particular stock, Doral Financial (ticker DRL) provides a good example of how H&S patterns may be rather unusual in shape. Figure 13.25 illustrates the left shoulder, a very high head, and a right shoulder. The neckline has been drawn for the sake of clarity. In spite of the rather distorted shape of the H&S, there was no diminishment in the power of this pattern as the stock fell from about $40 to $5.

Doral, as well as Epix Pharmaceuticals (Figure 13.26), provides proof that a higher right shoulder doesn't mean the H&S pattern should be

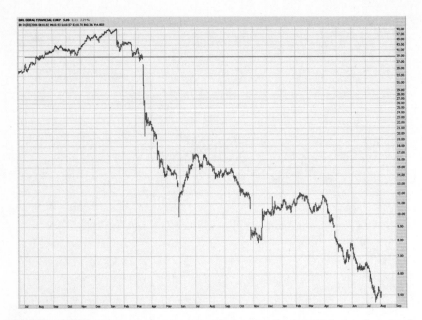

FIGURE 13.25 Patterns can sometimes be strangely shaped, but as long as the basic rules are still applied for analysis, the pattern is valid.

FIGURE 13.26 Just because the right shoulder is higher than the left does not negate the H&S pattern.

FIGURE 13.27 The day that the price broke below this stock's neckline would have been, in retrospect, a perfect time to get in, because the very next day the stock gapped down and never looked back.

ignored. Epix also illustrates how vital the neckline is to monitoring the stock's possible breakdown. On January 13, 2005, the stock fell below its neckline. For those who did not want to wait for a possible retracement, this would have been an ideal time to enter a short position on the stock, because the neckline was decisively violated. The very next day, the stock gapped down in price, almost instantly demonstrating the validity and strength of this pattern for this stock.

Subsequent to this break in price, the stock fell substantially before regaining some strength. However, instead of retracing to the neckline, it only retraced to the vicinity of the price gap before resuming its fall (Figure 13.27). Those waiting for a retracement to the neckline would have never taken a position in this stock, but those who executed their trades on the day of the neckline break would have enjoyed handsome gains.

It isn't practical, of course, to monitor hundreds of stocks to see what necklines have been broken. There are many web sites that provide free stock alert services on the Internet. Many online brokers also provide the ability to enter a stock order contingent on a stock's price. The neckline for EPIX, for instance, was at \$15.43. You might have entered an order to

FIGURE 13.28 Some H&S patterns can precede gigantic price declines, such as this one, which led the stock almost to $0.

sell the stock short if the price went below, for instance, $15.40 (or some other price low enough that you felt confident the neckline had indeed been violated). This way, you could put the trade on automatic pilot if you were confident enough in the pattern.

Generally speaking, it is indeed better for the right shoulder to be lower in an H&S pattern. Given the choice between two otherwise identical H&S charts, one with a higher right shoulder and one with a lower right shoulder, the latter is probably the more profitable choice. Fedders Corp (Figure 13.28) sported a very high left shoulder, a head, and a much lower right shoulder. The stock broke the neckline, retraced almost back to it, and then spent many subsequent months plotting out a series of lower lows and lower highs. The damage to the stock was tremendous, bringing the price almost down to zero.

A decision you will face every time you find an H&S pattern is whether to place a trade the moment the neckline is broken or instead wait for a retracement. A variety of factors will contribute to your decision, such as how high the potential profit is, how volatile the stock is, how well-formed the pattern is, and your own past experience with similar patterns. There is no one right answer, since every chart and opportunity are different. If you

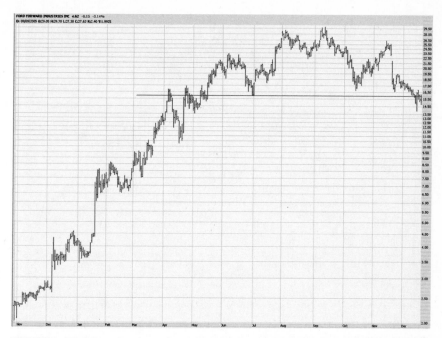

FIGURE 13.29 Entering a short position immediately upon the neckline break can yield better profits, but it also brings higher risk.

were looking at the chart shown in Figure 13.29, you might want to consider what you would do—short it at once, or wait to see what happened?

As Figure 13.30 shows, the best decision in this case would have been to place the trade at once, perhaps using a contingent order with your broker to execute the trade the moment the price dipped beneath the neckline. The stock never made a full retracement, but it did fall substantially. Only those bold enough to make the trade without hesitation maximized their profits.

Express Scripts (symbol ESRX) behaved quite differently, since its retracement was orderly and didn't even take very long to complete. The arrows on the chart (Figure 13.31) simplify the stock's behavior after the trendline break, first moving from $80 to $64, a 20 percent drop in price, and then returning to the neckline at $80 once more. It is possible that the cleaner shape of the H&S pattern contributed to this more orderly behavior.

A similar retracement can be seen with the small carrier Frontier Airlines (symbol FRNT). Figure 13.32 shows the stock running up in price from $3.75 to nearly $20. Between the $15 and $19 range, the stock built a relatively clean H&S pattern, although the neckline is a little rough.

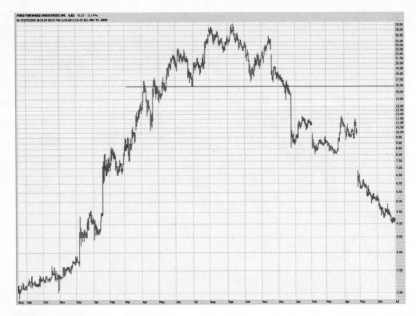

FIGURE 13.30 There are many occasions where a retracement is only partial, not making its way all the way back to the neckline.

FIGURE 13.31 Here ESRX goes full circle from $80 down to $64 and then back to $80 again.

FIGURE 13.32 The typical movement seen here is a break beneath the neckline followed by a strengthening of the stock back to a point just underneath the same line.

The stock broke down, falling rapidly for five days, then it spent the next several weeks fighting its way back to the neckline.

The longer-term graph in Figure 13.33 reveals the aftermath of this neckline break, with the arrow indicating the retracement point. This also helps illustrate how valuable it is for an H&S pattern to be preceded by a swift run-up in price, because there was virtually no meaningful support on the way down. It took longer for the stock to fall than it did to rise, which is somewhat unusual, but the downtrend was orderly as the stock lost about 60 percent of its value after the break.

Many of the examples used in this chapter are from companies that perhaps you had not heard of before. Important technical patterns such as the H&S certainly are not restricted to small stocks, however. In Figure 13.34, General Electric's stock price carved out a very good H&S pattern with predictable results. Even though the H&S pattern is widely recognized, the vast majority of traders—even those involved with gigantic stocks like GE—do not understand its power and application.

On some occasions you will see an H&S pattern form above a price gap. A price gap is an instance, in this case, where a stock's price opens

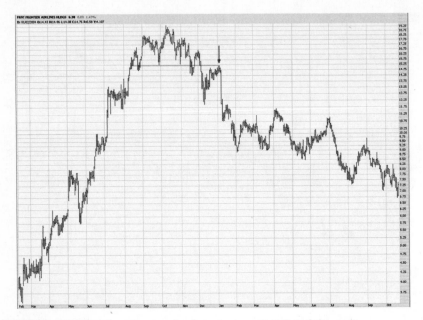

FIGURE 13.33 The arrow marks the retracement point of this pattern.

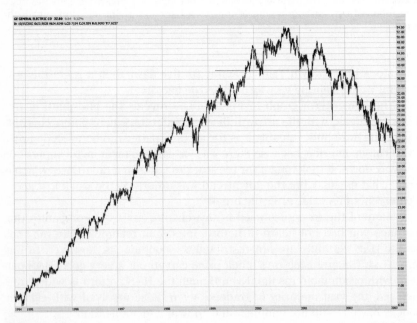

FIGURE 13.34 Even the largest cap stocks, such as gigantic GE, can fall badly after an H&S pattern is complete.

FIGURE 13.35 This neckline at $78 was just above the level where the price had gapped up late the prior July.

at a price far above the prior day's close and its trading remains at or higher than the opening price, thus creating a gap in the price graph between where the previous day's price has closed and where the current day's price had opened.

An H&S pattern will usually form a neckline at or above the high point of the gap. An example of this is shown in Figure 13.35, where the $78 neckline is just above the price gap. It is not surprising that this level represents support for the stock's price, since whatever event caused the stock to gap up in the first place must have been so powerful as to create tremendous demand for the stock at that price level.

Since a break of the neckline can close the price gap, however, it won't matter that there was a prior gap in price. The result for this particular stock, shown in Figure 13.36, is that a year's worth of gains were destroyed in just a month, and the stock went down to price levels that had not been seen in years.

As with trendlines, necklines have the two-faced, Janus-like property of representing both resistance and support. When a stock is climbing up, it may find resistance at the neckline level (even though the neckline hasn't even been established yet). During the formation of the H&S, the

FIGURE 13.36   It took only a month to wipe out a year's worth of price increase this stock had enjoyed earlier.

neckline undoubtedly represents support, since that's the very basis of the pattern. Once the neckline is broken, the line changes again to be resistance, and if the buyers of the stock manage to push it up again in price, it will likely reach a formidable level of resistance at the neckline once again. Figure 13.37 shows the neckline acting in both manners, with the price bouncing off resistance before the H&S was created.

If the price action before the H&S seems to treat the neckline as resistance, it is more likely that the H&S pattern's behavior will be more predictable and orderly. Figure 13.38 shows that in early September this stock, Hot Topic, backed away from the exact price level that would later be the neckline. The H&S formed, and the stock began falling, not even pausing to retrace.

Before turning our attention to some specific trading techniques, let us examine three more examples of the H&S pattern. Figure 13.39 is the stock for Juniper Networks (symbol JNPR), which had a fate similar to Broadcom back in 2000 and 2001. As with Broadcom, the neckline that formed was not perfectly clean. The price dipped below the neckline three different times.

Again, as with Broadcom, the stock fell fantastically (Figure 13.40) once the neckline was decisively broken. The drop is so severe that

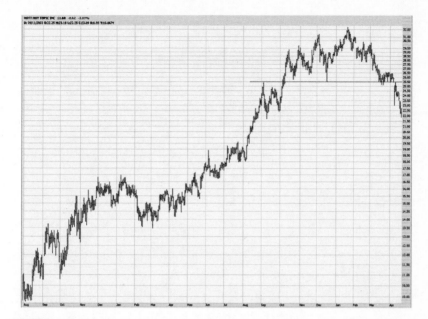

FIGURE 13.37 Notice how the neckline, which represented support during the H&S formation, also represented resistance before the H&S even began forming.

FIGURE 13.38 Here we see an exceptionally well-defined neckline at $25.50.

FIGURE 13.39 As with BRCM, the breakdown beneath the neckline of JNPR was not perfectly clean.

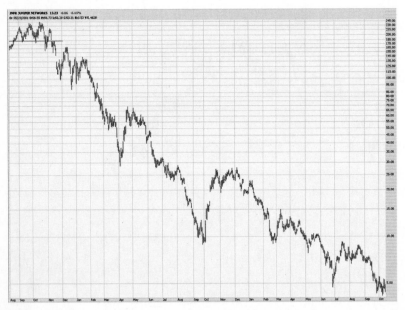

FIGURE 13.40 One of the most visible and catastrophic falls of a big-name stock from the Internet mania was predicted by an H&S pattern.

FIGURE 13.41 The left and right shoulders are more difficult to see here, since they do not touch the neckline cleanly.

the H&S pattern, which in Figure 13.39 was quite substantial, appears as just a tiny feature in Figure 13.40. You can see the small neckline in the upper-left corner of the chart.

Trading experience based on the H&S pattern will give you more discernment when it comes to unusual pattern recognition. The stock for Movie Gallery, Inc (Figure 13.41) formed a pattern that has the markings of an H&S. It is not a perfect pattern by any stretch of the imagination, particularly since the neckline isn't even contacted on either side of the pattern's head. In spite of the coarseness of this pattern, there are several signs that this is a good stock to short—the right shoulder being lower than the left, the clean retracement back to the neckline, and the substantial run-up in price before the pattern formed.

Being able to see past the imperfections of Movie Gallery's H&S pattern would have been a profitable observation (Figure 13.42). The stock fell away from the pattern and didn't stop making new lows until it was beneath $2.

Sometimes the H&S pattern can express itself in a somewhat mutated form, sporting more than one shoulder. This is sometimes referred to as a Complex Head and Shoulders pattern. Figure 13.43, for instance, shows

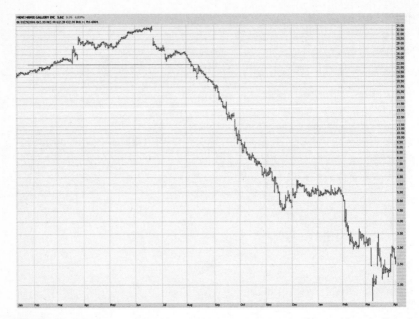

FIGURE 13.42   This stock fell virtually non-stop to under $2 per share before the selling was over.

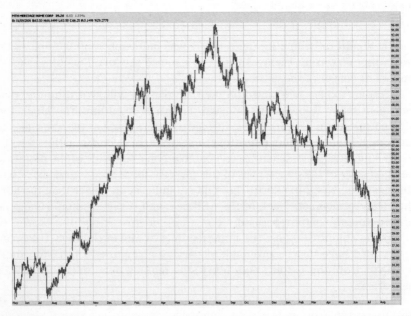

FIGURE 13.43   This pattern isn't quite as clean, as it has two shoulders on the right side.

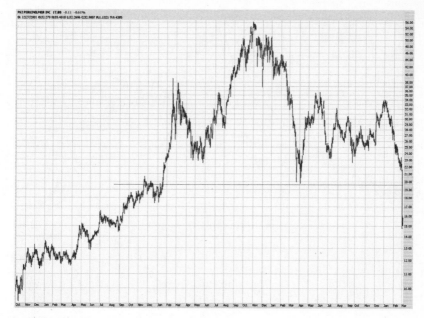

FIGURE 13.44 The break beneath this neckline was extremely swift.

a pattern that has two right shoulders. Having a nonstandard pattern takes away some of the validity, but it is still worth watching a chart like this to see if the neckline is clearly broken. The fact that the rightmost shoulder is lower than the earlier right shoulder is a positive sign for the bears, since it emphasizes the general weakness of the stock.

It has been pointed out that trades made immediately upon a neckline break are often the most profitable. It should be remembered that sometimes these breaks are so swift (Figure 13.44) you can find yourself at a relatively bad entry point, in spite of your intentions to get into a short position quickly. As of this writing, there is still an uptick rule in place for selling a stock short, which means that if a stock is falling straight down, your order will not be filled until the stock moves up a bit. For this reason, you may want to limit the price you will accept when you construct the order to enter the short position, since you do not want to sell it at too low (and risky) a price.

TRADING ON THE H&S PATTERN

Because the H&S pattern is so reliant on its neckline for support, a breakdown in this pattern can happen more swiftly than others. If you are highly

FIGURE 13.45 A contingent order on this security would probably have produced a better execution for a person trying to short this stock.

confident about a particular trade, you might want to place a contingent order on the stock you are following. This allows you to enter a market order to sell the stock short if it crosses below a certain price value (Figure 13.45), which means you do not have to monitor the stock constantly for your entry opportunity.

The more difficult issue is when to take profits on your position. Any position creates the two emotions that all traders know well: fear and greed. The fear comes about because you are afraid of profits diminishing (or, even worse, changing into losses). And the greed comes into play since you want to make as much as you can on the position. But there is no way to know with certainty that when you close a position it will be at the best possible time.

To understand some of the analysis that can help with the crucial issue of when to close a position, we will examine the formation of the pattern in the first place. Figure 13.46 shows how a typical H&S pattern is formed, which is as a series of higher highs and higher lows. It is the cessation of this series that creates the first shoulder, when the price sinks back down to equal the prior low point, thus establishing what will be the neckline for the pattern.

FIGURE 13.46 A series of higher highs and higher lows is broken, which was the beginning of the H&S pattern.

The nature of this ascent in price is what is so important in evaluating your target price for the position. If the rise in price was rapid, the stock is more prone to fall quickly. If the rise was steady and had a number of plateaus in price along the way, it is more likely that the stock will pause during its descent at those levels as well. Figure 13.47 shows a stock whose climb in price prior to the pattern was devoid of much support, which is a very positive sign for those taking a bearish position on the security.

If and when the stock does break below the neckline, it should form a series of lower lows and lower highs (Figure 13.48). As long as it is in such a mode, it is wise to hang onto the position. What you want to look for are areas of meaningful support during the rise preceding the pattern. You do not necessarily have to close out the position when it reaches those levels, but you can expect the descent to slow, and you should be more vigilant than normal about closing the position should the lower lows and lower highs pattern be violated. Since it is usually impractical to watch a stock chart all day, you can reset your stop-loss orders with your broker so that the position is closed automatically if a certain price is violated. That price can be determined by what would constitute a break in the lower lows, lower highs cycle.

FIGURE 13.47 There is very little in the way of support beneath this stock's neckline.

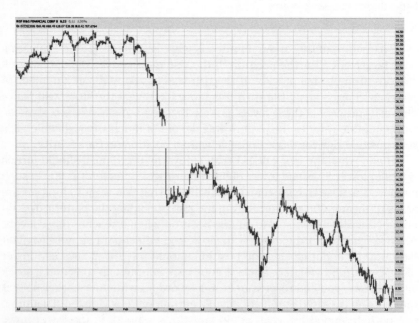

FIGURE 13.48 A series of lower lows and lower highs followed this stock's break.

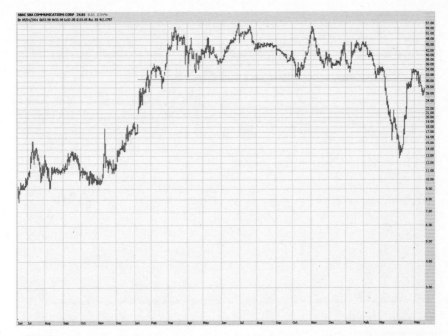

FIGURE 13.49 After a very clean break, the stock price pushes a little above the neckline on the retracement.

If you enter a position immediately after the neckline break, the logical place to put a stop is above the neckline. The question of how much to put it above the neckline is important, because that is where you control how much risk you will take. The most conservative stop-loss order would be set a penny above the neckline, since the assumption is that once the neckline is violated, any price action above the neckline renders the H&S pattern moot. That is probably too draconian an approach. It is riskier, but in a way more prudent, to give the stock a little wiggle room on the stop-loss order (Figure 13.49), perhaps setting the stop-loss a couple of percentage points above the neckline.

In the case of the stock shown in Figure 13.50, allowing a small amount of overage above the neckline would have been a profitable decision, because even though the retracement went a little above the neckline, the stock softened up again and fell dramatically, losing almost its entire value. If a person had set a very tight stop just above the neckline, the position would have been closed at a loss, and a marvelous profit would have been abandoned.

One relatively remote possibility is that a stock will gap down in price and break its neckline (Figure 13.51). For example, suppose a neckline was

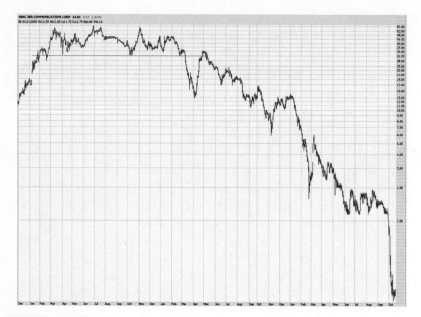

FIGURE 13.50 Allowing for a small amount of safety margin during this retracement would have been a lucrative decision.

FIGURE 13.51 This stock broke its neckline suddenly with a gap down in price.

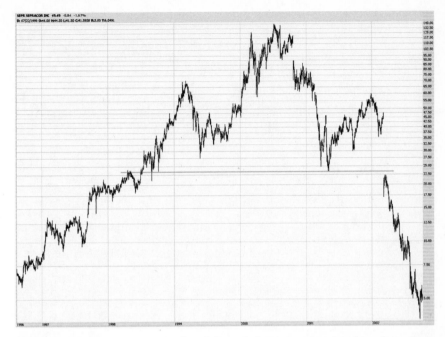

FIGURE 13.52 A stock can often fall much faster in price than it took to climb there in the first place.

at $50, and a stock had a partially completed H&S pattern with a left shoulder, a head, and most of a right shoulder. Further assume that the stock closed on Wednesday at a price of $60, and after the market closed, the company announced very bad earnings. The next morning, on Thursday, the opening price for the stock is $38. This is a gap down in price, because there is no trading activity between $60 and $38, and all of that equity value was instantly lost.

It is important to understand this if you plan to leave a contingent order open for a stock. Although it is not very likely such a dramatic gap down will occur, its chance of occurring makes it more prudent to enter the order as a day-order each day, instead of a good-until-cancelled order, which will remain until you specifically cancel it. This gives you a better measure of control over your trading.

For the stock that was shown in Figure 13.51, the gap down in price didn't make the result of the H&S pattern any less valuable (Figure 13.52). The general point, however, is that it is better to put in your contingent orders at the start of each day on a day-only basis instead of having an open risk of a radically different opening price triggering your standing order.

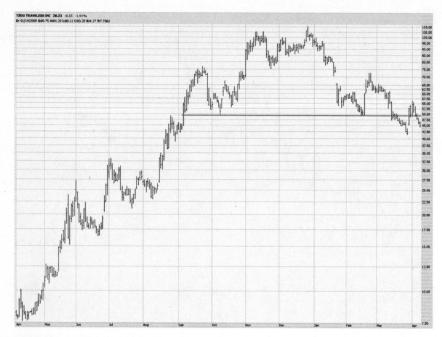

FIGURE 13.53 A price will sometimes bobble around a neckline before breaking cleanly. It is safest to wait for a clean break.

Although being somewhat forgiving with how far a retracement will go is a wise idea, you should be careful not to enter an order if the price of the security seems to be clinging to the neckline instead of clearly breaking beneath it (Figure 13.53). The neckline, after all, represents an important level of support. In other words, this price level is a line of equilibrium between bulls and bears, and it needs to be plainly violated to the downside for the bears to be plausibly in control of the price action.

If a gap down in price takes place after the neckline has already been violated, that is good news for those who are short the stock (Figure 13.54). But it should also be noted that the chance of a retracement piercing through that price gap is greatly diminished, so those waiting for a retracement to the neckline will probably be disappointed. Instead, the bottom of the price gap should be respected as an important area of resistance that should be heeded as much as the neckline would have been.

One final note on the H&S pattern is that the neckline doesn't necessarily have to be horizontal. Although it is most logical as a horizontal line, since this represents an agreed-upon line in the sand dividing bulls and bears, you can also recognize modestly angled necklines as legitimate definers of H&S patterns. In Figure 13.55, for instance, Hershey

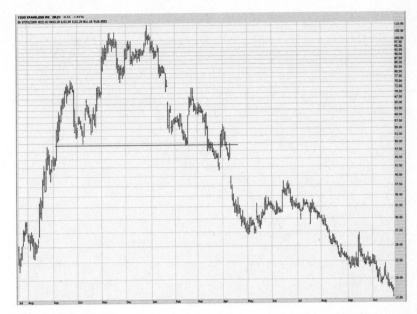

FIGURE 13.54 The gap-down following this neckline break indicated a retracement was probably not going to happen.

FIGURE 13.55 Necklines do not necessarily have to be horizontal to indicate a valid H&S pattern.

FIGURE 13.56 The retracement of Hershey's touched the sloped line perfectly.

(symbol HSY) sports an H&S pattern with an upward-sloping neckline. The pattern is quite well formed, and after the break beneath the neckline, the price moves neatly up to perfectly touch the underside of the neckline, which has now changed from support to resistance.

As illustrated in Figure 13.56, Hershey's price continued to move down once the retracement was complete. The same rules apply to an H&S with a slanted neckline as would apply to a horizontal one. The neckline is simply drawn differently, and the retracement (should it happen at all) will correspondingly move to a slightly different level than if the line were perfectly flat.

THE INVERTED HEAD AND SHOULDERS PATTERN

Whereas the H&S pattern is a reliable bearish pattern, there is a version of the H&S that is instead bullish; it is called the Inverted Head and Shoulders pattern (for the sake of brevity, IHS). As the name implies, it is similar to the H&S pattern, except that it is upside down. It has a left shoulder, a head,

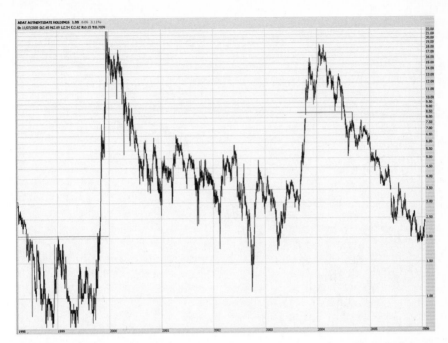

FIGURE 13.57 This chart shows, within a relatively short amount of time, an inverted H&S and a regular H&S on the same stock.

and a right shoulder, all of which are topped by a neckline. The principal difference is that the neckline represents resistance instead of support, and bulls watching this pattern want to see the price break above resistance.

As an initial illustration of this pattern, Figure 13.57 shows a stock with both an IHS pattern as well as, later, a regular H&S pattern. The inverted H&S, shown on the left side of the chart, precedes a dramatic rise in price. The H&S pattern, shown on the right side of the chart, precedes a big plunge in price. Even though this is the same stock, it offers both patterns at different points in time, each of which had the expected result.

Instead of starting with a perfect example, let us look at a more typical, real-life example in Figure 13.58. The neckline is drawn for the sake of clarity. There is a left shoulder, a very deep descent in price to create the head, and then a right shoulder. Although the stock very briefly peaks above the $3.40 neckline, it dips below it and spends a few months gaining strength. When it finally breaks above the neckline for real, the stock enjoys a nearly 10-fold increase in price over the next six years.

Two rules have been mentioned about H&S patterns that apply to its inverted cousin as well: (1) the longer the pattern, the more powerful it is, and (2) the price action prior to the pattern should be significant (to the

FIGURE 13.58 The initial breakout above the neckline for this stock was weak, and it took a second, more earnest attempt to truly break above the pattern formation.

upside for the H&S pattern and to the downside for the inverted version) for the break in the pattern to have much potential.

The stock for C. R. Bard (Figure 13.59) provides an example of both these properties. The stock had gone through a long, grinding descent in price during the infamous 1973–1974 bear market. It then spent the entire rest of the decade churning between a split-adjusted price of 45 cents and 90 cents. In the course of doing so, it produced a very potent IHS pattern. The neckline has been drawn horizontally across the chart for clarity, and although the pattern isn't perfect in all respects, you should be able to clearly make out the components of the pattern.

When the price broke above the neckline, the results were profound. For literally decades following the break, the stock moved up in price by thousands and thousands of percent (Figure 13.60). A $15,000 investment at the breakout would have grown to over $1 million by 2005, since the stock made a powerful and reliable series of higher highs and higher lows all through the 1980s and 1990s.

Volume plays a more important role in the inverted H&S pattern than it does with the H&S. The reason is that a stock needs power to rise, but it

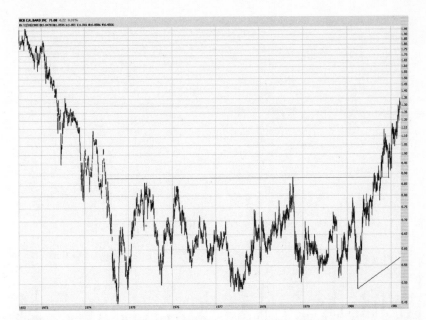

FIGURE 13.59 This massive inverted H&S pattern hammered out a critical bottom for this stock after a long descent.

FIGURE 13.60 This pattern spans years, and its effects were felt for decades to come.

FIGURE 13.61 The volume of this stock dried up near the bottom, as the selling pressure exhausted itself. A surge came during the initial breakout.

can fall of its own weight to the downside. Ideally, you will want to see a surge in volume at the breakout, and if there is a retracement back to the neckline, you should probably see a tapering off in price before it begins its rise anew.

The broker optionsXpress (Figure 13.61) gives us a nice example of volume in the context of an IHS pattern. During the formation of the left shoulder and head, the volume dried up, indicating that the selling pressure was diminishing. During the creation of the right shoulder, volume started to rise, which was a good sign for the bulls since it indicated more buying interest at a slightly higher price point. The real surge in volume came when the stock broke out above its neckline.

As the stock proceeded to triple in price, the volume continued growing, indicating a widening base of interest in the stock (Figure 13.62). The simple monitoring of a neckline was all that was required to get in on this stock early enough to enjoy virtually the entire upside of this move.

The stock for RosTelecom (Figure 13.63) gives another illustration of volume versus price action. There are two big bursts of volume here. The first is during the completion of the head part of the pattern, which

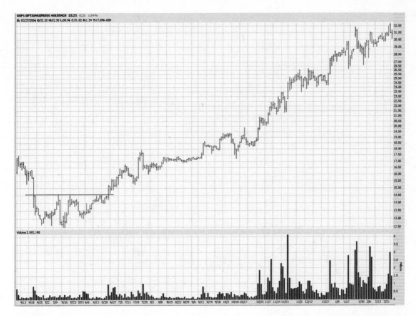

FIGURE 13.62 Surging volume during an upturn is an indication of strength.

FIGURE 13.63 The surge in volume here comes at the right time, which is when the stock is pushing off its lows and moving toward the neckline.

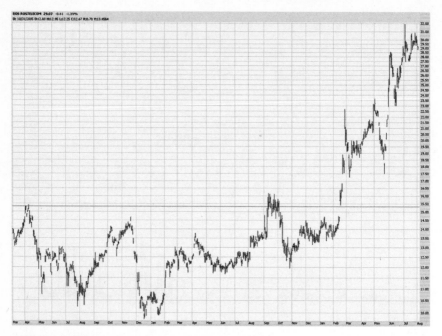

FIGURE 13.64 Patterns aren't always perfectly clean, so it is important to work on your analysis skills to help filter out the random noise built within a chart and still see the valid pattern clearly.

indicates a surge of buying interest after the stock has bottomed out. The next surge is during an attempted (but failed) breakout above the neckline.

The aftermath of this inverted H&S was a terrific upside for bulls (Figure 13.64). This pattern is a little unusual since there are two right shoulders (or one large right shoulder with a false breakout in the middle), but the neckline drawn makes plain the pattern's shape and location.

With the normal H&S pattern, it is a good sign when the right shoulder is lower than the left shoulder, since that suggests waning strength in the stock's price. The inverted H&S pattern has a corollary—it is a better pattern if the right shoulder is higher than the left shoulder (Figure 13.65). In other words, the prices on the right shoulder should not dip as far down as the prices on the left shoulder, since a higher right shoulder suggests more strength.

The result of this pattern was a nearly fivefold increase in price for AES Corporation (Figure 13.66). All the elements were in place for a positive outcome: a substantial decrease in price prior to the pattern, a clean IHS, a high right shoulder, and a good breakout above the neckline.

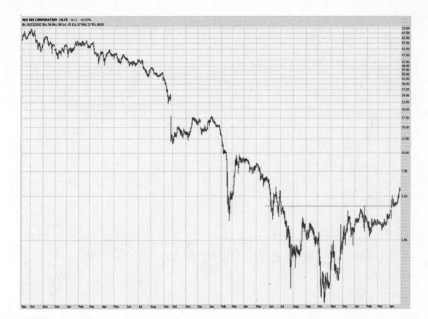

FIGURE 13.65 The right shoulder being shallower than the left shoulder is an indication of strength, which enhances the power of the inverted H&S.

FIGURE 13.66 The inverted H&S marked the end of a substantial decline for this stock.

FIGURE 13.67 This stock shows an almost perfect inverted H&S pattern: a shoulder, a head, a somewhat higher right shoulder, a breakout, and then a retracement.

Perhaps one of the cleanest IHS patterns in recent history was for the stock of Asyst Technologies (Figure 13.67). The neckline is at $5.50, and the pattern below it is perfectly formed. After the price breaks above the neckline, a retracement precisely down to the neckline takes place.

Following the formation of this pattern, Asyst Technologies (ASYT) swiftly doubled in price (Figure 13.68), in spite of the fact that it had recently been in a severe downturn. This pattern was easy to recognize and profitable to trade.

The importance of a volume surge during a price breakout is difficult to overstate. A volume surge confirms that there is a strong interest in the stock, and volume often begets more volume. When a stock explodes in volume, it appears on "Most Active" lists and other scans that traders follow. Figure 13.69 shows a particularly strong explosion in volume following a breakout.

For an inverted H&S pattern to have two right shoulders isn't uncommon, since there will still be hesitation and skepticism surrounding a stock that has spent so much time going down in price. Those waiting on the sidelines will want the stock to prove it is capable of sustained upward price movement before they are willing to commit to purchasing it, so it may

FIGURE 13.68 ASYT doubled in price after its breakout, in spite of a relatively recent severe decline in price.

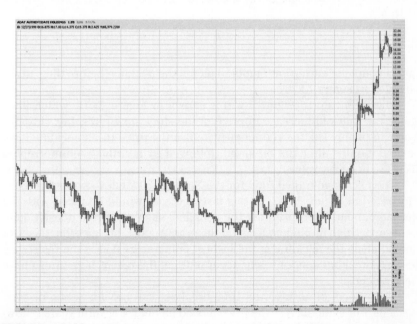

FIGURE 13.69 Notice the exceptional surge in volume following the breakout.

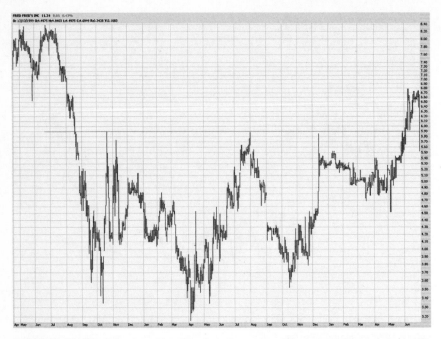

FIGURE 13.70 This could be interpreted as two patterns in one: an inverted H&S as well as a cup with handle, since the inverted H&S makes up the cup portion of the pattern.

take a couple of earnest attempts to pierce the neckline before the pattern completes (Figure 13.70).

The follow-up to Figure 13.70 is shown in Figure 13.71, which illustrates the fourfold increase in price of the stock for Fred's, Inc. (FRED). You can plainly see the retracement return the price to its neckline level several months after the breakout, followed by a virtually uninterrupted increase in equity value.

The exchange-traded fund for the Russell 1000 index (symbol IWD) is illustrated in Figure 13.72. In this instance, you would be faced with the decision about where to draw the neckline, since the price doesn't quite come up as high in January as it did the prior August. In cases like this, you should place the neckline at the highest point, since that is the resistance level. A breakout cannot really occur until all the recent high prices have been bested.

The effects of an inverted H&S breakout can last for years, or even decades. For symbol IWD, the price moved higher for several years following the breakout (Figure 13.73).

FIGURE 13.71   FRED increased in value fourfold once it broke above its neckline.

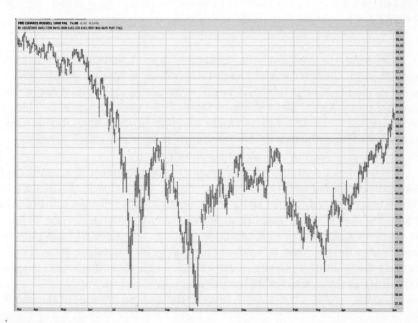

FIGURE 13.72   Here we see an extremely well-formed inverted H&S with the neckline at $47.50.

FIGURE 13.73   The price progress following the breakout was steady and consistent for years.

Knowing where to place the neckline isn't as obvious as the earlier examples in this chapter would suggest. Of course, if figuring out the placement of the neckline is too hard, perhaps the pattern is not well-defined in the first place. Figure 13.74 shows a chart whose neckline could be placed at either $22.75 or $26. Either would be appropriate, although the more conservative approach is to assume a higher neckline, which generates a more difficult-to-achieve breakout for the stock.

Sometimes a pattern can take on such a shape that it is actually two patterns combined into one. Examine Figure 13.75 closely, for instance. There is a very well-formed IHS pattern spanning the leftmost third of this chart. Yet if you look at the portion of the chart beneath the horizontal line, it also resembles a cup-with-handle formation. The inverted H&S pattern constitutes the cup, and a handle is formed to its immediate right. These are complementary patterns—both bullish—and their prediction played out nicely as the stock doubled in price.

You may wonder if the width (that is, the amount of time) of the shoulders and head need to be similar. It makes for an easier-to-find pattern when their widths are relatively close, but it is not a necessity of the pattern. Even a very narrow element of the pattern is acceptable, such as the

FIGURE 13.74 Finding the right place to place the neckline is something you will get better at with experience.

FIGURE 13.75 The owners of KMG enjoyed more than a doubling of price following this breakout above the neckline.

FIGURE 13.76 The right shoulder of this pattern is very narrow, but it qualifies nonetheless.

chart shown in Figure 13.76. In this case, the right shoulder is just a fraction of the width of the head and left shoulder, but because the basic rules of the pattern are still intact, this is a perfectly legitimate bullish shape.

The follow-through to the chart shown in Figure 13.76 is illustrated in Figure 13.77. After a picture-perfect retracement to the neckline, the price moved solidly higher. It is more common for a retracement to take place with an inverted H&S pattern, simply because there is a built-in caution in the market about pushing a stock higher that has been depressed for a while. Whereas a stock in an H&S pattern can quickly fall based on fear and panic, a stock shaping up for a solid breakout higher has to fight the traditional wall of worry, thus often providing a second chance to get in with the form of a retracement.

One extremely well-known stock that provided perhaps the most ideal inverted H&S pattern in years was that of Qwest Communications (symbol Q), shown in Figure 13.78. Two horizontal lines have been drawn here—the lower one to emphasize the lower bounds of the shoulders, and the upper one to show the location of the neckline. On the extreme right of the graph, you can see a very clean retracement that was executed very soon after the first breakout.

FIGURE 13.77 Symbol LVLT had a perfect retracement to its neckline at approximately $2.70.

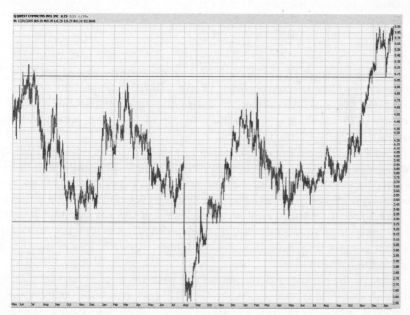

FIGURE 13.78 The stock for Qwest, symbol Q, had about the most perfect inverted H&S example you could want.

FIGURE 13.79 Following its breakout, Q moved much higher and never violated its neckline to the downside.

With such an exceptional pattern, it is no surprise that Q performed marvelously after the retracement (Figure 13.79). The pattern was two-and-a-half years in the making, but during that time the psychology of the holders of the stock gradually shifted to one of optimism, which was fed by more new buyers into the stock.

Most charts aren't nearly as perfect as that of Q. The neckline, for example, doesn't have to touch every element of each IHS component to the penny. You need to use your own judgment and experience to assess if a pattern is acceptably clean and clear enough to warrant making a trade. In Figure 13.80, the pattern is otherwise clean, but the left shoulder doesn't quite make it up to the neckline on both sides. That is all right, however, since it is more important that the stock build strength later in time, as it did on the right shoulder.

Just as the earlier example shows two patterns in one chart simultaneously, you also may sometimes see two IHS patterns within one another. Having a pattern with two necklines—one lower, one higher—usually

FIGURE 13.80   The left shoulder in this pattern isn't quite perfect, because it doesn't touch the neckline entirely, but that didn't make the breakout any less predictive.

means the pattern is that much more powerful, since the larger pattern is affirming and strengthening the smaller one. Redback Networks (RBAK), in Figure 13.81, has an exceptionally good inverted H&S pattern, and the lower horizontal line clearly shows the neckline of the smaller pattern.

In a longer-term view (Figure 13.82), two necklines can be seen. The behavior of the price above each neckline was similar—a breakout, a partial retracement, and then continued strength. An observer of this stock need not have waited for the formation and penetration of the higher neckline. The second, higher neckline simply confirms the strength of the chart, as can be seen with the steady upward direction following both breakouts.

Let's round out our examination of head and shoulders patterns with Figures 13.83 through 13.90, which will be captioned with the length (in time) and strength (in percentage) of their respective breakouts, from the neckline to the point of maximum change.

FIGURE 13.81 Here is the initial breakout of RBAK from its inverted H&S pattern.

FIGURE 13.82 There are two necklines in this stock, which is somewhat unusual.

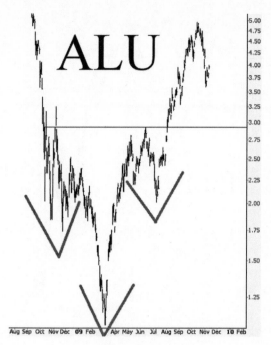

FIGURE 13.83 Allied Capital—length of move 70 days; strength of move +69 percent.

FIGURE 13.84 Melco Crown—length of move 348 days; strength of move −87 percent.

FIGURE 13.85 Isle of Capri Casinos—length of move 364 days; strength of move −88 percent.

FIGURE 13.86 Hutchinson Technology—length of move 397 days; strength of move −69 percent.

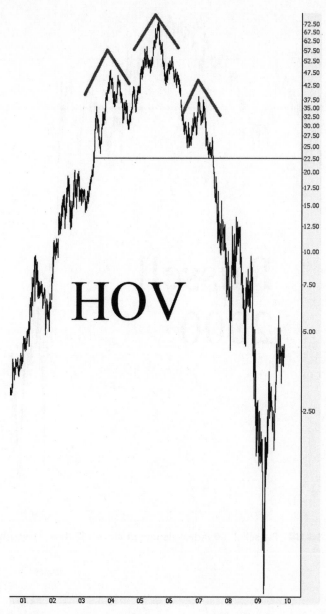

FIGURE 13.87 Hovnanian Enterprises—length of move 639 days; strength of move −98 percent.

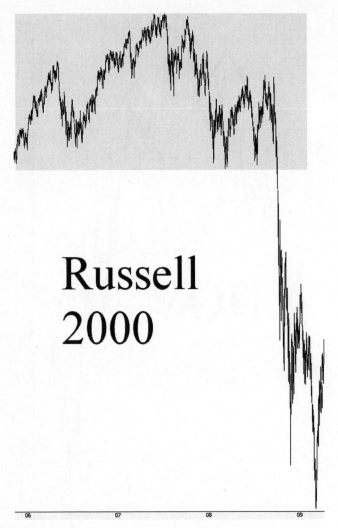

FIGURE 13.88   Russell 2000 index—length of move 157 days; strength of move −47 percent.

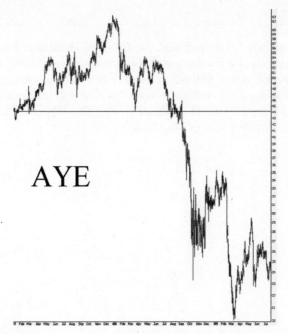

FIGURE 13.89 Allegheny Energy—length of move 188 days; strength of move −55 percent.

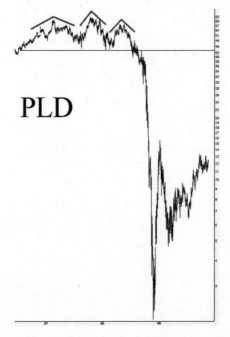

FIGURE 13.90 Prologis—length of move 129 days; strength of move −95 percent.

SUMMARY

Both the Head and Shoulders and the Inverted Head and Shoulders patterns are easy to recognize and profitable tools in your trading arsenal. You have seen dozens of real-life examples of how powerful these patterns can be with both bearish and bullish moves. We now will turn our attention to the final set of drawing tools available to you, the Fibonacci objects—the retracement, time series, arcs, and fans.

CHAPTER 14

Pattern Recognition

T he basis of a large portion of technical analysis is pattern recognition—that is, the ability to spot one of the classic technical patterns (such as a wedge, a head and shoulders, or a triple bottom) and estimate in what direction and by what amount the price is likely to move.

There are a couple of disadvantages to looking for patterns manually. First, it takes a lot of experience. Getting the ability to look at a chart and accurately discern what pattern, if any, is present, takes years of experience as a technical analyst. Second, it takes a lot of time. Going through hundreds of charts to look for a handful of high-probability patterns could easily consume hours of your time, and even if you decided to make a serious time commitment, you could not as a practical matter go through all the stocks that trade on the major exchanges.

Fortunately, ProphetCharts has a couple of tools that automatically find patterns in stock charts. One tool locates the classic technical analysis patterns over the course of many years of stock data, and the other tool finds short-term candlestick patterns. This chapter will introduce you to both of these tools and their effective use.

HOW TO FIND PATTERNS

The ProphetCharts historical price database automatically keeps track of patterns as they emerge. Getting to this information is simply a matter of

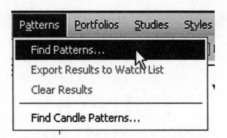

FIGURE 14.1 You can access up-to-date patterns results by clicking Find Patterns.

establishing the parameters of your search so the qualifying symbols can be delivered to your copy of ProphetCharts.

The first thing you do is choose Find Patterns from the Patterns menu, as shown in Figure 14.1.

The Find Patterns dialog box comes up, and within that box there are five different tabs: General, Patterns, Ratings, Watch Lists, and Filters. You can choose any of these five tabs to fine-tune the nature of your pattern search. We will go through each of these tabs individually.

The first tab, General, is the one that shows up when you first bring up the Find Patterns dialog box (Figure 14.2). It has a variety of checkboxes, dropdown menus, and radio buttons. As with the vast majority of the choices available in Find Patterns, you don't have to make selections in every single one of these parameters. They are mostly there to give you the ability to customize your search.

The General tab has the following parameters:

- **Find Symbols with Patterns:** You need to check this box to activate the search function. As the description indicates, the resulting symbols will show up in the Patterns module.
- **Order results by:** There is a dropdown menu here with eight different choices for you to establish the basis of sorting the results. The default, sorting by Symbol, is usually best.
- **Show Patterns on Charted Symbol:** If you check this box, ProphetCharts will automatically draw the lines that constitute the basis for the symbols found. It is very likely you'll want to check this box, since the whole point of the pattern recognition engine is to see the patterns.
- **Limit Search Result:** You can restrict the quantity of symbols that are displayed here. If you enter a number that is smaller than the resulting list, the excess symbols will not be displayed.

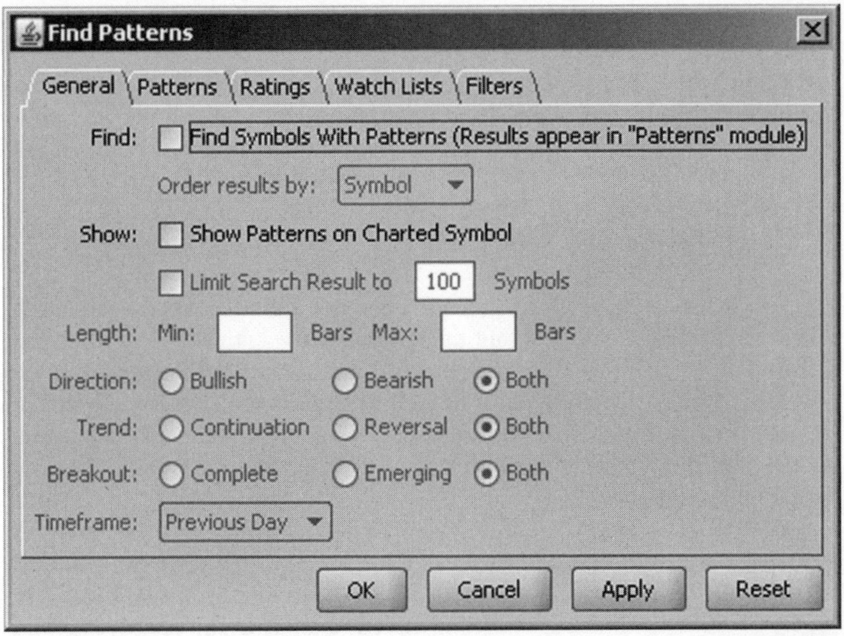

Find Patterns ☒

General \ Patterns \ Ratings \ Watch Lists \ Filters \

Find: ☐ Find Symbols With Patterns (Results appear in "Patterns" module)

Order results by: Symbol ▼

Show: ☐ Show Patterns on Charted Symbol

☐ Limit Search Result to 100 Symbols

Length: Min: [ ] Bars Max: [ ] Bars

Direction: ○ Bullish ○ Bearish ◉ Both

Trend: ○ Continuation ○ Reversal ◉ Both

Breakout: ○ Complete ○ Emerging ◉ Both

Timeframe: Previous Day ▼

[OK] [Cancel] [Apply] [Reset]

FIGURE 14.2 Of the five tabs, General has the most important parameters.

- **Length:** There are two fields here—Min and Max Bars—that let you state the number of price bars that will make up your search. For instance, if you were searching daily charts for patterns, and you wanted to see only patterns between 50 and 200 days in length, you would enter 50 in the Min box and 200 in the Max box. It is a pretty good idea to set a Min value, because the longer the price pattern, the stronger and more reliable it tends to be.
- **Direction:** Here are three radio buttons: Bullish, Bearish, and Both. You must choose one of these to state whether you want to seek bullish patterns, bearish patterns, or both.
- **Trend:** There are also three radio buttons here: Continuation, Reversal, and Both. Trend is an important distinction when seeking patterns. If you want to seek patterns that are echoing their general trend (for instance, if you want to seek bullish patterns that are in stocks that are already behaving bullishly), choose Continuation; if you are looking for changes in direction (such as bearish patterns in bullish stocks), choose Reversal; if it doesn't matter, choose Both.
- **Breakout:** The pattern recognition engine is always monitoring prices, including patterns that are in development but may not necessarily complete. You can choose to seek only patterns that have completed

(Breakout), those that are in the process of being formed (Emerging), or Both.

• **Timeframe:** This dropdown menu gives you a series of choices of time frames to search, ranging from just the previous day all the way up to the past five years. Choose the range of data of interest to you: if you are a very short-term trader, you might want to look for patterns over just the past couple of days; if you are a longer-term trader or a swing trader, you probably want to use a much longer time frame.

You don't have to go to any of the other tabs to execute a search. Whether you use any of the other tabs or not, the way to execute the search is the same: click either the Apply button (to populate the Patterns module with the resulting symbols but remain in the dialog box) or the OK button (to execute the search). You can also click Reset to change all the parameters to their default settings or click Cancel to get out of the Find Patterns dialog box altogether.

The Patterns tab, shown in Figure 14.3, lets you choose which of the 16 available patterns you'd like to seek. You can choose anywhere from 1 to all 16 of the checkboxes; the Select All and Clear All buttons will save you time by checking all (or unchecking all) the boxes. If you are just looking

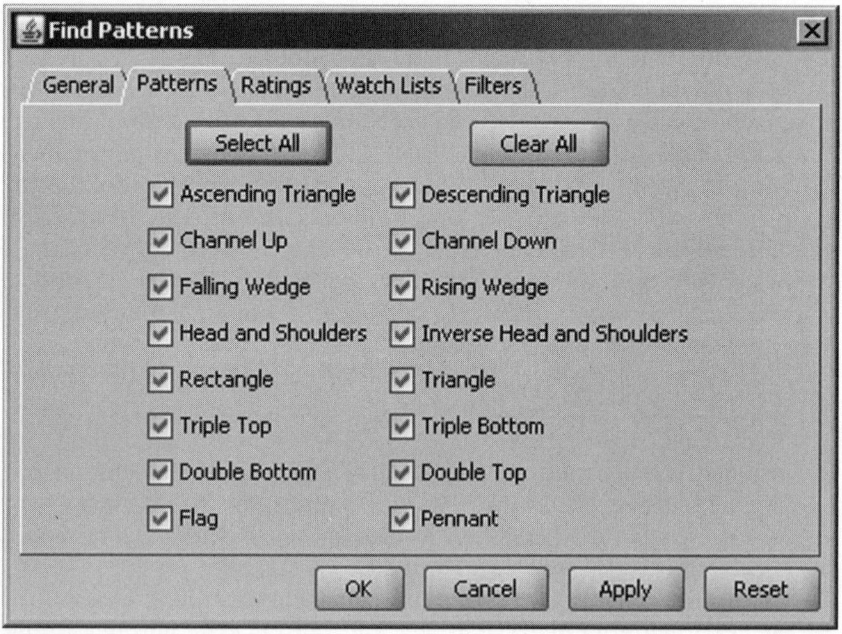

FIGURE 14.3 There are 16 patterns available in the recognition engine.

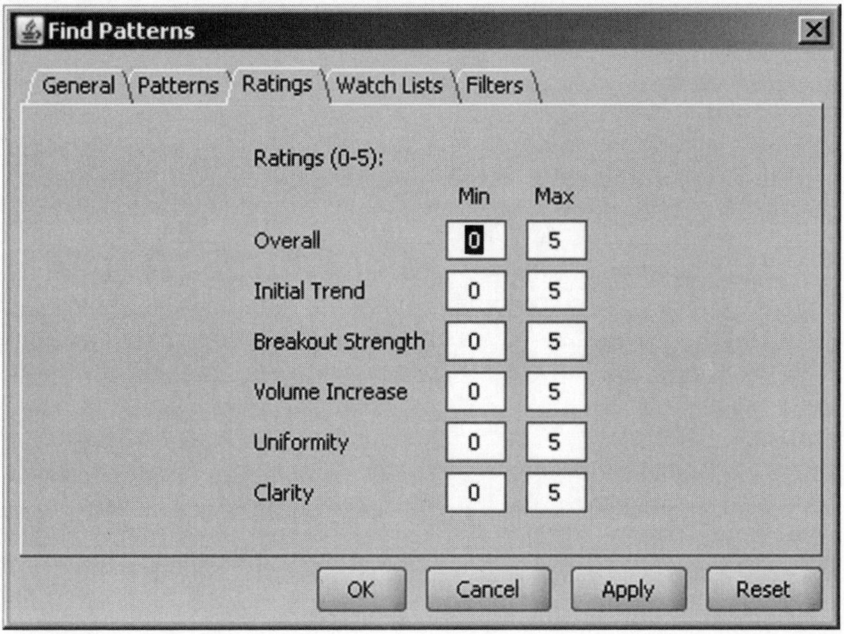

FIGURE 14.4 Most of the time, you probably will want to just keep the default settings.

for interesting patterns, you might as well leave all of them checked, but if you are homing in on a favorite (such as the inverse head and shoulders), just check the specific patterns you want.

The third tab, Ratings (Figure 14.4), lets you establish a minimum and maximum value for the quality of patterns you are seeking. These figures range from 0 (lowest quality) to 5 (highest quality), and the default is 0 for minimum and 5 for maximum for all six parameters (which means nothing is filtered out).

The six parameters dictate how clean the patterns are in several respects: Overall is the general quality of the pattern; Initial Trend is how clean the price action was leading up to the pattern; Breakout Strength is how much power the price has when moving out of the pattern; Volume Increase is how strong the volume increase was during the breakout; Uniformity is how well shaped the pattern is, compared with the ideal; and clarity indicates the confidence level that the price will move to the target.

Generally speaking, you should just keep these settings as they are, but if you'd like to tighten up the search to look for higher-quality patterns, you can change the Min value in the Overall parameter to 4 (or even 5), which will greatly limit the results.

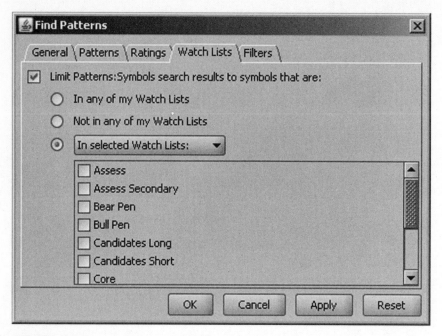

FIGURE 14.5 Including or excluding your watch list contents from the patterns search will save you time.

The fourth tab, Watch Lists (Figure 14.5) is extremely helpful, because it lets you constrict a search to only symbols found within or without your watch lists. For instance, if you wanted to seek patterns only for symbols that you were already following, you would choose the radio button "In any of my Watch Lists" (you would also check the checkbox titled Limit Patterns). This way, *only* symbols that you already follow would be displayed in the resulting patterns module.

You may instead want to seek symbols that aren't in any of your watch lists. After all, you are looking for new opportunities, so you might want to exclude those items you are following already, anyway. In this case, you would click the "Not in any of my Watch Lists" radio button.

You might even choose something not quite so stark as total inclusion or exclusion; instead, you might want to include (or exclude) specific watch lists. In this case, you would click the third radio button, which also includes a dropdown menu, to seek symbols that are already in (or not in) the watch lists that you specify by clicking the checkboxes beneath.

The final tab in the Find Patterns dialog box, Filters (Figure 14.6), can also save you time by not bothering to show you symbols that you don't

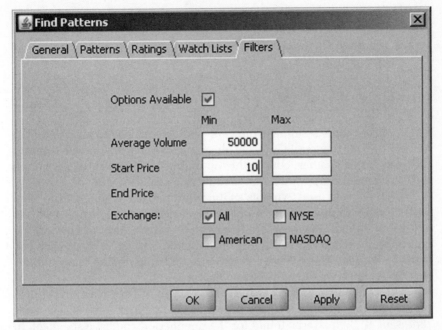

FIGURE 14.6 You should restrict your search to seek only stocks you would consider trading anyway.

find interesting in the first place. It offers a number of parameters to refine the search:

- **Options Available:** If this box is checked, only stocks for which options are available will be presented. This is particularly valuable if you are an options trader, but even if you are not, it will at least focus the search on stocks that are traded widely enough to have options in the first place.
- **Average Volume:** You can set a Min and Max level for the average volume. The main benefit of this parameter is to set a Min amount so that you are not looking at thinly traded stocks.
- **Start Price:** You can set a Min and Max for the price at the beginning of the pattern, which is probably not that important since it is the ending price that is more crucial.
- **End Price:** If you want to avoid stocks that are out of a certain price range (for instance, stocks less than $5), you can set Min and Max levels for the ending price of a stock.
- **Exchange:** By default, this setting is All, but if for some reason you want to find stocks that trade only on the NYSE, American, or NASDAQ stock exchanges, you can choose the appropriate checkboxes here.

Doing a Pattern search is quick, easy, and intuitive. Most of the time, you'll probably need to use only a few of the parameters to construct the search you want. Once you're ready, just click OK.

WORKING WITH THE RESULTS

To see the symbols resulting from your search, you need to make sure the Patterns: Symbols module is turned on. Figure 14.7 shows the two relevant modules to this chapter, both at the top of the list. If there is a checkmark next to a module name, then that module is available to you.

Assuming you used Symbols as the basis for your symbol sorting, you will see a list similar to Figure 14.8. It resembles a watch list, in that you can scroll up and down the symbols with the arrow keys to view all the charts, and you can right-click any of the symbols to add it to a watch list. The object of such an exercise is to find interesting trading opportunities that would not have otherwise been known to you.

When you begin looking at the symbols, you will see blue lines drawn on the charts (in addition to any drawn objects of your own). These lines represent all the patterns found for the time period you have specified. In many cases, you will see multiple patterns on the same stock, such as in Figure 14.9. If you mouse over any particular line, it will display an information box telling you the pattern found, its start and end dates, and its anticipated target.

Something else interesting and useful happens when you mouse over a pattern line: a rectangle appears, showing the target zone. If the target is bullish, the rectangle is tinted green; if the target is bearish, the rectangle

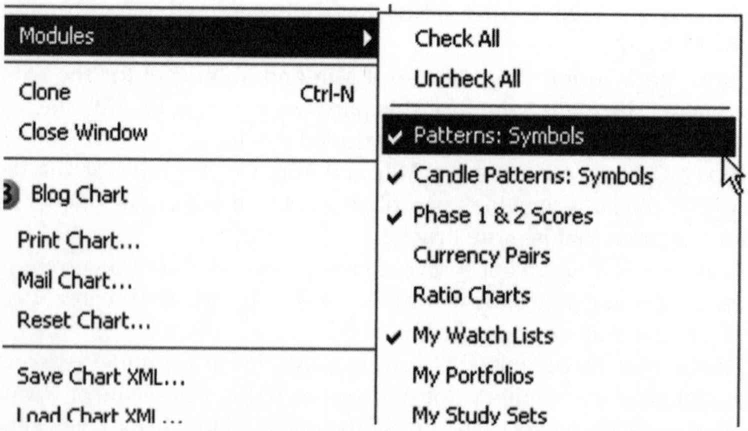

FIGURE 14.7 The top two modules in the list are relevant to this chapter.

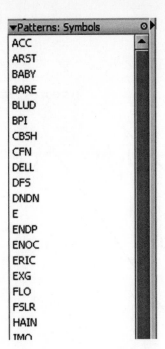

FIGURE 14.8 The symbols resulting from your patterns search are shown in this module.

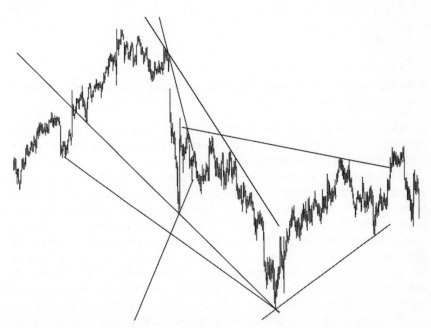

FIGURE 14.9 If you decide to Show Patterns on Chart Symbol in the dialog box, you will see blue lines automatically drawn on your charts showing any discovered patterns.

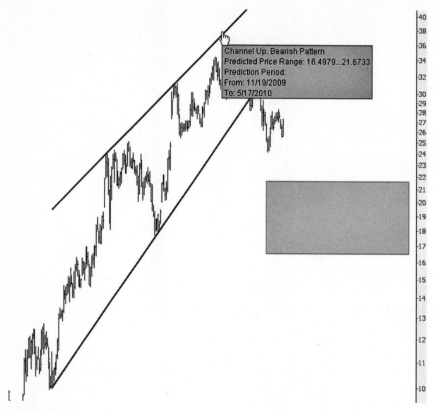

FIGURE 14.10 The rectangle shows the anticipated range of the price move.

is tinted red. The rectangle is placed on the chart appropriate for the target time range (which is the width of the rectangle) and the target price (which is the height). Figure 14.10 provides a bearish example.

The important thing to keep in mind when you view historical patterns is that the completion of a pattern typically happens when the price crosses beneath the supporting trend line (for bearish patterns) or above the resisting trend line (for bullish patterns). In Figure 14.11, for instance, the pattern was completed at a price of about $14.50 when the stock gapped down and pierced its lower trend line. At that time, the prediction system called for the stock to fall somewhere between $12.1188 and $13.3853 between the dates of 11/20/2009 and 2/7/2010. As you can see, the price did indeed fall within that date and price range, indicating a successful prediction.

We've seen a couple of bearish examples, so let's look at some bullish ones. Figure 14.12 shows a bullish projection (the green rectangle), calling for a stock that was about $34 at the time of the signal to climb above

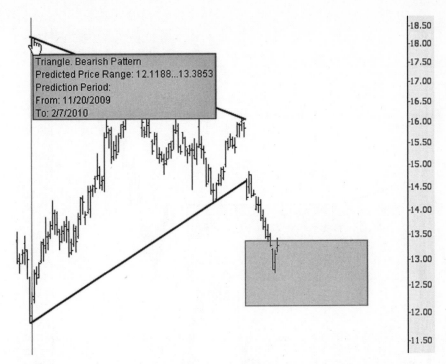

Triangle. Bearish Pattern
Predicted Price Range: 12.1188...13.3853
Prediction Period:
From: 11/20/2009
To: 2/7/2010

FIGURE 14.11 This is an example of a successful bearish prediction.

$40. Mousing over the pattern shows us the name of the pattern (Triangle), its direction (Bullish), its predicted price range, and its prediction period. Because some time has passed since the pattern was predicted, we can see the result, which was that the prediction succeeded. (Just to be clear: some predictions succeed, and some do not; there is no such thing as a 100 percent reliable system.)

Of course, even when a price moves into its prediction rectangle, there is no reason it will not keep going the same direction. Figure 14.13 illustrates that the price kept moving up after the time range of the rectangle. If you were making use of this prediction in a real trade, you would probably want to seriously consider closing the position once the price entered the rectangle. After all, anything inside the rectangle is considered a success, and there is no guarantee that the price will move into the upper boundary of the projected price movement. (Indeed, there is no guarantee that the rectangle will be penetrated by the prices at all.)

The pattern search engine isn't meant to be a substitute for your own thoughtful analysis; it is intended primarily as a source of ideas that you might not have had without access to this tool.

Triangle. Bullish Pattern
Predicted Price Range: 40.3016...47.4579
Prediction Period:
From: 7/22/2009
To: 5/12/2010

FIGURE 14.12 Here is an example of a successful bullish prediction.

PATTERN FAILURES

It's important to understand that plenty of patterns are not realized. Stocks that are projected to have bullish moves might plunge in value, and bearish projections might instead be faced with a soaring stock price. So, again, the results from a patterns search should be viewed as nothing more than a list of symbols to chart and consider on your own.

FIGURE 14.13 There is no reason prices cannot move above their bullish projections or below their bearish ones.

Figure 14.14 illustrates a failed bullish prediction. The entire time span has been traversed, but the price didn't even come close to getting inside the rectangle.

Figure 14.15 provides an even more interesting example, because not only did the price not get into the rectangle but also it subsequently fell away sharply once the projected time range had passed. This is a good

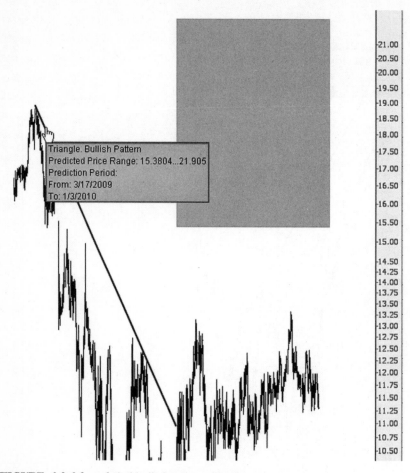

FIGURE 14.14 A failed bullish price projection.

illustration of why you should not simply hold on to a position based on a hoped-for outcome. If you were to enter a position based on a projection, and the time span passes entirely without the anticipated price being realized, it's probably time to move on (all other aspects of the chart being equal).

GRIDS AND EXPORTING

Later, in Chapter 16, you learn about the Grid Charts feature, but it should be noted here that you can right-click on any of the resulting symbols in the Patterns module and choose to view them in grid mode. This can be

FIGURE 14.15 The price fell away sharply after the predicted price movement was not realized.

a helpful time-saver, since you'll probably just want to thumb through the resulting charts fairly quickly to see if any patterns catch your attention. Figure 14.16 provides an example of what a quartet of charts with patterns looks like in grid mode.

As mentioned before, the best way to use the results of a pattern search is to examine the symbols yourself. You can do this directly from the

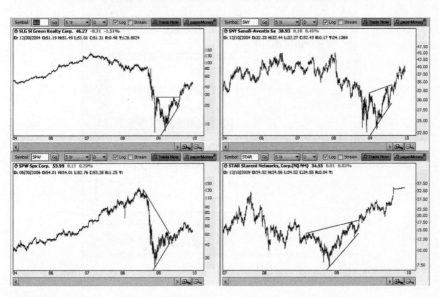

FIGURE 14.16 You can view four charts at a time in grid mode.

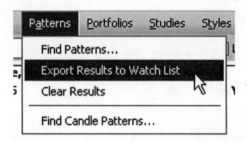

FIGURE 14.17 You can export all the symbols with patterns found in them to your own watch list.

module, or you can move all the symbols to your own watch list. As shown in Figure 14.17, the Patterns menu has a feature, Export Results to Watch List, that lets you take all the symbols you have found and put them in the watch list of your choice.

After you make this selection, you can either create a newly named watch list for the symbols or click on an existing watch list to add the symbols there (Figure 14.18).

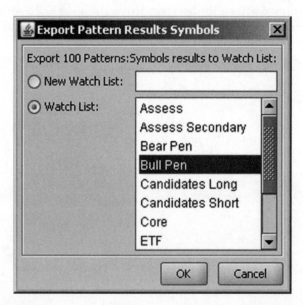

FIGURE 14.18 Choose the destination for the symbols with patterns that have been found.

Pattern recognition is good for long-term patterns. If you would rather focus on very short-term patterns, you might want to use the Candle Patterns feature instead.

CANDLESTICK PATTERNS

The second style of pattern search available in ProphetCharts is candlestick patterns, which you can access at the bottom of the Patterns menu (Figure 14.19). The number of patterns available is larger than the standard pattern engine, but the signals are for a much shorter time horizon.

After you choose Find Candle Patterns, a dialog box like the one in Figure 14.20 appears. There are several parameters on the first tab, general, and their functions are similar to those on the General tab in the standard Find Patterns box. The most important is the first checkbox, Find Symbols With Patterns. You also will probably want to click the last checkbox, Show Patterns on Charted Symbol, since otherwise there will be nothing different about the chart.

As shown in Figure 14.21, there are dozens of candlestick patterns tracked by the data engine. You can select all of them (with the Select All button) or handpick certain ones (by clicking Clear All and then checking only those you want). When you are ready to execute the candlestick search, click OK, and the resulting symbols will very quickly be displayed in the Candle Patterns module.

The patterns themselves span only one or two days, but their effects can be long-lived. Figure 14.22 shows a bearish engulfing pattern (highlighted at the top of the chart), which preceded a slump of more than 50 percent in the price of the equity shown. As with regular patterns, mousing over a candlestick pattern yields the pattern name. Any of the symbols from the Candle Patterns module will have at least one pattern (highlighted

FIGURE 14.19 Candlestick patterns can be found using the Candle Patterns search feature.

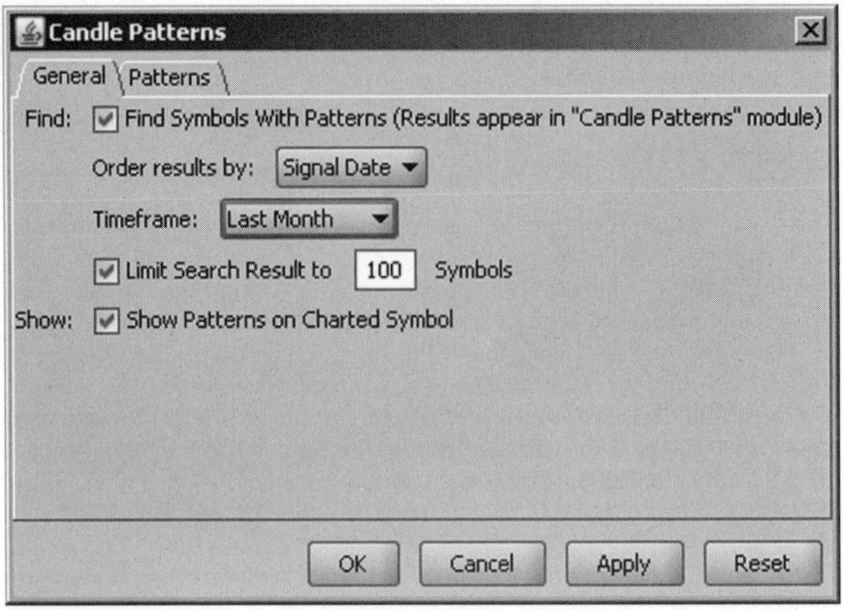

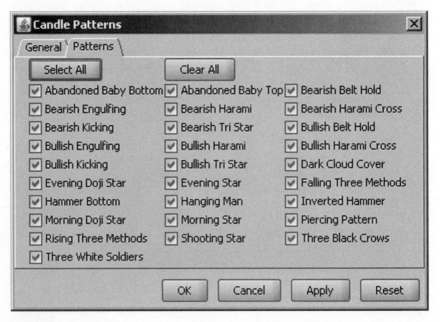

FIGURE 14.20 The General tab for candlestick patterns is very similar to the same tab in the standard pattern search dialog box.

FIGURE 14.21 All the major candlestick patterns are available in the search engine.

FIGURE 14.22 Mouse over the highlighted pattern to see its name.

with yellow) but may have many more, depending on how far in time you executed the search.

Figure 14.23 shows a couple of highlighted patterns. The leftmost one is a Bullish Harami, and the stock climbs about 25 percent after this pattern is identified. Clearly, the price did not sustain itself after that point. Take note that a key difference between the standard pattern search and

FIGURE 14.23 There is no time or price projection given with candlestick patterns.

the candlestick style is that the former provides price and time projections, whereas the latter simply tells you what candlestick pattern has been found.

Finally, if you are using candlestick charts and have color bars turned on, you may notice that several color combinations appear. These colors have the following meanings:

- **White with Black Outline:** The stock closed at a higher price than the candlestick's opening price and also higher than the previous candlestick's close.
- **White with Red Outline:** The stock closed at a higher price than the candlestick's opening price and at a price lower than the previous candlestick's close.

- **Red:** The stock closed at a lower price than the candlestick's opening price and also lower than the previous candlestick's close.
- **Black:** The stock closed at a lower price than the candlestick's opening price and at a price higher than the previous candlestick's close.

So there you have it—two powerful tools to find patterns that would be impractical to locate manually. Equipped with this knowledge, you now have a time-saving method for locating new trading opportunities, all built within your charting program. In the next chapter, we will explore an entirely new kind of pattern—those within the realm of Fibonacci drawings.

CHAPTER 15

Fibonacci Drawings

I n all the many years I've been learning and performing technical analysis, there is no set of studies which has interested me more than those of Fibonacci. In ProphetCharts, there are four kinds of Fibonacci studies available: retracements, fans, time zones, and arcs. In this chapter we will explore each of these, as always, with actual examples from the recent past. But first, let us learn a little about the namesake of these studies.

A BRIEF HISTORY LESSON

Leonardo of Pisa lived from 1170 to 1250, and he is regarded as perhaps the greatest mathematician of the Middle Ages. His father, William, had the nickname "Bonaccio," which means good-natured, so Leonardo was subsequently known by the nickname of "Fibonacci" (short for *filius Bonacci*, or the son of Bonaccio).

William worked in North Africa at a trading post, and even though his home country of Italy had used the Roman numeral system for centuries, he came into contact with traders who instead used the Arabic method of numbers (which is what we use today—1, 2, 3, 4, and so forth, as opposed to numbers such as XI and MMC). Leonardo helped his father with his work, and in the course of doing so, he became acquainted with and enamored by the Arabic style of numbering, which seemed far more sensible and efficient than the Roman style. The world owes Leonardo a debt of gratitude for helping to popularize this system of numbers, since it's doubtful anyone today would appreciate having to use Roman numerals in everyday life.

Another great contribution Leonardo made was with respect to his writings related to what we today call Fibonacci numbers. This is a sequence of numbers which begins like this: 0, 1, 1, 2, 3, 5, 8, 13, 21, 34, 55, 89, 144, 233, 377, 610, 987, 1,597. Each number is the sum of the two preceding numbers. These numbers have a variety of interesting properties, including the fact that, as the sequence progresses, each number divided by its preceding number approaches the mathematical figure *phi* (approximately 1.618033989), known as the golden ratio, which has a wide variety of expressions in nature.

In the world of stock charts, the concepts put forth by Fibonacci are manifested in drawn objects—retracements, time zones, arcs, and fans. We will explore each of these. There are entire volumes written on the golden ratio and Fibonacci numbers, including their relationship to nature. We will focus on how these mathematical insights can make us better, more profitable traders.

THE FIBONACCI RETRACEMENT

By far the most popular and easiest to interpret Fibonacci study is the retracement. The retracement study is performed by drawing a line between two extreme points on a graph (a significant high point and low point), which then creates the drawing of a series of horizontal lines set at key Fibonacci ratios (23.6 percent, 38.2 percent, 50 percent, 61.8 percent, and 100 percent). These ratios represent a certain proportion of the vertical distance between the extreme high and low you have identified.

The impact of these levels on a financial chart can be profound, since they represent significant areas of support and resistance. In many instances, you will see a stock price bounce off these lines until it penetrates one of them, only to behave the same way with the next line. The predictive power of retracements is that you can anticipate levels of support and resistance where prices will tend to cling.

To draw a retracement, you need to use the Fibonacci retracement tool in the toolbar. All four Fibonacci tools are located at the right side of the toolbar (Figure 15.1). They are, in order, the Retracement, Time Zones, Arcs, and Fans. To draw a Fibonacci retracement study on a chart, you would follow these steps:

1. Click on the Retracement icon in the toolbar. Your cursor will change into crosshairs.

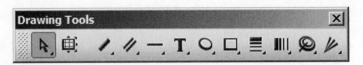

FIGURE 15.1   The four Fibonacci tools are located at the right side of the toolbar: Retracement, Time Zones, Arcs, and Fans.

2. Find an extreme trough or peak in the chart and click on it to establish one end of the reference line you are going to use.
3. Drag the mouse. As you do, the retracement lines will automatically be displayed. Once you have found the other extreme for your reference line, click the mouse again.

It should be stated early on that not all charts are Fibonacci-friendly. Some charts perform better with Fibonacci studies than others. Luckily, there is a fairly easy way to determine whether a stock is Fibonacci-friendly, and that is to lay down the study and examine whether past price behavior seems to comply with the study. If it does, chances are that it will continue to do so.

To make this assessment, it's valuable to understand the reference line and its relationship to time on the chart. The reference line is the line drawn between two extremes. Whichever of those two points is more recent creates a division between the before and after of the retracement. For instance, if you drew a line from January 1998 to March 2001, then the point at March 2001 is the more recent one, and the part of the chart prior to March 2001 would be before the study and the part after March 2001 would be after the study.

The reason this is important to note is that it helps establish how good the predictive power of the study is for that particular stock. The before time is useful only insofar as determining how Fibonacci-friendly the stock is, because the study could not have been laid down in this time period. In other words, because the entire reference line could not have been drawn until March 2001 had taken place, there would have been no Fibonacci study in existence until that date, which means that it could not have been used as a guide in trading.

After March 2001, however, the study could have been used, and that time period is valid to consider how strong a predictor the study had been. Study Figure 15.2, for instance. The reference line begins in autumn 1998 and ends in spring 2004. A thick vertical line has been drawn on this chart to distinguish the area before the study (left of the line) and after the study (right of the line).

FIGURE 15.2 The areas highlighted with rectangles show just some of the many instances where the price pauses or reverses based on the retracement level.

Rounded rectangles have been drawn on top of the chart to show areas where prices seem to cling to retracement levels. There are six clear instances before the study where the prices did this, which indicates this is a very Fibonacci-friendly chart. The eight highlighted areas to the right of the line confirm that the predictive power of this study for this stock is, as expected, quite strong. The conclusion is that, for this particular stock, this retracement study has a lot of power, and it would be useful to leave this study on the chart to anticipate future reversal points in the price action.

Unlike the other drawn objects, which tend to be a single, simple line, the Fibonacci studies draw relatively complex objects. In the case of a retracement, there are a number of pieces to the completed object. There is the reference line, which you draw from one extreme to another. There are the horizontal retracement lines, each of which can be the thickness and pattern of your choice. And there are the price and percentage references that accompany each of the lines so you can see what price value and percentage value each line has. You can control each of these elements to achieve the appearance you want.

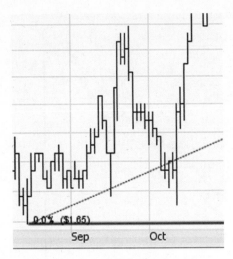

FIGURE 15.3 There are two extremes to drawing a retracement, and a dotted line references the distance between these two points.

Figure 15.3 shows the lowest extreme of a Fibonacci retracement. You can see the percentage (0.0 percent), the dollar price at that level ($1.65), the horizontal line that constitutes the 0 percent level, and the dotted reference line, which extends diagonally.

Whether you want to see the reference line is up to you and is controlled by the retracement preferences dialog box. Figure 15.4 shows a stock with a retracement drawn and the reference line visible. The rounded rectangles (which are drawn here for illustrative purposes and are not normally displayed in the charting program) highlight the various turning points in price that correspond to the retracement levels. Follow with your eye the entire price move for this graph, and notice how powerful the retracement levels are. You can appreciate what a good predictive tool this can be if you look at all the turning and pausing points that follow the reference line.

Figure 15.5 explicitly shows the motion from level to level with a series of rectangles and arrows. Obviously, the price doesn't move in a straight line from one level to another. What it does do, though, is (1) bounce off, (2) cling to, or (3) pierce each level. If you have a position in a stock, it pays to carefully watch a chart as it nears a retracement level. Especially strong (or weak, if moving downward) stocks will pierce the retracement without hesitation. Otherwise, the retracement will represent a wall of support or resistance to the price action, either repelling the price or at least stalling it at that level.

FIGURE 15.4 This retracement is shown with a reference line. You can choose whether you want the retracement line to be displayed for any drawing.

There are many different ways to apply the predictive power of the Fibonacci retracement. Let's mentally return to the autumn of 2003, a time when all the U.S. markets had suffered a severe downturn. Texas Instruments (symbol TXN) was especially hard-hit, losing nearly 90 percent of its value.

Let us further suppose you felt the selling was done with, and you wanted to take a large, long position in TXN. You know where you want to set your stop price—that's easy—you will set it just beneath the all-time low set in October. But how long do you hold onto the position? When do you take profits off the table?

That question is virtually impossible to answer unless you tell yourself to buy and hold in perpetuity. A Fibonacci retracement, however, proves to be invaluable in this decision. As Figure 15.6 shows, the stock seems to be Fibonacci-friendly. During the stock's entire descent, it seems to bounce off or cling to the various retracement levels. During its last gasp before the final fall, it hangs on to the 23.6 percent level before finally succumbing and bottoming out at $13. Let us suppose you bought the stock at $15.

As a skilled chartist, you would know to take profits off the table—at least some of them—at around $33 per share, since that is the level that

FIGURE 15.5 These arrows help illustrate how the price bounces from level to level, both before and after the reference line.

represents major resistance to the price moving higher. In about a year's time, the stock pushed up to that level, and sure enough, it started to fall again. It repeated this behavior again and again and again. By taking profits at the appropriate time, you would have bagged a very healthy gain and been able to invest your money elsewhere (or, if you were particularly confident, perhaps even short TXN as it bounced off the retracement).

The more obedient the price action is with respect to the Fibonacci retracement levels, the more likely it is that these lines will have power over future price action. From 1986 to 1991, the prices bounced very firmly off the various retracement levels (Figure 15.7), and having done so, the prices likewise continued to comply with these retracements after the termination of the reference line.

FIGURE 15.6 After a severe decline in a stock, the retracement level represents a formidable area of resistance.

But here is the remarkable thing—and you may want to read this several times for it to fully sink in—the reference line didn't even exist until 1991. In other words, the market was obviously blind to these Fibonacci levels in 1986, 1987, 1988, 1989, 1990, and most of 1991. Once the stock had peaked and clearly was heading south, a person could lay down a pattern like this only to discover at that time the almost eerie behavior of the prices relative to the Fibonacci retracement that was only now just laid down. This provides a very clear affirmation that these levels should be respected on a going-forward basis with this stock.

If you hold the mouse cursor over any element of a retracement, more information about that element will be displayed. For instance, Figure 15.8 shows the result of mousing over the 23.6 percent retracement level. A box appears that displays the date and value at the start of the reference line, the date and value at the end of the reference line, and the percentage and dollar value of the particular retracement being moused over.

Because the Fibonacci retracement is a relatively complex drawn object, there are many aspects of it you can control. There are two ways to invoke the Customize Fibonacci Retracements dialog box (Figure 15.9): you can right-click on a retracement and select Customize Fibonacci Retracements from the pop-up menu, or you can hold down your mouse button

FIGURE 15.7 If a price seems to bounce off retracement levels consistently before the reference line, the odds are much stronger it will do so as well after the reference line.

while pointing at the retracement tool in the toolbar to get the same selection. This dialog box lets you control these aspects of the retracement:

> *Color:* Controls the color of the entire Fibonacci drawing.
> *Opacity:* Controls the transparency of the retracement, ranging from 0 (invisible) to 1 (solid).

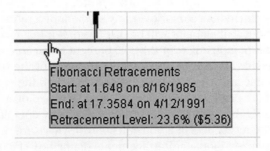

FIGURE 15.8 Mousing over any retracement level will reveal information about that level and the entire drawn object.

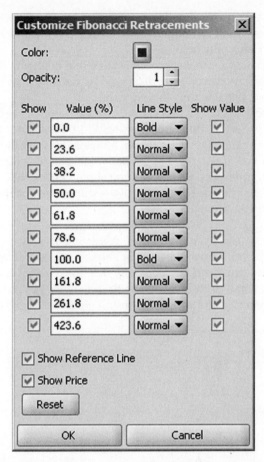

FIGURE 15.9 The wide variety of choices in the Customize Fibonacci Retracements dialog box control its appearance and settings.

Show checkboxes: Checking each of these will make particular retracement levels display. At first, all of them are checked. You can turn any levels on or off with these checkboxes.

Value entry boxes: These are the percentage values used to lay down the retracements. It is very unlikely you will want to change these.

Line Style dropdowns: You can choose from three line styles: normal, bold, and dotted. If you want to emphasize or de-emphasize any particular level, you may want to change the kind of line displayed.

Show Value checkboxes: This controls which of the retracement lines will have their percentage value displayed. These are all on by default. You can simplify the drawing by turning off any of these that you want, although knowing the percentage levels being displayed is usually helpful.

Show Reference Line checkbox: The line that connects the two points you click as extremes is displayed by default. If you want to hide this line, you can turn this checkbox off.

Show Price checkbox: If you want the dollar value of each retracement level displayed, this checkbox should be checked. Normally you get the percentage value shown for each line for which Show Value is checked. If you want the dollar value as well, which can be helpful when setting a stop price, you should check this, too.

Reset button: Clicking this resets all the values and checkboxes to their default condition.

Figure 15.10 shows a Fibonacci retracement with all the normal settings, except the Show Value checkboxes are all off and the Show Reference Line has been unchecked. This makes for a clean, simple look, although some of the key information is being suppressed. You can still access numeric data about any retracement level by mousing over

FIGURE 15.10 A sample Fibonacci retracement drawn on a stock chart.

FIGURE 15.11 A stock will not necessarily follow a retracement path all the way back down, but it may still pause at certain levels before reversing direction.

any particular line of interest to you. (As before, the rounded rectangles highlighting the reversal and resistance points are drawn here for emphasis and are not normally displayed in the charting program.)

It is impossible to know, of course, when a stock has reached a long-term peak or trough. Just because you are able to draw a good Fibonacci retracement that seems to line up well with prior price action doesn't mean a major reversal is in the works. What the lines do tell you, however, is that if the stock does start moving firmly either up or down, its next natural stopping point (either to pause or reverse) is going to be the next Fibonacci level.

Take Figure 15.11 as an example. The very top line represents the termination point of the reference line. A person deciding to sell this stock short around this point would need to pay close attention to the retracement levels beneath the current price. In this instance, the price moved down two retracement levels before reversing and moving higher. A trader short this stock would want to be especially watchful when the stock reached any retracement level, because each of them represents a potential reversal point, as was the case here.

FIGURE 15.12 A retracement will not indicate how long a price will remain at any given level, but it provides clear boundaries of support and resistance in both directions.

The longer and more substantial a prior price move, the longer it will probably take prices to move through the retracement levels in the opposite direction. Figure 15.12 shows the stock chart for Duke Energy, and the reference line is displayed. Notice the price action that took place to the right of the reference line. It took years, but the price pushed higher and higher through the various retracement levels.

First the price reached the 23.6 percent level, then it backed off. The next time, it pierced this level, almost reaching the 38.2 percent level, at which time it eased back to the 23.6 percent level (this time as support instead of resistance). It then pushed through the 38.2 percent level to pause at the 50 percent level, and so forth. You can follow the steady progression on the chart, but it is clear what an invaluable perspective the retracement levels would give to a person trading this stock. Without it, a trader is essentially flying blind.

Fairchild Semiconductor (Figure 15.13) provides another good example of using retracement levels as anticipated reversal points. After a very broad downward move from 2000 to 2002, the stock bounces within a very wide range. The lower three retracement levels, however, provided excellent indications as to the reversal points during those postcrash gyrations.

FIGURE 15.13 A stock does not necessarily make a broad down move and then a correlating broad up move. It may instead remain range-bound among the Fibonacci levels.

As always, drawn objects can be used in combination. If more than one object suggests a reversal point, that only strengthens the argument that the price will pause or reverse at that level. Healthnet (Figure 15.14) has both a retracement and a trend line drawn. There are four rectangles drawn on top of the chart. Reading from left to right: the first rectangle shows the price bouncing off the supporting trend line as well as the retracement level. Once the stock breaks beneath the trend line, the next stopping point is two more retracement levels down.

At this point, the price action becomes very interesting, because a trader would want to anticipate how far the stock is going to retrace upward after its recent plunge. The trend line and Fibonacci retracement, acting in concert, provide an excellent clue. The third rectangle shows how the price clung tightly to the retracement line, never getting higher than the former supporting trend line (which has changed roles and is now resistance). As the stock weakens again, it falls to the next retracement level beneath.

Used properly, well-drawn retracements are akin to getting tomorrow's newspaper today: you have a very strong predictor as to what price level will be reached next.

FIGURE 15.14 This chart has two helpful drawn objects: the retracement levels and a trend line, which provides clear resistance when the price tries to move upward again.

One instance where the Fibonacci retracement is especially useful is after a stock has made a major move, either up or down. After a large movement with a lot of volatility, traders are extremely uncertain as to where the next support or resistance level is going to be.

Take yourself back to the autumn of 2002. All the U.S. stock indexes, particularly the NASDAQ, had suffered a brutal bear market. The NASDAQ 100 ETF, better known as the QQQ (or cubes) had lost about 80 percent of its value. Suppose you believed the selling was overdone and you took a major long position in this security. (Take note that even though the financial instrument is known as the QQQ, the symbol is QQQQ.)

The QQQ begins to move higher, producing a profit for you. But how long do you hold on? Unless your intent is to hold it forever, you should probably try to optimize your holding period so that you get out when the recovery seems to have been fully realized. In this instance, the retracement is once again invaluable. Figure 15.15 shows the retracement levels placed on top of the QQQQ graph. The stock bottomed out at about $20, and the first retracement level is at about $43, a more than 100 percent gain.

FIGURE 15.15 After the gigantic slide of QQQ, which represents the NASDAQ 100 stocks, virtually no study except the Fibonacci retracement could have provided a good prediction as to how high QQQ would be able to climb back.

It took three years to get there, but as the arrow indicates, the QQQ came within pennies of the retracement point, at which time it eased away.

You may have noticed in the dialog box that the Fibonacci retracements do not end at 100 percent. They can go on to higher ratio levels, such as 161.8 percent, 261.8 percent, and higher. So not only can these retracement levels guide you in terms of price action between the two extremes of the reference line but also they can give you guidance as to how high or low a price may move outside those extremes.

The stock graph shown in Figure 15.16 provides a fitting example of this. The graph encompasses the time range 1985 to 2006, a period of more than two decades. The retracement was drawn based on points in 1985 (the low) and 1991 (the high). From 1987 through 1999, there are many instances—just a few of which are highlighted—where the retracement levels have been obeyed.

What's more interesting is what happens when the price breaks above the 100 percent level. There are three times when the stock paused and consolidated, and in each of those three instances, it matched the retracement

FIGURE 15.16 Fibonacci levels beyond 100 percent can be an invaluable predictive tool, as illustrated here.

level perfectly. Thus, the retracements are not only able to provide interpolation between two extremes but also able to extrapolate to price levels that haven't even been experienced by a stock yet. This obviously doubles the power and value of a well-placed Fibonacci retracement object.

Figure 15.17 is a powerful illustration of Fibonacci retracements, as well as intermarket analysis. What is shown is the ratio between the New Zealand currency (the kiwi) and the U.S. dollar. The retracement levels are established based on the extremes of 2001 and 2008, with important hits to those levels highlighted in yellow.

During the financial crisis of 2008–2009, a trader might have put this chart to good use in trying to find a good entry point to go long. Although NZD/USD fell very hard, it finally found stabilization in early March 2009 at the 23.6 percent retracement level, almost to the day that the equity market bottomed.

The retailer Nordstrom has a very Fibonacci-friendly stock chart, illustrated in Figure 15.18. Based on the extreme high (in 2007) and low (in 2008), the retracements provided multiple opportunities for a trader to profit from both long and short positions, as there was a strong tendency to bounce off these levels in both directions.

FIGURE 15.17 The currency chart NZD/USD provided a powerful indication that the equity market had bottomed in early March 2009.

When price levels approach multiple points of support or resistance that are in agreement, those levels should be heeded more than if simply one tool was being used. In Figure 15.19, the NASDAQ Composite ($COMPQ) is approaching both the 38.2 percent Fibonacci retracement and the underside of a broken trend line that was started almost 20 years earlier. The resolution of this resistance will be history long after the publication of this book, but as of this chart's capture, prices will have difficulty pushing easily past those levels.

FIBONACCI FANS

By now it should be clear how to draw and use the Fibonacci retracement. We now turn our attention to an equally useful tool, the Fibonacci fan. The

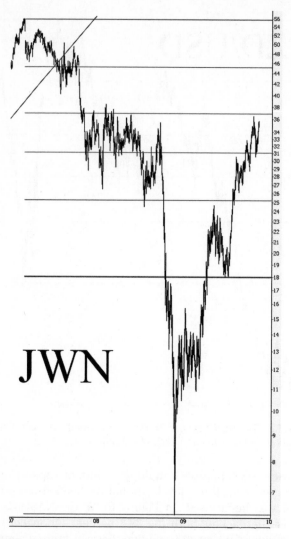

FIGURE 15.18 Nordstrom's price action is well-bounded between the retracement levels.

application and interpretation of fans is very similar to retracements. As with a retracement, you need to identify a low and a high extreme to place your reference line, at which point the fans will be automatically placed for you. As with retracement, the fan lines indicate important support, resistance, and consolidation points for price action.

Except for the fact that fan lines are at an angle, the interpretation of these lines is very similar to the application of retracements. Examine

FIGURE 15.19 Both the failed trend line and the retracement levels suggest the NASDAQ Composite faces difficulty at present prices.

the chart for Hansen Natural (symbol HANS) in Figure 15.20. To draw this Fibonacci fan, a user would:

1. Choose the Fibonacci fan tool from the toolbar.
2. Draw a line from the low on February 12, 2003, at 40.62 cents all the way up to the extreme high of $52.72 on July 6, 2006 (an amazing 130-fold increase in price in just over three years).
3. Release the mouse, thus displaying the Fibonacci fans.

The three arrows on the chart indicate where the price reversed off the highest fan line. This is a good confirmation of the Fibonacci-friendly nature of this stock with respect to these fan lines. Now suppose you had sold this stock short in July as it started to ease. As sensational a run-up as this stock has had, it's obviously very strong and has no clear areas of support. The question is: when do you take profits?

FIGURE 15.20 These Fibonacci fans are drawn from one extreme to another on the symbol HANS. The arrows indicate points where the price touched the top of the highest fan line, at which point it reversed each time.

On August 7, 2006, HANS started to plunge on record volume. If you owned puts on this stock or had a short position, you would be in the happy predicament of wondering when to take profits. Fibonacci fans would have yielded a ready answer: because the stock opened beneath one of the fan lines, that level of support was clearly already taken out. The next fan line down, therefore, would be the next level of support. As Figure 15.21 illustrates, this level offered formidable support for HANS in spite of the high-volume plunge in price. Traders covering their positions in this area would have had good timing, and those empowered with the insight of the Fibonacci fan probably would have done so.

Although the trading public is obviously not aware of where Fibonacci fan lines are placed, there is still a remarkable tendency on the part of prices to either cling to a certain fan line or be plainly bounded between two lines, bouncing between the two of them. This applies even when fan lines span years, or even decades, which makes them positively remarkable, particularly considering they are sloped (as opposed to horizontal zones of support and resistance, which are easier to explain away).

FIGURE 15.21 When HANS got hammered after its earnings announcement, the fan line provided a natural stopping point during the plunge.

A number of the following examples are drawn from extremely large Fibonacci fans that span many decades. The chart shown in Figure 15.22 is just a portion of the Dow Jones Industrial Average on which a 70-year-old fan has been drawn. The rectangle has been drawn to highlight how the price action not only is bounded by two fan lines but also, for many years, tends to cling to one of the lines. This particular section is following the dramatic crash of 1987. In spite of all the chaos and tumult surrounding that crash, the prices continue their orderly motion between and along the fan lines.

One should pause to consider how simply remarkable this is. The fan lines were drawn from the depths of the Great Depression to the peak of the Internet bubble (1932 to 2000). The market had no awareness—at least none of which it was conscious—of these boundaries. Over the decades, billions upon billions of individual decisions are made that move this index up and down every day. And in spite of all of these variables, which number on an astronomical scale, the index performs in a stunningly orderly and systematic fashion.

Looking at another, broader index—the S&P 500—we can see similar fascinating phenomena (Figure 15.23). The arrows show how the highest

FIGURE 15.22 Prices will often become bound between the support and resistance provided by fan lines.

and lowest fan lines constrict the price movement. Keep in mind the graph is showing a period of more than 70 years. The price reverses on various fan lines in many instances, and the two rectangles that are drawn here highlight two multidecade years when the prices were bound between two fan lines.

Looking at a specific portion of this index (from 1954 to 1985), we can see a neat, tidy progression of tilted rectangles (Figure 15.24). The rectangles move slightly down each time, since this period of market history included several vicious bear markets, including the infamous 1973–1974 bear market. Even when prices made extreme moves, pushing outside the bounds of the rectangle, the fan lines still provided support against the price moving any lower.

Experimenting with Fibonacci studies, particularly the fans, can be a mesmerizing experience because they seem to wield an almost mysterious power over the markets. Figure 15.25 shows a close-up of the Dow Jones Industrial Average from 1988 to 1994, which includes the minicrash of 1989. This close-up view shows the remarkable tendency, again and again, for

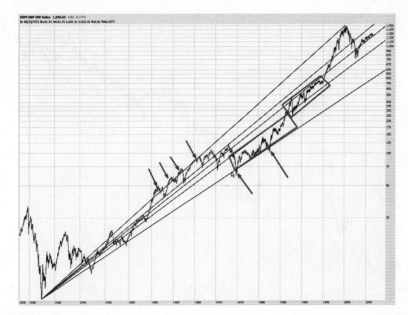

FIGURE 15.23 The arrows here indicate extreme levels of support and resistance during this multidecade movement of the S&P 500, with the rectangles showing just a couple of the bounded areas.

FIGURE 15.24 Here we can see a neat and tidy progression of rectangles that are bounded by the fan lines.

FIGURE 15.25 A close-up of the Dow Jones Industrial Average shows the remarkable ability of the fan lines to dictate where resistance will be, even when it was predicted decades in the past.

the price to move upward toward and then move away from the higher fan line. During the minicrash, the price collapse was stopped short by the fan line beneath it.

The China index, symbol $CZH, had remarkable behavior with respect to its fan lines (Figure 15.26). There are eight specific instances highlighted in the chart where the price bounced almost perfectly off the fan line. Although prices eventually broke free of this confinement, as they always will, for a while this drawing provided remarkable insight into what was most likely to happen next with this index.

The fan lines for American Electric Power (AEP), with points between October 10, 2002, and April 5, 2007, also provided potent levels of support and resistance as the equity generally turned downward for several years (Figure 15.27).

Emerson Electric's (EMR) fan lines were established from much longer-range data points, beginning at October 4, 1974, and ending December 4, 2007 (Figure 15.28). We see again that selling short when the price was at the upper range of fan lines and going long when the price

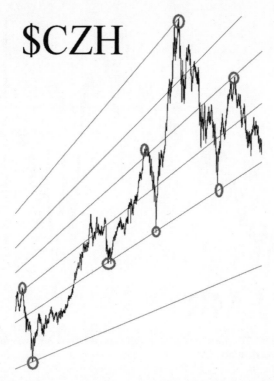

FIGURE 15.26 The Chinese stock market had remarkable behavior with respect to the Fibonacci fan lines.

FIGURE 15.27 Symbol AEP offered good long and short opportunities for those watching its fan lines.

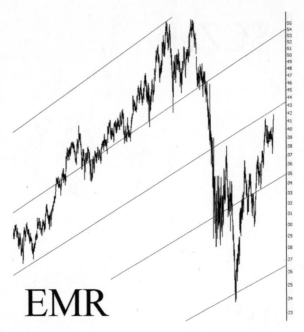

FIGURE 15.28 The fan lines shown here were based on two points that were more than 23 years apart.

was at the bottom range of a fan line pair would have been repeatedly profitable.

By their nature, the space between fan lines gets larger, as illustrated in Figure 15.29, which is for Apple Computer (AAPL). Although prices are obviously able to escape the ranges defined by the pairs of lines eventually, these ranges make helpful trading guideposts. Take note in particular of the earlier part of the chart, which shows how well-bounded the prices were. In the rightmost part of the fan lines, the range is much wider, which was appropriate, given Apple's steady rise from the upper $70s to over $200.

Certainly the most import foreign exchange graph a trader wants to monitor is the EUR/USD (Figure 15.30), measuring the ratio of the euro to the U.S. dollar. Fibonacci fans have shown themselves to be instructive on this instrument, which tends to have a positive correlation with U.S. equities. During 2008's financial crisis, the EUR/USD plunged to its 61.8 percent fan line and seemed to firm up there. This was a good indication that equities were turning safer. Although the ultimate low in some indexes took place four months later, November 2008 would have been an excellent medium-term entry point for equities, as suggested by the EUR/USD's relationship to its fan lines.

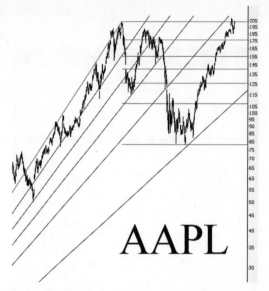

FIGURE 15.29 Apple Computer's fan lines were helpful in providing likely ranges for price movement.

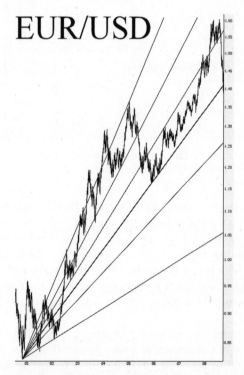

FIGURE 15.30 The EUR/USD was in a free fall from July to November 2008, at which time it stabilized at its 61.8 percent fan line. This proved to be a good turning point for some major stock indexes.

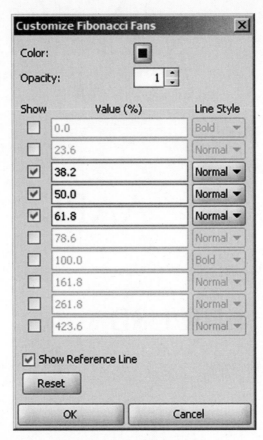

FIGURE 15.31 Fibonacci fans can be customized for color, opacity, whether certain lines are shown, and many other parameters.

The dialog box to customize Fibonacci fans is virtually identical to, although somewhat simpler than, the one for retracements. Because the lines are diagonal, there is no need to display a price level (since it is changing constantly). Figure 15.31 shows all the adjustments available in the dialog box, which can be accessed either by right-clicking a fan object and choosing Customize Fibonacci or by selecting the same choice by clicking and holding down the mouse button on top of the Fibonacci Fans button.

One of the most extraordinary charts in this entire book is shown in Figure 15.32. What is shown is quite simple: the Dow Jones Industrial Average from 1900 to 2006 and two Fibonacci fans. The first fan is drawn between the low in 1903 (the Rich Man's Panic) and the peak in 1929 (the Roaring Twenties). The second fan is drawn between the low in the

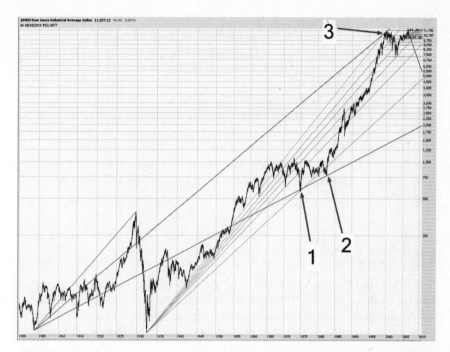

FIGURE 15.32 The point marked 1 is where these two fans intersected, which corresponded to a perfect prediction of the low of the 1973–1974 bear market. Point 2 was the beginning of the gigantic 1980s and 1990s bull market. And point 3, amazingly, was the very top of the bull market, predicted by a Fibonacci fan nearly a century old.

summer of 1932 (the Great Depression) and the peak in 2000 (the Internet bubble).

Just as combining different kinds of drawn objects can yield new insights, combining multiple instances of the same object (using different time frames) can do the same. The reason is that the multiple objects can agree with one another, emphasizing similar levels of support or resistance, and their intersections can be indicative of major turning points in the market.

In the graph there are three particular points of interest, labeled 1, 2, and 3. Point 1 marks where the two lower fan lines cross. This is an extremely important point in this chart, because it is the only place the two lower fans cross. The location that they cross is December 1974, which, remarkably, is the exact bottom of the tremendous 1973–1974 bear market (which bottomed on December 9, 1974).

This is positively remarkable. A fan that was started in the same year that Orville and Wilbur Wright flew at Kitty Hawk and a fan that was started when Herbert Hoover was still in office coincided with one of the most pivotal points in the century's market history, decades later.

Point 2 is the last time that the price touched the lower fan line. It also turns out to be the exact point where the tremendous secular bull market of the 1980s and 1990s began.

Finally, point 3 is the last time the price touched the upper fan and, amazingly, marked the exact peak of the stock market. At the risk of driving the point too heavily, it should be noted that this peak was predicted by a fan that was commenced 97 years earlier. And unlike some other instances, this fan was in place since 1929. Therefore, a person watching the broad stock market would have had a very useful insight as to where the peak might be.

FIBONACCI ARCS

The other two Fibonacci studies, arcs and time zones, warrant a somewhat briefer look, principally because the instances when they provide strong predictive power are less common. They are still useful, however, particularly in conjunction with other Fibonacci studies. Using fans and arcs together, for instance, is a common technique.

As with retracements and fans, the arcs are drawn by clicking on two points (an extreme low and extreme high), thus creating a reference line. Instead of straight lines based on these points, concentric circles are drawn using the Fibonacci ratios, basing the distance on the difference between the two extreme points.

Figure 15.33 shows the line being drawn from the autumn of 1998 (low) to the winter of 2000 (high). Three arcs are drawn automatically, suggesting possible support and resistance levels. The circled areas (which do not appear on the chart but are shown here for clarity) illustrate the price behavior proximal to these arcs.

In the case of Figure 15.33, a trader would have had helpful information about how high the stock might be going before reversing direction. In three instances after the major tumble the stock took in 2001, the stock pushed up to the retracement arc, either pausing or reversing after touching it.

The dialog box for the arcs is identical to the one for the fans. Figure 15.34 shows that only three levels have been selected for display, which is what was used for Figure 15.33. This makes a cleaner, easier-to-read chart.

The Dow Jones Industrial Average is shown in Figure 15.35 with arcs based on points between October 11, 2007, and March 6, 2009. Tinted in yellow are the areas where prices clung to the arcs, indicating support (on the way down) or resistance (on the way up).

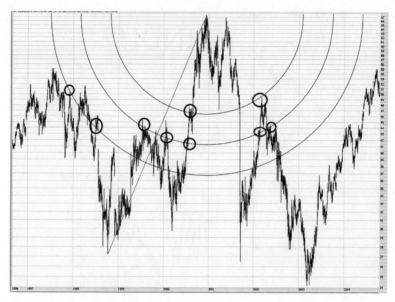

FIGURE 15.33 Arcs are used in a similar fashion, with each arc representing a locus of support or resistance.

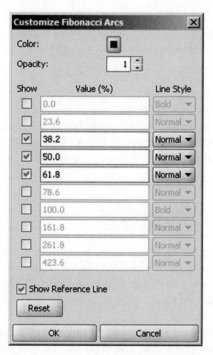

FIGURE 15.34 Arcs can be customized in much the same way that fans can.

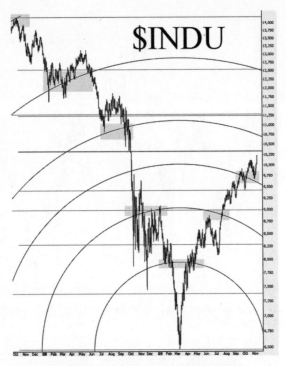

FIGURE 15.35 Fibonacci arcs, based on extreme minimum and maximum price points, can suggest areas of strong support and resistance.

Even more remarkable is the fact that extensions of these arcs, accessed via the customization dialog box, can also amplify the importance of a particular arc formation by showing how price movements in the distant past still clung to these levels. In Figure 15.36, a greatly expanded view of the Dow Jones illustrates past prices climbing the long-term arcs.

FIBONACCI TIME ZONES

The Fibonacci time zones is the only Fibonacci study that requires the selection of one (instead of two) data point. It is also the only one that expresses itself as a series of vertical lines meant to measure time instead of price. The purpose of time zones is to predict major turning points for a given financial instrument.

To draw a Fibonacci time zone, you need only choose the Fibonacci time zones tool (the third from the right on the tool bar) and click on an

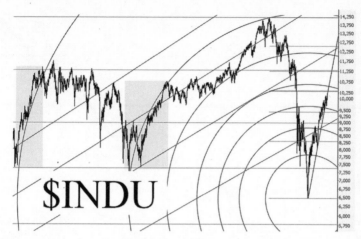

FIGURE 15.36 Sometimes Fibonacci arcs show a relationship to prices even from years earlier.

extreme low or high on a graph. When you do, a series of vertical lines, each of which is farther to the right than the previous one, will be drawn. As with other studies, the time series does not work equally well with all graphs. Judging how friendly the study is by assessing its past predictive value will dictate how useful the study is on a forward-looking basis.

Figure 15.37 provides a superb example of an excellent time series. The graph is the S&P 500, and the low selected is at the deepest level of the Great Depression in the early 1930s. The four downward-pointing arrows (provided on this chart for easy interpretation of the graph) show that the time series study did a prophetic job in pinpointing four crucial peaks in the market that took place over a 70-year period. Having affirmed the accuracy of these turning points, you could expand the chart's time scale to look into the future to see when the next turning point would be. Of course, there may be turning points before then, but this study would offer at least one forthcoming major turning point with a strong likelihood of taking place.

As with the other three Fibonacci studies, the time series can be customized (Figure 15.38), but the customization choices are limited to its color, its opacity, and whether you want a reference line displayed.

When a time zone study is placed, a large number of vertical lines are drawn, especially near the placement point. Most of the time, the leftmost vertical lines don't correspond to any particular turning point (Figure 15.39). Do not let this dissuade you from the predictive power of a given study. As long as the rightmost vertical lines appear to correlate with major turning points in the market, the study should be perceived as having value when used with whatever security you are analyzing.

FIGURE 15.37 This time zones chart, started at the low point of the early 1930s, accurately predicted the turning point at four major junctures.

COMBINING OBJECTS

Fibonacci studies are at their best when they are paired. The intersection points of studies can be exponentially more powerful since they offer affirmation from two different perspectives of a support or resistance level. Figure 15.40 shows the Dow Jones Industrial Average with two Fibonacci

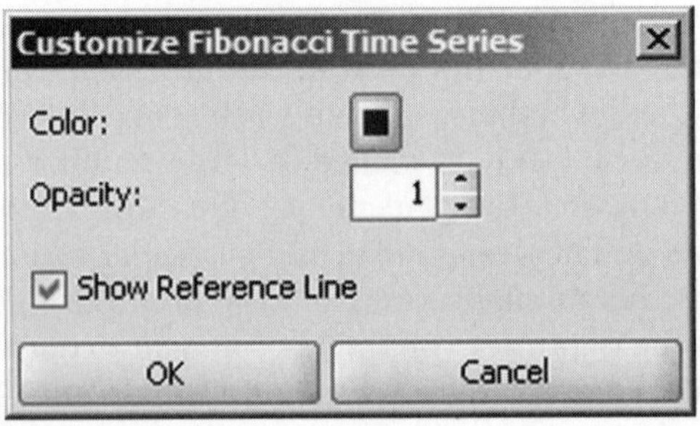

FIGURE 15.38 The simplicity of the time zones also means its customization choices are very limited.

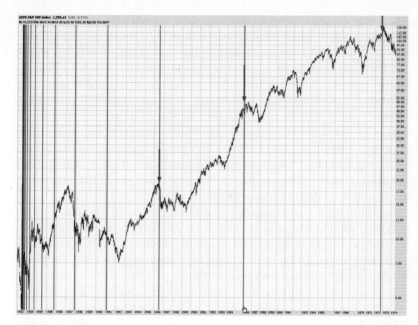

FIGURE 15.39 Earlier time zones do not tend to be as useful and should typically be ignored.

FIGURE 15.40 Combining Fibonacci studies can yield greater insight. Here the fans and retracements are being used as a combination.

studies on it: a retracement and fan lines. The six rounded rectangles drawn for emphasis show major turning points anticipated by the studies. The left-most three rectangles show turning points predicted by the retracement lines. The rightmost three rectangles have the benefit of being affirmed by both the fans and the lines. Whenever you are approaching an area where two studies agree, you should consider that an especially potent price level.

There is no reason to limit yourself to Fibonacci studies when analyz-ing a graph, of course. Although you do not want to apply so many drawn objects that the chart becomes too noisy with information, the judicious application of well-drawn studies can improve your predictive powers over a stock, index, or any other financial instrument.

In Figure 15.41, a variety of trend lines, channels, Fibonacci retrace-ments, and Fibonacci fan lines have been applied against the S&P 500 in-dex. Working together, these studies are helpful in monitoring and predict-ing the price behavior on both a large time scale and, as seen on the right side of the chart, a shorter-term time scale.

FIGURE 15.41 Trend lines, channels, retracements, and fans are all being used on this graph of the S&P 500.

SUMMARY

We have now completed our journey through the four Fibonacci drawn objects. As you have seen, the Fibonacci studies are some of the most amazing and, used correctly, powerful predictive tools in your trading arsenal. To round out our knowledge of the ProphetCharts system, the next chapter will address the newest power features that have been introduced to ProphetCharts.

CHAPTER 16

Power Features

B ecause it is a web-based product, ProphetCharts can be updated with new features automatically for all its users. It is therefore very much a living product and has a steady stream of new features being added to it.

A printed book, on the other hand, is a snapshot in time, and by the time you read this, ProphetCharts will surely be capable of doing some things not mentioned on these pages. However, since the first edition of *Chart Your Way to Profits* was published, some major new features have been introduced, and we can learn about them here. These include the ability to apply multiple labels to symbols, create customized ratio charts, observe four charts at a time in grid mode, and look at charts flipped upside down.

LABELS

As you know, watch lists are a crucial part of keeping your trading world organized. Built correctly, watch lists give you the opportunity to maximize the observations and opportunities you take from the market.

However, a list of symbols is a one-dimensional way of organizing things, because you are simply putting stocks (or other financial instruments) into folders (that is, watch lists) of a certain name. If you want to earmark symbols in a more meaningful way, you would formerly have to make a large number of watch lists, each of which had the very specific category or classification you sought. In addition, one particular symbol—GLD, for instance—might have to be put into multiple watch lists (such as "Precious Metals," "Commodities," and "ETFs"), making things messy.

With the new Labels feature, there is a much more elegant approach available to you. Using Labels, you can assign any given symbol as many properties as you like. A property—in ProphetCharts parlance, this is synonymous with label—can be any meaningful attribute. Some possibilities might be:

- Highly Liquid.
- Commodities-Related.
- Local Stock.
- Easy to Short.
- Excellent Dividend.
- Non-Marginable.
- Triple-Bullish Fund.

The symbols in your watch lists can have zero labels (the default) to multiple labels. If you take the time to assign labels to your securities, you will benefit later by being able to view only the items of specific interest to you at any given moment.

Applying a label to a symbol is very easy, and there are a couple of ways to do it. The most direct approach is to right-click on the symbol, as shown in Figure 16.1, and click the Apply Label item. A sub-menu appears, showing all the labels available. Note that when you first start using ProphetCharts, these are the default labels that are available to you, just to get you started. You will be able to add and delete from this list to your liking, as you shall soon see.

There are a few things to keep in mind about labels:

- You can apply as many labels as you like to each given symbol. A check mark will appear next to each label that has been applied to any given symbol. (Figure 16.1 shows a symbol with no labels applied to it and thus with no check marks.) The whole beauty of labels is that they add an entirely different dimension to how you organize your watch lists.
- The vast majority of work involved in labeling takes place when you initially go through your symbols and mark them. It is very time-consuming, but you will probably find that the investment of time pays off handsomely since it will make viewing your lists a much richer experience.

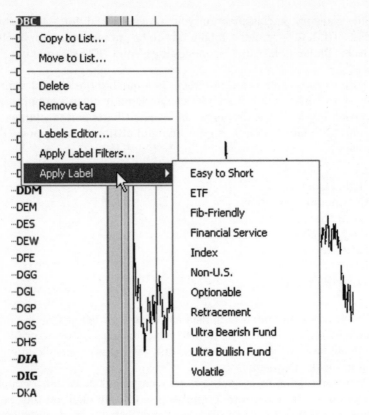

FIGURE 16.1 The most direct way to apply labels is right-clicking a symbol in a watch list.

- You don't necessarily have to label all your symbols. Label as few or as many as you want, and try to work with a list that is long enough to be detailed but not so overly long as to be redundant (e.g., having a label for Gold, another for Silver, and another for Precious Metals would be a waste; you might simply want to use Precious Metals instead).

There is a much faster, more efficient way to apply labels, though, and that is through the labels editor, shown in Figure 16.2. The labels editor lets you do several useful things:

- Add or remove multiple labels quickly for a given symbol with just a mouse click.
- Scroll through all the symbols, one at a time, to make applying labels to a large group of symbols faster.
- Add customized labels.

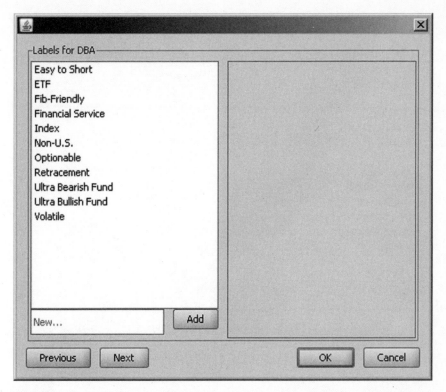

FIGURE 16.2 The labels editor is the most powerful way of applying labels to symbols.

To access this editor, right-click on any symbol and choose Labels Editor.

Here are the various things you can do with this editor:

- **Apply a label**—Double-click on the label you want to use, and it will show up in the right side of the dialog box, indicating that the label is now applied to this symbol.
- **Remove a label**—Click on the red X next to the label name on the right side of the dialog box; it will instantly be deleted.
- **Add a custom label**—Type in the label you want to use in the box with the word "New." Once you are done, click the Add button. Not only will this label be added to the right side, showing it is used for this symbol, but it will also be permanently added to your list of labels so you can access it for other symbols as well.
- **Go to the next symbol in the Watch list**—Click the Next button.

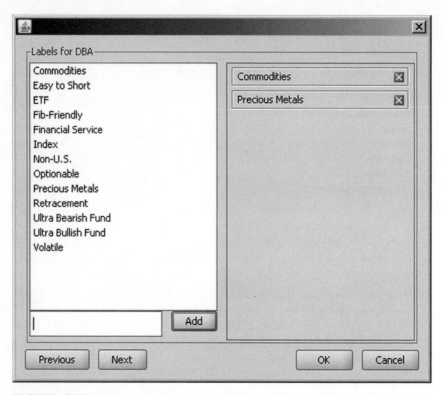

FIGURE 16.3   This is what the Labels Editor looks like after two labels have been applied to a symbol.

- **Go to the prior symbol in the Watch list**—Click the Previous button.
- **Accept all the changes**—Click the OK button.
- **Ignore all the changes**—Click the Cancel button.

Figure 16.3 illustrates what the Labels Editor looks like after a couple of labels have been applied. You will see a red X next to the labels in the right column, which would delete them.

There might be labels that you never use and therefore want to delete. If you want to delete a label, choose Delete Label from the Watch Lists menu, and a Delete Label dialog box will appear, as shown in Figure 16.4. When you do, a warning box states that deleting the label will remove it from all the symbols and watch lists, giving you a chance to change your mind if you realize that you do in fact want to retain that label.

As mentioned earlier, if you follow a lot of symbols, then labeling them properly will take a lot of time. In the end, though, it will be worth it,

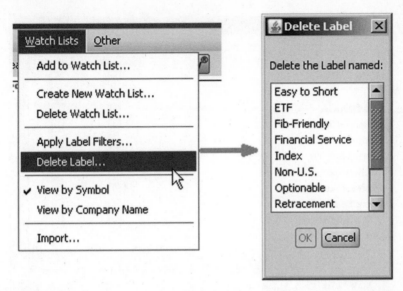

FIGURE 16.4 You can delete any labels that you decide you will not be using.

since—like the index of a book—they will make finding things much easier for you.

To make use of the labels, go to the Apply Label Filters dialog box. You can access it by choosing Apply Label Filters from the Watch Lists menu or by right-clicking any watch list item. The dialog box, shown in Figure 16.5, has a number of elements:

- The Label column—Shows, in alphabetical order, all the labels used.
- The Include column—Lets you put a check mark next to any label whose affiliated symbols you want to view; for instance, if you only want to see symbols with the label Easy to Short, check the checkbox next to that label. You can check as many checkboxes as you like, and all the symbols that have any of those labels would be displayed in the end.
- The Exclude column—The opposite of the Include column, it eliminates symbols that include the label in question. So, for example, if you did not want to see any symbols that had the Index label, you could click Exclude on the row corresponding to the Index label.
- The Select All button—Puts a check mark next to all the labels. If you have, for instance, 20 labels, and you want to apply 18 of them, it would save you time by letting you select all of them and then removing the check marks for the two labels that don't interest you.

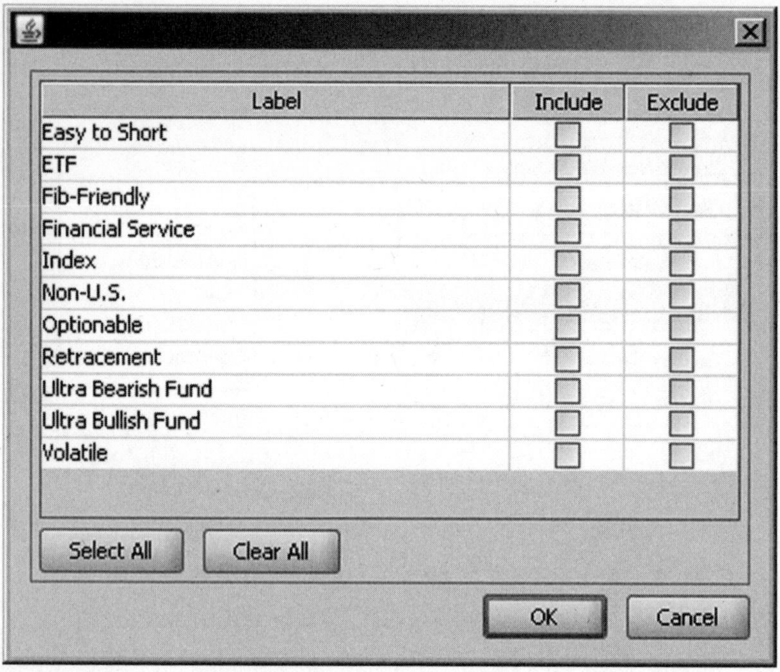

FIGURE 16.5 The Labels Filter lets you choose which labels you do and do not want applied to your watch lists.

- The Clear All button—Removes all the check marks from both the Include and Exclude columns.

If you have selected some items to include or exclude and click OK, the labels filters will be applied at once. You will notice a couple of big changes in your watch list module. First, any labels you have decided to include will be displayed at the very top of your watch list module in green, and any labels you have decided to exclude will be immediately below that, shown in red. The green and red labels at the top are shown in attention-getting colors to make it very clear that labels are being applied. The other change, obviously, is that only the symbols that comply with the parameters you have laid out are displayed.

So, for instance, if you have decided to include all the items with the label "Precious Metals" and exclude all the items labeled "Thinly Traded," you would only see (assuming you have done a good job of labeling) financial instruments related to precious metals that have decent volume. You would also see, at the top of the watch list module, "Precious Metals" in green and "Thinly Traded" in red.

Also take note of the X next to each of these labels shown in the module. You can instantly eliminate the application of any of these by clicking on the X, which is quicker than making the same change in the Labels Filter dialog box.

Used properly, the labels feature in ProphetCharts will dramatically increase the organization and utility of watch lists and make you more comfortable following even a large number of stocks, since you can home in on those items that are of greatest interest to you at any particular moment.

GRID CHARTS

If you follow a lot of stocks, one way to speed up viewing these stocks is with the grid mode. In this mode, you can view four charts at a time instead of just one.

There are a couple of reasons you might want to do this. One is to reduce the amount of time it takes you to look at all your charts. Of course, your examination of the charts is going to be somewhat less thorough, since you are looking at charts one-fourth the normal size, and you will probably be giving them a more cursory examination than you normally would.

The second reason is if you want to look at one stock at a time but using four different time periods or studies. This might give you a richer perspective on what a chart might do next.

As shown in Figure 16.6, there is a menu dedicated to this function called Grid Charts. Choosing the first item, Grid Mode, changes the regular ProphetCharts screen into one with four equally-sized panes.

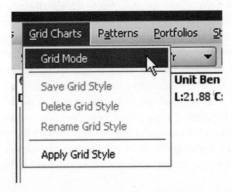

FIGURE 16.6 Choose Grid Mode to change ProphetCharts into a four-paneled layout.

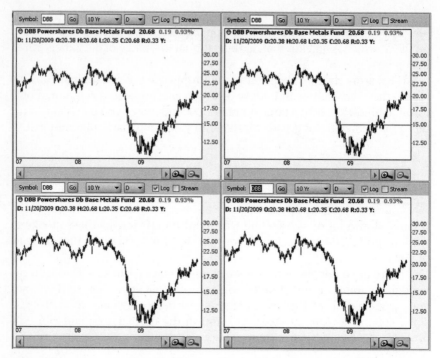

FIGURE 16.7 The initial result of using grid mode is four identical chart panes.

If you are looking at a single chart and choose Grid Mode, the result will be somewhat like Figure 16.7: four equally sized panes, each identical to the others. At that point, you can treat each of these panes independently, using any symbol, duration, frequency, or other settings in each of the four charts that you like. As you make other alterations to the default menu, such as adding technical studies, those embellishments will be applied to whichever of the four charts is currently active.

There is very little value in this, however, because all you've done is given yourself one-fourth the amount of workspace you had before. One useful thing to do, though, is to keep the same symbol in all four panes but change the amount of time displayed in each. This allows you to have a short-, medium-, long-, and very long-term perspective (or any other combination) when examining the contents of a watch list (typing a symbol into one of the panes doesn't change the other three panes, but thumbing through a watch list will populate all four panes with the same symbol).

In Figure 16.8, for instance, the same symbol, DBB, is shown as a 10-year daily chart, a 5-day/5-minute chart, a 30-day/30-minute chart, and a 3-month daily chart.

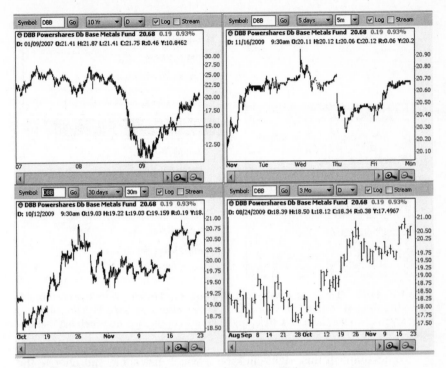

FIGURE 16.8 Multiple panes can provide you multiple perspectives.

Once you have established a quartet of useful settings, you can preserve them in a grid style, saving you the trouble of doing that work over again. Choose the item Save Grid Style from the Grid Charts menu, and the dialog box in Figure 16.9 appears. You have two choices here: you can choose the first radio button and type in a unique name for this style, or you can update an existing style with the radio button. You can also choose to include the accompanying technical studies as part of the style by checking the pertinent checkbox.

When you are in grid mode, you can examine the contents of a watch list, one symbol at a time, but displayed in the four panes you have customized. Looking at charts this way is performed the same way as you regularly look at a watch list: just open up the list you want to see, double-click on the first symbol, and press the down-arrow (or click the down-arrow button) to thumb through charts, one by one.

We've just learned one of the ways to use grid charts—that is, to examine a single financial instrument four different ways. The other use for grid charts is to look at four different charts at a time (usually with the same settings for each chart, since you want to be using consistent parameters when looking at different issues).

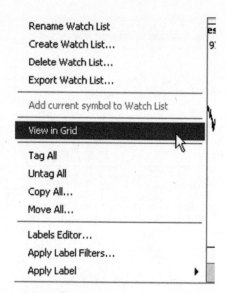

FIGURE 16.9 Once you have established the desired settings for your four charts, you can save them as a style.

FIGURE 16.10 You can view four different charts at once by choosing this item from the pop-up watch list menu.

To accomplish this, right-click on a watch list name and choose the View in Grid item, as shown in Figure 16.10. What this does is automatically populate the grid with the first four symbols of the selected watch list.

What is somewhat unusual in this mode is that the four symbols in the watch list are highlighted all at the same time, and when you click the up- or down-arrow (or button) to move up or down the list, you will move four symbols at a time (in chunks, so to speak). Figure 16.11 gives an example of this function; you can see on the watch list that four symbols are shown in inverse text, and the corresponding quartet of charts is displayed in a grid.

As suggested before, there is a price to pay for grid charts, which is thoroughness. If you are examining one large chart at a time, you are probably going to do a much better job of analyzing the stock, as opposed to viewing a quarter-size chart accompanied by three different instruments. However, if you want to do a more cursory examination of a long list of charts, the grid mode can be a valuable time-saver.

RATIO CHARTS

Charts do not necessarily need to be examined in a vacuum; analyzing how one chart is doing in relation to another can yield profitable insights.

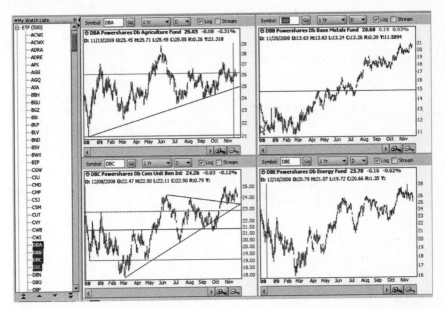

FIGURE 16.11 Viewing a watch list in a grid can greatly reduce the amount of time examining a long list requires.

Assume, for example, that you believed the value of gold and silver moved in such a way that, over the years, silver oscillated between worth half as much as gold (relatively speaking) to being worth twice as much as gold. (This example is overly simple, but it has a point.) That would be a powerful piece of knowledge because, assuming this cycle remained intact on an ongoing basis, you could go long silver (and short gold) at one extreme of the ratio and go long gold (and short silver) at the other extreme.

ProphetCharts provides the ability to combine multiple stock symbols with arithmetic operators to yield new graphs based on synthetic instruments. You can't actually trade the concocted symbols you create, but you can draw insights from them. Take Figure 16.12 as a simple example. In it, the user has typed in (GLD/SLV) in the symbol box, instead of just a regular symbol. The parentheses indicate that a formula is being used, and GLD/SLV divides the silver ETF (symbol SLV) into the gold ETF (symbol GLD). The result is a ratio chart—that is, the ratio of the symbol GLD to the symbol SLV. Although it doesn't yield the whimsical sine wave conjured up in the aforementioned example, it still provides an interesting illustration of how gold's value interacts with silver's (in this instance, gold is generally overpowering silver, although in this chart, its relative strength has recently been greatly diminished).

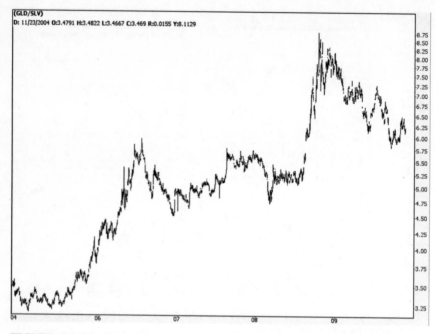

FIGURE 16.12 The formula GLD/SLV yields a chart of the gold/silver ratio.

There is a lot more power in ratio charts than simple division, however. The more powerful way of entering a formula is with the Ratio Charts dialog box, which you can access directly from the Chart Settings menu. Figure 16.13 provides an example of how to use this feature. In it is the formula (goog+rimm+aapl+amzn)/4; these four stock symbols are known as the four horsemen of the NASDAQ exchange, and they are surrounded by parentheses and followed by a division sign and the number 4. This formula, therefore, adds up the price values of all four of these stocks and finds their average, yielding a chart of the Four Horsemen Average (which doesn't exist, but it does for the sake of this example).

You can use all the standard basic math operators when constructing a formula: addition (+), subtraction (−), multiplication (∗), and division (/), along with parentheses, which take precedence over the other functions. Figure 16.14 provides a somewhat more complex example that uses nested parentheses. In this case, we are multiplying the value of SLV by 5 and dividing that result into the value of GLD. The reason for this is that, as of this writing, SLV is about one-fifth the price of GLD, and this formula helps normalize the ratio. Figure 16.14 is similar in appearance to 16.12, but the y-axis values are different since they are aligned to a more traditional value of 1.0 as being "normal" for the ratio.

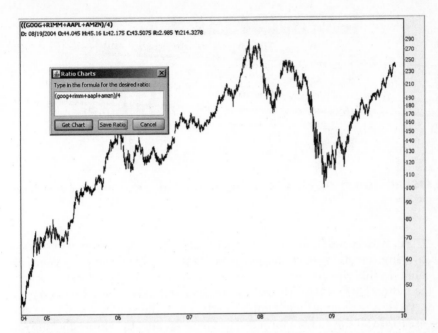

FIGURE 16.13 Arithmetic operators and symbols can be used to create your own custom indexes.

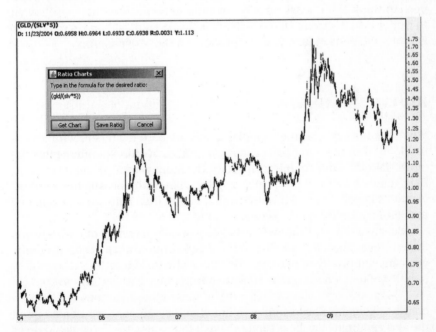

FIGURE 16.14 Using nested parentheses when constructing a formula.

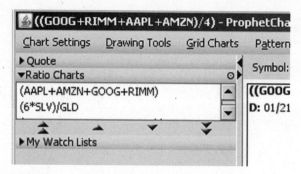

FIGURE 16.15 You can preserve all your customized charts in the Ratio Charts module.

As with most features in ProphetCharts, the work you put into constructing something customized can be permanently preserved in your account. In this case, when you are done with constructing a formula, click the button labeled Save Ratio. The formula you have entered will be preserved in the module called Ratio Charts. From then on, you will have access to any of the custom formulas you have created by double-clicking on them in the Ratio Charts module, shown in Figure 16.15.

The ratio charts feature calls for imagination and creativity, since you'll need to think about markets in a true intermarket sense; that is, you want to gather insights from what one financial instrument is doing in relation to another and deduce how you can profit from those dynamics.

HIDING ELEMENTS

When it comes to charting, simpler is usually better. Traders with access to a lot of different indicators and studies often overdo it, thinking that the more elaborate and complex the chart, the more powerful and useful it is. This simply isn't the case. A clean, spare chart with only the most crucial elements is going to be far more helpful to you than a fireworks display of indicators splashed on the screen.

Because of this, ProphetCharts lets you hide a variety of the elements that are displayed. To briefly see the chart without a particular property, you can temporarily or permanently hide features. Figure 16.16 shows how to hide an item: choosing the Hide item from the Chart Settings menu.

This menu also shows that most of these Hide functions have a keyboard equivalent. For example, to hide the volume pane, you could press the Ctrl and Spacebar keys (and to reveal the pane again, you would press

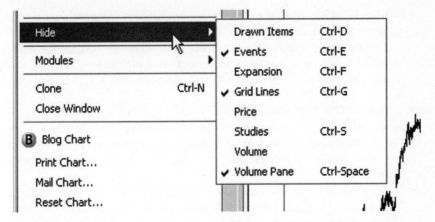

FIGURE 16.16 Any elements currently hidden will have a check mark next to them.

Ctrl-Space again; this is what is known as a toggle, since it turns something on and off alternately). The various items you can hide are:

- Drawn Items (Ctrl-D)—Hides all the objects you created with the drawing tools menu, such as trend lines, Fibonacci studies, and highlights.
- Events (Ctrl-E)—Hides all the event icons, such as earnings calls and dividend payments. Unless you consistently use these events as the basis for trading decisions, you'll probably want to hide events and leave them hidden, temporarily turning them on only when you need to glance at an event for a particular stock.
- Expansion (Ctrl-F)—As you know, you can add as much white space horizontally (for time) and vertically (for prices) as you like with the expansion tool. If you want to revert to a regular chart with no expansion, you can use this function (which doesn't so much hide an object as it undoes the effect of a particular feature in the program).
- Grid Lines (Ctrl-G)—By default, ProphetCharts displays a Cartesian grid of lines for the major x-axis and y-axis levels. You might have noticed in this book that there are virtually no gridlines shown; this is because eliminating them makes the charts simpler and cleaner to interpret for some people. You can toggle whether the grid is visible or not with this function.
- Price—This might be a surprising one for you, since it seems odd that a person would want to hide prices on a chart of prices. However, if you are using overlay studies (such as moving averages) and want to focus on them and their movement instead of the price, you can make the price bars disappear.

- Studies (Ctrl-S)—This is probably one of the most frequently used toggles, since a person generally doesn't want to see studies on their charts for every single viewing. Instead, studies are usually brought up when a person wants to examine a chart more deeply. Toggling the studies on and off is far more efficient than clearing and then reapplying studies repeatedly.
- Volume—This hide feature is similar to being able to hide price, since it will still keep the pane open in which volume is displayed, but the volume bars themselves will disappear. This is useful when you are performing overlay studies on volume and want to temporarily hide the bars.
- Volume Pane—Finally, this eliminates the volume pane altogether. This is also one of the most frequently used toggles, since many ProphetCharts users would rather use the space on their screen for their price chart, only turning on the volume pane on the occasions when they want to examine what volume action is going on with respect to the accompanying price data.

Figure 16.17 shows an example chart in which both prices and volume bars are hidden. Somewhat like the Cheshire cat's smile, only the studies remain.

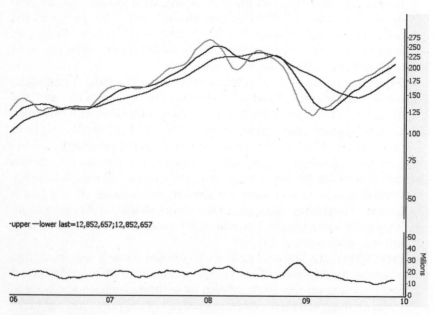

FIGURE 16.17 The result of hiding both price and volume bars.

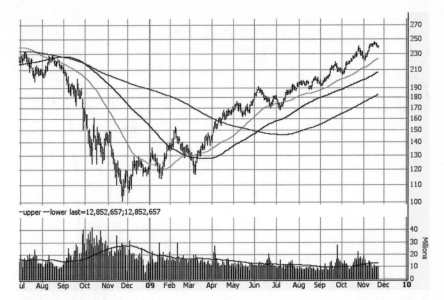

FIGURE 16.18 The volume and price bars are revealed, along with the Cartesian grid in the background.

Figure 16.18 shows the price and volume bars reinstated, accompanied by the grid. When you hide or unhide any particular element, the chosen state will remain intact until you make any other changes. Also note that the settings for the elements that are hidden or suppressed will be included in any ProphetCharts styles that you preserve, since these settings are considered critical elements of appearance.

UPSIDE-DOWN CHARTS

ProphetCharts now also has the ability to flip charts upside down. All you have to do is press Ctrl-U to toggle between upside down and right side up. Why would this be useful, you ask? It helps give you a new perspective on a stock's movement. Some people have a predisposition to bullish charts, and others are predisposed to bearish charts. But turning the chart on its head, you can see a graph with a totally new perspective, helping you get past any biases you might have in your own examination of a graph.

Let's take the extraordinary example of Dollar Thrifty rental car (symbol DTG), which fell from about $55 to about 60 cents in 2007 and 2008, only to soar thousands of percent higher in price in 2009. Figure 16.19 shows DTG over a lengthy period, and the horizontal line provides a nice

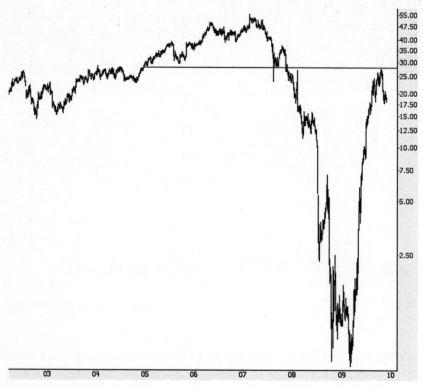

FIGURE 16.19 The extraordinary price movement of DTG over eight years.

demarcation as to when the price fell below support and, years later, pushed up against resistance.

Experienced traders will claim to be neither bulls nor bears, but the truth is that most people do tilt pretty strongly one way or the other. If someone has bull on the brain (or bear on the brain, for that matter), it might be instructive, when looking at a chart that has experienced such extreme movement, to flip it upside down and see if they feel any differently about it. Figure 16.20, for example, shows the result of pressing Ctrl-U on the DTG chart. As you can see, the prices and the y-axis are both flipped (although the logarithmic nature of the graph is retained). To someone very accomplished at picking out bullish charts, they might say that this chart is extraordinarily bullish, which, given the fact that it is upside down, means that this could be a compelling short-sale opportunity.

The upside-down feature is a toggle, but it only holds when you are actually pressing down the keys. The reason for this, naturally, is that you don't want to accidentally leave charts in upside-down mode and be basing your decisions on inverted charts.

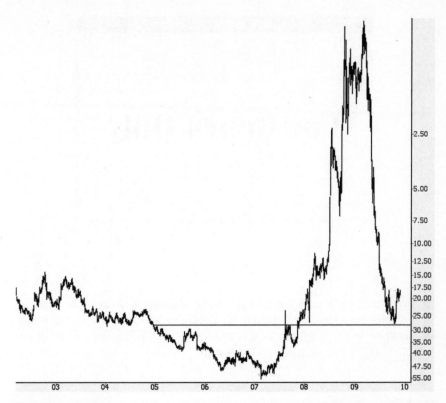

FIGURE 16.20 When a chart is flipped upside down, it still maintains its logarithmic properties.

MORE TO COME

As stated earlier in this chapter, ProphetCharts is a dynamic, ever-changing product. You can expect improvements to continue coming, and depending on your method of accessing the product, you will be notified of these improvements, and how to use them, in release notes and other announcements that are distributed by your platform provider.

CHAPTER 17

For Bears Only

I n my trading, I have made a specialty of being a short-seller (that is, betting that a security will go down), and I've learned a few things about short-selling in my many years of doing so. I'd like to share some of my personal experiences and knowledge here.

THE PHILOSOPHY OF SHORTING

Selling a stock short involves selling a security you do not own, pledging that you will buy back the same stock at a later date (and hopefully at a lower price). There are many financial instruments you can short (and many ways you can short the market by going long, such as purchasing put options), but I will use stocks as the focus in this chapter, since that is the simplest and most popular method.

Over the many years I've been trading and writing my blog, people have often asked me why I tend to be a bear in the first place. Let me first state that I am quite aware of a couple of reasons why a person *shouldn't* be a bear:

1. The whole world is against you. From the investment banks, to CNBC, to Jim Cramer, to the brokerage houses, everyone on the planet wants the market to go up forever. There is a huge, huge, huge vested interest in the markets going skyward for all eternity. So by being a bear, you are definitely going against the crowd.

2. No one gets rich being a bear. Fortunes like Warren Buffett's are made by investing in stocks that reap multithousand percent gains or more. There is virtually no one on the Forbes 400 list that got there by being a bear, although there are a couple of big hedge fund managers who have done so.

Having said that, allow me to explain myself and hopefully shed some light on my position. I have several reasons, some of which are rational, and others which are not:

Impatience: I'm not the most patient soul in the world. And the fact is that markets fall much faster than they rise. For instance, on February 27, 2009, the market plummeted over 500 points in just a few hours. It takes weeks to go up that much (usually). The financial turmoil in late 2007 and throughout 2008 is a fine example—it took only 15 months to wipe out gains that had required a decade to form. So I'm drawn to fast-moving markets.

Worrywart: I'm a worrier by nature. I wouldn't go so far as saying I'm a pessimist, but usually I tend to see the things that will go wrong faster than I see the things that will go right. (I will add this is a skill that is quite handy when one is raising young children.)

Unconventional: Somehow I'm wired to want to be different. I like to stand apart from the crowd. Per my introductory paragraph, being a bear is by its very nature weird and different. If you happened to be this way during the 1980s and 1990s, it's also terribly unprofitable!

Long-Term Charts: I'm a chartist. I believe in what charts can predict. And every long-term chart I see (and when I say long-term, I'm talking about over a century in some cases) absolutely screams TOP! to me. And if you study the charts well, it doesn't predict a few hundred points off the Dow. It predicts a cataclysm, and I want to profit from it.

Social Observation: One of the few verbs I remember from four years of Latin in high school is *speculare*, from which we derive the term *speculate*. This verb doesn't mean "to gamble" but instead means "to observe." I am a speculator, and as such, I am an observer. And what I am noticing in the present environment, based on my long-term analysis of markets, points to a multiyear downturn followed by remarkable, long-term growth.

Whatever a person's reasons for leaning one way or another in the never-ending bull-bear battle, my belief is that most traders are naturally inclined to be either bullish or bearish, and it's important to your development as a trader to have enough self-awareness to understand your inclinations and the reasons behind them. I hope some of the reasons I've offered for my own personal bias help shed some light on your own thinking as well.

PRACTICAL GUIDE TO SHORT-SELLING

In simplest terms, short-selling is no different than the normal buying and selling of a stock, except that you are doing it backwards. Bulls want to buy low and sell high; bears want to sell high and buy low.

There are obstacles, however, that exist for bears that bulls need not contend with. You should be aware of these pitfalls:

- **Locating the Stock**—If you want to buy a stock, your broker will always be happy to oblige. But if you want to sell a stock, they have to find it first. Typically, the larger the brokerage firm, the easier it is for them to locate a stock. Some brokerages can show you lists of stocks that are easy for them to borrow. Generally speaking, the more widely traded a stock is, the easier it will be to find. If you find yourself often frustrated with your broker's lack of inventory, and you are serious about short-selling, you might consider changing brokers.
- **The Uptick Rule**—As of this writing, this rule is no longer being used, but there is talk of bringing it back in some form. The uptick rule, in its prior form, deemed that a person could not sell a stock short unless there was an uptick in its price—that is, unless the stock traded at a price higher than it did before, indicating there was at least some level of buying happening. This is, sadly, an example of how the market is constructed to be against the bears—notice there is no *downtick* rule on the books—but the logic was that the markets should not permit a stock to go down mercilessly, aided by the incessant selling pressure of the bears.
- **Buy-Ins**—Once you are in a short position, your brokerage can force you out of that position, even at a price that you'd prefer not to take. This is known as a buy-in. Recall that, in order to sell a stock that you do not own, you need to borrow it from someone else. Well, that someone else might want it back; more particularly, if the broker's inventory of that given stock shrinks to the point that they need to recover shares that are sold short, they may need to take you out of that position.
- **Dividends**—If you own a dividend-paying stock, you enjoy being paid a (usually small) dividend periodically from the company. If you are short a stock, the reverse is true—you actually have to pay the dividend

yourself, on behalf of the company, since the rightful owner of the stock is still due that dividend. So this creates a true cash cost to being short a particular security (which means you might want to focus on stocks that don't pay a dividend in the first place).

- **Squeezes**—You have probably heard the term "short squeeze" before, but perhaps you're not sure what it meant. When a large number of individuals have short positions in a given stock, they all are obliged to buy back that stock at some point. But let's assume that a stock has been performing well, and it keeps pushing to new highs (or at least technical levels that are damaging to bears). Those who are short the stock will be compelled to close their positions in order to stop the pain, and that creates more buying pressure on the stock. This buying pressure, in turn, compels other shorts to cover their positions, and this cascade of buying feeds on itself. This is what is known as a short squeeze, because eventually all the bears on that stock are falling all over themselves to get out, which, ironically, is terrific for the bulls. So it is best to avoid stocks that are already heavily short (there are entire web sites devoted to tracking the short interest on stocks, showing, relatively speaking, how many shares are short for a given company's stock float).

- **Emergency Rules**—There are times when extraordinary circumstances in the market lead to extraordinary measures being taken. Since those who regulate markets tend to be in favor of upward markets, and opposed to down markets, these measures are almost without exception designed against bears. During the historic week of September 15, 2008, the SEC put rules in place banning short-selling on an entire class of widely traded financial stocks. This caused havoc in the markets, particularly on securities based on bearish financial positions. So during tumultuous times, be warned that the laws and regulations might be changed right under your feet.

There is one other risk often mentioned when the topic of short-selling arises, and that is how potential losses are infinite. In other words, if a person pays $10 a share for a stock, the most he is risking is $10 per share, because a stock can never be worth less than zero. However, if a person is short a stock and pledges to buy it back, there is no limit to how high the stock can go, and thus a person's theoretical risk is unlimited.

I think this argument has a point, but in general it's pretty silly. I remember when I was learning to scuba dive that some people would get completely unhinged at the vastness of the ocean. The ocean is gigantic, it can be miles deep in places, and even in a normal dive spot, there is a hundred feet of uninterrupted water beneath you. Yes, that's all true, but you're *buoyant*, and it's a bit preposterous to equate being a hundred feet above the sea floor with being a hundred feet in the air.

By the same token, although one's potential risk of loss is indeed unlimited, there are a few basic risk-management tools that can render this point virtually moot:

- **Position Size**—There's no reason any particular position has to constitute a large percentage of your portfolio. I personally tend to have a very large number of positions, so even if I get a nasty surprise in one stock, it has a very minor effect on my overall portfolio.
- **Stop-Losses**—If a person has no stop-loss order and is content to let a stock he has sold short rise forever, then, yes, he can lose much more than the sum of his original investment. But that would be foolish; you should always have a stop-loss order on all your positions, if you want to remain prudent.
- **Price Ranges**—The simple fact of the matter is that, even with an earnings blowout or a corporate takeover, it is very rare that a stock (unless it is a penny stock) pushes up hundreds of percent in value overnight. Even if a short position moves against you, the percentage loss is usually going to be quite modest. I try to keep my risk to less than 10 percent for any one position, which is far enough away from "unlimited" to make me comfortable.

EXCHANGE-TRADED FUNDS

Prior to 1993, there was no such thing as an exchange-traded fund (ETF), but as of this writing, there are more than 1,500 of them. These are financial instruments that trade very much like stocks but can represent a wide variety of slices of the financial world, including sectors, countries, and inverse funds (which are of interest to us in this chapter).

Prior to their creation, the function of ETFs was largely covered by mutual funds, but mutual funds have some pretty big disadvantages for active traders, not the least of which is that they can be bought or sold only at the end of the trading day. On the other hand, ETFs trade through the day (and, for the most popular issues, after hours as well), and some ETFs are among the most popular investment vehicles in the world.

For those looking to take on bearish positions, there is an added benefit: because of the existence of inverse funds, one can take on a long position while actually being short the market. This was useful to me, for instance, in 2008, because I had money in a 401(k) that I wanted to use on the short side, but the custodian forbade anything except long positions. I took advantage of inverse funds to produce an extremely substantial gain that year. (Regrettably, in extending its mission of apparently protecting investors from themselves, the same custodian went so far as to ban trading of ETFs altogether in 2009.)

A number of firms offer inverse funds, a couple of which are Rydex and ProShares. With a regular brokerage account, you should be able to buy and sell pretty much any ETF, and even if you are required to have only long positions, you can still be short the market.

There are many ways to take on bearish positions by using ETFs. While new ETFs are being created all the time, listed here are several of the existing categories:

- Index ETFs—These were the first ETFs ever created, with SPY being the original back in 1993: SPY, for example, follows the movement of the S&P 500, QQQQ follows the NASDAQ 100, and IWM follows the Russell 2000. Most index ETFs are extremely heavily traded and thus very liquid, and these represent the most direct way to short an entire market. You could sell short the SPY, for instance, to be short the S&P 500 index.
- Sector ETFs—These cover entire sectors, such as semiconductors, consumer staples, and so forth. These represent a good way (for bulls and bears alike) to take a position on an entire industry as opposed to a single stock or a whole index.
- Commodity ETFs—Most stock traders aren't interested in getting directly involved in the commodities market by opening a futures account; these ETFs allow you to take advantage of price swings in gold, silver, agricultural commodities, or a variety of other baskets. If you wanted to take a bearish position on gold, for instance, the symbols GLD and GDX are both very heavily traded gold ETFs.
- Inverse ETFs—These are similar to other ETFs, except that they go up when the underlying instruments go down. For example, the symbol DOG is the inverse of the Dow 30 index, so if on a given day the Dow 30 goes down by 2 percent, then DOG would climb about 4 percent.
- Leveraged ETFs—Finally, leveraged ETFs are supercharged versions of regular ETFs, since they move more than 100 percent of the direction of the underlying instrument. Various coefficients are available, such as 1.5 times, 2 times, 3 times, and even 4 times. For instance, the symbol TWM is a double inverse fund on the Russell 2000, so if on a given day the Russell went down 1.5 percent, meaning its ETF the IWM would also be down 1.5 percent, then the TWM would be up about 3 percent, since the movement is doubled. Likewise, if the Russell went up 1.5 percent, the TWM would go down 3 percent.

Now let's take a moment to review a very important point about leveraged ETFs. There is a very insidious reality about leveraged ETFs that it seems a lot of people do not understand, which is that unless a given index or sector (on which the ETF is based) moves very consistently in the direction you desire, the value of your ETF will probably suffer even if, over the long haul, the direction you want it to move is realized.

Let's take an oversimplified example: let's suppose you had a double-inverse ETF on a given index, and let's give it the value of $100. On a Monday, the index goes up 5 percent, meaning your ETF goes down to $90. On Tuesday, to your relief, the index goes down 5 percent. Are you back to where you started, since the index has moved in your direction by precisely the same amount it moved against you the prior day? No, because your $90 ETF goes up 10 percent in value, which is $99. So you are down 1 percent, even though, over the course of those two days, the index hasn't budged.

Now imagine this process repeated over and over, and you will soon realize that the value of the ETF can wither away, even if the market is generally moving in your direction. If the index kept wiggling up and down, day after day, the ETF would be down 40 percent in 100 trading days (and this isn't even taking into account fund expenses and other slippage, which would damage the fund even more).

A surprising number of supposedly sophisticated investors didn't realize this when they bought into ultra ETFs, because both bullish- and bearish-oriented leveraged funds tended to suffer unless their movement was relatively consistent in the intended direction. Late in 2008, two new instruments based on financial stocks were introduced; their symbols were FAS (triple-bullish) and FAZ (triple-bearish). The extraordinary thing is that *both funds lost most of their value* even though they are opposites. Amateur observers would have assumed that one would prosper while the other suffered, but both of them did poorly (and very savvy traders shorted as much of both of them as they could when they were initially brought to market).

PUTS FOR LEVERAGED PROFITS

If you are not well acquainted with options, here is a simple explanation: options give you the right (but not the obligation) to buy (in the case of a call option) or sell (in the case of a put option) a particular financial instrument at a particular price within a certain amount of time. Options are derivative instruments, meaning they are based on something else (which might be an index, a stock, a commodity, or the like).

An option's price is crudely composed of two components: intrinsic value and time premium. Let's take the example of a call option on Apple

Computer that expires in June of a certain year (for the purpose of this example, let's say that it is currently April) and gives you the right to buy 100 shares of Apple at $200 per share. Let's further assume that Apple is currently trading at $210 and the option in question has a value of $15. In this instance, the intrinsic value of the call is $10 (because it is worth $10 to pay $200 for a stock which has a market price of $210), and its time premium is $5 (because there is uncertainty about what the price will do between April and June, and people are willing to pay a premium for that uncertainty). The option itself, by the way, would cost $1,500, since it controls 100 shares, not just one.

A put option is similar, except it gives you the right to sell something at a given price (which is known as the strike price). Let's use the Apple example again, only this time we're dealing with a put instead of a call, and let's suppose the price of the option is $5. In this case, there is no intrinsic value, since having the right to sell Apple at $200 when the market price is $210 isn't of interest to any economically rational person. In fact, there is *negative* intrinsic value of $10, which means the time premium is $15.

As you might guess, one of the appealing things about options is the leverage they provide. And, generally speaking, the calmer a market is, the greater the leverage. The reason for this is that time premiums will be much higher in volatile markets because people are scared and willing to pay a high premium. It's not much different than the cost of hurricane insurance in Florida versus Iowa—the premiums are going to be vastly different.

So let's return to Apple again and assume that we thought the stock was going to fall. Let's further suppose that the market has been extremely benign, and faith in Apple's upward price trajectory is deeply embedded among investors, so a June put option with a strike at $200 is selling for just 10 cents (the stock price, as with the earlier incarnation of this example, is still $210). An option priced at 10 cents means each contract (which controls 100 shares) is $10, so let's say you took an aggressively bearish position and bought 1,000 of these contracts for a total cost of $10,000.

The next morning, Apple announces something very bad for its stock price, and it plunges $20 to $190 per share. You have put options with a $20 strike, and these now have an intrinsic value of $10 each. In addition, because people are suddenly very nervous about Apple, there is a $5 time premium, making the price $15. You are now the (ecstatic) owner of $1.5 million in Apple puts, which you promptly sell for a breathtaking profit. Later that day, you buy everyone in your town the latest iPod.

Now, this is a bit of a silly example, but it shows you the power of leverage. If you took the same $10,000 and shorted 48 shares of Apple (which is what you could do in a cash account at $210 per share), even with the $20 plunge, you would have netted $960—a far cry from a million and a half dollars. Of course, the reality is that your $10,000 in options will in all likelihood expire worth $0, netting a $10,000 loss if you hold on to them until the very end, but sometimes options holders can experience astronomical gains.

If you do decide to give options a try, here are several words of advice:

- *Don't get stars in your eyes*—Stories like this one are compelling, but so is reading about lottery winners. The vast majority of the time, those purchasing high-risk options wind up losing the entire investment. It's better to start small and aim low.
- *Avoid out-of-the-money options*—Try to get options with some intrinsic value. Buying cheap out-of-the-money options makes for hypothetically higher percentage returns, but the odds are stacked much more heavily against you, and the time premium you will be paying will be much greater. Buying in-the-money options is safer and more conservative, and (at least at the time of purchase) it gives you the assurance that you are purchasing something that has worth.
- *Avoid nearby expiration dates*—As with out-of-the-money options, options that expire relatively soon are going to be very cheap and tempting to beginning traders. There is a phenomenon in options pricing known as theta burn, which essentially is the rate at which a time premium decays as the expiration date nears. The decay looks like a plunging roller coaster as the final weeks of an option's lifespan take place, so it is best to get an option that is at least a couple months out to give your position a reasonable chance of working out.

Buying in-the-money, far-out options is duller than getting out-of-the-money options that expire in a week, but it's radically safer. You might miss a "hit it out of the ballpark" trade now and then, but you will probably avoid a lot of losses, too. The bottom line is that leverage is a two-edged sword, and the same power that makes breathtaking returns possible is also able to provide you 100 percent losses.

GOOD AND EVIL

The nature, definition, and manifestation of good and evil are subjects I have pondered many times in my life. All cultures, philosophies, and religions have their own views on these subjects. Some of them dismiss the idea that evil even exists. I disagree.

The best definition of *evil* I remember reading was this: "That which destroys life and liveliness."

But how does one comprehend goodness? Do we simply invert the aforementioned definition, yielding "That which *creates* life and liveliness"?

I think that is a step in the right direction. But the thought of goodness conjures up, for me, a variety of other properties. In no particular order—and this list is far from complete—goodness is:

- Balance
- Harmony
- Order
- Love
- Faith
- Compassion
- Generosity
- Kindness
- Honesty
- Bravery
- Moderation

None of this is terribly controversial. But there are some subtleties in human nature and behavior that make the topic less simple.

Self-Perception

The mass of individuals on Earth don't align themselves to a standard yardstick of principles and behaviors in order to present themselves as being on a particular point on the continuum of good and evil. People are, in my view, self-interested creatures; it's tempting to consider another person evil simply because he is different (or has a different worldview). I seriously doubt Osama bin Laden stares at his fragment of a mirror hanging in the cave, cackles mischievously to himself, and declares, "*Oh, what a fine life it is to be evil. I shall crush all those goody-two shoes that oppose me!*" Nor do I think the likes of Hitler or Stalin considered themselves to be evil. They were consumed with their own motives, and those in opposition to those motives were going to either get out of the way or be destroyed.

I think the vast majority of humanity would agree that such individuals were, in fact, evil. But what's required to make this sort of assertion is some perspective.

Is Heroism Chosen?

What constitutes a hero?

On a regular basis, newspapers and television shows have stories of individuals who, in the face of danger to themselves or loved ones, decided to act with remarkable courage and strength in order to achieve a positive outcome. A man runs into a burning building to save the life of a stranger; a woman dives into a frozen lake to rescue someone who fell in; a dog drags an injured dog off a road to prevent it from being killed.

These are all heartwarming, and as sentimental as I am, I'm probably even more affected and moved by these stories than most others. But do heroes *choose* to be good, or are they simply wired that way? And if they are wired that way, are they any more deserving of our praise than anyone else blessed by other genetic dispositions, such as having blond hair or a nice singing voice?

In the end, I don't think anyone really cares if it was a person's *conscious* choice to behave heroically. The fact is that they *did*, and the action itself gives that person heroic attributes. It is all the more alluring and praiseworthy to the public that these decisions are usually made in a split second, because deep inside we're all wondering if we would have done the same thing; we ponder, no matter what our self-image, if we have that goodness within *us* that we so admire in others.

What Does This Have to Do with Trading?

The reason I bring this subject up in a book about trading is that I believe there is a big misunderstanding about the actions of traders and what those actions represent: specifically, the notion that buying stocks (and being bullish) is good whereas selling or shorting stocks (and being bearish) is bad.

Let's start with a few basic suppositions:

- Unless one's trading size is so gigantic compared to a given security's volume that you are going to push the market substantially up or down, your actions are immaterial to the market as a whole.
- Unless you are actively and effectively spreading malicious untruths about a given organization or security, you are trading morally.
- Your participation in an aftermarket does nothing to help or hinder a public company.

Let's focus on that last point. If you buy 5,000 shares of Apple (AAPL), the company Apple doesn't care. You're not helping them, their employees, their sales, their customers, or their management of expenses. If you short 5,000 shares of AAPL, likewise, the company doesn't care.

Now, if it were 1976, and Steve Jobs and Steve Wozniak came to you for start-up funding, and you gave it to them, Apple would care very much—because you are providing them what they need to create a business. And if, in 1980, you as an investment bank agree to underwrite their public offering, Apple again cares, because you are providing them with a source of financing that will help them grow as a business.

But once a company's public, your actions as a trader really have nothing to do with them. Sure, a company (and, more particularly, its shareholding employees) *like* to have a stock bid up to higher prices. But your actions as a trader aren't creating any good (or evil) for that organization. You are operating in a realm outside the bounds of that enterprise.

Creation and Destruction

Some people get the idea that bears are malicious, nasty, grubby creatures that relish the thought of destruction and collapse. I can't speak for all bearish traders, but I would say for myself—and I would think most sane people—that this notion is absolute junk.

An objective technical trader does the following:

1. Examines a chart.
2. Reaches a conclusion.
3. Acts upon that conclusion.

There is nothing malevolent in the list. *Nothing.* If I believe the stock BIDU is going to fall, and I short it, then I am taking actions that I hope will be profitable for me. I am taking a risk. Yes, I am *hoping* the stock will fall, because that benefits me and aligns with my analysis. It feels good to be right, and it feels good to take a profit. But this hope has nothing to do with wishing ill on others; it is simply a supposition made based on analysis.

Others might say bears want America to fail, or that they hate America. Again: nonsense. I love this country. I built a business here, creating employment, products, and profits—and I sold it to a much bigger firm. I raise my family here. There is, on the whole, no other place I'd rather live.

But my perception that this country is going very bad places doesn't make me un-American. If anything, my willingness to perceive and talk about these concerns makes me that much *more* of an American. I would like to see this country come out on the other side of this mess in one piece. I would say blind optimists who figure things will get better just because they ought to get better are unpatriotic by way of their apathy.

As for corporations: if you really want to destroy a company—if that's your fondest wish—then create a better competitor! Who do you think had a more destructive effect on Yahoo!: short-sellers or the founders of Google? I think even a *million* short-sellers couldn't even approach the damage that the *two* co-founders of Google created. So Joseph Schumpeter's notion of Creative Destruction wins the day.

The Amorality of Trading

For 99.9 percent of traders out there, trading is an *amoral* act. You're not *good* for buying; you're not *evil* for selling; you're not *virtuous* by being bullish; you're not *malevolent* by being bearish.

What about the circumstance where you actually make a profit as a direct result of the suffering of others?

Let's suppose that, on September 10, 2001, you were strongly of the opinion that airlines were going to go down in price, so you put all of your trading capital into puts on American Airlines, United Airlines, and the like. September 11 happens and when the market finally reopens on the 17th, your puts soar in value hundreds of percent (I do not know what the options actually did during that month, but I am guessing this is close to the truth).

Was there evil intent in your trade? Did you contribute to an evil cause? Did you assist the terrorists? No, of course not.

Did you (unwittingly) profit because of a terrorist act? Yes. Does this make you evil? Based on hypothetical circumstances I have described, I would say the answer is no.

Now, it certainly might *feel* unseemly if you were in this position (and we won't even go into a potential visit from federal authorities, curious about your prescient timing). Your profits might feel like blood money to you—you might even donate all the profits to the Red Cross, since it would seem like the right thing to do.

I propose that you have no sin you need purge, although I do agree it might be fitting, and erase a perceived stain on your soul, to surrender the profits, since the circumstance would be profoundly unusual.

But, let's face it, 9,999 times out of 10,000, a profitable short sale or put position doesn't do well because of an event that causes human suffering. But I think the wise bear keeps his mouth shut about profiting from a company's troubles. No matter how morally neutral a trade might be, there is still room in this world for decorum and common sense.

The bottom line, for me, can be expressed simply as this: you simply *are*, your trading *is*, and the markets *are*. These things are neutral, and it is your *relationship* to the market that will dictate your profits and losses. Outside of those boundaries, nothing matters, and no one need care.

THE SLOPE OF HOPE

In 1995, I had been trading stocks and options for about 17 years, and I had also sold the company I founded, Prophet Financial Systems. I was spending a lot of time trading, and a family member suggested that I start a blog about it.

Although blogging was relatively new at the time, I was hesitant to do my own blog, mainly because it seemed a bit too trendy. I really didn't see the point of writing a blog, particularly since the handful of friends and family that might check it out didn't really have an interest in stocks in the first place. But I decided to give it a shot and did my first post on March 27, 2005.

From the very beginning, I made my blog—which I initially called Technically Speaking, but later renamed Slope of Hope—all about my own trading ideas. For the most part, I would post charts and talk about how I felt about these charts, whether I was buying or selling them, and what kinds of stop price I was using. I would also periodically post the kinds of things you would see on any personal blog, such as funny videos, anecdotes from my life, and the occasional picture.

As I predicted, my blog's traffic—if one could even call it that—was only about a hundred views per day. Almost no one knew about Slope, but I kept doing posts on a regular basis. Generally speaking, I would do one post per day, although on occasion I might do a couple of posts. It was rare that I would skip a day, since even with a small audience I felt a certain obligation to put something new up.

As the years went on, traffic went from a few hundred views to a few thousand to a few tens of thousands. As the traffic grew, I began to post more actively (since the need to keep the blog stocked with fresh content was something I felt more keenly), and more important, conversation within the blog became more active. In my blog's first year, I would get excited if anyone at all would post a comment. By the time Slope was popular, it was getting over 1,000 comments every day.

The reason I am bringing this story up is to stress the importance of community. I have been part of the online social network scene since 1981, which was a quarter-century before "social network" was a commonplace term. And as much as the technology has changed over those years, the nature of the interaction really hasn't changed that much. The kinds of interactions, camaraderie, and inside jokes I remember from CompuServe's CB Radio chat room was little different than the most modern discussion platform on the Internet.

What I would encourage you to do is go to www.SlopeOfHope.com in your browser and join the discussion. Reading the blog and participating are free, and you'll probably find that the topics being discussed and the articles being shared are instructive to your trading. The blog also has a reputation for having a bearish bend to it, which is why I'm making a point of mentioning it in this chapter.

Speaking for myself as a trader, there are two major benefits I have received from doing the blog: first, since I have a large audience, I think much more deeply and critically about any trading ideas I have than if

I only had to convince myself of their wisdom. Second, the audience on the blog makes a terrific sounding board for ideas and knowledge base for trading information. It's like having a non-stop convention of active traders constantly talking, sharing, and guiding one another. The collective mind of the blog has been invaluable to me, and I am very proud of the culture that I have cultivated over the years on Slope of Hope. I hope to see you there.

CHAPTER 18

A Practical Guide to Trading

I n this book, we've covered a lot of ground with respect to technical analysis, charting, and the ProphetCharts product. There are hundreds of books written about other aspects of trading, including books about technical indicators, the psychology of trading, futures, options, and just about every other imaginable subject.

We shall not endeavor to incorporate the vast knowledge and information from those books here, since it is the principal goal of this volume to make you comfortable and confident using ProphetCharts. However, there are some basic guidelines about any kind of trading that will be helpful to most people who decide to trade, be it professionally or casually, and we will review those in this final chapter.

TRADING RULES

It is often tempting for people to keep a list of their own trading rules, particularly as they generate losses they regret and wish to avoid in the future. Keeping a diary of trading experiences is a valuable exercise, but what often happens with a list of rules is that the list grows so long and arcane as to be almost useless. The old saying about how you can never step into the same stream twice holds true for trading, and over the months and years that you are trading, you will be faced with a never-ending set of changing circumstances.

I've got my own list, but it is short and sweet. I ignore some of these rules from time to time, and virtually every time I do, I regret it. If one day

I can follow these rules consistently, I'll be a much better trader for it. An acronym for the rules below is SOB FEES, which is appropriate considering how many tears were spent attaining them.

- **Stops**—A stop price must be in place at all times for all positions.
- **Opening Bell**—No new positions should be initiated in the first 30 minutes of any trading session. In addition, after-hours trading is to be avoided altogether, since the volume is terribly thin and thus prone to easy manipulation.
- **Balance**—This one is the hardest of all to define, but because it is impossible to know with certainty the future direction of the market, a balance between bullish and bearish positions is the most prudent. In addition, if you are heavily weighted, either bullish or bearish, and if the market moves strongly in your favor intraday, you should consider taking on a large opposite day-trade position for insurance profits in case that intraday move reverses.
- **Freshness**—Positions should be regularly refreshed for the sake of updated stops. This is especially important when the market has moved in your direction a meaningful amount so that you can lock in some profits with tighter stops.
- **Emotional Awareness**—Use emotional awareness to your advantage, understanding that fear often accompanies reversals in your favor and hubris often accompanies reversals against your positions.
- **Exits**—The only acceptable exit is either being stopped out of a position or reaching a target price that has a clear technical rationale, and even in cases of the latter, partial exits are preferable to outright closes.
- **Sizing**—Initial position sizing must be consistent among instrument types irrespective of anticipated opportunity.

Following these rules consistently isn't easy. But every year I get a little better at it, and every year I do better in my trading. I urge you to consider making these rules an important part of your trading life.

Let us now examine some of these rules more deeply and from a different angle with three simple components: how to open a position, how to hold a position, and how to close a position.

HOW TO OPEN A POSITION

When traders open up a position, they are at their most optimistic. There are many different profit possibilities available: the classic Buy Low/Sell

High; the oft-ignored Buy High/Sell Higher (such as is the case with strong performers that seem too expensive to much of the investing public); and for short-sellers, Sell High/Buy Low.

No matter what your disposition is on a stock, there are five easy-to-follow rules that will probably save you a lot of trouble and money.

Don't Enter a Trade in the First 30 Minutes of the Day

Although you may be eager to jump into a trade the very moment the market opens, it is wise not to do so. There is a tremendous amount of noise in the first 30 minutes of the trading day. Amazingly, a significant percentage of stock orders are placed even before the opening bell. This creates a rather distorted picture of the market in the first part of the day.

It is, of course, all right to let a stop order close out a position for you (more on this later) in the first 30 minutes. After all, it is the job of a stop order to get you out of a trade if it needs to do so. But letting the smoke clear out of the market is essential before you enter any new positions. Even if you pay a little more for a stock by waiting out the first half hour, it will be immaterial if the position turns out to be a good one.

Pay a Good Price

This may seem like absurd advice, akin to never lose money. But the point is simply this: when you examine a chart, you have an opportunity to see what constitutes an attractive price for a security. This will depend strictly on the chart, so there is no predetermined rule for all securities. If, for example, a stock explodes out of a basing pattern and quickly rises from its former resistance level of $15 to $25, you may decide to wait until the stock is $17 or less before purchasing it. It may never reach that level again, and you may find yourself denied the opportunity of profiting from future growth. But rushing into a stock just after it has had a major price ascent may put you in a position of unnecessary risk.

The key is to make a decision for yourself (preferably not during market hours, so that you can calmly and rationally decide what a fair price would be) as to what price you are willing to pay for the security. You want to seek a good risk/reward ratio. The risk is measured by calculating the price you would pay for a security versus the price at which you would be stopped out of the position; the reward is based on the difference between the target price for the security and the price you would pay for it.

For example, assume you were willing to pay $16 for a stock with a target price of $36 and a stop price of $14. The risk is $2 and the potential reward is $20, which is a risk/reward ratio of 10. In other words, you are risking $1 for every $10 in reward you are seeking. That's a very attractive ratio. On the other hand, it is unlikely you would want to buy into a stock at $34 with a stop price of $15 and a target price of $40. Even though there's still a potential profit to be had, the risk/reward profile doesn't make it worthwhile.

You cannot control how high the stock will go, but you can certainly control what you pay for it. Therefore, you have much more say in the risk you are willing to undertake as opposed to the reward you may or may not make. Determine your price in advance and don't pay anything higher, as tempting as it might be. It often pays to wait for the stock to return to the level you seek.

Trade Only Active Securities

Although there are many tens of thousands of stocks and options that trade in the U.S. equity markets, only a few thousand of them trade in significant enough volume to be worthwhile. Although you may find a chart with a very alluring pattern, be sure to check its average daily volume to ensure you don't get stuck with a security that has too thin a market.

The problem with a thin market is twofold: first, there is typically a substantial bid/ask ratio. In other words, for a heavily traded security, you will enjoy a very tight bid/ask ratio. The NASDAQ 100 index (QQQQ), for example, might trade with a bid of $36.02 and an ask of $36.03, because there are so many people making a market in this security that a penny spread is sufficient. On the other hand, a security that trades just a few thousand shares a day might have a bid of $43.20 and an ask of $45.00. This means that the moment you enter the position, you have a $1.80 per share loss on your hands.

The other problem is that you are far more vulnerable to someone gunning for your stop price. As you will read next, having a stop price is crucial for responsible trading. But if a market is extremely thin, it becomes very little trouble for others in the market to push the market either up or down and execute orders based on existing stop prices. You will not experience this kind of problem in actively traded shares.

As for what defines "actively traded," securities that trade at least a million shares a day are best, but at a minimum, you should avoid anything that trades less than 250,000 shares per day unless the chart is so spectacular that it is worth the extra risk.

Have a Stop and Target Determined in Advance

Just as you should have a price you are willing to pay determined in advance, you should likewise figure out a stop price and a target price.

As a reminder, a stop price is a price below which (or, if you are short, above which) a market order will be instantly executed. For instance, let's say you bought 5,000 shares of Apple (AAPL) at $50, and you set a stop price of $47.99. As long as AAPL trades at $48 or above, your order will not be executed. But if any trade at $47.99 or lower goes through, there will be an instant order submitted to the market to sell your position at the best available price.

The reason stops are so crucial is that they allow you to dispassionately get out of bad trades. You should never, ever have a position without a stop price. In fact, the moment you get your order filled, you should place the stop order. It is far too tempting to talk yourself out of selling a stock if it falls and you don't have a stop order in place. By automating the process, you remove the emotional element from getting out of a bad trade.

The target price is less important, because it is much harder to judge how far a stock will go, and it is likely that if a stock moves in the direction you anticipate, you will update your target. But a target is important to judge the risk/reward ratio of a potential position.

If you are trading options, there is a special point. It isn't wise to place a stop order based on the option price itself. Options are typically far too thinly traded to make this a reasonable approach. What makes more sense is to go with a broker that offers contingent orders. This means that if the underlying security falls above or below a certain price, then the order to close the option position is placed. Stocks are far, far more heavily traded than their options, so this is absolutely the best way to go to protect your option positions.

Trade Only Based on Completed Patterns

Patterns do not form overnight. They take weeks, months, or even years to form. And when they are about 70 percent to 80 percent complete, it becomes easy to see what pattern might ultimately take shape.

In a situation like this, it is very tempting to enter a trade based on the supposition that a pattern will complete. For example, perhaps you are looking at a head and shoulders chart that has the left shoulder, the head, and about half of the right shoulder. You can clearly see what the pattern would look like if it were to complete as expected. You can also see that you will make more money getting into the position now, since the area between the neckline and the current price of the stock represents that much more profit to you. In other words, you want to beat the crowd before they realize the pattern has broken.

As tempting as this is, you should wait for the pattern to complete before taking action. An incomplete pattern isn't a pattern at all—it's simply something that may become a pattern. You will find that jumping the gun like this will backfire so many times that it simply doesn't become worth the extra profit you might make. So wait for the trend line to be crossed, the neckline to be violated, and the resistance level to be overcome. Don't rush in before the chart is ready for you.

HOW TO HOLD A POSITION

Once you're in a position, having steadfastly followed these five rules, now what do you do? The easiest thing to do is sit back and let your positions take care of themselves. If your stock reaches your target, terrific, you can cash in your profits. If your stock gets stopped out, that's okay, because you've managed your loss and kept it reasonable. But too often people meddle in their portfolios and cause themselves harm they never intended. Let us review some rules to avoid this.

Let the Winners Run

This is one of the most basic rules offered to traders (more completely, cut your losses and let your winners run). It would seem obvious for people to let profits grow. The reason this often doesn't happen is based on a human impulse articulated by another old saying: You'll never go broke taking a profit.

People love to take profits, and often they take them far too soon. For every person who enjoyed a 1,000 percent return on a stock, there are hundreds of other people who bought the exact same stock at the exact same time, took a 10 percent profitm and felt they were financial geniuses (until the stock kept moving higher). It feels good to take a profit, because it means you not only get to pocket the extra cash but also you eliminate the risk of holding the position in the first place.

Unfortunately, instead of letting winners run and cutting losses short, it is human nature to let losers run and cut winners short. A person holding a losing stock will always find many reasons to hold onto that position, hoping that it will turn around, and a person with a profit has the urge to bank that profit as swiftly as possible. But small profits can never pay for large losses, and in the end, taking this approach will create a shrinking portfolio.

So what you should do instead is simply hang on to the position as long as it doesn't violate your stop price (or until such time as it reaches your target). This is how multihundred percent returns are created.

Let Your Stops Manage Your Losers

Stop orders are your friend. Placing a stop order the moment you are in a position does a couple of very good things for you. First, it relieves you from the duty of staring at a computer screen, monitoring your positions. If the stop price is hit, you'll be taken out at once. Second, it injects a healthy dose of responsibility into your trading. Determining and setting a stop price with a calm, rational, objective mind-set will save you a fortune in the long run.

For years there has been a late-night TV ad for a kitchen appliance where the host says to the audience, "Set it, and forget it!" This is, for the most part, also true of stop orders for your positions.

Keep Your Stops Updated

When you initially establish a stop price, you are doing so at a price below the current value of the stock (or above the current value, if it is a short position). But if the stock moves in the direction you anticipate, the stop price is going to become less and less relevant. As a position matures, a stop price's function should change from minimizing your loss to instead preserving your profit.

For example, if you bought 1,000 shares of a $20 stock and set a stop price of $18, you have $2,000 at risk. If the stock moves up over time to $100, it would be silly to continue to have an $18 stop in place. There is no reason to risk the entirety of your profits after a stock has moved that much.

Instead, it pays to check your charts on a regular basis and update the stop prices based on the most recent chart activity. For example, let's say the same stock just mentioned traded at about $25 for several weeks before moving higher. You may decide to update your stop price to $24.99 since there seems to be a strong new level of support at $25. You could therefore lock in $5 of profit and still allow the stock to go higher.

Some brokers offer trailing stops, which base the stop price on a percentage of the stock's current value. This is much like laying down a moving average on top of a chart and stating to sell the stock if it crosses below that moving average. If you don't have time to update your stops regularly, this is a nice compromise, since it automates the act and ensures that you can lock in some profits. The only trouble is that trailing stops aren't really based on the pattern per se, since they are little more than a raw moving average based on recent price activity. But they are certainly better than leaving your initial fixed stop price in place forever.

HOW TO CLOSE A POSITION

Saint Teresa of Avila wrote: "More tears are shed over answered prayers than unanswered ones." A trader might paraphrase that by saying: "More tears are shed over profits than losses." The reason is that a closed profitable position often goes on to a wildly profitable position, and you missed most of the ride.

There were five rules for opening a position and three rules for holding a position, but there's really only one rule for closing a position: close it when your target has been reached or your stop has been violated. It's as simple as that.

Never do an ad hoc close. In other words, don't decide in the moment to rush out of a position for any reason—that reason might be the thrill of a sudden profit, the shock of a sudden loss, or anything in between. As long as your stop is in place, let the position run, and if your target is met, terrific—close it out. Until then, allow the seeds you've planted to grow, undisturbed.

When you do close a position, you may want to jot down some notes about what you learned from that particular trade. If you lost money, can you figure out if your analysis was wrong? If you made money, are there things you did correctly that you want to emphasize for future trades? There is always something to be learned from a properly closed position, whether you made money or lost it. Over the course of time, these trading lessons will form a helpful mosaic for your ongoing career.

TIME AND MONEY

One aspect of being a trader that is simultaneously appealing and nerve-wracking is that the results a trader generates are just about the purest reflection of whatever talent the trader might have. In other words, the talent is almost perfectly correlated with the result.

This is not the case with most other endeavors. Let's say you are a fifth-grade schoolteacher. You have certain talents that are germane to the job: patience, discipline, knowledge, a rapport with young people, a rapport with their parents, the ability to wake up and get to school on time, and so forth. There are dozens of attributes that factor into your potential success in that occupation.

How does one measure the result? That's a tough question right there. It could be measured by the change in test scores from the start of the year to the end, by the relative performance of that class versus similarly aged classes in the same school, by the results of a satisfaction survey that the students fill out, or a similar survey by the parents. As you can see, even defining "success" in this occupation is very hard.

Similar challenges would be seen for a lawyer, a dentist, or a bricklayer.

In addition, what happens between input (skills) and output (results) is subject to the interaction of the person with the environment. In the case of the teacher, the environment is mainly the students and the school's culture; for a lawyer, it is clients and coworkers; for a bricklayer, it is the job site, the tools, and other subcontractors.

But the perception of success in any given occupation can be fudged quite a bit. You can be a lousy Congressman but still seem quite competent and get elected repeatedly. You can be a crummy teacher but thrive simply because your students like how permissive you are.

A trader, though, really has just one asset: their ability to apply their edge, whatever it might be, in the never-ending turmoil that represents a given market. Their edge might be skillful charting, insightful fundamental analysis, or a deep understanding of a certain industry.

But since a trader's measurement of success is simple—their profit/ loss statement—there's no fudge factor allowed. All you've got is talent, and all you've got to show for it is a numeric result.

So let's say you were hired to sit on a manhole cover to prevent zombies from coming out of it. You are being paid 100 percent for your time. You are applying no talent at all to this occupation; the only asset you are bringing to the job is your body's mass. (It could be argued that some folks are more talented than others even in this respect, but let's keep it simple!)

If you are a salesclerk at a high-end clothing store, you are being paid partly for your time (someone needs to be there to make the place look open for business and to make sure people don't just steal things) but also partly for your talent (your knowledge of clothes, what looks good on a particular person, etc.).

No one is going to pay for a trader's time. You can sit there all year long, working your tail off, and if the talent isn't there, you're not going to get a stipend. In fact, you are going to work very hard for the privilege of losing money.

Of course, the market's behavior has a direct relationship to what kinds of results your talent brings, but that is the biggest task of all: honing your skills so that the market's behavior becomes, ultimately, irrelevant to your ability to generate profits.

THERE IS NO HOLY GRAIL

My philosophy on trading has this important premise: it's all about the relationship between you and the market. The market you cannot control, but yourself—to a degree—you can. And it is the complexity of yourself vis-à-vis an ever-changing market that makes the entire enterprise of being a trader simultaneously fascinating, exasperating, and thought-provoking.

Instead of latching on to one particular trading method, I have, over the years, adopted a handful of methods, and I've put them into my own unique trading stew. I am refining it all the time, weighting some vectors I am monitoring more, weighting some less. But the concoction is best suited for me and who I am. It wouldn't work as well for most other people.

It's important to embrace one's perpetual ignorance. I seek mastery by considering myself a dunce who is in search of knowledge. By no means am I suggesting piling on rule after rule, method after method. I view the act of trading as not much different than making an ongoing series of bread loaves. I'm changing the recipe a little each time, and I'm kneading, kneading, kneading the dough (that is, my positions, their weighting, and their stops) to try to get the result I'm after: metaphorically, a delicious loaf of bread; realistically, a nice, outsize profit.

The fact that learning to be a great trader is a very personal journey is why I stopped buying business books many years ago. When I was in my late teens and early twenties, I bought business books all the time. I figured they would help me become a more successful businessperson. They didn't.

I've got shelves of these books, and I don't think I learned a thing from any of them. It's not because I didn't read them carefully. But most how-to books are based on the notion that if you do what this person did, you will be like this person. But you know what? That person is that person. He isn't you. And the circumstances he found himself in (whether he's Jack Welch, Tom Peters, Steve Jobs, Mark Zuckerberg, or God-knows-who-else) are unique to that person. If you want to read a biography, great, read a biography. But if you want to be like that person, well, that spot's already been taken.

This isn't to say there's nothing to learn from books. But I think books related to business or trading are best applied to either (1) the actual mechanics of trading techniques and their application and (2) learning from the successes and failures of others in order to template those events to your own personal experience. I don't have any illusions that I'm going to be a Paul Tudor Jones, but I do draw inspiration from his resilience in the face of defeat and his successful use of past markets to understand present ones.

CHARTING YOUR WAY TO PROFITS

Making money in the market isn't easy. So much of human nature is geared to poor trading habits that it is difficult to overcome the challenges to being a good trader.

You have some advantages on your side now, however. You have a very powerful charting tool at your disposal to calmly and rationally judge securities. You have seen hundreds of examples of technical analysis in real-life charts to understand how to observe and apply these lessons. And you know some critically important rules of the road that lead to sound trading.

Good luck in your endeavors, and make a point of revisiting this book whenever you need a refresher. I hope it will be a powerful guide as you chart your way to more profitable and consistent trading.

And stay in touch! You can learn more by visiting my blog (www.slopeofhope.com), and if you want to write me, I am at trader.tim.knight@gmail.com.

The Kirk Report Interview

Charles Kirk is the widely read blogger who writes The Kirk Report (www.thekirkreport.com/). In August 2009, he conducted a lengthy interview with me, which he has kindly permitted me to republish here. I think this interview does a good job of answering a lot of questions about my trading style.

People read trading blogs for all sorts of reasons. Some do it to learn something new, others do it to find new trading ideas and many do it simply for entertainment. For me, Tim Knight's Slope of Hope has been a great source of interesting perspectives as well as pure enjoyment.

Tim is an interesting fellow and his blog is worthwhile. He has been actively trading since 1987 and uses technical analysis as a key part of his approach. However, you can expect to see much more than charts there. In fact, every time you visit his blog you can count on Tim saying or sharing something that is likely to amuse you and/or at least get you thinking about something. His perspectives are always fresh, witty, and clearly different than the typical "we're always in a bull market" garbage found within the mainstream financial press. That's why Tim's blog has always been among the blogs I read and one of the main reasons why I've invited Tim to participate in this month's Q&A.

Tim's "Slope of Hope" is one of those must-read blogs for anyone interested in the market.

We sincerely hope you find this Q&A both enjoyable and helpful.

Q&A WITH TIM KNIGHT

Kirk: Hi, Tim. Thank-you for taking the time away from your daily trading routine to answer our questions. I speak for many members who have a great deal of respect for you and we sincerely welcome you to this Q&A series!

Tim Knight: Thanks, Kirk. It's just about impossible to look at a list of top trading blogs and not see the Kirk Report, so it's really an honor for me to be mentioned on your site.

Kirk: For those who don't know you, please tell us a little about your professional and educational background.

Tim Knight: My educational background is nothing glorious—I was eager to get into the world of work, so I got my four year degree in two and a half years from Santa Clara University, which is a Jesuit college in California (and the state's first higher education institution). My experience with computers, though, began long before that—I got serious about computers back in 1980, and I wrote my first book about them—*The World Connection*—when I was 16 years old. I went on to write twenty different books about computers, which allowed me to pay for my own college education and living expenses, and I had a brief stint with "real" jobs at Apple Computer and Montgomery Securities.

The first trade I ever placed was on Black Monday in 1987; perhaps that experience etched bearishness into my head permanently. I traded casually for years, but I didn't get really serious about it until 1992 when I founded Prophet, which is where I've been ever since.

Kirk: How did you get interested in trading?

Tim Knight: This may seem like a random reference, but it's not. When I was a young boy growing up in Louisiana, where it rains a lot, I would always get mesmerized by the beads of water bobbing up and down the side of the car's window. Since the car was in motion, the water droplets would jiggle up and down, clinging to the window, and watching the random movement of the water fascinated me.

Maybe that's why I was predisposed to technical analysis. I like to see relationships of time and motion, and I find the ability to predict the future to be empowering. I fail at those predictions part of the time, obviously, but I am on a constant quest to improve my skills as a trader, one of the most important being to draw probabilistic conclusions from a given chart.

Kirk: How would you describe your style of trading?

Tim Knight: I guess the words I'd use to describe my trading would be "technical analysis-based," "swing," and "broadly directional." I use charts pretty much exclusively as the basis of my rationale on any given position, and I'm looking for broad moves either up or down. I don't get fancy with my positions—just straight-up equity plays or options.

Kirk: In an average week how many trades do you make? What is your average hold time and how many positions do you have open at any given time?

Tim Knight: It really depends on the week, but I'd say a weekly range would be anywhere from a couple dozen trades to maybe a hundred. The number of positions I have open at any one time can range from as few as eighty to as many as a couple hundred.

Kirk: That's pretty active, Tim. I'd go crazy trying to manage a portfolio of more than a dozen stocks! What would you say is your average win/loss ratio for your trades?

Tim Knight: That's something I've never really tracked, since I'm much more interested in my equity curve. I've got plenty of losers, believe me, but I go out of my way to keep them on the small side.

Kirk: How has your overall performance been recently, as well as the past few years?

Tim Knight: I've been doing pretty well, but so far 2008 was my stand-out year. At the end of 2008, my personal account was up something like +180 percent, and my 401(k), which is self-directed, was up about +438 percent.

Kirk: No doubt your bearish perspectives helped generate those recent returns! Tell us a little about your initial learning process and anything significant you learned within the first year or two of trading.

Tim Knight: My learning process was a lot longer than a year or two—I've been at this twenty years, and I'm still learning! I think the most important thing I've learned is this—the synopsis of what it takes to be a good trader can easily fit on one page, if not one paragraph. But actually executing those principles consistently is something which runs completely against basic human nature, so it is a tremendous challenge for most people to actually adhere to those principles. The paradox of trading is that what feels right is usually the wrong decision.

Kirk: Indeed, this is something we've learned from others like William Eckhardt who said that "if you're playing for emotional satisfaction, you're bound to lose, because what feels good is often the wrong thing to do." So, where do you think most traders go wrong in the first couple of years?

Tim Knight: All the "classic" mistakes one hears about—off the top of my head, I'd say averaging down, not having stops, over-committing to a particular position. At its core, however, the biggest mistake is that people take the most important rule of trading—Cut Losses Short and Let Winners Run—and do exactly the opposite. Taking profits quickly (because it feels good) and letting losers run (because it is hard to admit defeat) is how most people operate, and it's understandable, given the way human beings tick.

Kirk: After the initial learning curve, what do you think marked the next stage of your progress in becoming a successful trader?

Tim Knight: The real sea change for me came when I started blogging. After I sold Prophet, my wife thought people might find it interesting to read what I had to say about the market. Since I didn't have an audience, I thought it would be a waste of time, but I finally started doing a post a day. The blog grew really slowly, at first just read by friends and family. But I made a real habit of it, and the pressure of being "on stage" with my trading made me a much more astute trader. I had to think hard about what I was doing, because I don't get my jollies out of looking foolish, and I wanted to write things and do things which made sense in the long run.

Kirk: So, in a way, the blog held you accountable for your ideas and analysis much like many find through trading journals.

Since you began trading in 1987, do you feel like you have perfected your system?

Tim Knight: I don't have a system, and even if I thought I did, I'd never claim to have perfected it. The markets are ever-changing, just like anything else. An amazing campaign manager from 1968 might find himself completely lost in today's political world, and a superb mutual fund manager from 1975 might be a colossal failure today. To me, the entire act of trading is a constant examination of the relationship between (1) you and (2) the market. That may sound simple, but to my way of thinking it's just as complex and challenging as any deeply personal relationship.

Kirk: Over the past few years, what would you say is the most significant lesson you've learned about yourself and trading?

Tim Knight: Speaking for myself, I'd say the biggest lesson—or, more accurately, challenge—is fighting my bearish tendencies. I'm sure the "permabulls" had a devil of a time in 2000–2002 and mid 2007–early 2009, but by the same token, we bearish types had it really rough in all the other years. I've worked really hard to open my eyes up to both bullish and bearish opportunities, going so far as to add a feature in

ProphetCharts which literally flips it upside down so people with "bear on the brain" like me can view charts more objectively.

Kirk: That's very interesting, Tim. I have often recommended others to flip the chart upside down to discover any bias. Frankly, I'm surprised that more charting software doesn't enable this feature. So, good for you for recognizing the importance of understanding yourself in relation to your analysis of the charts.

Also, I have to tell you that I really love it when traders like you have provided their trading rules especially when they are concise and to the point as you have done.

So, here's my first question—how do you set your stops?

Tim Knight: A lot of people ask me this, and my answer—it depends on the chart—is surely very unsatisfying. But it really does depend on the chart, and I am very specific about where I place stops; I've never used trailing stops or anything else automatic like that.

The whole purpose of a stop is, once crossed, to tell me that my analysis is wrong; in other words, it tells me that the rationale I used to get into a given position is no longer valid, and thus the trade should no longer be held. It's as simple as that.

Kirk: Fair enough, Tim. You've also said that "partial exits are preferable to outright closes." Can you take us through a trade you've made recently in order to show how a partial exit was the best approach?

Tim Knight: I can't think of a recent one which springs to mind, but I'll give you a very simplistic hypothetical. Let's say you bought 1,000 shares of a stock at $5, and you're fortunate enough to see it move up to $10. You aren't certain if it's going to go any higher, so you sell half your position, 500 shares, and recapture your entire initial investment. You are now in a very powerful place, psychologically, because all of your risk capital has been eliminated: in other words, you can let the position trade more freely (in spite of your uncertainty of its direction) without being concerned about taking any kind of hit on the position; added to which, it's virtually impossible the stock will find its way down to $0, so you are virtually guaranteed a profit. The point is that if the stock eventually gets up to $25, you've got a wonderful profit without having had to second-guess the position on the way up.

Kirk: As the saying goes—when in doubt, sell half—because if it keeps going up, you still are right because you have a position on. Likewise, if the stock goes down at least you sold some.

So, do you believe in scaling into a new trading position? Why or why not?

Tim Knight: Scaling into a position makes sense for a couple of reasons: first, it reduces your risk. If you are wrong, then the loss you take is going to be more modest, and if you are right, then "averaging up" into a winning trade is just as smart as "averaging down" a losing trade is dumb. And second, I think it's rare that a person enters a trade at exactly the perfect time, so scaling into it allows some forgiveness (and less stress) as the position hopefully starts to move in your direction.

Kirk: Do you ever average down into a losing trade?

Tim Knight: I really try to avoid this, and I'm pretty good about it, mainly because my stops do the work for me. I never use a "mental stop"—my stop prices are real, and if something is not going my way, I'll simply be taken out.

Kirk: As outlined by your trading rules, your trend analysis is both simple and straightforward—that is, the trend of the market is defined by the 13-week EWA and 52-week EWA of the $SPX. Based on the relative position of the 13-week EWA, the market is either Up-Trending (13-week EWA above the 52-week) or Down-Trending, and no more than 20 percent of the value of all your positions may be positioned against that trend at any one time. Where can traders track the EWA online based on this simple trend system?

Tim Knight: Well, it probably comes as no surprise that I use ProphetCharts, and I use that product more than any computer product I've ever touched. There are, of course, other good sites on the Internet, and quite a few folks on my blog use StockCharts.com, which is a site I've always respected.

Kirk: I like that you've placed a restriction that says that 20 percent of your positions must not be positioned against the trend. How did you arrive at that number and why do you think that's important?

Tim Knight: It isn't a number derived from any scientific method; it just seemed right to not be 100 percent in one particular direction. During bear markets, some extraordinary stocks push higher, and during bull markets, some stocks are prone to falling. So I came up with that 80/20 split to give myself some latitude to "hedge" a portfolio instead of being utterly bullish or bearish.

Kirk: To be clear, do you think that it is a good idea to always have 20 percent of your assets positioned against the prevailing trend? Why or why not?

Tim Knight: I suppose there are a couple of good reasons. One of them is that I believe in any given market, there are opportunities in both directions, and it keeps you sharper as a trader to be able to play positions both ways. Secondly, let's face it, all trends eventually end, and being able to capture a portion of a trend change will help soften the blow to your other positions. In other words, if you're 80 percent long and 20 percent short, and the market starts to turn down in earnest, the 20 percent shorts are going to be a helpful save (and a good signal) for the losing longs.

Kirk: Another rule says that positions should be regularly updated for the sake of updated stops. How do you recommend traders do this?

Tim Knight: It's a lot of work, but it doesn't have to be a daily exercise. I typically do a "clean sweep" of all my stops whenever the indexes have moved in my direction some meaningful amount. For instance, if I have a bunch of short positions, and the Dow 30 has moved down, say, 500 points since I entered them, then it's high time I get in there and review those charts, one by one, and tighten up those stops. This allows me to at least lock in some partial profits if I'm stopped out, and it lets me sleep easier at night knowing that I'm not going to expose myself to, in this case, a subsequent 700 point rise in the Dow and see all those profits turn into losses.

Kirk: You also have a rule against trading within the first 30 minutes of the trading day. Are there any other times you try to avoid and when are you typically most active?

Tim Knight: The first 30 minutes are the only "hands off" time for me. Sometimes people ask if I permit my stops to do their work during that half hour; absolutely! The point is for me not to be trading, but by all means my stops have to be there doing their job.

These days, the last 90 minutes of the trading day have become their own alternative universe, although that may change at some point. But the "end of day run-up" has become almost a cliché in this market. I also tend to back off during Fed days (FOMC announcements), since the markets typically go completely spastic after the Fed announcement, and it takes at least an hour for them to figure out which direction they want to go.

Kirk: Emotions are a large component of trading. Your rule is first to "be aware" of your emotions and the importance of keeping fear and hubris in control in order to have a "carefree and fearless" state of mind. This is easier said than done. In your view, how do traders learn the level of emotional control to trade well?

Tim Knight: The area of emotional control is something I think a person can only partly handle, because some of us are simply more emotional than others. Making money can be euphoric, and losing money can be devastating, and swaying between those two feelings can be very challenging for most individuals. My own "self-improvement course" in this area is to read good books on the topic. I really like *Trading In the Zone*, and I'm currently reading *Enhancing Trading Performance* by Dr. Brett Steenbarger.

Kirk: Your last rule speaks of position sizing and that it must "*be consistent among instrument types irrespective of anticipated opportunity.*" Can you provide an example of a recent trade and explain your method for determining the size relative to your own trading portfolio?

Tim Knight: Well, I really try to keep things simple. Given my current portfolio size, I try to keep individual equity positions at $10,000, options positions at $5,000, and ETF positions at anywhere from $100,000 to $250,000, depending on how strongly I feel about its potential direction. That's probably about the least sophisticated portfolio management system on the planet, but it at least assures me that no single equity's surprise move is going to severely affect my overall portfolio.

Kirk: What mistakes do you think most traders make concerning position sizing?

Tim Knight: Probably looking for home runs—maybe they put all their eggs into one basket. To be honest, I don't really have exposure to the portfolios of others, so this is just speculation on my part.

Kirk: As you've said, creating rules is great, but it isn't easy to follow them. In your experience, which is the most difficult rule to follow and why?

Tim Knight: The most difficult rule to follow is to let your profits run. That one, for me, has been atrociously difficult. I can't tell you how many times I've taken a profit, patted myself on the back, and watched the same position continue to move dramatically higher (or lower, in the case of shorts).

Kirk: Are there any techniques that you are using to let winners run?

Tim Knight: The core technique I use for letting my winners run is to keep my stop prices fresh. Assuming a position is moving in my direction, I will periodically ratchet the stop price up (or down, as the case may be) to a technically significant level so that I can at least preserve a portion of my profits if things move against me. This has been for me the only reliable way to fight the urge to take all my profits. I have found this to be much easier on bearish positions than bullish ones, since it is sometimes hard to accept the possibility that something on the long side can move up hundreds—or even thousands—of percent.

Kirk: Now that we've talked about your trading rules, what are some of the key rules or factors that you consider before selecting any potential trading opportunity?

Tim Knight: I really want the risk/reward to be in my favor, so the most important thing to me is that the stop price is relatively close and the potential profit is relatively far away (in other words, the potential profit dwarfs the potential loss, because I like operating from the assumption that the trade will probably go wrong). One really great position can make up for a lot of trading "sins" in the past.

Kirk: Please explain the process of how you go about finding your trades. Can you take us through a relatively new trade of yours from the very beginning starting with how you discovered the idea to the first position through the final sell?

Tim Knight: It's all about organization. I'm a pretty organized person by nature, and I'm pretty manic when it comes to my watch lists. In ProphetCharts, I've got a series of watch lists set up, and stocks move from place to place depending on my disposition toward each of them.

First, I've got my "Core List," which is the general holding bin for stocks. If something looks like it's starting to "gel" as a good short opportunity, I'll move it to a watch list I call Bear Pen, and if it's starting to look good on the long side, it goes into the Bull Pen. That way, I can really focus on those two holding pens.

If and when an item in those pens actually looks ready to trade, I'll move it to either Candidate Longs or Candidate Shorts, and once the trade is actually in place, the symbol will move to whatever portfolio is appropriate (I manage several personal portfolios). So my watch lists are in a constant migratory state.

As for actually looking for trading ideas, I follow about 800 stocks, and that gives me all the ideas I need. I virtually never do a scan or use any of the other services on the Web to smoke out trading ideas, simply because I've already got a very good universe of tradable instruments that I already follow.

Kirk: What would you say are your favorite kinds of technical setups?

Tim Knight: The classic head and shoulders—both normal and inverted—is probably my favorite. It's pretty easy to identify, has a good risk/reward ratio, and it has worked out well for me historically. I also like upside breakouts with strong volume for bullish positions, for obvious reasons.

Kirk: In recent years, have you discovered any new patterns that have been helping you achieve more success?

Tim Knight: It isn't a pattern, per se, but there's a service called Retracement Levels that was created by a regular reader on my blog which I like quite a lot. These are simply horizontal levels on various markets which represent meaningful support and resistance levels. During the insanity of autumn 2008, I found them to be indispensible, particularly since the market was so volatile.

Kirk: I know you utilize Fibonacci in your analysis. In your experience, what is the strength and weakness from this type of analysis?

Tim Knight: The principal weakness is they have to be applied correctly, and that takes a certain amount of experience and an "eye" for the chart. Of the four Fibonacci studies in ProphetCharts—retracements, fan lines, arcs, and time series—I've found retracements to be by far the most useful. Fans work from time to time, but frankly I hardly ever have found utility from the other two.

Kirk: In your book *Chart Your Way to Profits*, you talk about essential indicators like moving averages, Bollinger bands, the parabolic stop and reversal (PSAR), and moving average convergence divergence (MACD). Among all of these methods, which are your favorites and why?

Tim Knight: Some people may find this surprising, but I don't use any of them. It's not because I've tried them and they don't work; it's simply that my style of charting is quite vanilla, and I haven't found the use of derived information to be helpful for me personally.

Kirk: Very interesting. So, do you use different time frames in your technical analysis? If so, what time frames do you like to use and why?

Tim Knight: I'm pretty consistent these days using a 10-year daily chart. That might seem like a lot, but it captures the past two bear markets and the big bull run in between. I like to keep an eye on the 10-day minute bar chart for indexes during the trading day, but otherwise the 10-year daily is my reference.

Kirk: All good traders dedicate a lot of time and effort to improvement and to reducing mistakes. How has your trading method evolved and improved over the years?

Tim Knight: I think my organization skills and my psychological discipline have improved the most. If anything, I've simplified my method and approach.

Kirk: Can you provide an example of something you thought was true when trading early in your career and now believe is just dead wrong?

Tim Knight: I used to think individual stocks could have minds of their own and act independently of the market, but I now know that a huge part of what any stock does depends on what the market as a whole is doing. There are always exceptions—I remember that, for whatever reason, Krispy Kreme's stock did fantastically well during the bursting of the tech bubble—but on the whole it's really, really tough to fight the general trend.

Kirk: How much time and attention do you pay attention to others' opinions about the market and/or stocks you are trading?

Tim Knight: I'm not especially interested in other opinions about individual stocks, but there are a few places I respect for opinions on the market in general. I enjoy Elliott Wave International's publications, particularly their Short-Term Update, and of course I draw a lot of knowledge and perspective from the comments section of Slope, since there are tens of thousands of readers on a regular basis.

Kirk: I know you've said you like to do "hand-chart analysis." In fact, you shared a very interesting chart some time ago about the future of the market. What can traders accomplish by charting stocks and the markets in this manner and, by the way, how did you create that chart?

Tim Knight: I created the chart by comparing the 1937–1941 market to our own market, since I felt it was the closest historical "template." So far, it's proved remarkably prescient, but we'll have to see how the next few years pan out. I have hardly ever done something like this before, but I felt inspired on that particular day about the future direction of the market. I only wish I had paid closer attention to my own work, since I missed a good chunk of the run-up from March through August of 2009, even though my own chart totally nailed it.

Kirk: It is human nature to think the markets must conform to our view of reality, but as we've both seen, the market is not rational but emotional. Over the years and, especially recently, I've witnessed many traders suffer performance anxiety because of their negative views about the economy and the skepticism over the bailouts and from just fighting the short-term trends. In your view, how do traders learn to separate their opinions and bias and still profit from the market while having a large amount of skepticism? I'm asking this question of you particularly because I think this is one of your strengths.

Tim Knight: I'm appreciative that you think it's one of my strengths, although my bias about what's been going on with all the government bailouts is tough for me to shake. My point of view, the more tunnel vision you can have with respect to the charts, the better. If you can focus on your own analysis—in my case, purely charts—and filter out all the other noise, it's bound to help. And I never, ever flick on the television to hear what the financial news networks are talking about.

Kirk: Please describe a typical trading day for you. How do you organize and dedicate your time?

Tim Knight: I live on the West Coast, so my day starts early. I am usually up at about 5:30 or 6 A.M. to catch up on e-mails, check out the overnight markets, and look at comments on my blog. I'll typically do a quick post before the market opens. The first half hour of the day, I'm simply watching what's going on and going through my key watch lists. Once the first half hour is done, I'm usually ready to execute some ideas.

I spend the trading day doing blog posts, answering e-mails, working on new product features, and managing trades. I like to do an end-of-day wrap-up after the markets have closed, and then I'll catch up on other work in general. The 6:30 A.M. to 1:00 P.M. time block is precious to me, because that's when I'm really focused on trading and writing.

Kirk: Can you give us some idea of what tools you use to monitor the markets (i.e. your trading platform, software, websites, etc.)?

Tim Knight: It's actually very simple. I've got two computers—a high-end Dell laptop and a Mac PowerBook. Each of them drives two monitors, my favorite of which is my honkin' big 30-inch Apple monitor whose sole purpose in life is to show me the S&P e-mini future bob along. I am very loyal to Prophet's own products, so I use MarketMatrix to track my portfolios and ProphetCharts—of course!—to make my trading decisions and keep my watch lists in order.

Kirk: What would you say are the biggest changes in the markets and trading in general you've seen during your career both good and bad?

Tim Knight: Recently the biggest change has been the huge influence of the government and investment banks in trying to turn the economy around. The government has never, at least in my lifetime, intervened so radically in the markets, and that has caused a lot of methods and systems that used to work very reliably to be set aside as useless until this whole thing blows over and we can all return to a semblance of normalcy.

Kirk: Do you think it is easier or more challenging to trade for a living now than in the past?

Tim Knight: I think it's somewhat easier, but only because there is such a better selection of trading vehicles. Traders have an amazing set of tools to work with in the form of all the new ETFs that have come out, in addition to the e-mini futures, and the product selection just keeps getting better. It wasn't long ago that the biggest innovation around were the inverse mutual funds which set their prices just twice a day, and you had to place the order something like 30 minutes in advance.

Kirk: What kind of advice would you give a person just now beginning in trading the markets?

Tim Knight: I would spend a lot of time hanging out in a quality online community. Slope of Hope comes to mind, naturally, but there are plenty of other good blogs and forums out there where people can either lurk and learn or actually get in there and participate. Continuing the learning once you start trading is even more important.

Kirk: A number of people who read my web site desire to trade for a living. Like you, I receive a lot of questions concerning capital requirements needed to start and how to make the transition to trade full-time. Do you have any words of wisdom or rules of thumb to share along these lines?

Tim Knight: I'm sorry, I really don't. Some people have taken small sums and made fortunes, and some people have done just the opposite. It's like the old joke—"How do you make a small fortune trading commodities? Start with a large one." So I don't know of any magic number, and there certainly isn't any dollar figure that will guarantee you are immune to being badly damaged if you don't trade well.

Kirk: What are the things you like best about the trading business?

Tim Knight: The fact that I and I alone am responsible for the results. To some people, that might be a negative, since it's always more comforting to say that such-and-so caused a bad thing to happen to you. But to be able to look in the mirror and know that you are the only person who is going to create a result, whether for good or bad, can be very empowering.

Kirk: What are the downsides to trading for a living?

Tim Knight: The uncertainty—you have absolutely no control of the market, and even though it's very easy for a person to say "just trade what you see," that advice is about as useful as telling a newly married couple, "Don't ever have a fight." People and markets are complex creatures, and things aren't always going to go as you plan.

Kirk: How does a person know it is the right time and the right decision for them to trade for a living?

Tim Knight: I think most of us would agree that it's important to have the basics in place for core living expenses. You don't want to be trading the children's tuition or the family grocery money. No matter how unlikely you may think it is, you have to be in a position to lose 100 percent of your trading capital and not have it affect your lifestyle. Otherwise, the pressure will simply screw up your mind-set.

How long a person trades before getting really serious about it depends on the person's innate ability, and I do think that varies widely. Just as some people are born to be musicians, I think some people were born to be traders. I was not a "born" trader, so it's taken me many, many years. But there are surely 21-year-olds out there who are ready to trade for a living, and I'm sure there are 70-year-old people with 50 years of trading experience that still should just keep it as an amusing hobby and nothing more.

Kirk: Because of your web site I'm sure you are privileged to know a lot of different kinds of traders. Where do you see traders missing the boat?

Tim Knight: I think the biggest boat missed is underestimating just how far a market or an individual security can go. There seems to be nothing more common than someone buying a stock at $5, selling it at $7, congratulating themselves on a terrific profit, and then seeing the stock go up to $30 (or, for a bear, similar figures in the opposite direction). I am quite guilty of this myself—I bought the stock Avis Budget Group (CAR) on March 2 for 42 cents, got stopped out the next day for a tiny loss, and then watched the stock move up to over $10 in just a few months. Now that was a big boat to miss!

Kirk: Likewise, what are some qualities you frequently find among the most successful traders you know?

Tim Knight: I'd say "evenhandedness." There's a regular reader on my site, Brinkley, who has a knack for having a very impartial view of the market, no matter what it's doing. I really admire that, and I think a lot of my readers look up to her for the same quality which is pretty difficult to find among traders.

Kirk: Thinking back, what was most instrumental in your development into becoming a successful trader?

Tim Knight: There's no doubt that writing Slope of Hope has been the biggest development for me, simply because I have to not only answer to myself but also to the several tens of thousands of people who read my work. It has made me a much more careful, thoughtful, and logical trader.

Kirk: When all is said and done, in your experience what is the best way to learn how to trade?

Tim Knight: I have long been a "learning by doing" sort of person. The tricky thing about doing this with trading is that you're dealing with actual money. Some people are big believers in paper trading, but I'm afraid that's just not the same. I suppose it helps a person acquaint themselves with the actual mechanics of placing orders, watching charts, and placing stops—all of which are healthy—but I don't think one really starts learning how to be a trader until they are actually trading with their own dollars and cents.

Kirk: I suspect like all good traders you are working on improving your performance in some manner. Can you share what you're specifically working on right now?

Tim Knight: At the risk of sounding repetitious, my personal challenge is to balance the bear in with me with some bull. I'm afraid I enjoy bear markets way too much for my own good, particularly since they move so quickly, which tends to agree with my impatient nature. But the fact is that bull markets are more common and longer-lasting than bear markets, and I won't be a consistently successful trader unless I can be as good a bull as I am a bear. That's my ongoing goal.

Kirk: At this point of your career, who do you look up to for inspiration and guidance?

Tim Knight: I don't have a particular mentor or role model, so books about traders and trading are my stand-in. I enjoy books about trading psychology, successful traders, and interesting charting techniques. I'm in the final throes of getting my Chartered Market Technician certification, so that is exposing me to a lot of required reading that I normally might not have discovered.

Kirk: Although I know both of us share love for the markets and trading, what are your long-term career plans and future for your web site?

Tim Knight: My overriding principle in anything I do is that work should never actually seem like work. Doing what you love seems like a common truism these days, but I have lived that credo for my entire life. The popularity of my blog has opened up some new opportunities that I'm going to be exploring very soon, but one thing I'm pretty certain about is that I'm going to keep writing Slope of Hope as long as my readers will continue to put up with me.

Kirk: Finally, if you had one piece of advice to share with all investors and traders, what would it be?

Tim Knight: Be patient! Learning how to trade profitably and consistently isn't something you do after attending a weekend seminar. It can be a lifelong journey of self-discovery and self-improvement. Give yourself time, and keep your risk capital sensible so that you don't hurt yourself in the process. Good luck!

Kirk: Thank you for all of the perspectives about how you trade. We look forward to reading your blog updates. Trade well!

MarketMatrix

The MarketMatrix applet is a streaming quote and portfolio system that is made available on the Investools Investor Toolbox (www.investools.com). The purpose of this section is not to teach you how to use MarketMatrix but to illustrate how the portfolio management system is tied to the charting systems.

Each line in MarketMatrix displays a symbol as well as a quote for that symbol (in the case of a watch list) or a profit/loss for your position in that symbol (in the case of a portfolio). When you right-click on a symbol, a pop-up menu appears, and one of the choices offered is ProphetCharts (Figure B.1). You can select this or, for the same result, double-click that line to make a chart appear.

You are not limited to displaying just one chart on your screen. You can have multiple charts displayed, each of which can have its own properties. There does not need to be any correlation between the charts at all: they can have different symbols, different time periods, some streaming and some not streaming, and so forth. The goal is for you to get a view into the market that is helpful without being overwhelming.

You can create multiple chart instances by repeatedly invoking ProphetCharts from MarketMatrix, or you can use the clone feature (discussed in Chapter 2) to create new charts using any existing chart style. Figure B.2 illustrates how all the available chart styles appear when the down-arrow next to Clone is clicked. Choosing any of these styles will produce another chart instance using the specified style.

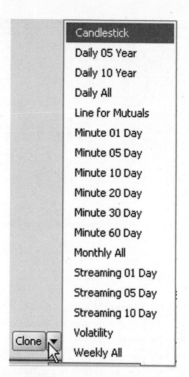

FIGURE B.1 This is the pop-up menu that appears when you right-click an item in a portfolio within MarketMatrix.

FIGURE B.2 When you clone a chart, you can select any of the chart styles you have made as the basis for the clone.

As a simple example, Figure B.3 shows two charts simultaneously displayed. The top one is a streaming five-day minute-bar chart of the S&P 500 index, which also includes streaming real-time quotes. The lower one is a five-year daily chart of the S&P 500 ETFs (symbol SPY). This kind of conjoint short-term/long-term view is popular among swing traders who need two perspectives at once.

No matter how many charts you have, you will find it time-consuming to create, resize, and position each and every chart day after day. This is particularly true if you use multiple video screens, since arranging the various elements that are available with MarketMatrix (such as multiple Watch Lists, multiple Portfolios, Options Chains, Time & Sales, Level 2, and multiple ProphetCharts) takes a lot of time and care.

For this reason, there is a time-saving feature called Desktop in MarketMatrix that allows you to preserve all the elements you have laid out on the screen into a custom-named desktop. Therefore, when you call up this desktop again, everything you've laid out—particularly including the

FIGURE B.3 These two charts appear on the same screen, the top showing an intraday streaming graph and the bottom showing a daily multiyear graph.

charts—will be put back in the same place using the same size, symbols, and other parameters. All you need to do is click the Desktop dropdown menu and choose the Save option to get the dialog box as shown in Figure B.4.

Once your layout is saved, you can access it from the same pop-up menu in MarketMatrix. Just click on Desktop and choose Layouts (Figure B.5). Any desktops you have saved already will be shown in a sub-menu, and all you need to do to create it is click on the desktop name you want to invoke.

FIGURE B.4 You should save a desktop with a name describing the purpose or layout of the desktop.

PORTFOLIO INTEGRATION

On the Investor Toolbox, there is another level of integration that makes ProphetCharts more helpful as a trading tool, and that is the integration of portfolio data directly within the applet. You may recall that one of the modules available on the left panel is My Portfolios (located between My Watch Lists and My Study Sets). If you choose to display this module, it will show you the name and contents of every portfolio you have created on the Investor Toolbox, along with the size and entry price of each position (Figure B.6).

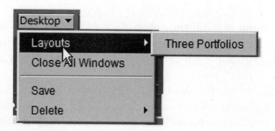

FIGURE B.5 Any layouts you have created already will be presented in the pop-up so you can bring up that layout with one click.

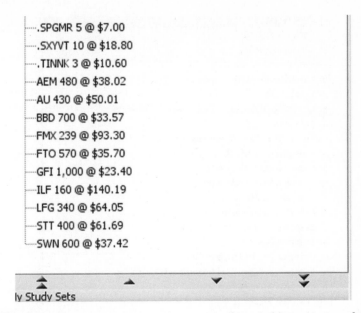

.SPGMR 5 @ $7.00
.SXYVT 10 @ $18.80
.TINNK 3 @ $10.60
AEM 480 @ $38.02
AU 430 @ $50.01
BBD 700 @ $33.57
FMX 239 @ $93.30
FTO 570 @ $35.70
GFI 1,000 @ $23.40
ILF 160 @ $140.19
LFG 340 @ $64.05
STT 400 @ $61.69
SWN 600 @ $37.42

ly Study Sets

FIGURE B.6 The quantity and purchase price of any holdings in a portfolio are displayed in the module.

Prophet.Net : MarketMatrix : Trust

Watch Lists   **Portfolios**   **Options**

View [Trust ▼]   Action ▼   Show [All Positions ▼]   ☑ Based on Bid/Ask

Add Symbol(s) [   ] [Go] Search   *Position Count: 34 (10 Short/24 Options)*

Symbol	Last	$Ch-PC	%Ch-PC	P/L-Today	Bid	Ask	Volume
⊖ $INDU	11,382.910	+12.970	+0.11%				180,097,000
⊖ $SPX	1,304.270	-0.010	-0.00%				
⊖ $NDX	1,5⬚950	+8.300	+0.53%				
⊖ $XAU	144.750	+0.760	+0.53%				
⊖ $XOI	1,158.450	-16.700	-1.42%				
⊖ .ADQVH	5.800	-0.700	-10.77%	-350.00	5.700	5.900	31
⊖ .AGNVD	6.300	+0.500	+8.62%	+0.00	6.200	6.400	20
⊖ .ALXJ	5.800	+0.000	+0.00%	+0.00	6.500	6.700	N/A
⊖ .APAVO	9.900	+3.200	+47.76%	+1,280.00	9.100	9.300	12
⊖ .AQMVJ	6.500	+0.800	+14.04%	+400.00	6.300	6.500	12

FIGURE B.7 At the top of the MarketMatrix display is a count of all Long, Short, and Options positions in the currently-displayed portfolio.

FIGURE B.8 ProphetCharts can display the sum total of items following the name of each watch list or portfolio.

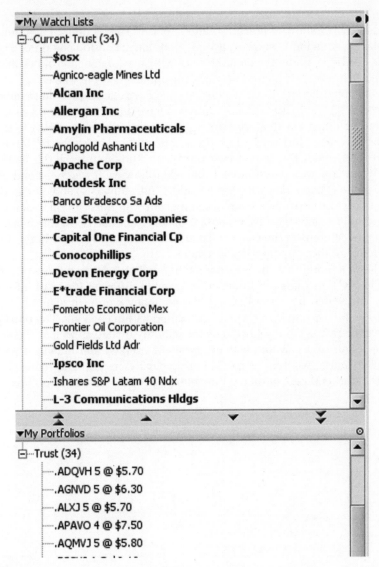

FIGURE B.9 The watch lists show just the company names of the watch list contents, whereas the portfolio lists display the basic information about the positions being held.

You will see the same portfolio reflected in MarketMatrix. For example, Figure B.7 shows a portfolio called "Trust." The number of positions is displayed, showing 10 short equity positions and 24 option positions. These same positions, under the name "Trust," will be available in ProphetCharts, since all the data are shared between the applets and the web site.

One helpful thing about Watch Lists and Portfolios both being available as modules is that you can make sure you have an accurate representation of your holdings. One feature ProphetCharts provides is the ability to show a quantity count for each watch list and portfolio. Under the Preferences dialog box, check the Show Item Counts checkbox to turn on this feature.

When you do, a parenthetical sum will follow each watch list and portfolio name (Figure B.8, with arrows added for emphasis) so you can confirm that your portfolio's contents in a given watch list are in synch with the actual holdings you have entered into MarketMatrix. In this instance, there are 34 items in the Current Trust watch list and 34 items in the Trust portfolio, so they appear to be in synch.

Keep in mind that the information in My Watch Lists and the information in My Portfolios are intended to provide different kinds of information. The watch list shows simply the company name (or symbol, if you have elected that style of display) contained within each list. The portfolio shows the raw symbol followed by the quantity owned as well as the entry price (Figure B.9). Watch lists are typically created and managed within ProphetCharts, whereas portfolios are typically created and managed either in MarketMatrix or on the Portfolio page of the Investor Toolbox.

Index